CHINA'S "PEACEFUL RISE" IN THE 21ST CENTURY

China's "Peaceful Rise" in the 21st Century
Domestic and International Conditions

Edited by
SUJIAN GUO
San Francisco State University, USA

ASHGATE

© Sujian Guo 2006

All rights reserved. No part of this publication may be reproduced, stored in a retrieval system or transmitted in any form or by any means, electronic, mechanical, photocopying, recording or otherwise without the prior permission of the publisher.

Sujian Guo has asserted his moral right under the Copyright, Designs and Patents Act, 1988, to be identified as the editor of this work.

Published by
Ashgate Publishing Limited
Gower House
Croft Road
Aldershot
Hampshire GU11 3HR
England

Ashgate Publishing Company
Suite 420
101 Cherry Street
Burlington, VT 05401-4405
USA

Ashgate website: http://www.ashgate.com

British Library Cataloguing in Publication Data
China's "peaceful rise" in the 21st century : domestic and
    international conditions
    1. China - Politics and government - 2002- 2. China - Foreign
    relations - 21st century 3. China - Economic conditions -
    2000-
    I. Guo, Sujian, 1957-
    951'.06

Library of Congress Control Number: 2006922671

ISBN-13: 978-0-7546-4847-5
ISBN-10: 0-7546-4847-8

Printed and bound in Great Britain by Antony Rowe Ltd, Chippenham, Wiltshire.

Contents

List of Figures and Tables		*vii*
List of Contributors		*ix*
Acknowledgments		*xi*
Introduction	Challenges and Opportunities for China's "Peaceful Rise" *Sujian Guo*	1

Part 1   **Domestic Conditions of China's Peaceful Rise**

1	The Dialectic Relationship between Peaceful Development and China's Deep Reform *Guoli Liu*	17
2	China's Peaceful Development, Regime Stability and Political Legitimacy *Baogang Guo*	39
3	Corruption, Economic Growth and Regime Stability in China's Peaceful Rise *Shawn Shieh*	61
4	Strategic Repression and Regime Stability in China's Peaceful Development *Andrew Wedeman*	89
5	Hybrid Regime and Peaceful Development in China *Zhengxu Wang*	117

Part 2   **International Conditions of China's Peaceful Rise**

6	The International Conditions of China's Peaceful Rise: Challenges and Opportunities *Li Qingsi*	141

7	Maintaining an Asymmetric but Stable China-U.S. Military Relationship *Xuetang Guo*	159
8	A Rising China: Catalysts for Chinese Military Modernization *Bang Quan Zheng*	183
9	China's Peaceful Rise and Sino-Japanese Territorial and Maritime Tensions *Jean-Marc F. Blanchard*	211
10	China's Rise and Contemporary Geopolitics in Central Asia *Oliver M. Lee*	237

Index   *263*

List of Figures and Tables

Figures

1.1	China's Gross Domestic Product (selected years between 1978–2003)	19
1.2	China's GDP Growth Rate in Comparative Perspective (1990–2001)	19
3.1	Spectrum of Destructive and Development Corruption	88
4.1	Strategic Repression	92
4.2	Arrests of Protestants	102
4.3	Arrests of Catholics	102
4.4	Arrests for Sectarian Activity	104
8.1	U.S. Exports of Goods	189

Tables

1.1	Total Value of Imports and Exports (U.S.$ billion)	21
1.2	Chinese Utilization of Foreign Capital (U.S.$ billion)	21
1.3	Chinese Household Consumption (Yuan)	30
2.1	Political Stability Indicator for Selected Countries (1996–2002)	42
2.2	Traditional Chinese Cognitive Model of Legitimacy	43
2.3	China's Position in Corruption Perception Index	51
2.4	World Happiness Rank (1995–2005)	55
2.5	Regional Income Disparity in China (in Yuan)	57
3.1	Governance Indicators for China (1996–2004)	62
3.2	Typologies of State-Society Structures and Their Effect on Corruption	83
4.1	Assessments of China's Human Rights Record	96
4.2	Dui Hua Foundation Documented Detainees and Arrests	98
4.3	Length of Detention	105
4.4	Variations in Sentencing	106
4.5	Sentences Handed Down for Separatism in Xinjiang	107
4.6	Spatial Distribution of Arrests of Protestants, 2001–2003	111
4.7	Spatial Distribution of Arrests of Catholics, 1994–2003	112
8.1	China's Top Export Destinations ($ million)	188
8.2	China's Defense Expenditure	193
8.3	Selected Chinese Arms Production Programs	195

List of Contributors

Jean-Marc F. Blanchard, Assistant Professor of International Relations at San Francisco State University, San Francisco, California. He earned his Ph.D. degree from University of Pennsylvania. His research interests include territorial and maritime issues, Chinese foreign economic and security policy, multinational corporations, economic statecraft, and globalization. He is a co-editor of and contributor to *Power and the Purse: Economic Statecraft, Interdependence, and National Security* (London: Frank Cass, 2000) and the author of more than a dozen book chapters and refereed articles. His articles have appeared in the *China Quarterly*, *Journal of Contemporary China*, *Geopolitics*, *Security Studies*, and *International Interactions*.

Baogang Guo, Associate Professor of Political Science at Dalton State College in Georgia, Associate Editor of the *Journal of Chinese Political Science*, and research associate at the China Research Center in Kennesaw, GA. He received a Ph.D. degree from Brandeis University and a Master's degree from Zhengzhou University. He is the author of numerous publications on Chinese political culture, political legitimacy, and public policies. His recent publications have appeared in *Asian Survey*, *Journal of Chinese Political Science*, *Modern China Studies*, *Journal of Comparative Asian Development*, *US-China Review*, and *Twenty-first Century*.

Sujian Guo, Associate Professor in the Department of Political Science at San Francisco State University and Editor of the *Journal of Chinese Political Science*. His areas of specialization include Comparative Politics, International Relations and Methodology. His research interests include Chinese/Asian politics, communist and post-communist studies, democratic transitions, and the political economy of East and Southeast Asia. He has published more than two dozens articles both in English and Chinese. He is the author of *Post-Mao China: from Totalitarianism to Authoritarianism?* and *The Political Economy of Asian Transition from Communism*.

Xuetang Guo, Associate Professor and Deputy Director of Institute of International Politics at Tongji University, with areas of specialization in China-US relations, China's foreign strategy, geopolitics, and United Nations. He has published extensively in the above areas. He teaches courses of China-US Relations, American Foreign Policy, International Political Economy, and International Organization. He is co-author of *Is China a Threat? Interpreting "China Threat Theory"* (Shanghai: Xuelin Publishing House, 2004).

Oliver M. Lee, Professor Emeritus of Political Science at the University of Hawaii at Manoa, with areas of specialization in Chinese Foreign Policy, U.S.-China Relations, and International Politics. He has published in both English and Chinese journals.

Li Qingsi, Associate Professor of School of International Studies, Renmin University of China, Beijing, China. His areas of specialization include American Studies, China-US relations and International Relations. He has numerous Chinese publications in the above areas.

Guoli Liu, Associate Professor of Political Science at the College of Charleston, with specializations in comparative politics and international relations. He is author of *States and Markets: Comparing Japan and Russia* (Westview Press), editor of *Chinese Foreign Policy in Transition* (Aldine de Gruyter), co-editor (with Lowell Dittmer) of *China's Deep Reform: Domestic Politics in Transition* (Rowman & Littlefield, forthcoming), and co-editor (with Weixing Chen) of *New Directions in Chinese Politics for the New Millennium* (Edwin Mellen).

Shawn Shieh, Associate Professor of Political Science at Marist College. He has written several book chapters on provincial leadership and center-local relations in China and articles on economic policy, local property rights and corruption in reform China in *The China Business Review*, *Issues and Studies*, and *Journal of Contemporary China*.

Zhengxu Wang, Research Fellow in the East Asian Institute at National University of Singapore. He holds a Ph.D. degree from the University of Michigan. His research interests include democratization, development, and regime change. His recent publications focus on the changing citizen attitudes and behaviors and their impacts on political changes in developing countries. He is currently working on a book project on political development in China.

Andrew Wedeman, Associate Professor of Political Science at the University of Nebraska, Lincoln, where he is also the Director of International Studies and the Director of Asian Studies. His research focuses on the political economy of reform in China and specifically the effects of corruption on development, both in China and elsewhere in the developing world. Recent publications include: *From Mao to Market: Rent Seeking, Local Protectionism, and Marketization in China* (Cambridge University Press) as well as articles in *China Quarterly*, *Journal of Contemporary China*, and *China Review*.

Bang Quan Zheng, Asian Studies Program at the University of Michigan, Ann Arbor, with specializations in Chinese political, foreign and security policy, Chinese military modernization, and Chinese defense industrial reform.

Acknowledgments

The authors owe a special debt of gratitude to Dean Joel Kassiola, the College of Behavioral and Social Sciences at San Francisco State University, and Professor Jie Chen, the International Graduate Programs of Old Dominion University, for their generous funding for making this volume possible.

Introduction

Challenges and Opportunities for China's "Peaceful Rise"

Sujian Guo*

Introduction

China's rapid development has attracted worldwide attention in recent years. The implications of various aspects of China's rise, from its expanding influence and military muscle to its growing demand for energy supplies, are being heatedly debated in the international community as well as in the United States. Facing a rising China, there have been increasing wariness, fear, and suspicion from the world, particularly from the United States. The Bush Administration has been advised to adopt a new containment strategy to counterbalance the "China Threat."[1]

In response to the "China Threat" and U.S. pressure, the Chinese government proposed "peaceful development" (*heping fazhan*), which has become a new thinking (*xinsiwei*) in Chinese foreign policy under the Fourth Generation Leadership. The concept "*heping fazhan*" was derived from the Chinese academic debate on the term "peaceful rise" (*heping jueqi*) which was officially introduced at the 2003 Bo'ao Forum by Zheng Bijian, Chairman of China Reform Forum.[2] "The only choice for China under the current international situation is to rise peacefully, namely, to

---

* The author owes special thanks to Andrew Wedeman for his able editing of this chapter and Guoli Liu for his helpful comments and suggestions.

1   Robert D. Kaplan, "How We Would Fight China," *The Atlantic Monthly*, vol. 295, no. 5, June 2005, pp. 49–64, http://www.theatlantic.com/doc/prem/200506/kaplan.

2   The concept, "China's rise" or "the rise of China," was first used by a Chinese distinguished scholar, Yan Xuetong of Tsinghua University, in his controversial book titled *International Environment of China's Rise* published by Tianjing Renmin Chubanshe in 1998, and then in his English article titled "The Rise of China in Chinese Eyes" published in *Journal of Contemporary China* (vol. 10, no. 26, 2001, pp. 33–44). The concept was developed not only in terms of the Chinese history and the international environment but also from the perspective of China's foreign policy strategies under the new generations of Chinese leadership at the present and in the future. However, the concept of "China's rise" caused internal debates in China after the book was published in 1988. The Chinese government under Jiang rejected this concept and the word "rise" (*Jueqi*) was forbidden to appear in official documents. The concept "peaceful rise" was later re-introduced at the 2003 Bo'ao Forum by Zheng Bijian, Chairman of China Reform Forum.

develop by taking advantage of the peaceful international environment, and at the same time, to maintain world peace through its development," explained by Zheng in his speech at the 2003 Bo'ao Forum.[3] However, there was continued disagreement on use of the term "peaceful rise" both in the Chinese government and academia, particularly about possible misinterpretation of the term "rise" that could boost the "China Threat." As a result, at the 2004 Bo'ao Forum, Hu Jintao changed the terms, calling for "peaceful development." Since then, "peaceful development" has set the tone for Beijing's official statement of its foreign policy.[4]

The adoption of "peaceful development" foreign policy strategy is a continuity of Deng Xiaoping's concept "*taoguang yanghui*" (keep a low profile and never take the lead) but a break away from Jiang Zemin's "*duoji shijie*" (multipolar world). Under Jiang, building a multipolar world implies to "multipolarize" the American unipolarity and counterbalance the U.S. hegemony. This "peaceful development" foreign policy strategy is, in fact, to accept the unipolar structure of international system and that the U.S. will continue to be the hegemonic power in the long term. It proposes that China must avoid direct confrontation with the U.S. in order to secure a favorable external environment for its rise, although China can adopt a multilateral and bilateral diplomatic approach in the unipolar world dominated by a single hegemony.[5]

"Peaceful development" thus seeks to reassure the U.S. and other countries that China's rise will not be a threat to peace and stability in the region and the world and that the U.S. and other countries can benefit from China's peaceful development. China's development is mutually beneficial to China and the world in the process of globalization. The new policy emphasizes "economic development first" and breaks away from ideological doctrines in Chinese foreign policy. China's foreign policy in the Asian Pacific regions has become more flexible and cooperative with multilateral organizations, such as the ASEAN+3 and ASEAN+1, Shanghai Cooperation Organization (SCO), EU, NATO, G7, and UN. The new policy also seeks negotiated settlement of regional problems such as the nuclear crisis on the Korean peninsula and South China Sea dispute with Vietnam and Malaysia.[6]

The new foreign policy stresses that China is a peace-loving, people-based (*yiren weiben*), cooperative, tolerant, confident, and responsible power. However, China also recognizes that its "soft power" – "1.3 billion population + 1 purchase order," international trade and cooperation, economy, and culture – can be used to enhance

---

3 "China's Road of Peaceful Rise," *China View*, http://news.xinhuanet.com/english/2004-04/23/content_1436850.htm.

4 Hu Jintao replaced the term "peaceful rise" with "peaceful development" also because of Jiang's opposition to the term "rise" (*jueqi*). Hu's final decision is that the rise of China should be discussed freely by scholars in their writings but the term of "rise" is no longer used in government statements.

5 Xiaoxiong Yi, "Chinese Foreign Policy in Transition: Understanding China's 'Peaceful Development'," The *Journal of East Asian Affairs*, vol. 19, no. 1, 2005.

6 Ibid.

China's role as a rising power in the regional and world affairs and to facilitate China's economic development and modernization.

The "peaceful development" strategy has also had an obvious impact on Beijing's Taiwan policy. Beijing has quietly shifted its Taiwan policy to "*budu buwu*" (no independence, no war) – aimed at maintaining the status quo and putting aside the "*tongyi*" (unification) for the time being. Deng Xiaoping made the unification one of the central tasks for the Chinese government, and Jiang Zemin pressed Taiwan for the unification by declaring that the resolution of the "Taiwan issue" would not be delayed indefinitely. However, Hu Jintao declared during his visit to Canada in September 2005 that the resolution of the Taiwan issue was complicated and would take a long time, and that "*fangtaidu*" (struggle against the "Taiwan independence") would be a long fight – without setting a time table for the unification. This is a departure from Jiang's "*jitong*" (hasty unification) to a new thinking in the Taiwan policy that seeks "peace," "reconciliation," "cooperation," and "win-win situation" (*heping, hexie, hezuo, shuangying*) across the Taiwan Strait that could lead to a future of "peaceful development" and "common prosperity."[7] In the year 2005, Beijing invited Taiwan's two top opposition leaders, Lien Chan (KMT) and James Soong (PFP), to visit mainland China, accompanied by Taiwanese legislators, politicians, businessmen and media leaders, and embarked on the first major historical dialogue and political interaction across the Taiwan-Straits since 1949. The new shift in the Taiwan policy is an integral part of Beijing's "peaceful development" strategy.

Apparently, the Chinese leaders have made clear to the world that China has no interest in seeking regional hegemony or a change in the existing world order and China is committed to "peaceful development." However, is the "peaceful development" possible given existing domestic and international conditions? This is the central question this book attempts to address. In what follows, we will highlight how each of the chapters addresses this central question and related issues from different perspectives and to what extent the authors as a whole contribute to our understanding of the issues related to the rise of China and the significant implications for the world in the 21st century. Finally, we will conclude the chapter with an overall assessment and prediction into the future.

Domestic and International Conditions

The central theme of all chapters of the book is centered on the question of whether it is possible for China to have "peaceful development" given domestic and international challenges, including American efforts to "constrain" or "contain" it. Chapters in Part 1 address the domestic dimension and what factors could affect the peaceful development while chapters in Part 2 discuss the international challenges and how China can meet these challenges. In world history, no major power has risen

---

7 http://www.ccforum.org.cn/archiver/?tid-36534.html; http://www.huaxia.com/zt/rdzz/05-020/2005/00303455.html; http://news.xinhuanet.com/taiwan/2005-04/29/content_2895458.htm.

"peacefully." From the early colonial powers Spain and Britain, to late industrializers, Germany and Japan, all new powers fought their way to their power status. "The history of the United States is the history of confrontation, even conflict, with the other great powers of the earth," first with Britain and France in the 19th century and then with Germany, Japan, and then Russia in the 20th century, not to mention many wars fought by proxy.[8] Moreover, the past experience of great powers suggest that dominant powers have typically seen rising powers as potential threats and have sought to thwart their rise. Containment, however, has often produced a nationalist backlash in the rising power that has intensified its desire to revise the status quo. The rapid economic development associated with rising power also tends to produce complex domestic political pressures that can prove destabilizing. China's "peaceful development," therefore, will only occur if both external power relationships and internal political changes are carefully and skillfully managed. Otherwise peaceful development could end up in instability and conflict. The pre- and post-Second World War experiences of Germany and Japan have provided both positive and negative lessons for China. Globalization, economic interdependence, and changes in the post-Cold War international system have brought new opportunities and challenges for China. Therefore, the authors of this book believe that the peaceful rise could be possible if China can strategically overcome challenges and leverage opportunities at both domestic and international fronts.

In Chapter 1, "The Dialectic Relationship between Peaceful Development and China's Reform," Guoli Liu examines the connection between China's domestic politics and foreign policy orientation. In recent years, there have been significant debates about the rise of China and its implications for international relations. One of the key issues is whether China's rapid rise will be peaceful or will disrupt the international order. Liu argues that China's deep reform, i.e., profound political and socioeconomic changes, requires a peaceful international environment while a largely peaceful environment has contributed to China's successful economic reform. However, without meaningful political reform, China's growth may not be sustainable. If socioeconomic development runs into deep trouble, China might not be able to maintain its peaceful orientation in foreign policy. China's deep reform and peaceful development are thus mutually dependent. If deep reform fails, China's peaceful development will be interrupted. If peaceful development is blocked or interrupted, deep reform will suffer a serious setback. The symbiotic relationship between peaceful development and deep reform requires China to simultaneously deepen its domestic reforms and pursue a peaceful diplomacy. The ultimate success of this new grand strategy of peaceful development, therefore, demands not only the persistent hard work of many generations of Chinese people but also a true spirit of cooperation from the other great powers.

In Chapter 2, "China's Peaceful Development, Regime Stability, and Political Legitimacy," Baogang Guo examines regime stability and political legitimacy as

---

8 James P. Pinkerton, "Superpower Showdown," *The American Conservative*, November 7, 2005.

the domestic preconditions of China's peaceful development. The relationship between regime stability and political legitimacy is analyzed by developing an analytical framework of Chinese system of legitimation. A number of hypotheses are then examined through analyses of changes in the regime's political ideologies, official ethics, and eudemonic appeals, which demonstrates how the Chinese system of legitimacy has helped the regime enhance state capacity and maintain stability. However, he also argues that the extent to which the Chinese Communist Party can sustain its regime stability and achieve its goal of peaceful rise is dependent upon its ability to bring up to date its system of legitimation and turn itself from an authoritarian power to a democratic one. A failure to continue to modernize its bases of political legitimacy at home may compromise its stability, and consequently undermine the peaceful nature of its development.

In Chapter 3, "Corruption, Economic Growth and Regime Stability in China's Peaceful Development," Shawn Shieh looks at the threat that corruption poses to economic growth and thereby regime stability by surveying the comparative literature on corruption and state-business relations, focusing primarily on countries in East and Southeast Asia. Shieh identifies those conditions in which clientelism and corruption have had a harmful effect on economic growth and stability in these countries. He then uses these conditions to assess the danger that corruption poses to the market reforms and peaceful development in China.

In Chapter 4, "Strategic Repression and Regime Stability in China's Peaceful Development," Andrew Wedeman documents the strategic nature of repression in contemporary China showing that whereas the regime continues to crack down hard on separatist movements and overt challengers such as Falun Gong, it has adopted a mixed policy toward other heterodox groups, suppressing them in some instances but coexisting with them in other instances. Although this shift toward strategic repression does not foretell an imminent end to repression, Wedeman suggests that by helping to maintain regime stability, it is a necessary condition for the success of "peaceful development" strategy.

In Chapter 5, "Hybrid Regime and Peaceful Development in China," Zhengxu Wang argues that politically China is evolving into a "hybrid regime," that is, a regime that is neither democratic nor strictly authoritarian. Facing increasing pressure for political opening and increasing difficulty in maintaining legitimacy, the Party is considering expanding elections from local to upper level governments and opening more channels for political participation. Such incremental reforms are intended to alleviate public pressures and help the Party renew its rule. Nevertheless, such changes, with expanded political rights and political resources for citizens, are transforming the regime into a hybrid regime, and will continue to push the regime toward democracy. This direction should help the goal of "peaceful development."

In Chapter 6, "The International Conditions of China's Peaceful Rise," the focus shifts from the domestic to international. Li Qingsi explores the advantages and disadvantages of the international conditions China faces as a rising power and how China will be able to rise peacefully facing external challenges. The author attempts to simplify the international environment as a U.S.-centered world system, constituted by the United States, its allies, and the rest of the world. Since the world is highly interdependent, China would be able to navigate through the complex international relations to attain the goal through peaceful means, for nations not only compete with but also rely upon each other in the age of economic interdependence and globalization.

In Chapter 7, "Maintaining an Asymmetric but Stable China-U.S. Military Relationship," Guo Xuetang argues that China-U.S. military relationship has maintained an asymmetric but stable status quo for about 30 years. However, the asymmetric and stable relationship could become uncertain in the early 21st century if the Bush administration shifts its military focus toward China, deploying a missile defense system in the West Pacific region, strengthening its military alliance with Japan and even encouraging Japanese remilitarization and involvement in a potential Taiwan military conflict. According to Guo, the United States has begun preparing militarily for a worst case scenario involving a confrontation with China. It has thus made military deterrence and prevention a core of its strategic thinking. And yet, there is a non-confrontational dimension to the Sino-American relationship that provides opportunities for bilateral military exchanges and cooperation. Guo explains the sources of American military strategy toward China and efforts to maintain an asymmetric but stable China-U.S. military relationship that affects the overall bilateral relationship and the peaceful development in China as well.

In Chapter 8, "A Rising China: Catalysts for Chinese Military Modernization," Bang Quan Zheng points out that the world is increasingly concerned about China's emerging military power and its impact on regional stability in the Asia-Pacific. Contrary to structural realism, which argues that a stronger China will strive to change the current international system, Zheng argues that even although China has embarked on a program of military modernization, it does not have the ambition and capability to rival the United States or challenge the established international order. Although China has one of the largest armed forces in the world, its weaponry systems are obsolete, and it is "natural" for China to upgrade it for the national defense purpose. However, the main factors that have stimulated China's military modernization are Washington's global efforts to counter a rising China by deepening its military and security cooperation with Japan, and a perceived American tilt toward Taiwan. Fear of a tightening of American containment, in other words, has compelled the Chinese military to upgrade its weaponry systems and enhance its deterrence capabilities.

In Chapter 9, "China's Peaceful Rise and Sino-Japanese Territorial and Maritime Tensions," Jean-Marc F. Blanchard observes that China's peaceful rise depends upon a variety of factors including a good working relationship with Japan. Unfortunately, Sino-Japanese relations are quite frigid these days as a result of frictions over history, China's military modernization, Japan's quest for a permanent seat on the U.N. Security Council, and an ongoing competition for friends in South and Southeast Asia. A highly important source of tension is the Sino-Japanese dispute over ownership of the Diaoyu (Senkaku) Islands as well as the delimitation of the East China Sea. Blanchard argues that the Sino-Japanese dispute over Diaoyu/Senkaku Islands has the potential to generate serious conflict because of its links to national identity, energy, and national security. This territorial quarrel, he argues, could escalate as both Japan and China has historically used force to resolve territorial disputes. In this study, Blanchard examines the likelihood that Sino-Japanese territorial and maritime tensions may erupt in militarized conflict. To provide a basis for this analysis, he develops a three-variable analytical framework, using both the history of the quarrels as well as the literature on boundary disputes (particularly institutionalist-statist theory). This analytical framework focuses on China's interests in its boundaries with Japan, China's capability to pursue these interests, and the politico-economic environment in which Chinese leaders construct policy towards the disputes. He concludes that there is both good and bad news. In the short- to medium-term, the likelihood of violent boundary conflict is low. In the long run, however, the potential for militarized conflict could increase if conditions and factors were to change. Therefore, the escalation or resolution of Sino-Japanese tensions could handicap or promote China's "peaceful rise."

In Chapter 10, "China's Rise and Contemporary Geopolitics in Central Asia," Oliver Lee observes that, since the collapse of the Soviet Union, and especially since 9/11, American power has penetrated into Central Asia for the first time. The U.S. has thus encroached on areas that both the Chinese and Russians have traditionally considered their backyards. Lee observes that because both China and Russia place a greater strategic value on Central Asia and the U.S. remains a seapower, it is unlikely that the U.S. will fight major landpowers in Eurasia or make serious inroads in this region. He thus concludes that given careful implementation of the peaceful development strategy China will likely continue to enjoy sufficient leverage in the region and this will afford China the access to Central Asian oil and gas it needs for continued rapid economic development.

All the ten chapters, five on domestic conditions and five on international conditions, address the significance of both the domestic and international conditions for China's "peaceful rise." The five chapters on domestic conditions address major factors and problems that could significantly impact China's peaceful development: reform, legitimacy, corruption, repression, and regime type. The five chapters on international conditions address another set of major factors and problems: general international conditions, China-U.S. military relations, China's military modernization, Sino-Japan relations, and Central Asian geopolitics. All the factors constitute the most important challenges faced by China in the 21st century and will affect the general conditions for China's peaceful development although the book might not address all of the factors and issues that could affect China's future development.

Conclusion

One of the central questions in the discussion of China's peaceful rise is therefore whether "peaceful development" is possible given the domestic and international challenges China faces in the 21st century? The rise of past great powers has led the realists or realpolitik pessimists to believe that China's rise will inevitably collide with the existing great powers and China and the United States are likely to engage in an intense security competition with considerable potential for war.[9] Liberal theorists, however, argue that in an era of deepening globalization, integration, and democratization, peaceful development may be possible but only if China can overcome the challenges and leverage the opportunities at both domestic and international fronts.

To many realists world history suggests that "global power shifts happen rarely and are even less often peaceful."[10] Thus they assume that China's rise will inevitably collide with the existing great powers, particularly the United States, and China and the United States are likely to engage in an intense security competition with considerable potential for war.[11] This assumption, however, seems contradicted by the peaceful rise of Japan, Germany, and Europe after World War II. Because they were fully integrated into the international system and economy, these "new" powers did not emerge as aggrieved, anti-status quo revisionist power, but instead they emerged as status quo powers and key supporters of the established world order and contributed heavily to the stability of international financial, monetary, trade, and security systems. China could also become a status quo power and play a similar role in the international system if it is allowed to be fully integrated into the established international system and economy.

From a constructivist perspective, the Chinese leaders have moved toward a more comfortable embrace of liberal values, norms and institutions in their contacts with the Western countries since China's reform and open door policy, and shifted away from cognitive rigidity and dogmatism to flexibility and pragmatism in Beijing's foreign policy thinking and behavior. China's embrace of the "peaceful development" policy suggests that its leaders have learned from historical lessons that China must avoid the path of pre-World War II Germany and Japan and the Soviet Union in the Cold War and proceed on the path of peaceful development.[12] As Robert G. Sutter points out, "Chinese leaders reviewed the negative experiences of China's past confrontations with neighbors and other powers, and the negative experiences of earlier rising powers, such as Germany and Japan in the twentieth century, to conclude that China cannot reach its goal of economic modernization and development through confrontation and conflict.[13] They believe that China has directly benefited from the past two decades of international stability and that

---

9   John Mearsheimer, "Better to Be Godzilla than Bambi," *Foreign Policy* (FP), January/February 2005, http://www.foreignpolicy.com/story/cms.php?story_id=2740&page=2.

10 James F. Hoge, "A Global Power Shift in the Making," *Foreign Affairs*, July/August 2004.

11 John Mearsheimer.

12 Huang Renwei, "Zhongguo heping jueqide daolu xuanze he zhanlue guannian," *Jiefang Ribao* (Liberation Daily), April 26, 2004.

13 Robert G. Sutter, *China's Rise in Asia: Promises and Perils* (Lanham, MD: Rowman & Littlefield Publishers, 2005), p. 266.

China's ability to sustain rapid economic development depends on sustaining a peaceful international environment that has enabled China to focus on an export-led strategy of rapid economic growth and allowed for massive inflows of FDI and ready access to export markets in the developed world.[14] Thus rather than seeing China as disadvantaged by the established international system dominated by the U.S. superpower, the new leadership under Hu Juntao believes that China can take advantage of the benefits and public goods provided by the existing world order. In short, peaceful development defines a rising China as a status quo power, not a threat to the status quo. As Avery Goldstein points out, "China's foreign policy behavior continues to conform closely to that typical of a status quo state."[15]

However, although the Chinese leadership may believe that it is possible for China to rise peacefully, in reality China faces a series of challenges, both at home and in the international system, that if not properly and skillfully handled could lead China down the revisionist path associated with previous rising powers. China does not, of course, entirely control the fate of peaceful development and even if it embraces peaceful development, a containment policy directed by the dominant powers against China could derail even the best intensions. As Avery Goldstein points out, "even if both China and the United States strive for cooperation, missteps by either or conflicts provoked by third parties that neither controls (such as North Korea or Taiwan) may ultimately foil the attempt to nurture a Sino-American modus vivendi for the twenty-first century."[16]

The Taiwan issue could be a potential peace breaker that could frustrate China's peaceful rise. The forces for independence on the island have grown and sought an independent political and cultural identity for the island. If Taiwan declares independence, peace across the Taiwan Strait could breakdown, a cross-strait conflict could, in turn, escalate into war between China and the United States. Maintaining peace across the Taiwan Straits is thus an important precondition for China's peaceful rise. Separatist movements in Tibet and Xinjiang have constantly sought independence from China, and it also poses challenges to China's political stability and international images.

Border and territorial disputes with the neighboring states have created additional threats to China's national security and sovereignty, particularly the Sino-Japanese tension over the gas and oil reserves beneath the East China Sea and territory quarrel over the Diaoyu/Senkaku Islands. While China and Japan are major trading partners, Sino-Japanese political relations have deteriorated recently, causing suspicion and rivalry between the two Asian powers to grow. Some analysts have used the phrase, "economically hot and politically cold," to describe the current Sino-Japan relations. As Jean-Marc F. Blanchard discussed in his chapter, the Sino-Japanese dispute over the Diaoyu/Senkaku Islands has national identity, energy, and national security

---

14 Ibid., p. 4.

15 Avery Goldstein, *Rising to the Challenge: China's Grand Strategy and International Security* (Stanford, CA: Stanford University Press, 2005), p. 213.

16 Ibid., p. 219.

dimensions, and the presence of a territorial quarrel between China and Japan has the potential to worsen. Escalation is, however, not favorable for China because it would face the combined forces of Japan and the United States and hence a high probability of significant geopolitical turbulence if the tensions and conflicts cannot be resolved but get escalated into armed conflicts. The success or failure in the resolution of these disputes and conflicts could handicap or promote China's "peaceful rise."

Managing the "American factor" could be the most crucial factor in China's peaceful rise. The United States has in fact long maintained a security circle or a strategic hedge against China not only along the Asian Pacific rim through bilateral military agreements with Japan, South Korea, and other Asian Pacific countries. As Oliver Lee suggests, more recently the United States has begun building a new network of military partnerships in South Asia and Central Asia. To many Chinese, the U.S. has already begun constructing a new containment structure whose purpose is to block China's rise. To some Americans, however, China's military modernization is viewed as a harbinger of a more aggressive China, leading the American strategic planners to adopt policies aimed at containing the potential threat from China. At the same time, economic ties between the U.S. and China have deepened, thus creating a situation of complex interdependence that has, on the one hand, drawn the two economies together while at the same time creating new friction over trade. Competition for access to energy has also increased in recent years as China's military upgrading efforts and global search for oil and resources are perceived to be assertive and threatening to the U.S. interests in the region and around the globe. Mutual suspicion and misperception could, therefore, destabilize Sino-American relations and jeopardize the goal of "peaceful development." If China were to find its access to U.S. and its Western allies' markets, capital, and technology, worsened Sino-U.S. relations would have a negative effect on China's economic and military modernization.

Despite the real or potential conflicts, the United States and China also has significant common interests and most of these shared interests correspond with China's interest in maintaining a peaceful international environment. Both countries have tremendous shared interests in many global issues (terrorism, nuclear proliferation, energy, environmental protection, and public health), regional security issues (nuclear crisis on the Korean peninsula and peace across the Taiwan Strait), and bilateral economic, business and market benefits. Thus, challenges and opportunities co-exist in China's foreign relations, and advantages and disadvantages also co-exist in its foreign policy, which could be utilized by the Chinese leadership to advance China's peaceful rise, as discussed by Qingsi Li. Aaron L. Friedberg recently points out, "the contemporary U.S.-China relationship is clearly mixed, consisting of an array of cooperative and competitive elements."[17] There are two opposing sets of causal forces at work that are pushing the relationship toward conflict and peace. But, the two opposing causal forces tend to be "mutually offsetting," and the forces

---

17 Aaron L. Friedberg, "The Future of U.S.-China Relations: Is Conflict Inevitable?" *International Security*, vol. 30, no. 2, Fall 2005, p. 40.

tending toward cooperation appear stronger than those pointing toward competition.[18] In fact, there is ample evidence of increasing cooperation. As Guo Xuetang points out, even as the United States has adopted policies aimed at military deterrence and prevention, there exists a non-confrontational dimension to Sino-U.S. military relations that would provide opportunities for bilateral military exchanges and cooperation. The coexistence of challenges and opportunities for cooperation are also evident in regional and bilateral hot issues. Even though Taiwan poses a most serious security challenge to the U.S.-China relations, both countries have sought to avoid conflict across the Taiwan Strait, and have made clear that both oppose a change in the status quo across the Taiwan Strait. The nuclear crisis on the Korean peninsula could be potentially an explosive security issue for China and the United States, but once again we have found the two countries have worked together for years to manage the crisis and bring all parties to the negotiating table. Economic and trade conflicts have recently increased between the two countries. Nonetheless, both sides have sought to avoid a trade war, looking instead to negotiations to resolve bilateral economic conflicts. The U.S.-Japan security alliance poses a threat to China, and to Chinese people, it encourages Japan to adopt a tougher position toward China. Yet at the same time, a stable and constructive Sino-U.S. relationship would provide opportunities for maintaining stable Sino-Japanese relations because postwar Japan has maintained strong security ties with the U.S. and become dependent upon the U.S. for its security shield which places constraints on Japanese foreign policy making. In fact, the United States has historically played a vital balancing role in this region, and will likely continue to play such a role. The extensive mutual dependence of Sino-American and Sino-Japanese commercial relations and interests has created common interests which could shield each of them from excessive offensive actions and military adventurism that could put peace and economic growth at risk, particularly in the nuclear age in which each major actor has a significant nuclear deterrent. As Zbigniew Brzezinski put it, "the nuclear age has altered power politics in a way that was already evident in the U.S.-Soviet competition."[19]

As a matter of fact, all five major powers involved in this region, the United States, China, Japan, Russia, and India, could find common interests, and these common interests would provide opportunities and incentives for each power to maintain a stable and constructive relationship, if not strategic partnership, with the other great powers of this region. The United States, which would continue to play a role of balancer, could be an important stabilizing factor in maintaining peace in Asia. China itself can also be a stabilizing factor in the region since it is also in China's fundamental interest to maintain the stability and prosperity in Asia. As Bang Quan Zheng argues in his chapter, China's "peaceful development" is based on the stability of current international economic, political and security orders, and thus the rise of China need not be a threat to the U.S. and the international system.

---

18 Ibid., pp. 40–45.
19 Zbigniew Brzezinski, "Nukes Change Everything," *Foreign Policy* (FP), January/February 2005.

In a fundamental sense, in fact, China's adoption of a new "peaceful development" foreign policy strategy suggests that Chinese new leadership already recognizes the importance of maintaining peace with all actors involved in this region for China's further development and modernization. In the December 2005 White Paper, titled "China's Peaceful Development Road," published by the Information Office of China's State Council, Beijing explains the inevitability for Beijing to pursue "peaceful development," outlines the major policies the Chinese government has taken to achieve the goal, and demonstrates its resolve to stick to the road of "peaceful development" now and in the future.[20] Therefore, the new foreign policy strategy is defensive in nature, aimed at decreasing the fear of a "China Threat," promoting good neighbor relations and multilateral relations in the region and around the globe, and creating a peaceful and stable external environment for its economic development. According to Robert Sutter, "even Chinese leaders seem to understand this in their acceptance of U.S. leadership in Asian and world affairs as part of China's recent long-term strategy to develop 'peacefully' without upsetting the United States. This represents a sharp reversal from China's post-Cold War efforts to wear down the U.S. superpower and seek to create a 'multipolar' world."[21]

The domestic challenges facing China during the next few decades are also enormous. China faces serious corruption, increasing mass unrest, enlarged polarization in the personal and regional income distribution, increased unemployment and an insufficient social safety net, shortages of energy and key resources for economic modernization, massive migrations from rural areas to urban areas, extensive bad debt held by state banks and deep problems in the financial sector, excessive public debt, environmental deterioration, etc. All these problems and obstacles could lead to political instability and disrupt economic growth. As Shawn Shieh argues, although corruption in China is less harmful to economic growth than in countries like Indonesia and the Philippines, a failure to combat corruption would endanger market reforms and "peaceful development" by undermining public confidence in the regime, weakening bureaucratic competence, and aggravating social inequality. Thus a more transparent and democratic political system is needed in reducing corruption in China. The resolution of the above problems, as Guoli Liu discusses, depends on China's deepening domestic reform and peaceful international environment. This is described as the dialectical relationship between the two aspects of Chinese politics: China's peaceful development is a necessary condition for domestic political and economic reforms while deeper reforms and open-door policy ensure the continuity of "peaceful development" policy.

It is evident that considerable changes in economic, cultural, social, and legal areas have taken place in China, and an open-minded leadership has contributed to such changes. Politically, however, both Chinese and foreign scholars on China have pointed out the contradiction between China's "peaceful development" foreign policy and its lack of significant democratic and liberal reforms in domestic politics.

---

20 http://news.xinhuanet.com/english/2005-12/22/content_3955754.htm.
21 http://www.apcss.org/Publications/Ocasional%20Papers/OPChinas%20Rise.pdf.

A well known China analyst, Willy Wo-Lap Lam, wrote on CNN online quoting Cao Siyuan, a constitutional scholar and ardent reformer, who has raised queries about the viability of *heping jueqi* in the absence of real liberalization in domestic politics, "it is doubtful that foreign countries will be convinced about China's peaceful ascendancy if it sticks to a non-transparent and undemocratic political system," and "a leadership's commitment to global fraternity and solidarity will be called into doubt if it is so reluctant to give its own people adequate human rights."[22] Cao thus implies that "peaceful development" would be impossible without fundamental democratic reforms because the regime faces increasing domestic unrest and challenges from various social groups. Increasing mass unrest would undermine the regime stability that is vital to China's "peaceful development."

However, Andrew Wedeman, in his chapter on regime stability and repression, points out that regime stability lies less in the level of unrest, than in how the regime responds to the proliferation of challenges. In his observation, the Chinese government has strategically differentiated among a variety of emerging groups, threats and challenges, and adopted different policies toward dissident groups. While it continues to crack down on prominent dissident groups and eminent challengers, the regime has adopted more tolerant and flexible policy toward more benign heterodoxies and local incidents. Wedeman concludes that this reflects a shift away from a strategy of comprehensive control to one of unrest management. This also suggests that the regime has attempted to make a shift from a revolutionary party to a ruling party that attempts to manage the crises and unrest situations rather than harshly suppress them all as it did in the earlier time.

Zhengxu Wang has observed that some significant grassroots political changes have taken place, and that the party leadership is considering expanding the scope of local elections and opening more channels for political participation. Such incremental reforms are transforming the regime into a hybrid regime and as such would continue to push the regime toward democracy. If this trend continues, it should help the goal of "peaceful development."

Moreover, Baogang Guo argues that the Chinese system of political legitimation based on the Chinese Confucian tradition and the ruling party's successful economic performance and efforts to renew its "mandate" to govern has strengthened rather than weakened the regime. This renewed legitimacy has helped the regime maintain political stability and enhance state capacity, which could also help China achieve the goal of "peaceful development." However, he also argues that the past success can not guarantee future success. Therefore, the extent to which China can maintain long-term stability and fulfill its promise of becoming a peaceful power depends on its ability to update its system of legitimation and turn itself from an authoritarian power to a democratic one.

To ensure a "peaceful rise" for China, it would be in Beijing's fundamental interest to deepen its political reform and move China toward a more transparent

---

22 Willy Wo-Lap Lam, "China aiming for 'Peaceful Rise'," http://edition.cnn.com/2004/WORLD/asiapcf/02/02/willy.column/.

and democratic political system. This does not necessarily mean that "democracy with Chinese characteristics" would be exactly the kind of liberal democracy found in the west. But even an "illiberal" Chinese democracy would look less threatening or more acceptable to the United States and other great powers. Thus even limited political reforms would reduce the possibility that China's rise would intensify fears and suspicions of a "China Threat" and fuel efforts to contain and constrain it. "Peaceful development" could degenerate into wishful thinking if China cannot dispel suspicion and concerns about the rise of China in an undemocratic political context and thus about the kind of role a more powerful China would play in the region and in the world affairs. As Evan S. Medeiros put it, "the future evolution of China's new external strategy of peaceful rise is unclear.... Regardless of how peace-loving the Chinese people feel they are, Chinese leaders need to take into account the legitimate concerns of its Asian neighbors and major powers in the region. Whether Chinese leaders can translate this new expression into tangible policies and deeds of reassurance remains an open question.[23]

---

23 Evan S. Medeiros, "China Debates Its 'Peaceful Rise' Strategy," *YaleGlobal*, June 22, 2004, http://yaleglobal.yale.edu/display.article?id=4118.

PART 1
Domestic Conditions of China's Peaceful Rise

Chapter 1

The Dialectic Relationship between Peaceful Development and China's Deep Reform

Guoli Liu*

This chapter examines the connection between China's domestic reform and foreign policy orientation. In recent years, there have been significant debates about the rise of China and its implications for international relations. One of the key issues is whether China's rapid rise will be peaceful or disruptive to the existing international order. The argument of this paper is that China's deep reform, i.e., profound political and socioeconomic changes, requires a peaceful international environment while a largely peaceful environment has contributed to China's successful economic reform. However, without meaningful political reform, China's growth may not be sustainable. When socioeconomic development runs into deep trouble, China might not be able to maintain its peaceful orientation in foreign policy. Thus, the relationship between peaceful development and China's deep reform is interdependent. Success in one will strengthen the other. On the other hand, failure or crisis in one aspect will certainly have serious consequences on the other.

China's Development Requires a Peaceful Environment

A peaceful international environment is essential for achieving sustained economic development. Domestic sources of foreign policy are a very important but understudied subject in China studies.[1] In a centralized political system, domestic factors including

---

* An earlier version of this paper was presented at the 2005 annual meeting of the Association of Chinese Political Studies. I would like to thank Lowell Dittmer, Sujian Guo, Gregory J. Moore and Brantly Womack for their thoughtful comments and suggestions.

1 For insightful analysis of this subject, see the chapters by William C. Kirby on traditions, Steven I. Levine on perception and ideology, and Carol Lee Hamrin on elite politics in *Chinese Foreign Policy: Theory and Practice*, edited by Thomas W. Robinson and David Shambaugh (New York: Oxford University Press, 1995). For comparative perspectives, see the excellent essays in Eugene R. Wittkopf and James M. McCormick eds., *The Domestic Sources of American Foreign Policy: Insights and Evidence* (Lanham, MD: Rowman & Littlefield Publishers, 2004).

elite politics tend to play a more significant role in foreign policy than in a pluralist system. In the era of Mao Zedong, Mao himself played a dominant role in China's key foreign policy decisions. One of Mao's key assumptions in the 1960s and early 1970s was that war was inevitable and China must be prepared against wars.[2] When Deng Xiaoping emerged as China's paramount leader in 1978, he made a fundamentally different assumption that world war would not break out in the foreseeable future. Thus, China should stop its "class struggle" and end its active preparation for armed conflict. Instead, the core task should shift to economic development aimed at "the four modernizations" – modernization of industry, agriculture, national defense, and science and technology. Since then, economic development has been a core objective for the Chinese leadership. As a result, domestic economic consideration has played a greater role in China's foreign policy. In pursuit of economic goals, China moved to improve relations with the broadest possible range of countries. Ideological obstacles to better relations were largely eliminated, and a pragmatic approach helped in general to resolve problems with foreign powers. Economic considerations accelerated the normalization of diplomatic relations with the United States in 1979 and led to a gradual expansion of normal relations.[3]

China has truly enjoyed the benefit of dynamic growth in a peaceful environment for more than a quarter century. As Figure 1.1 indicates, Chinese GDP has experienced continuous high growth rates. In aggregated terms China is an economic power whose rapid growth is felt by the whole world. From 1979 to 2004, China's average annual growth rate was 9.4 percent. From 1978 to 2003, China's per capita income grew from 379 yuan to 9101 yuan.[4] According to the World Bank, China saw a six-fold increase in GDP from 1984 through 2004. China contributed one-third of global economic growth in 2004.[5] The national economic survey conducted in 2005 revised China's GDP for 2004 to 15.9878 trillion yuan (about 2 trillion U.S. dollars), up 2.3 trillion yuan, or 16.8 percent from the preliminary figures.[6]

Having suffered a scourge of wars and civil conflicts, the Chinese people know full well that peace is precious and that development is important. After more than a century of Western invasion starting with the Opium War in 1839, large scale peasant

---

2 One of the most widely publicized slogans during the Cultural Revolution was Mao's saying of "*Beizhan, beihuang, wei renmin*" (Be prepared against war, be prepared against natural disaster, and do everything for the people). In contrast, one of Deng Xiaoping's most famous statements is "taking economic development as the central task."

3 See Barry Naughton, "The Foreign Policy Implications of China's Economic Development Strategy," in *Chinese Foreign Policy: Theory and Practice*, edited by Thomas W. Robinson and David Shambaugh (New York: Oxford University Press, 1995), pp. 47–69.

4 All the data in this article come from *China Statistical Yearbook 2004* (Beijing: China Statistics Press, 2004) unless otherwise noted.

5 See http://web.worldbank.org/WBSITE/EXTERNAL/COUNTRIES/EAST ASIAPACIFICEXT/CHINAEXTN/0,,contentMDK:20680895~menuPK: 1497618~piPK:217854~theSitePK:318950,00.html#Facts (Accessed on December 7, 2005).

6 See http://news.xinhuanet.com/english/2005-12/20/content_3947262.htm (Viewed on December 20, 2005).

The Dialectic Relationship between Peaceful Development and China's Deep Reform 19

Figure 1.1 China's Gross Domestic Product (selected years between 1978–2003)

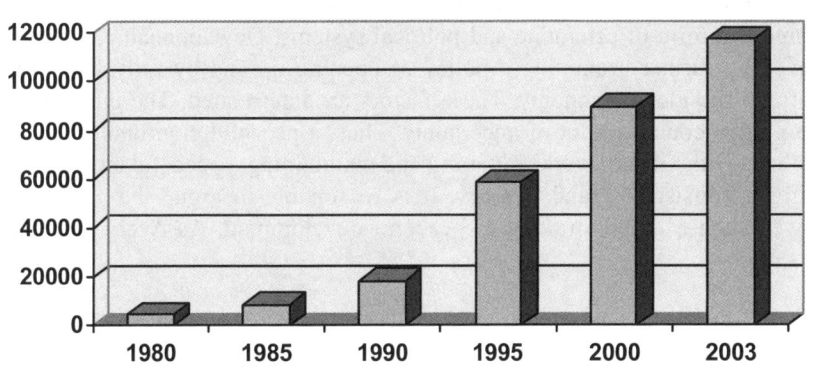

Note: Unit = 100 million Yuan
Sources: Adapted from *China Statistical Yearbook 2004*. Beijing: China Statistics Press, 2004. Data in this table are calculated at current prices except otherwise noted. Exchange rate from 1994 to 2004 has been around U.S.$1=8.26 to 8.61 yuan.

Figure 1.2 China's GDP Growth Rate in Comparative Perspective (1990–2001)

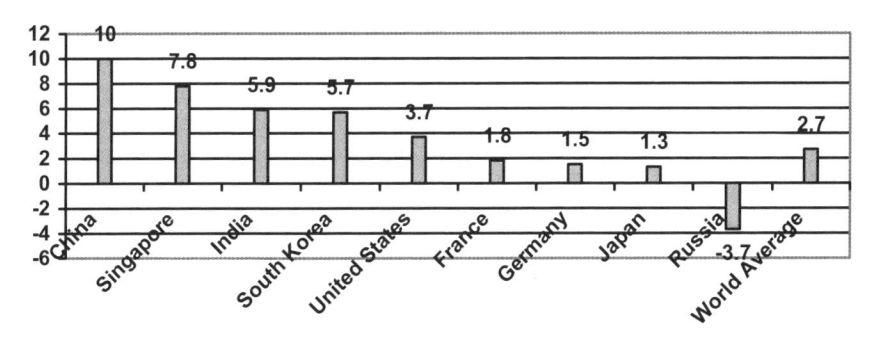

Sources: Adapted from World Bank, *World Development Report 2003* (New York: Oxford University Press, 2003), Table 3, pp. 238–239.

rebellions, dynastic decline and collapse, violent warlord politics, bloody civil war, imperialist Japanese invasion, civil war between the Nationalists and the Communists, and seemingly endless internal political struggles that peaked in the Cultural Revolution, China desperately needed peace and stability. Modern history has taught the Chinese a very clear lesson, i.e., China cannot develop well without a peaceful environment. Since Deng Xiaoping's "independent peaceful foreign policy" came into being in the early 1980s, China has followed a peaceful foreign policy. China's most fundamental policy since the Deng era has been "reform and opening" aimed at building a strong and prosperous country. As Figure 1.2 indicates, this policy has led to an extraordinary GDP growth rate almost four times higher than the world average rate between 1990 and 2001.

China's development requires several key factors. Social and political stability is crucial for development. Development and stability should be achieved through continuous reform of economic and political systems. Development can only be achieved by further promoting a policy of opening up and by fully integrating China into the global economy. These factors are interrelated. The international system today contains a lot of uncertainty. Thus, a peaceful environment cannot be realized without hard work.[7] Creating and maintaining a peaceful environment requires a consistent grand strategy. It is reasonable to argue that China has followed such a grand strategy of peaceful development. As Avery Goldstein points out:

> China's emerging grand strategy links political, economic and military means in an effort to advance the PRC's twin goals of security and great-power status. Politically, China pursues multilateral and bilateral diplomacy to mute threat perceptions and to convince others of the benefits of engagement and the counterproductive consequences of containment. Economically, China nurtures relations with diverse trading partners and sources of foreign investment, weaving a network of economic relations to limit the leverage of any single partner in setting the terms of China's international economic involvement. Militarily, China seeks to create some breathing space for modernization of its armed forces.[8]

China's open door policy is not a short term tactic but a long term strategy. This strategy is best demonstrated by China's firm commitment to comprehensive opening beginning with the Special Economic Zones in the southern costal areas in the late 1970s and extending to 14 open cities in 1984. The opening was expanded to Shanghai Pudong in the early 1990s and then further expanded to inland areas. Such SEZs and open cities have played important roles in promoting foreign trade, opening up markets, and attracting FDI.[9]

As Tables 1.1 and 1.2 clearly demonstrate, foreign trade and foreign investment have played very important roles in China's economic development. China's dynamic and fruitful participation in the world economy is the result of peaceful and relatively stable global trading and financial systems. There is no doubt that China could not enjoy such fruits of globalization without the reform

---

7 Liu Jianfei, "Heping waijiao shi Zhongguo de changqi guoce" (Peace Diplomacy is China's Longterm National Policy), in *Zhongguo Heping Jueqi Xindaolu* (New Path of China's Peaceful Rise), Institute of International Strategic Studies, CCP Central Party School (Beijing: CCP Central Party School Press, 2004), pp. 102–117.

8 Avery Goldstein, "An Emerging China's Emerging Grand Strategy: A Neo-Bismarckian Turn?" in *International Relations Theory and the Asia-Pacific*, edited by G. John Ikenberry and Michael Mastanduno (New York: Columbia University Press, 2003), p. 83. For more in depth analysis, see Avery Goldstein, *Rising to the Challenge: China's Grand Strategy and International Security* (Stanford, CA: Stanford University Press, 2005).

9 See Sujian Guo and Han Gyu Lheem, "Political Economy of FDI and Economic Growth in China: A Longitudinal Test at Provincial Level," *Journal of Chinese Political Science*, vol. 9, no. 1, Spring 2004, pp. 43–62.

Table 1.1 Total Value of Imports and Exports (U.S.$ billion)

Year	Total Imports and Exports	Total Exports	Total Imports
1978	20.64	9.75	10.89
1980	38.14	18.12	20.02
1985	69.60	27.35	42.25
1990	115.44	62.09	53.35
1995	280.86	148.78	132.08
2000	474.29	249.20	225.09
2003	850.99	438.23	412.76

Source: Adapted from *China Statistical Yearbook 2004*. Beijing: China Statistics Press, 2004.

Table 1.2 Chinese Utilization of Foreign Capital (U.S.$ billion)

Year	Total	Foreign Loans	Direct Foreign Investment	Other Foreign Investment
1979–1984	17.14	13.04	3.06	1.04
1985	4.46	2.51	1.66	0.30
1990	10.29	6.53	3.49	0.27
1995	48.133	10.327	37.521	0.285
2000	59.356	10.0	40.715	8.64
2003	56.14		53.505	2.635
1979–2003	679.58	147.57	499.76	32.64

Source: Adapted from *China Statistical Yearbook 2004*. Beijing: China Statistics Press, 2004.

and opening policy. The opening policy is dependent on a peaceful international environment. China's open door policy is based on the strategic assumption that there will be no major wars in the foreseeable future. Foreign trade and FDI will both be disrupted or even completely stopped if major armed conflict involving China occurs.

Peaceful Development and China's Deep Reform

China's peaceful development requires not only a peaceful international environment but also "deep reform." [10] China's reform since 1989 and especially since 1992 has been quite different from previous reform. The most appropriate term to define this recent stage of China's reform is "deep reform." Deep reform has been transforming the nature of Chinese politics, economics, and society. Thus it is important to ask the following questions: What is deep reform? Where does it come from? What is distinctive about reform since 1989? Since 1978, reform has been a key theme of China's economic and political development.[11] After one decade of rapid economic growth, China's reforms encountered serious obstacles. By 1988 Deng Xiaoping himself had realized the urgent need for deeper reform:

> China is conducting deep reform in order to create better conditions for future development. We do not just set our sights on the twentieth century but also think about the new century. The problem is that if we do not move ahead we have to retreat. Only deep and comprehensive reform can guarantee that we can build a well-to-do (*xiaokang*) society by the end the twentieth century and make more progress in the next century.[12]

The third plenary session of the 13th CCP Congress in September 1988 first proposed "comprehensive deep reform." Deep reform has multiple international and domestic causes, preeminently including the need to reconcile the contradictions and conflicts of earlier reforms. The 1989 Tiananmen crisis and the collapse of the Soviet bloc forced the Chinese leaders to carefully consider their options. Some conservative officials in Beijing thought all the domestic and international crises were results of too much reform, too soon. But Deng and other reformers drew a totally different conclusion. They saw the collapse of the U.S.S.R. as a result of not having had effective reforms soon enough. Deng clearly realized that it was a dead end not to reform. Only fundamental and comprehensive reform could save China from a Soviet type train wreck. After the 1989 crisis in Beijing, Deng strongly urged Jiang Zemin and other Chinese leaders to uphold the policy of reform and opening.

As he became increasingly impatient with the slow and cautious pace of reform pursued by his successors in 1990–1991, Deng made the famous southern tour in 1992 to publicly promote further opening and reform. He emphasized that whoever did not firmly support reform and opening should be removed from power. Jiang Zemin, Li Peng, and the rest of the Politburo leadership promptly and publicly agreed. Since then, deep reform has been the phrase that best catches the spirit and substance of political change and economic development in China. The 14th CCP

---

10 The analysis of China's deep reform in this section draws from the introductory essay by Guoli Liu and Lowell Dittmer in *China's Deep Reform: Domestic Politics in Transition*, edited by Lowell Dittmer and Guoli Liu (Lanham: Rowman & Littlefield, 2006), pp. 1–24.

11 Lowell Dittmer, *China under Reform* (Boulder, CO: Westview Press, 1994).

12 Deng Xiaoping, *Deng Xiaoping wenxuan*, vol. III (Selected Works of Deng Xiaoping, vol. III), (Beijing: Renmin chubanshe, 1993), p. 268.

Congress in September 1992 decided to establish a "socialist market economy with Chinese characteristics." The 15th CCP Congress in 1997 set the goal of building "a state based on the rule of law." Building a market economy and a "rule of law" state are two fundamental goals of China's deep reform, which includes the following core features.

First, the most fundamental development is to build a complete market economy instead of an economy halfway between planned and market. Marketization has become a clear goal and the growth of mixed ownership has been encouraged. Unlike the earlier stage of experimental reform aptly described as "crossing the river by feeling the stones," since 1992 Chinese reformers have set a clear goal of establishing a socialist market economy. In addition to lifting state control and allowing prices to float, the rapid growth of the private economy, joint ventures, solely foreign owned enterprises, and the reorganization of state-owned assets have led to a truly "mixed ownership economy." The range of the economic reform has been much broader. Initially, the economic system was reformed incrementally to improve incentives and increase the scope of the market. The new reform has penetrated much more deeply into fiscal, financial, and administrative matters, as well as property rights and other key aspects of the Chinese economy. Many formerly forbidden rules were broken and many closed areas were opened up. The reformers initiated a financial reform in 1994 in order to increase state capacity. Since then, there has been more centralization of financial power and a shift from central planning to market regulation. State revenue has increased significantly as a result of the nation-wide collection of the value added tax. The reformers have aimed at more centrally controlled managed growth and left behind the boom and bust cycles of the 1980s. State capacity has grown as a result of these financial reforms. Such deep reform has allowed China to sustain high growth rates despite the Asian financial crisis in 1997 (though it is true that it also helped that China's currency is not yet directly exchangeable on world markets). Market reform has both positive and negative consequences. On the one hand, reform has led to greater efficiency and higher productivity. On the negative side, incomplete market reform has resulted in widespread corruption and a growing disparity between the rich and the poor.

Second, the open-door policy has progressed to comprehensive opening in the context of globalization. Having learned the tough lessons of Mao Zedong's self-reliance policy, having known both the extremes of the Cultural Revolution (1966–1976) and the first fruits of Deng's opening policy after 1978, Chinese reformers realized that isolationism was a dead end and that comprehensive opening provided the best opportunity for socioeconomic development. After a temporary retrenchment from opening to the outside world in 1989–1991 related to the Tiananmen incident and its aftermath, China began a bold new phase of opening to all countries in the world in 1992. Such dramatic and decisive opening has led to a sharp rise in both foreign trade and direct foreign investment. The rapidly growing connections between China and the outside world have had a profound impact on all major institutions and aspects of social behavior. The scope and speed of China's opening to the outside world has accelerated since 1992, leading to China's entry into the

World Trade Organization (WTO) in 2001. Comprehensive opening is reflected in the growing volume of trade, financial transactions, travel, and other exchanges between China and all major regions of the world. China's total imports and exports have increased from U.S.$135.7 billion in 1991 to more than U.S.$1.1 trillion in 2004. In 2004 China became the world's third largest foreign trader behind the U.S. and Germany. This is truly extraordinary considering the fact that China ranked 32nd with a small trade volume of $20 billion in 1978. China has also become the largest recipient of direct foreign investment in the world, receiving a total of more than $570 billion. The degree of interdependence between China and the world economy has grown to an unprecedented level. As a consequence, China has gained multiple benefits, chiefly an accelerated economic growth rate. On the other hand, China has also been exposed to the growing pressure and risks of globalization. The 1997 Asian financial crisis and the 2003 SARS epidemic were two examples of the new challenges confronting the Chinese.

Third, "the rule of law" has been transformed from a governing instrument to a fundamental goal of reform. Chinese reformers have taken the legal system more seriously than ever before. They realized that their legitimacy and governance must have a legal and constitutional foundation. Numerous new laws have been enacted and put into practice. But China still has a long way to go before solidly establishing the rule of law. Although the Constitution has been amended several times, many parts of the 1982 Constitution (written under the context of highly centralized political power and a command economy) have become outdated. The next stage of deep reform may require more fundamental constitutional change.

Fourth, meaningful political reforms including political institutionalization and systemic leadership transition have taken place. Tiananmen destroyed forever the myth that China could engage in economic reform without touching the political system. In reaction to that traumatic event, the leadership not only emphasized a certain amount of recentralization and popular control but a renewed focus on political reform and improved governance. Indeed, any significant economic reform would be impossible without some political change of the formerly highly centralized Chinese political system. Deng Xiaoping initiated the first round of political change in 1978–1981, and after temporary setbacks in 1986 Zhao Ziyang unleashed new initiatives at the 13th Party Congress in 1987. In the 1990s, political reform has adjusted its direction, now focusing on: (1) relatively smooth leadership transition from the third generation to the fourth generation; (2) institutionalization of political elite selection from the top to the basic levels; (3) further separation of political and administrative functions of the party-state; (4) gradual expansion of the range of political discourse associated with the information revolution; (5) village elections and experiments of self-governance in residential communities, and (6) reformulation of official ideology including the emergence of the "three represents." Thus deep reform has led to a new level of ideological pragmatism and re-legitimization through development. Productivity and prosperity have become the ultimate criteria for economic and political success. Jiang Zemin formalized this in his contribution to official ideology, the "three represents." This formulation stresses that the CCP's mission is to represent the most advanced productive forces, the most advanced culture, and the fundamental interests of the overwhelming majority of the Chinese people. Though apparently bland and innocuous, this dramatic departure from proletarian revolution and class warfare has allowed the leadership to refocus its tasks on modernization without institutional breakdown. As a result, Chinese politics today is more institutionalized, more predictable, and more performance oriented. In contrast to deep reform in financial and trading sectors, China's political change, though extensive, has been relatively slow. The contradiction between deep economic reform and slow political reform has become a bottleneck for the next stage of China's reform. And there are some indications that the "fourth generation" leadership will make political reform a higher priority. For instance, fighting against corruption is one of the biggest challenges facing the CCP leadership, threatening to undermine the legitimacy of the government and erode the basis of the ruling party. And Hu Jintao said that in order to resolve the corruption issue, the CCP must "deepen reform to create a new system."[13] This would be a further step in the direction of deep reform.

Finally, deep reform is linked to a new grand strategy for the "peaceful rise" (*heping jueqi*) of China. Deng Xiaoping initiated China's "peace and development" line in the 1980s, and since that time China has been one of the biggest beneficiaries of the post-Cold War reduction of inter-state violence.[14] On the other hand, China's deep reform and rapid growth have made a growing contribution to regional and world economic vitality. Whereas the rise and fall of nations has often been accompanied by crisis and instability (as in the cases of Germany and Japan in the first half of the 20th century), China's deep reform is based on the premise of a peaceful rise. It remains to be seen whether this paradigm shift will materialize. Considered separately, many of the elements of deep reform emerged before 1992. Taken together, however, it is clear that the reform since 1992 has reached a qualitatively new level of development.

Chinese cultural tradition, featuring "unity in diversity" (*he er butong*) and "priority to peace" (*he wei gui*), goes a long way toward facilitating China's harmonious coexistence and sharing of prosperity with the Asia-Pacific region and the world at large. China's peaceful rise brings to the Asia-Pacific region opportunities for development, conditions for peace, and space for cooperation.[15] In the process of its peaceful rise, according to Zheng Bijian,

> China has formed a new security concept that differs from any traditional concept. With mutual trust, mutual benefit, equality, and cooperation as its core notions, our new

---

13 *Remin Ribao*, January 12, 2005, 1.

14 For various perspectives on this issue, see Guoli Liu ed., *Chinese Foreign Policy in Transition* (New York: Aldine de Gruyter, 2004).

15 Zheng Bijian, "China's Peaceful Rise and Opportunity for the Asia-Pacific Region," Roundtable Meeting between the Bo'ao Forum for Asia and the China Reform Forum (April 18, 2004). http://www.brook.edu/dybdocroot/FP/events/20050616bijianlunch.pdf#search=`china's%20peaceful%rise'.

paradigm firmly abandons the strategic framework in which big powers in the past vied for spheres of influence, engaged in military confrontation, or exported ideologies. Ours is a comprehensive and strategic concept with peaceful existence as its precondition, common interests as its basis, strategic cooperation as its bond, and common development as its objective. History and experience have repeatedly proved that armed forces cannot make peace, and that power politics cannot ensure security. The collective security achieved through cooperation among the Asia-Pacific countries will surely lead to universal, lasting peace and rapid, sustained development.[16]

Deep reform also implies that China will be fully integrated into the international system. Liu Jie sees China's participation in international regimes as an essential part of peaceful rise.[17] International regimes refer to the norms, procedures, and standards of decision making in various issue areas. The regimes have played constructive roles in stabilizing and facilitating international economic interaction, human rights protection, and even peace and security. Participation in international regimes is an indicator of a country's openness. For a long time, China was an "outsider" to international regimes. As China's reform deepens and opening expands, Beijing has adopted much more positive attitudes toward international regimes. China today has joined most international organizations and their related regimes. The current international regimes are dominated by Western countries. The core values, systemic structure, standards of behavior and decision making procedures are not necessarily consistent with China's strategic goals. Nevertheless, the Chinese leaders have realized that there is no viable alternative to participating in international regimes. Although China is under the influence and restraint of the current international regimes, it will make the necessary reforms and adjustments and might have some impact on the evolution of international regimes. From another perspective, joining international regimes such as the WTO will provide powerful incentives for China to deepen its domestic reforms because China will not be able to succeed in the tough global competition without making its institutions compatible with international regimes.

Internal and External Challenges to China's Peaceful Rise

In the post-Cold War era and especially since the mid-1990s, the rise of China has become a very controversial topic in international studies. With the world's fastest economic growth in the last two decades, rising China has sired many debates in

---

16 Zheng Bijian, "China's Peaceful Rise and Opportunity for the Asia-Pacific Region," Roundtable Meeting between the Bo'ao Forum for Asia and the China Reform Forum (April 18, 2004). http://www.brook.edu/dybdocroot/FP/events/20050616bijianlunch.pdf#search=`china's%20peaceful%rise'.

17 Liu Jie, *Jizhihua Shengcun: Zhongguo heping jueqi de zhanlue juece* (Living under Regimes: The Strategic Choice in the Course of China's Peaceful Rise) (Beijing: shishi chubashe, 2004).

the world.[18] According to Joseph S. Nye, the "rise of China" is a misnomer: "re-emergence" is more accurate.[19] Inside China, both "rise" (*jueqi*) and "national rejuvenation" (*minzu fuxing*) have been hotly discussed.[20]

"China's peaceful rise" is a relatively new concept in Chinese public discourse. On November 3, 2003, Zheng Bijian, the former vice president of the CCP Central Party School and now Chairman of the China Reform Forum, addressed a plenary session of the Bo'ao Forum for Asia. In his speech, titled "A New Path for China's Peaceful Rise and the Future of Asia," Zheng introduced the concept of China's "peaceful rise" (*heping jueqi*):

> In the 25 years since the inception of its reform and opening up, China has blazed a new strategic path that only suits its national conditions but also conforms to the tide of the times. This new strategic path is China's peaceful rise through independently building socialism with Chinese characteristics, while participating in rather than detaching from economic globalization.[21]

Zheng insisted that although China would rely mainly on its own strength, it needed a peaceful international environment to accomplish the task of lifting its enormous population out of a condition of underdevelopment. He also pledged that China

---

18 For contending views on the rise of China, see Samuel S. Kim, "China's Path to Great Power Status in the Globalization Era," *Asian Perspective*, 27: 1 (2003): 35–75; Stuart Harris and Gary Klintworth, eds., *China as a Great Power: Myths, Realities and Challenges in the Asia-Pacific Region* (New York: St. Martin's Press, 1995); Avery Goldstein, "Great Expectations: Interpreting China's Arrival," *International Security* 22: 3 (Winter 1997–1998): 36–73; Michael Brown et al., eds., *The Rise of China* (Cambridge, MA: MIT Press, 2000); and Gordon G. Chang, *The Coming Collapse of China* (New York: Random House, 2001). It is interesting that *Newsweek*, *U.S. New & World Report*, and *Time* had cover stories and special reports respectively on "China's Century," China Challenge," and "China's New Revolution" in May and June 2005. For a Chinese view, see Peng Peng ed., *Heping Jueqi lun* (Peaceful Rising Theory: The Path of China Becoming a Great Power) (Guangzhou: Guangdong renmin chubanshe, 2005).

19 Joseph S. Nye, "China's Re-emergence and the Future of the Asia-Pacific," *Survival* 39 (1997–1998): 65–79. Historian Jonathan Spence also prefers to call China's recent development as "reemergence." In a series of essays published in *Foreign* Policy (Jan–Feb 2005, pp. 44–58), Jonathan Spence, Martin Wolf, Minxin Pei, Zbigniew Brezezinski, and John J. Mearsheimer discuss how China is changing the world. They debate whether China is more interested in economic development than war, whether China can rise peacefully, and whether China needs to be "contained."

20 For instance, both Jiang Zemin and Hu Jintao frequently talk about *zhonghua minzu de weida fuxing* (great rejuvenation of the Chinese nation). The theme of the 2005 annual meeting of the Chinese Association of Diplomacy is "China's Peaceful Rise." The meeting was held on August 13-14, 2005 in Kunming, China.

21 Zheng Bijian, "A New Path for China's Peaceful Rise and the Future of Asia," November 3, 2003, http://hisotry.boaoforum.org/English/E2003nh/dhwj/t20031103_184101.btk.

would rise to the status of a great power without destabilizing the international order or oppressing its neighbors:

> The rise of a major power often results in drastic change in international configuration and world order, even triggers a world war. An important reason behind this is that these major powers followed a path of aggressive war and external expansion. Such a path is doomed to failure. In today's world, how could we follow such a totally erroneous path that is injurious to all, China included? China's only choice is to strive for rise, more importantly strive for a peaceful rise.[22]

Premier Wen Jiabao took the initiative to push the concept of peaceful rise further toward a policy formulation when he used the term in a speech at Harvard University on December 10, 2003.

> There are many challenges to China's peaceful rise. It is neither proper nor possible for us to rely on foreign countries for development. ...While opening still wider to the outside world, we must more fully and more consciously depend on our own structural innovation, on constantly expanding the domestic market, on converting the huge savings of the citizens into investment, and on improving the quality of the population and scientific and technological progress to solve the problems of resources and the environment. Here lies the essence of China's road of peaceful rise and development.[23]

It is beyond dispute that China has enjoyed extraordinary high growth rate over a quarter century. The key question is whether China's strong growth is sustainable. China faces multiple challenges to its development. The first is that of natural resources. Currently, China's exploitable oil and natural gas reserves, water resources, and arable land are all well below world average in per capita terms. The second challenge is the environment. Serious pollution, the wasteful use of resources, and low rates of recycling are bottlenecks for sustainable economic development. The third is the lack of coordination between economic and social development. These major challenges, alongside rapid growth, mean that China is facing both a period of development and a period of tough choices.[24]

Energy shortages and especially low energy efficiency have become serious bottlenecks for Chinese growth. In 1990, China net exported 24 million tons of crude oil. Very soon China became an oil importer rather than exporter. The country's net imports of crude oil by 2002 were 80 million tons annually. In 2003, oil only accounted for 23 percent of China's total energy consumption. In the same year, coal accounted for 67 percent of China's energy consumption. China produced and

---

22 Ibid. Quoted in Robert L. Suettinger, "The rise and descent of 'peaceful rise'," *Chinese Leadership Monitor*, no. 12 (2004).

23 "Turn Your Eyes to China," full text of Premier Wen's December 10, 2003, speech at Harvard University, *People's Daily* online, December 12, 2003.

24 Zheng Bijian, "China's Development and Her New Path to a Peaceful Rise," Villa d'Este Forum (September 2004). http://www.brook.edu/dybdocroot/FP/events/20050616bijianlunch.pdf #search='china's%20peaceful%rise'.

consumed close to 1.3 billion tons of coal in 2003. That is about 1 ton of coal for every Chinese. The heavy reliance on coal has very serious environmental and health consequences. Chinese electricity consumption jumped from 623 billion kwh in 1990 to 1633 billion kwh in 2002. When more and more manufacturing facilities are moving to China, energy consumption is also increasing rapidly. China has become the second largest consumer of energy resources in the world, only behind the United States. In 2004, each U.S. citizen consumed about 25 barrels of oil while each Chinese citizen used about 1 and a half barrels of oil. It is not hard to imagine what kind of a global oil crisis will occur if the Chinese per capita oil consumption gets closer to the U.S. level. Obviously, China cannot and should not blindly follow the U.S. pattern of heavy consumption of oil. China must find a new pattern of growth that relies on less energy. However, China's energy efficiency is far behind that of the United States and even further behind that of Japan. China has tremendous troubles with extensive growth. According to China's top statistician, Li Deshui, China only produced 4.4 percent of the world's total GDP in 2004, yet the crude oil it devoured accounted for 7.4 percent of the world's total; coal, 31 percent; iron ore, 30 percent; rolled steel, 27 percent; and cement, 40 percent.[25]

It is difficult but absolutely necessary to make a transition to intensive growth. A closely related issue is ecological and environmental challenge. Environmental pollution in China is very serious. The ecological situation is deteriorating. Enormous energy consumption with low returns has become a severe problem. China's ecological and environmental challenge has become a serious bottleneck for Chinese sustainable economic development.[26]

With the structural transition of the Chinese economy and especially the reform of state-owned enterprises, millions of workers have been laid off. China has been experiencing a paradoxical phenomenon: on the one hand there is a growing demand of skilled workers, on the other hand there is an increasing number of "surplus laborers." At the same time, labor migration is natural. But China is experiencing the largest movement of rural labor in history. In recent years, Chinese cities have absorbed more than 100 million rural workers, and they are expected to see an influx of another 250 to 300 million in the next two or three decades. Under the circumstances, it is hardly surprising that China's effort to establish a new social

---

25 See http://news.xinhuanet.com/english/2005-12/20/content_3947262.htm (Viewed on December 20, 2005).

26 Elizabeth C. Economy, *The River Runs Black* (Ithca: Cornell University Press, 2004). One city after the next is offloading its polluting industries outside its city limits, and polluting industries themselves are seeking poorer areas. Heavy air pollution contributes to respiratory illnesses that kill up to 300,000 people a year. "Over the past 20 years in China, there has been a single-minded focus on economic growth with the belief that economic growth can solve all problems," said Pan Yue, the outspoken deputy director of China's State Environmental Protection Administration. "But this has left environmental protection badly behind." Quoted in Jim Yardley's "Rivers Run Black, and Chinese Die of Cancer," *New York Times*, September 12, 2004, pp. A1, 8.

Table 1.3 Chinese Household Consumption (Yuan)

Year	Households	Rural Households	Urban Households
1978	184	138	405
1980	236	178	496
1985	437	347	802
1990	803	571	1686
1995	2236	1434	4874
1996	2641	1768	5430
1997	2834	1876	5796
1998	2972	1895	6217
1999	3138	1927	6796
2000	3397	2037	7402
2001	3609	2156	7761
2002	3818	2269	8047
2003	4089	2361	8471
Region (2003)			
Beijing	10584	5041	12775
Tianjin	7836	4321	10266
Hebei	3452	2305	7082
Shanxi	2934	1535	5173
Inner Mongolia	3742	1667	7263
Liaoning	5159	2630	7147
Jilin	4557	2161	6830
Heilongjiang	4645	2008	7614
Shanghai	15866	8141	18175
Jiangsu	5274	3293	8126
Zhejiang	6451	4665	11688
Anhui	3312	2572	4933
Fujian	5324	4358	8731
Jiangxi	2739	1964	5127
Shandong	4385	2943	7740
Henan	3129	1897	6544
Hubei	3985	2179	8402
Hunan	3284	2227	7040
Guangdong	6190	3086	10471
Guangxi	2567	1678	6843
Hainan	3275	2400	5642
Chongqing	3217	1599	8447
Sichuan	2839	1926	6404
Guizhou	1770	1213	4964
Yunnan	2495	1821	5979
Tibet	2825	1272	9112
Shaanxi	2548	1395	6080
Gansu	2171	1211	5542
Qinghai	2895	1529	6102
Ningxia	2927	1695	5558
Xinjiang	3237	1619	6330

Source: *China Statistical Yearbook 2004* (Beijing: China Statistics Press, 2004). Data in this table are calculated at current prices.

safety net has fallen short, especially given its socialist roots. The lack of social safety net for large sectors of the population has become a source of social instability.

At a time of rapid growth and growing prosperity, the issues of income disparity become more conspicuous. Table 1.3 on household consumption clearly demonstrates the growing disparity of income between urban and rural households and severe disparities among regions. For instance, the consumption gap between rural households and urban households jumped from 227 yuan in 1978 to 5365 yuan in 2000 and 6110 yuan in 2003. The household consumption gap between the wealthiest cities (Beijing 10,584 yuan, Shanghai 15,866 yuan) and the poorest provinces (Guizhou 1770 yuan, Gansu 2171 yuan) are extraordinarily large. Such gaps far exceed the disparity between the advanced cities and less developed states in the United States. Chinese leaders have realized the growing regional disparity and proposed a grand plan to develop the big West. There has been a lot of talk but not enough actions to adequately address the growing regional disparity.

For many years, the reforms promoted the idea of "getting rich is glorious" and encouraged some people and some regions to become rich first. Such policies naturally favored the people with better education and greater skills. The opening policy especially favored the costal areas with good infrastructure and strong entrepreneurial tradition.

As new leaders with working backgrounds in the poor provinces of Gansu, Guizhou and Tibet, Hu Jintao and Wen Jiabao formulated a new direction in China's development path away from a blind pursuit of economic growth toward "scientific development," a variation on the idea of sustainable development. This new model stresses improving people's livelihoods and protecting the environment. This new direction included both symbolic gestures and real action, but it remains to be seen whether the path will depart substantially from an economic development program that is based fundamentally on inequality and tends to further it.[27] "The most pressing challenges in the years to come may spring directly from the rising expectations created by the regime's own professions of belief in a more compassionate development model."[28] China needs sustained rapid growth of the economy, but it also needs speed up social development; it wants to maintain dynamic growth trend in East China, it also wants to achieve common development of Eastern, Central, and Western China. Reformers must confront the dilemmas between equity and dynamic growth, between deepening of reform and maintaining social stability.

Zheng Bijian proposed three strategies to deal with the above challenges. The first grand strategy refers to a new pattern of industrialization. China's development cannot rely on old patterns of industrialization of high input, high energy consumption, and heavy pollution. Instead, China should take a new path of industrialization with more high technology, higher economic efficiency, low resource consumption, less environmental pollution, and full utilization of human

---

27 Mary E. Gallagher, "China in 2004: Stability above All," *Asian Survey* 45: 1 (2005), p. 28.

28 Gallagher, "China in 2004: Stability above All," p. 32.

resources advantages. The second grand strategy is to actively participate in economic globalization by transcending the path of modern latecomers of great powers and the Cold War mentality. Zheng says China will not repeat the German road of World War I, and the German and Japanese road of World War II. Both Germany and Japan resorted to seeking world hegemony via violent struggle over resources. He says China will also not repeat the old path of Cold War confrontation and struggle for hegemony after World War II. The third grand strategy is to build a society of socialist harmony by transcending the outdated model of social governance. In sum, China's strategy is aimed at peace and harmony, i.e., internal harmony and external peace.[29]

This peaceful strategy has affected Beijing's policy of "one country, two systems," and peaceful unification with Taiwan. Beijing's focus has been on peaceful means. In recent years, cross Taiwan Strait economic relations have expanded very drastically. Economic interdependence between Taiwan and the mainland has become a fact of life. Leaders of Taiwan's opposition parties, including the Nationalist Party, People First Party, and the New Party, have conducted historic visits to the mainland and held fruitful talks with the top CCP leaders in 2005. However, serious differences remain between the CCP and the ruling Democratic Progressive Party (DPP). The issue of Taiwan continues to be potentially explosive and very dangerous. If Taiwan declares independence, Chinese leaders cannot afford to stand idle. Pro-independence forces in Taiwan constitute a serious threat to peace and stability in the Taiwan Strait. If Beijing has to respond with military means to Taiwan independence, the peaceful environment in the Taiwan Strait and in East Asia more generally will be seriously affected.

China has followed a good neighbor policy and built friendly relations with almost all of its neighbors. The only major neighboring country that has serious political differences with China is Japan. Militarism and right-wing political extremism are growing in Japan. China is surrounded by a number of countries with troubled bilateral or multilateral relations. For instance, India and Pakistan have long been in territorial and religious disputes. The fact that both India and Pakistan are armed with nuclear weapons now makes the situation more intense. North Korea has been developing a nuclear program. It is difficult to tell whether the six party talks can achieve positive results in the near future. A nuclear North Korea will seriously disrupt the regional security order and have negative consequences for Beijing's peaceful foreign policy. China and Russia are enjoying their best relations in decades. However, there is no certainty that Sino-Russian relations will always remain trouble free. In fact, both sides have some deeply rooted mistrust and mutual suspicion. Russia is also concerned with the growth of Chinese immigration to the Russian Far East. Nevertheless, it seems that common interests between Russia and China exceed their differences. China and Russia conducted a joint military exercise in 2005 and the two countries share some strategic concerns especially

---

29 Zheng Bijian, "Using 'Three Strategies' to Meet 'Three Challenges'," *Renmin Ribao*, June 22, 2005, p.1.

on the common fight against terrorism, Islamic fundamentalism, and separatism in Chechnya and Taiwan.

The potential for a peaceful rise does not depend on China alone. It also demands that the rest of the world help China create an international environment where this sort of rise can take place. Internationally, China faces a host of established powers, most notably the United States, with their own economic and political concerns. The most important bilateral relationship for China is Sino-American relations. A healthy relationship with the United States is critical for creating a favorable international environment for reform and opening, for defending China's national security, and for achieving China's modernization with assistance of U.S. capital, technology, and management experience.

Sino-American relations have entered a new period of stability in recent years due to the following factors. First, the U.S. strategy of anti-terrorism has broadened the foundation of Sino-American cooperation. In the near future, the U.S. is not likely to treat China as a main competitor. Second, both China and the United States are seriously concerned of the proliferation of weapons of mass destruction. Both sides do not want to see nuclear weapons in the Korean peninsula. Beijing has played a critical role in making the six party talk about North Korea's nuclear issue. Third, both Beijing and Washington have realized the sensitivity of the Taiwan issue. The Bush administration has reemphasized the One China policy. Beijing has demonstrated greater determination against Taiwan independence on the one hand and greater flexibility in exploring peaceful means to solve the Taiwan issue on the other hand. Fourth, rapid development of trade relations between China and the United States has created a broad and strong economic foundation for bilateral relations. At the same time, a lot of tensions have intensified because of the growing frictions of trade deficits and China's proposed purchase of sensitive companies such as Unocal. Managing Sino-American relations is a priority of Chinese diplomacy. In the view of Gong Li, a professor at the CCP Central Party School, "the fundamental interests of China in the 21st century includes peaceful rise, modernization, and national unification. None of these strategic issues can be resolved by getting around (*raokai*) the Untied States."[30] If Gong's view is right, success or failure in managing Sino-American relations might affect the fate of China's development and peaceful rise. A similar argument can be made that the United States cannot resolve many important regional, especially East Asian and global, issues without actively engaging China.

Can the new stability in Sino-American relations last? According to David Shambaugh, neither the U.S. nor China seeks a deterioration of relations. Indeed,

---

30 Gong Li, "Zhongguo de duimei zhengce yu Zhonguo heping jueqi xindaolu" (China's Policy toward the United States and China's New Path of Peaceful Rise), in *Zhongguo Heping Jueqi Xindaolu* (New Path of China's Peaceful Rise), Institute of International Strategic Studies, CCP Central Party School (Beijing: CCP Central Party School Press, 2004), p. 252. See also Yasheng Huang, "Sino-U.S. Relations: The Economic Dimensions," in *In the Eyes of the Dragon: China Views the World*, edited by Yong Deng and Fei-Ling Wang (Lanham, MD: Rowman & Littlefield Publishers, 1999), pp. 159–181.

both countries are otherwise preoccupied. The United States is committed to the war against terrorism and improving the domestic economy. China faces the tough challenges of deep reform and is in the early stages of a prolonged and wrenching process of implementing the terms of its accession to the World Trade Organization. Shambaugh concludes: "If wisely managed by both sides – and if the key sensitivities of each are respected rather than provoked – the new stability in Sino-American relations may endure."[31] But Shambaugh's optimistic vision is rejected by the likes of "offensive realist" John J. Mearsheimer, who believes that the United States will not tolerate the rise of China as the dominant power in Asia.[32]

The Symbiotic Relationship between Peaceful Development and Deep Reform

China's peaceful development requires deep reform that will provide both institutional and technological innovations. In more than 20 years, China has made enormous progress and built a firm foundation for the development of a great power in the future. At the same time, China has accumulated a large number of domestic problems while going through a series of profound changes. As discussed above, many urgent problems need to be solved in China. These problems include rising unemployment, rampant official corruption, weak legal system, growing regional disparity, a growing gap between the rich and the poor, unequal access to education, population problems, energy bottlenecks, and severe environmental problems. If the critical problems cannot be solved or alleviated effectively, they may cause crisis and lead to calamitous impact on political and social stability. In recent times, Chinese citizens often put corruption, bureaucratism, increase in unemployment and laid-off workers, and the widening gap between the rich and the poor as the four main factors affecting social stability in China.

The tough problems that China is confronting today can only be resolved through the deepening of reform. Widespread corruption has in fact weakened the Chinese government's managerial ability, but the Chinese political system still retains certain mobilization power. China may prevent a major social crisis if it properly manages politics, implements system innovation, overcomes corruption and polarization, and distributes the fruits of the economic growth more rationally among all social members. If the reformers improve the supervising system effectively, via the democratic construction at the basic level, and pursue an inner-party power check and balance mechanism, China will move in the direction of democratization with

---

31 David Shambaugh, "Sino-American Relations since September 11," *Current History* (September 2002): 243–249.

32 This is the conclusion of Mearsheimer's book, *The Tragedy of Great Power Politics* (New York: Norton, 2001), pp. 401–402. Mearsheimer argues that the United States does not tolerate peer competitors. As it is demonstrated in the 20th century, it is determined to remain the world's only regional hegemon. Therefore, the United States will seek to contain China and ultimately weaken it to the point where it is no longer capable of dominating Asia.

Chinese characteristics.[33] "China's political future depends on conducting reform in development, and seeking stability through change."[34] Brantly Womack provides an insightful analysis of the theoretical and practical issues in regard to the "party-state democracy." It is important to examine the transition from a revolutionary party to a "governing party" and "democracy" under the new leadership.[35]

In China today, fundamental political change could start from the grassroots creeping democratization and the intra-party democracy and move to a more open and free election at higher levels of the government while allowing the Chinese government to maintain stability for economic development. There will be no real "checks and balances" without democracy. Without checks and balances, there will be no real solution to corruption, and there will be no real peace and stability in China in the long term. Suppression works temporarily, but not in a long-term, and the cost is too high and it undermines the credibility and legitimacy of the government. That is why "deep reform" is necessary. The "deep reform" is not simply "rectification of party discipline," "mass line," "people-oriented" etc. propaganda, but real political reform, which is not simply "administrative" in nature, but "political" in nature – transforming the relationship between the party and the government, between the party leaders and the rank-file members, and between the government and the citizens. Such fundamental political reform will continue to affect the international environment of China. As China becomes more democratic and provides better protection of human rights, it will be more conducive for the Chinese leadership to achieve its strategic goals (such as high tech imports and transfer, a long-term "strategic relationship" with the U.S. and the West, and energy supplies) and create a favorable international environment for China's "peaceful development." The above analysis indicates that domestic reform and external environment are dialectic and interrelated with each other. Therefore, democratic reform is essential both for maintaining a long-term domestic stability and for maintaining a peaceful international environment that would allow China to achieve its foreign policy strategic goals.[36]

Deep reform cannot be successful without a peaceful environment. Zbigniew Brzezinski provided an insightful analysis of the connections between peace and China's development. Chinese leaders fully understand that a confrontational foreign policy could disrupt that growth, harm hundreds of millions of Chinese, and threaten the CCP's hold on power. China's leadership appears rational, calculating, and conscious not only of China's rise but also of its continued weakness. "Even

---

33 For more in depth analysis along this line of thinking, see Ye Zicheng, *Zhongguo da Zhanlue: Zhongguo chengwei shijie daguo de zhuyao weiti ji zhanlue xuanze* (China's Grand Strategy: Key Issues and Strategic Choices in China's Development as a World Power) (Beijing: China Social Science Press, 2003).

34 Xiao Gongqin, "China is not likely to have political turmoil," *Strategy and Management*, 2003, no. 6.

35 Brantly Womack, "Democracy and the Governing Party: A Theoretical Perspective," *Journal of Chinese Political Science*, vol. 10, no. 1, 2004, pp. 23–42.

36 Sujian Guo contributed to this critical argument.

beyond the realm of strategic warfare, a country must have the capacity to attain its political objectives before it will engage in limited war. It is hard to envisage how China could promote its objectives when it is acutely vulnerable to a blockade and isolation enforced by the United States. In a conflict, Chinese maritime trade would stop entirely. The flow of oil would cease, and the Chinese economy would be paralyzed."[37] Fundamentally speaking, a peaceful diplomacy is the only correct choice for China in the era of globalization.

The strategy of peaceful development is not only a logical extension of domestic reform, but also a result of historical learning. Wang Jisi, Dean of the School of International Studies at Peking University, examined the historical lessons of Soviet-American struggle for hegemony and concluded that China must not engage in a new Cold War with the United States.[38] Unlike the former Soviet Union, China has neither desire nor ability to contend for hegemony with the United States. The U.S. also does not treat China as a primary strategic threat. The Soviet Union followed the command economy. China has completely abandoned the command economy and moved toward a market economy. Having tasted the fruit of marketization and globalization, there is no reason for China to return to the command economy. This is a powerful reason that China will not be a Soviet type competitor against the United States. The former Soviet Union committed a fatal mistake by engaging in an extraordinarily costly arms race against the United States. Although Soviet GDP was only about half of that of the U.S., Soviet military spending of $175 billion actually exceeded U.S. military spending of $115 in 1980. Extremely high levels of military spending and a stagnant economy contributed to Soviet decline and final collapse. Wang's key conclusions are: First, Chinese leaders have a sober understanding of China's condition. They define China as an "economically and culturally backward developing country." The gap between the Chinese economy and U.S. economy today is greater than that between the Soviet Union and the U.S. during the Cold War. Militarily, in terms of defense spending, strategic nuclear missiles, Naval and Air forces, etc, the U.S. currently enjoys an absolute advantage. China has a realistic goal of becoming a country with a middle level per capita income by the mid 21st century. This forms a sharp contrast with the former Soviet Union, which claimed to have achieved "developed socialism" and aimed at overtaking the U.S. both economically and militarily. Second, China has a clear understanding of economic globalization and international strategic balance. As a result, it actively participates in globalization and advocates "win-win" in international cooperation and competition. China has joined almost all major international organizations and regimes. Third,

---

37 Zbigniew Brzezinski, "Make Money, Not War," in Suzanne Ogden ed., *Global Studies: China*. Eleventh edition (Guilford, CT: McGraw-Hill/Dushkin, 2006), pp. 181–182.

38 Wang Jisi, "Sumei zhengba de lishi jiaoxun he Zhongguo de jueqi" (Historic Lessons of Soviet-U.S. Contending for Hegemony and the Path of China's Rise), in *Zhongguo Heping Jueqi Xindaolu* (New Path of China's Peaceful Rise), Institute of International Strategic Studies, CCP Central Party School (Beijing: CCP Central Party School Press, 2004), pp. 5–25.

while the fundamental goal of Soviet foreign policy was to "bury world capitalism," Chinese foreign policy is aimed at creating a favorable international environment for development, defending territorial sovereignty, and facilitating national unification. Thus, China truly appreciates the strategic opportunity for peace and development. It does not wish to lead any international effort against any great power. China is against U.S. hegemonism and unilateralism. Unlike the former Soviet Union, however, China does not base its foreign policy on ideology, nor does it build blocs or spheres of influence, form exclusive trading blocs, or form any military alliances. Furthermore, China pays special attention to strategic dialogue, communication and mutual understanding with the United States and other great powers. In the early 1990s, Chinese leaders proposed to U.S. leaders to use "increase mutual trust, reduce troubles, develop cooperation, and avoid confrontation" as principles for managing Sino-American relations. In the post-Cold War era, Sino-American relations has experienced several twists and turns. Fortunately, the two sides have been able to prevent the crises from getting out of control because leaders on both sides have put common interests above their differences. Since the end of the Cold War, China's national strength has increased significantly. At the same time, the position of the U.S. as the only superpower has not weakened but strengthened in some aspects. Such developments indicate that China and the U.S. not only can enjoy a win-win situation in economic relations, but also have a win-win situation in global security and political relations. All of this is better than "zero-sum games."[39]

Despite all that has been said about China's high speed economic growth," China's economy in 2004 was just one-seventh the size of the U.S. economy, and one-third the size of Japan's. In per capita terms, China is still a low-income developing country, ranking below one-hundredth in the world.

Currently China's security strategy has four main goals: (1) the basic goal is to maintain national territorial and sovereign integrity; (2) the core objective is to create a favorable external environment for economic development; (3) an important task is to create conditions for full national unification; and (4) China wishes to contribute to regional and global peace and stability. All goals are based on "peace."[40]

In sum, deep reform and peaceful development are mutually supportive and mutually enabling (*xiangfu xiangcheng*). If deep reform fails, China's peaceful development will be interrupted. If peaceful development is blocked or interrupted, deep reform will suffer a serious setback. The symbiotic relationship between peaceful development and deep reform requires China to simultaneously deepen its domestic reforms and pursue a peaceful diplomacy. The ultimate success of this grand strategy of peaceful development demands not only the persistent hard work of many generations of Chinese people but also a true spirit of cooperation from the other great powers.

---

39 Ibid.
40 Liu Jianfei, "Heping waijiao shi Zhongguo de changqi guoce," p. 107.

Chapter 2

China's Peaceful Development, Regime Stability and Political Legitimacy

Baogang Guo*

Introduction

Chinese leaders began promoting the idea of "peaceful rise" or "peaceful development" in 2002.[1] Their targeted audience is clearly those who advocate the "China threat theory." The intention is to calm the uneasiness shared by many Western nations over China's fast re-emergence as a great power. The supporters of the China threat theory have argued that China's rise as a non-democratic or an illiberal "communist" regime poses political, military, and economic threats to the status quo of the liberal world order.[2] The proponents of the peaceful rise theory dispute the claim that China is a threat, and insist that China's goal is to integrate with rather than isolate from or confront the existing liberal economic system. China's goal is to become a partner for peace and a force for continuity rather than a force of instability. According to this theory, China has no need to challenge the existing world system; rather, its own national interests will lead China to become an active participant in the on-going economic globalization. Indeed, China has openly welcomed the new expression used in describing China's new role coined by Robert Zoellick, Deputy Secretary of State of the United States, namely, a "responsible stakeholder." [3]

But the world cannot simply bet on China's promise, as Zoellick also cautiously pointed out. To many China watchers, China needs to take concrete actions to

---

* The author wishes to thank Douglas Reynolds, Andrew J. Waskey and He Li for their comments made on earlier drafts of this chapter.

1 Zheng Bijian, "The 16th National Congress of the Communist Party of China and China's Peaceful Rise-a New Path," speech at the Center for Strategic and International Studies in the U.S. (December 9, 2002); Information Office of the State Council, *White Paper on Peaceful Development*, available from: http://www.people.com.cn, accessed on Dec. 23, 2005.

2 Fareed Zakaria, "The Rise of Illiberal Democracy," *Foreign Affairs*, November/December, 1997; Bill Gertz, *The China Threat: How the People's Republic Targets America* (Washington D.C.: Regency Publishing, 2000).

3 Robert B. Zoellick, "Whither China: From Membership to Responsibility?" Remarks to National Committee on U.S.-China Relations, September 21, 2005, New York City.

contribute to world peace. China has suggested that it will take an unconventional path of development. The new path offers, among many other things, opportunities to expand democracy and individual freedom internally. However, as long as China remains an authoritarian regime, the uncertainty over China's intentions will not wither away easily. There are two reasons for this.

First, many people in the West are strongly influenced by the so-called "democratic peace" theory which holds that peace is only empirically evident within democracies.[4] It can be argued for this reason that peace is not assured until China becomes a member of the democratic club, and the lack of democracy is in itself the lack of legitimacy. Secondly, to some, a non-democratic regime has permanent flaws in legitimacy, thus, hinders its regime stability. An unstable regime has no credible claim to peace either.[5]

The aim of this paper is not to discuss the merits and fallacies contained in the two claims stated above. But those claims do raise the issue of domestic preconditions for the peaceful development. For example, in what way can the strengthening or weakening of a regime's political legitimacy affect the regime's political stability? What are the bases of political legitimacy? Are there alternatives to democratic theory of legitimacy? Since Beijing has maintained a consistent level of political stability since 1989, an assumption can be made that there must be some effective ways to maintain strong public support despite the lack of political freedom and democracy in that country. Is there a unique system of legitimation exiting in China which has apparently not been adequately understood by Western scholars? If so, how has the regime adapted to the system? Maybe it is the ability to adapt to the Chinese system of legitimation that has saved Communism from falling in the way their European counterparts experienced in the 1990s.

The research question to be explored in this paper is the relationship between regime stability and political legitimacy. It assumes that regime stability is a function of political legitimacy, and stability within is an important determent of China's behavior in international affairs. A peaceful development depends primarily on its ability to maintain its regime stability, and a failure to continue to rebuild and strengthen its bases of political legitimacy at home may compromise its stability, and consequently undermine the peaceful nature of its development. Unlike the conventional view which tends to believes that the use of coercion is the primary cause of Beijing's long-term regime stability, it will be argued that the prolonged stability has been achieved in large part through its successful efforts to renew and reinforce its right to govern internally. Chinese cultural environment and its traditional system of legitimation that are founded upon original and utilitarian

---

[4] Immanuel Kant, *Perpetual Peace*, translated by Lewis White Beck (New York: The Library of Liberal Arts, Bobbs-Merrill, 1957); Ray, Jamee Lee, "Does Democracy Cause Peace?" *Annual Review of Political Science*, vol. 1, 1998, pp. 27–46.

[5] Allan Buchanan, "Political Legitimacy and Democracy," *Ethics*, vol. 112, no. 4, July 2002, pp. 689–719.

justifications provide continued support for the regime in Beijing.[6] However, the past success cannot guarantee future success. Therefore, to what extent the Chinese Communist Party (CCP) can sustain its regime stability and fulfill its promise of becoming a peaceful global power is very much dependent on its ability to bring up to date its system of legitimation and turn itself from an authoritarian power to a democratic one. Not until then is the China-threat theory likely to fade away.

An Analytical Framework

Regime stability can be defined as a lack of political challenges and a high level of consistency and predictability in a state's behaviors in domestic and international affairs. Stability is a most wanted goal for all political regimes, and a necessary condition for a country's peaceful development. Yet stability itself does not always imply a policy for peace. The bases of political legitimacy upon which the regime is founded will shape state behaviors. Before examining the nature of China's system of legitimation, the question to be asked first is: has China been a stable state?

China has been undertaking two radical transformations simultaneously for some time, namely, from a command economy to a market economy and from a traditional society to a modern society. Empirical studies suggest that countries which have experienced either one or both of these transitions will more often than not produce a high level of political instability and turbulence. The task of preserving political order in changing societies is difficult because the development of political institutions tends to lag behind social and economic changes.[7]

There have been efforts made to measure political stability worldwide. In a study done by the World Bank, researchers developed a Political Stability Indicator (PSI) using a number of factors to measure levels of stability. The PSI indicator was one of six indices developed to measure overall governance in a country. The authors drew 194 different measures from 17 different sources of subjective governance data constructed by 15 different organizations. The PSI measures perceptions of the likelihood that the government in power will be destabilized or overthrown by possibly unconstitutional and/or violent means, including terrorism. The choice of units for governance ensures that the estimates of governance have a mean of zero, a standard deviation of one, and range from around -2.5 to around 2.5. Higher or positive values indicate greater political stability. Table 2.1 summarizes PSI figures for selected countries. The data indicates that China is a relative stable country comparing with most developing countries, but is less stable than most developed countries. Notably, the level of stability fluctuated little over the years.

---

6   Baogang Guo, "Political Legitimacy and China's Transition," *Journal of Chinese Political Science*, vol. 8, no. 1–2, Fall 2003, pp. 1–25.

7   Samuel P. Huntington, *Political Order in Changing Societies* (New Haven, CT: Yale University Press, 1868).

Table 2.1 Political Stability Indicator for Selected Countries (1996–2002)

Country	2002	2000	1998	1996
Afghanistan	-2.21	-2.44	-1.84	-1.51
Brazil	0.17	0.27	-0.43	-0.01
China	**0.22**	**0.27**	**0.29**	**0.23**
Czech	1.02	0.85	0.95	0.95
Germany	1.06	1.27	1.42	1.19
India	-0.84	-0.35	-0.34	-0.55
Russia	-0.40	-0.53	-0.49	-0.76
United States	0.34	1.26	1.13	0.92

Sources: Kaufmann, D., A. Kraay, and M. Mastruzzi, *Governance Matters III: Governance Indicators for 1996–2002*. World Bank, World Bank Policy Research Working Paper 3106. 2003. Available at: http://www.worldbank.org/wbi/governance/pubs/govmatters2001.htm.

State legitimacy is commonly believed to be a precondition of regime stability. Talcott Parsons contends that legitimacy is "the highest normative defense against the breakdown of a system of social order."[8] Its perpetuation is always a major preoccupation of the government.[9] In the West, political legitimacy is defined by some as "right to govern,"[10] or "moral justification,"[11] but more often it is defined instrumentally as "the capacity of the system to engender and maintain the belief that the existing political institutions are the most appropriate ones for the society,"[12] or "a power relationship justified in terms of people's beliefs."[13] Comparing with these Western conceptualizations, Chinese understanding of political legitimacy is much more systematic; it can be characterized as inward looking, two-dimensional, and moralistic in nature.

---

8 Talcott Parsons, "Some Reflections on the Place of Force in Social Process," in Harry Eckerstein, ed., *Internal War: Problems and Approaches* (New York: Free Press, 1963), p. 57.

9 James O'Connor, *The Fiscal Crisis of the State* (New York: St. Martin's Press, 1973), p. 7.

10 Coicaud, J.-M., *Legitimite et Politique*, Chinese translated by Dong Xinping and Wang Yuanfei (Beijing: Central Compilation and Translation Press, 2002), p. 12.

11 Buchanan, *op. cit.*, p. 689.

12 Seymour Martin Lipset, *Political man*, expanded ed. (Baltimore: Johns Hopkins University Press, 1981), p. 88.

13 David Beetham, *The Legitimation of Power* (Atlantic Highlands, NJ: Humanities Press International, Inc., 1991), p. 11.

Table 2.2 Traditional Chinese Cognitive Model of Legitimacy[14]

Justifications	Core Values	Expected Behaviors	Impact on Stability
Original "意莫高于爱民"	天命 Mandate of Heaven	唯天命 Observe the mandate	"顺天者昌, 逆天者亡" Survive if the mandate is followed, and vanish if it is forfeited
	仁君 Virtuous rulers	正德, 仁政 Cultivating morality, rule of virtue	"不仁则民不至" People will not follow you if you are not acting benevolently
	民本 Put people first	敬民, 爱民 Respect and love people	"民惟邦本, 本固邦宁" If people are peaceful and complacent so will be the state
	法礼 Rite, ancestral law	修礼 Cultivating ritual	"国家无礼不安" State will perish without observing ancestral rites
Utilitarian "行莫高于厚民"	厚民 Equality	"家给人足, 天下大治" The state will be at peace if all families and individuals prosper	"患不均而不患寡" People are not afraid of scarcity of wealth, but the unequal distribution of it.
	利民 Benefiting people	九功允治 There are nine policies leading towards good governance	"水则载舟, 水则覆舟" Water (people) can support and sink a boat (ruler)

---

14 Many of the quotes used here are contained in various classic writings. Since it is difficulty to translate them, I will quote the original here:

《老子》: "顺天者昌, 逆天者王"《孟子》: "民为贵, 社稷次之, 君为轻;"
"患不均而不患寡;"《国语》: "不仁则民不至;"《荀子》: "水则载舟, 水则覆舟;"
"国家无礼则不宁;"《管子》: "凡治国之道, 必先富民"《晏子春秋》
"意莫高于爱民, 行莫乐于厚民," "廉者, 政之本也;"《论语》 "政者, 正也."
《尚书》 "民惟邦本, 本固邦宁;"《尚书·大禹谟》把 "六府" (水,火,金,木,土,谷) 和 "三事" (正德, 利用, 厚生) 称为 "九功."

As anywhere else, legitimacy in China is constructed first and foremost as a function of trust.[15] The way in which people see their government to be trustworthy or not has always been influenced by a complex cognitive system of legitimation (Table 2.2). The system was developed during the pre-Qin era, canonized during the Spring-Autumn period, and institutionalized in the Han dynasty. It is centered on Confucian ideas of virtue and supported by two vital pillars: original (the *a priori* or prescriptive justice), and utilitarian (the *eudemonic* or substantive justice) justifications. Each pillar is further supported by a set of key values. Chinese rulers, including its communist ones, are preoccupied with attaining these values conscientiously, and take them as part of their "art of rulership."[16] Surprisingly, little attention has been given to this unique system of legitimation in academic circles. For that reason, many scholars in the West has consistently underestimated the level of political support the regime in Beijing is able to muster, and have made erroneous projections repeatedly for a "coming collapse" of the regime in Beijing.[17] In order to avoid making the same mistake, it will be necessary to take a closer look at the traditional system of legitimation. Table 2.2 is a summary of the key elements in the system and its impact on regime stability.

The two-dimensional view of political legitimacy provides both normative and substantive principles towards good governance. The original justification is based on four prescriptive values that were considered to be self-evident and truthful: Mandate of Heaven (*tian ming*), rule by virtue (*ren zhi*), put people first (*men ben*), and legality and ritual (*fa li*). The idea of *men ben* is especially of importance since a similar idea did not appear in the West until modern times.

The utilitarian justification says that individuals will approve or disapprove of a ruler's actions based on whether or not they increase or decrease the amount of happiness of the party whose interest is in question.[18] At least two values can be found that were used to qualify the meaning of the *eudemonic* reasoning: *hou min* and *li min*. *Hou min* implies the idea of prosperity for the people and a fair distribution of wealth. The idea of *li min* asks rulers to take less from people, and let people profit from what they are doing the best.

Based on the proceeding synthesis, a legitimate ruler needs to have the Mandate of Heaven, possesses the quality of virtue, shows respect to his subjects, follows the rules of the ancestors, always put people's interest first, and tries to win the hearts and minds of the people. Similarly, a just ruler will be instrumental to the attainment of benefits or values that are important to the people. There must be fairness in

---

15 Richard Flacks, "Protest or Conform: Some Social Psychological Perspectives on Legitimacy," *The Journal of Applied Behavior Science*, vol. 5, no. 2, 1969, pp. 127–150.

16 Roger T. Ames, *The Art of Rulership* (New York: State University of New York Press, 1994).

17 Gordon Chang, *The Coming Collapse of China* (New York: Random House, 2001).

18 Jeremy Bentham, *An Introduction to the Principles of Morals and Legislation* (New York: Hafner Publishing, 1948), p. 1.

distribution of these benefits and values as well. A set of hypotheses can be made according to this cognitive model of legitimation.

1. Linear Relationships

1.1 A legitimate government is the one which possesses both original and utilitarian justifications. This may be a pure ideal type since the achievement of a completed balance is always beyond the reach of any ruler. For most governments, it is always a constant struggle to maintain a delicate balance between the two sets of value justifications.

1.2 The violation of any one of the rules of legitimacy can lead to instability or even a regime change. This hypothesis can be further divided into several sub-hypotheses:

1.2.1 The diminishing Mandate of Heaven can lead to a regime change. The Mandate of Heaven establishes the divine right which makes the rulers legitimate. The Mandate of Heaven, however, is not permanent; it can be lost or acquired depending on if a ruler has followed the "heavenly ways."

1.2.2 Ethical rule enhances ruler's power of persuasion. The notion of *ren jun* gives a ruler a humane face. It requires the ruler to govern ethically. If the ruler's policies are unethical, immoral, or corrupted, then the ruler will lose the ability to lead since people will no longer obey the ruler.

3.3.3 A lack of eudemonic appeal may lead to regime instability. A government's policy should be for the benefits of a majority. Its ability to produce happiness can enhance a regime's stability.

The relationship between stability and legitimacy does not have to be a linear one. The following hypotheses deal with non-linear relationships:

2. Non-linear Relationships

1.1 Instability may be a result of the deliberated efforts made by a ruler to achieve certain objectives. A dynamic model of legitimacy must allow room for changes. A change intended to strength a regime's legitimacy may actually cause instability. Smaller and incremental changes may be a way to avoid creating unrest or potential crises.

1.2 A regime with proper original justification can still suffer from a crisis of legitimacy if the regime cannot effectively satisfy people's substantive needs. An authoritarian developmental state may prove to be highly efficient in balancing the needs for rapid economic growth on the one hand, and the needs for full employment and low inflation on the other. It thus may turn out to be very stable and popular.

The government in Beijing has consciously followed the traditional Chinese model of political legitimation. What's different is that it has used Marxist political ideology as *a priori* justification, idealistic altruism as the official ethics, and communist *eudemonic* appeals as its utilitarian validation. The following discussion will focus exclusively on these three key variables. Their impact on regime stability will be examined and several aforementioned hypotheses and sub-hypotheses will be tested.

Regime Stability and the Legitimizing Ideology

Regime instability was a chronic problem in China during the era of Mao Zedong but has been significantly improved since the time of Deng Xiaoping. Some of the crises that occurred during Mao's time were apparently the results of flaws in political legitimacy, but many were actually self-inflicted. Various political campaigns, launched under Mao's theory of "continuous revolution," were responsible for radical changes and occasionally chaos. Yet, even during the most hectic times, such as the Cultural Revolution (1966–1976), no political force was able to pose substantial challenges to the party and the state.

To explain this unique phenomenon, one must take a look at the importance of Marxist ideology in providing a new mandate for the communist state. The Chinese Communist Party (CCP) is very good at producing political ideologies needed to glorify its existence. From the orthodox Marxism to Mao Zedong Thought, and from Deng Xiaoping Theory to the present Theory of Three Represents, the constant modifications in the regime's ideology reflects the party's ability to adapt to new conditions and environments. Ideological and political work, a peculiar invention of the communists, has always played a critical role in legitimizing the state and the party. On the one hand, "without the ideology," wrote Peter Moody, "the Party would have no claim to legitimacy."[19] On the other, the gradual conversion from a revolutionary ideology to a programmatic one has remade the CCP as well.

When the CCP forcibly seized the power in 1949, it needed to legitimize itself quickly. A system of legitimation mixed with the traditional and Marxist revolutionary ideologies were put into place. To institute its original justification, the CCP replaced the Mandate of Heaven with Marxist mandate of history. According to Marx's theory of scientific socialism, the industrial working class, organized and conscious, is certain to bring down capitalism and create a society of abundance with universal brotherhood and true freedom.

The revolution-based political ideology served as a double-edged sword; it was both a tranquillizer as well as a source of political instability. Although communist propagandists occasionally depicted the party and its leaders as godlike saviors or "a never setting sun," it refused to use the ancient idea of divine right as a justification for its rule. Instead, Karl Marx's historical materialism and the scientific socialism were used to provide ideological authentications for the one-party state.

---

19 Peter R. Moody, *Tradition and Modernization in China and Japan* (Belmont, CA: Wadsworth, 1995), p. 172.

Maoists believed that the right to govern came from revolution and gun barrels. "A revolution is an insurrection, an act of violence by which one class overthrows another," Mao declared.[20] The CCP's logic is simple: the coming of a communist society is inevitable, and the new Mandate of Heaven is to wipe out capitalism and build a communist one.

Obviously, the Communist regime did not rely on ideology alone. *Eudemonic* appeal was also a factor. The CCP was able to gain popular support in the early and mid-1950s because of its success in the "liberation war" and the improvement of China's economy. The land reform, for example, benefited over 300 million peasants. A total of 700 million *mu* of farm land (about 1.15 million acres) and farming tools were confiscated from landowners and given to peasants for free.[21] Equality in land ownership was realized for the first time in Chinese history. This in turn generated a tremendous amount of support for the new regime.

In addition, the regime's legitimacy was assisted by the use of coercion. Challenges to the revolution were dealt with mercilessly. For instance, over half a million of the so-called "anti-party" rightists, mostly intellectuals, were purged during the anti-rightist campaign in 1957–1958, and a million were sent to the countryside to be reformed. The use of class struggle became the most sacred tactics to silence the critics of the communist regime.

The longest period of instability took place during the Cultural Revolution. Communist radicals, guided by Mao's theory of "continuous revolution," waged a cultural war against Chinese tradition and the apparatus of the communist establishment. For the first two years, the country became a battle ground filled with ideological clashes and factional wars. Mao initially supported the "Gang of Four" and Red Guards to make sweeping changes. But the situation was soon out of control. Mao himself eventually had to put a stop on all factional wars, and called for "stability and unity." This self-inflicted havoc was finally ended with the arrest of the "Gang of Four" after Mao's death in 1976.

As one of the victims of the Cultural Revolution, Deng Xiaoping soon reemerged and became a main advocate for a drastic revision of Mao's radical ideology. Deng's pragmatic philosophy, though lacking in rigorous theoretical cohesion, dominated the party and became its leading tenets in the 1980s. Deng realized that a decade of political turmoil had seriously damaged the country's economy and weakened the party's legitimacy. He warned the party that "in a country as big and as poor as ours, if we don't try to increase production, how can we survive? How is socialism superior, when our people have so many difficulties in their lives?"[22]

---

20 Mao Zedong, "Report on an Investigation of the Peasant Movement in Hunan" (March 1927), *Selected Works of Mao Zedong* (Beijing: Beijing Foreign Language Press, 1967) 2nd ed., vol. I, p. 28.

21 Sun Jian, *The Economic History of the People's Republic of China (1949–1990)* [Zhonghua renmin gongheguo jingji shi] (Beijing, Remin University Press, 1992).

22 Deng Xiaoping, "We Shall Concentrate on Economic Development," *Selected Works of Deng Xiaoping (1982–1992)* (Beijing: Beijing Foreign Language Press, 1994), vol. III.

Deng believed that only through some concrete improvement of people's standards of living could ordinary citizens become content and supportive of the regime again. The economic reform started in the 1980s was a tremendous success. The economy improved a great deal, and the Stalinist command economy was soon abandoned. People accepted the authority once more when the reform was perceived as beneficial to the people. However, Deng was reluctant to carry out meaningful political reform. The lopsided development soon led to another unwanted political crisis in 1989. Unlike the Cultural Revolution, this time the disorder was considered to be life-threatening by many CCP old guards.

The willingness to use coercion saved the regime from immediate danger, but the crack down took the limelight from the impressive economic success achieved in the previous decade. The regime gained some time to make self-corrections and policy changes to address some of the public criticisms. Before long, Deng retired and handed over his power to the so-called third generation of party leaders. His programmatic ideas are now being canonized as Deng Xiaoping Theory. Deng's success in stabilizing the state added to his charisma as a revolutionary veteran and a talented statesman. However, in the end he failed again to resolve the problem of periodical political instability. In spite of the drama in the last years of his political career, Deng will most likely be remembered as a strongman of the communist state.

In the aftermath of the Tiananmen Incident, CCP suffered from ideological disarray and the loss of confidence by many intellectuals and elite.[23] In the 1990s, Jiang Zemin, the new Party General Secretary, managed to restore order partly through authoritative measures, but most importantly by diverting people's energy from politics to economic development. A decade of changes consolidated the market-oriented reform, and elevated the standard of living of ordinary people to that of "small comfort." A full-fledged market economy has been put into place, which will ensure the economic vitality the country needs to keep on its ascendance to the great power status. Although trying very hard to cultivate an image of a "great man of the century," Jiang eventually acknowledged that he was neither a "strongman" nor a "dictator."

During his thirteen years in office he served as a true revisionist theorist and made some audacious moves to improve the traditional communist dogmas. According to Teng Wensheng, Jiang's major contributions lie in his embracement of the market economy in 1992, his effort to modernize Marxism through his theory of three represents in 2000, and his effort to modernize the CCP since 2001.[24]

In an effort to modernize outdated communist ideology, and most importantly, to defend and revitalize the CCP's ruling rationales, Jiang Zemin stepped up his own theory-building effort. When Jiang's group came to power in 1989, Deng Xiaoping told them to focus their energy on party rebuilding. But little was done in the next

---

23 Gilley, Bruce, *Tiger on the Brink* (Berkeley: University of California Press, 1998).
24 Robert L. Kuan, *The Man Who Changed China: The Life and Legacy of Jiang Zemin* (New York, Crown, 2005).

ten years. In January 1999 Jiang warned the party that it was the time to do so or it would be in danger of losing its political power if nothing was done to strengthen the party legitimacy basis.[25]

In the spring of 2000, Jiang made the move to conduct a systematic review of some strategic issues related to the party building. He reportedly studied many classical writings of Karl Marx and investigated the experiences of the former communist parties in East Europe. He reportedly laid out detailed research topics to the party's research departments.[26]

During his inspection tour of south China's Guangdong province in February 2000, Jiang proposed the ideas of "three represents" for the first time, which include "representing the developmental trend of advanced productive forces, the orientation of advanced culture, and the fundamental interests of the overwhelming majority of the people." He believed that the CCP would be invincible if the party could adhere to these principles. He attached a great deal of importance to the new thinking and wanted to make it the CCP's "guiding principle, legitimate basis of the ruling, and source of energy and power."[27]

The party's propaganda machine quickly responded by declaring this theory to be the party's new political declaration in the new millennium. A nation-wide campaign was launched to study the new theory. Jiang later used his influence assertively and convinced the party to revise CCP's party platform to include his theory. The National People's Congress also revised the country's Constitution in order to incorporate this new ideology.

Why did the leadership take the seemingly simply theory so seriously? In a widely publicized article, Pan Yue, a well-known party scholar and government official, praised the theory as a significant departure from the traditional Marxist dogma and called attention to the need for transforming the party from a revolutionary party to a ruling one.[28] Some observers have contemplated the possibility that the theory will pave a way for a peaceful evolution of the party from a Leninist party to a party of all people.[29] These speculations are not entirely groundless. Since 1921, the CCP has constantly claimed to be a pioneer party of the "proletarian" class. Since the 15th Party Congress, however, the CCP has replaced the term "proletarian" with "working class" in part because the proletarian class is no longer an accurate description of the working class.

Jiang's theory and the 16th Party Congress went even further by opening the membership door to entrepreneurs and business owners, and by re-naming the

---

25 CCTV 4, China News, September 8, 2001.
26 China News Agency, "The Theory of Three Represents is the Political Declaration of the Chinese Communist Party in the New Millennium," available from: http://chairmanjiang.com/sangedaibiao/pinlun8.htm, accessed on January 2, 2006.
27 *People's Daily (PD)*, October 30, 2001.
28 Chinesenewsnet.com, July 24, 2001.
29 Kwan, Chi Hung, "'Three Represents Theory' Aims for 'Peaceful Evolution'," available from: http://www.rieti.go.jp/en/china/02082301.html, accessed on December 23, 2005.

traditional concept of "capitalists" with "socialist builders." As one author pointed out, this new theory gives a "pivotal role to new economic elites in the country, and particularly to entrepreneurs and technology specialists.[30]

Nonetheless, the theory has generated much less enthusiasm among ordinary Chinese citizens than the official media. After all, the political ideology is losing its appeal to many people. Any speculation that Jiang's theory somehow will provide a permanent *a priori* justification for the CCP may turn out to be unrealistic.

Regime Stability and Official Ethics

The hypothesis that government ethics directly impacts regime stability has ample historical support. For instance, King Zhou of the Shang dynasty lost his power due to his immoral conduct. The Chinese communists believe that they have a strong moral appeal. As the proletarian pioneers, CCP members and government officials are asked to uphold idealistic altruism and adopt the highest code of conduct.

Numerous role models are selected to exemplify an ideal communist. Lei Feng, a soldier of the People's Liberation Army (PLA) who always rendered helping hands to people, became an ideal man. Jiao Yulu, a county-level party secretary who led peasants' fight against poverty until the very last minutes of his life, became an icon for government officials. Wang Jinxi, an oil worker whose work ethics won him a nickname "iron man," was turned into a national hero. The list can go on and on.

Role models became a source of inspiration during Mao's era. Higher morality, great achievement, and perfection were virtues of all heroic figures shown on movies, Beijing Opera shows, and in literature. The spirit of public services, devotion to one's work, unselfishness, and heroism kindled the passion of millions who wanted to make sacrifices for the cause of revolution. The idealistic altruism appeared to provide a firm moral foundation for the regime's legitimacy, and might have contributed to the regime stability at that time.

The transition to a market economy, however, has had profound impact on the official ethics. Idealism now has been replaced by profit-seeking or rent-seeking behaviors. Money and power have led to widespread corruption and abuse of power. It has been reported that from 1998 to 2002, 846,000 CCP members were disciplined and 137,700 expelled, of which 28,996 were officials at the county level, 2,422 at the bureau level and 98 at the provincial level, a big surge from previous years.[31] From 2003–2004, 34,000 party members were punished for corruption charges, of which 12,000 were officials at the county level, 836 at the bureau level, and 36 at the provincial or minister level (Li, 2005).[32] Although these numbers only represent

---

30 Li, Peilin, et al., *Social Conflicts and Class Consciousness in China Today* (in Chinese) (Beijing, Social Sciences Academy Press, 2005), p. 17.

31 Wang Ying, "CPC Enhance Fight against Corruption," *People's Daily*, September 15, 2004.

32 Li, Zhilun, "The state and task of anti-corruption campaign" [Guanyu fafu lichang de xingshi he renwu], available from: http://opinion.people.com.cn/, accessed on December 20, 2005.

Table 2.3 China's Position in Corruption Perception Index

Year	Rank	CPI Score
1998	52	3.5
1999	58	3.4
2000	63	3.1
2001	57	3.5
2002	59	3.5
2003	66	3.4
2004	71	3.4
2005	78	3.2

Sources: Transparency International, *Corruption Perception Index*, 1998-2005. CPI Score relates to perceptions of the degree of corruption as seen by business people and country analysts and ranges between 10 (highly clean) and 0 (highly corrupt). A higher number in the rank indicates the higher degree of corruption.

about 2% of all CCP members, it is believed the actual number of corruption cases could be much higher than these reported figures. According to one estimate, only about 10-20% of corruption cases were solved and only 6.6% of party officials who were disciplined for corruption received any criminal punishment.

The treatment of corruption is also unfair. Officials will be prosecuted for corruption only in cases involving more than 2,000 yuan ($240).[33] It is reported that after seeing a official-made anticorruption documentary film, *Live or Die*, in August, 2000, Jiang Zemin described the movie as a "powerful shock and a profound warning."[34] According to the Corruption Perception Index (CPI) developed by Transparency International, China now stands at 78, representing the worst score ever for China since the organization began to take the survey in 1998 (Table 2.3).

Waves of corruption cases have become the worst nightmare for the CCP. They damage the party's image as a servant to the people, and undercut its legitimacy. As a response, many new laws and policies have been put into place to fight corruption. Some of the high level government officials are jailed or given capital punishment.[35]

---

33 "The Heresy that Haunts the Communist Party," *Economist*, February 15, 2002.

34 Rose Brady, Mark Clifford, and Dexter Roberts, "Can China Tame the Corruption Beast?" *Business Week*, December 18, 2000, Issue 3712.

35 Chen Zewei, "New Trend in China's Anti-corruption Campaign" [Zhongguo fan fubai zhanlue de xindongciang], *Liaowang Magazine*, available from: http://news.sohu.com/20060102/n241252548.shtml, accessed on January 3, 2006.

But the anti-corruption campaign has yet to prove to be effective in reducing cases involving official corruption.

Official corruption is not new to China. For that reason, Confucian system of legitimation always put the rule of ethics as a core value of good governance. There are many causes for the increase of official corruption cases since 1980s. The prolonged existence of two economic systems, the excessive governmental power and involvement in business and society, the lack of adequate checks and balances, the existence of patron-client politics, the social-economic polarization, and lack of distinction between the public and private domains are responsible for the moral degeneration in contemporary China.[36] However, one reason that has not received adequate attention is the CCP's failure to transform itself from a totalitarian revolutionary party to a democratic socialist party. The disproportionate amount of power the party and the state has gives officials many opportunities to commit crimes such as embezzlement of public funds and bribery taking. The lack of inner party democracy has left the party officials unchecked and unaccountable to the public.

The CCP as a Leninist party relies heavily on its rank-and-file members to carry out its missions. The party is supposed to be made up by the advanced elements of the working class whose missions are to raise working class consciousness. As an elite party, CCP's membership is carefully controlled. Only 69 million people, or about 5–6% of the population, are CCP members today. But party members make up the majority of the ruling elite at all levels.

The party's claim of moral superiority has been challenged in the new market economy. Idealism fails to function as a behavior regulator of its members. The defect in human nature mentioned by Lord Acton in the 18th century suddenly became a cold reality: "power tends to corrupt and absolute power corrupts absolutely."[37] When the rule of man is replaced by the rule of law, corruptions have become unintended consequences of the modernization.[38] The idealistic communists are not immune to the lure of material world, and their altruistic spiritual world, if there was one at all, is falling apart.

Concerned about the impact of corruption scandals, the CCP and the state have tried to use various ways to reverse the trends. In June 2000, Jiang Zemin mentioned for the first time the needs of both rule of law and rule of ethics. On January 10, 2001, Jiang proposed the notion of "rule of ethics" and called for the establishment of a new ethical and moral system based on patriotism, collectivism, Marxism, and traditionalism. As one author points out the key to the return to the rule of ethics is

---

36 An Chen, "Social-economic Polarization and Political Corruption in China: A Study of Correlation," *Journal of Communist Studies and Transitional Politics*, vol. 18. no. 2, 2002, pp. 53–74; Julia Kong, *The Political Economy of Corruption in China* (Armonk, NY, M.E. Sharpe, Inc., 1997).

37 Lord Acton, "Letter to Bishop Mandell Creighton, 3 April 1887," see *Life and Letters of Mandell Creighton* (London: Longman, 1904).

38 Yufan Hao, "From Rule of Man to Rule of Law: the Unintended Consequences of Corruption in China in the 1990s," *Journal of Contemporary China*, vol. 8. no. 22, 1999, pp. 405–423.

to resort to the traditional "politics of virtue" to solve the immediate crisis of official morality.[39]

The CCP has realized that the lack of inner party democracy and inadequate checks and balances are linked with abuse of power and corruption. It is contemplating the possibility of promoting inner party reform.[40] However, no specific plan is known for how this process will be carried out.

Hu Jintao, who succeeded Jiang Zeming in 2003, has made limited moves so far in this regard. Reform of party conventions is under way with experiments being carried out to increase the role of party delegates to the party conventions at all levels and to conduct direct election of party chairs at local levels. Some cosmetic changes were made as well. Hu has established a precedent to report the work of the Politburo to the Central Party Committee. Its intention is to make the Politburo more accountable to the party's central committee.

The most significant effort to clean the party was the education and rectification campaign launched in 2005. This is the largest party rectification movement since the Yanan era in the 1930s. The campaign has several objectives. First of all, to renew the image of CCP as an advanced party made up by the pioneer of the working class. Secondly, to unify the party with its new ideology. Finally, to improve official ethics and party disciplines. However since the campaign involves 69 million people, the effectiveness of the campaign remains to be seen.

Nonetheless, the effort to restore idealistic altruism may prove to be illusive. It contradicts the rational-based pragmatism that has been prevailed in the economic arena. If revolution is no longer the desired goal of the party, then the idealistic ethics may be due for a major overhaul as well.

It will be interesting to see if the CCP will be able to truly transform itself from a revolutionary party to a social democratic one. As matter of fact, the differences between the two socialist movements have gradually converged since the 1980s.[41] Deng Xiaoping's market socialist theory echoes a lot of arguments made by European and American social democrats decades ago. For example, on the key question of public ownership, China has literally embraced the notion of socialization interpreted by Kautsky and the Congress of the Socialist International.[42] In addition, European and American social democrats also emphasized the continuity of bourgeoisie democratic institutions. Rosa Luxembourg, the left-wing revisionist of the German

---

39 Zhang, Jiayuan, "Correctly Understand the Content of 'Rule of Virtue" [Zunqian bawo yide shiguo de neihan], *Hubei Ribao*, December 20, 2002, available from: http://www.cnhubei.com/aa/ca191874.htm, accessed on December 23, 2005.

40 Jiang, Zemin, "Speech on the Celebration of the Eighty-Years' Anniversary of the CCP," July 1, 2001, available from http://www/,people.com.cn, accessed on Dec. 23, 2005.

41 Baogang Guo, "Old Paradigms, New Paradigms and Democratic Changes in China," in *China in the Post-Deng Era*, Ch. 4, eds. by Xiaobo Hu and Gang Lin (Singapore: University of Singapore Press, 2001).

42 "The Frankfurt Declaration," adopted at the Founding Congress of the Socialist International at Frankfurt, West German, July 1951. Reprinted as Appendix I in Norman Thomas, *Socialism Reexamined* (New York: W.W. Norton, 1963).

Communist Party once said when the communist comes to power it will "replace bourgeois democracy with socialist democracy, not to abolish democracy itself."[43]

The CCP always endorses democracy in public, but has never been able to materialize it at the national level for fear of potential challenges to its one-party rule. The latest effort to promote inner party democracy may be a conscious move by the party to find a way to break ground for more meaningful political reforms. "Only through promoting enlarged inner party democracy and people's democracy," as some party scholars claimed, "can we reach the goal of maintaining party's ruling legitimacy."[44] But it is still unclear as to how and when the reform is going to be carried out.

Despite the problems of corruptions and moral decay, the CCP continues to receive strong popular support. In a study of popular support in urban China, Jie Chen found that an overwhelming majority of urban residents still considered the regime in Beijing to be legitimate, and that support came from diffuse support rather than specific support of incumbent policy performance.[45] The diffuse support, defined as a person's conviction that the existence and functioning of the government conform to his or moral or ethical principles, may also be an indication that the official ideology and propaganda may have played a role in shaping people's attitude. This continued support may serve as an element of its political capital which will give the CCP much needed time to carry out more audacious reforms.

Regime Stability and Eudemonic Appeals

The discussion so far has focused on the relationship between regime stability and the original justification. Now what is the relationship between regime stability and the utilitarian justification? How to serve people's own material and non-material interests at times can be more important than the abstract value judgment based on *a priori* justification. Peasant rebellions happened frequently in Chinese history because of hardship they endured in their lives, and dynastical changes were often the result of these events. What about people today? Are they happy with their life and well-being?

On the whole, the level of satisfaction people have towards their life remains very high. More opportunities and individual freedom are apparent to everyone in China. The level of state control has been significantly reduced. Economic freedom has become a driving force for the economic development. A survey of the "happiness" in the world made by the Erasmues University Rotterdam found that Chinese have

---

43 Harrington, Michael, *Socialism: Past and Future* (New York: Penguin Group, 1994).

44 Zhen, Xiaoying, Li Qinghua, "Promoting popular democracy through inner party democracy and remove barrier to the system of development" [Cujing dangnei minzhu tuidon renmen menzhu, gechu fazhan tizhi zhangai], available from: http://www.china.org.cn/chinese/OP-c/348331, accessed on December 23, 2005.

45 Jian Chen, *Popular Political Support in Urban China* (Stanford: Stanford University Press, 2005), p. 183.

Table 2.4 World Happiness Rank (1995–2005)

Top *> 7.7*		*Middle range* *± 6.0*		*Bottom* *<4*	
Denmark	8.2	Brazil	6.8	Armenia	3.7
Switzerland	8.2	**China**	**6.3**	Ukraine	3.6
Iceland	7.8	South Korea	5.8	Moldova	3.5
Mexico	7.7	India	5.4	Zimbabwe	3.3
U.S.	7.4	Russia	4.3	Tanzania	3.2

Sources: Veenhoven, R., *Average happiness in 91 nations 1995–2005*, World Database of Happiness, Rank Report 2005/1, Internet: *worlddatabaseofhappiness.eur.nl.*

very positive opinions on their life. The data were collected from 91 nations between 1995 and 2005, and is based on answers to the question of "how much people enjoy their life-as-a-whole on scale 0 to 10."[46] This high-middle range of happiness in China is certainly one of the contributing factors to China's extended period of stability since the 1990s (Table 2.4).

The economic reform and CCP's policy achievements in recent years are largely responsible for the positive feeling people have towards their lives. But its successes have created new sets of problems such as income disparities. The latest focus on humane governance and building a harmonious society reflects top leaders' concerns over this issue. The policy goals for the foreseeable future seem to be a balanced development strategy that will guarantee a fair share of wealth for all, not just for a few. "A harmonious society," according to the Party Secretary Hu Jintao, "should feature democracy, the rule of law, equality, justice, sincerity, amity and vitality."[47]

Since 2002, the new Chinese political leaders have intensified their *eudemonic* appeals.[48] The 16th Party Congress of 2002 brought the first peaceful and

---

46 Veenhoven, R., "Average happiness in 91 nations 1995–2005," World Database of Happiness, Rank Report 2005/1, available from: www.worlddatabaseofhappiness.eur.nl, accessed on December 23, 2005.

47 Xinhua News Agency, "Beijing targets harmonious society," March 4, 2004, available from: http://chinadaily.com.cn/Xinhua/, accessed on December 20, 2005.

48 Zhao, Dingxing, "China Prolonged Stability and Political Future: Same Political System, Different Policies and Methods," *Journal of Contemporary China*, vol. 10, no. 8, 2001, pp. 427–444.

institutionalized power transfer in the history of the People's Republic of China (PRC) as well as the Chinese Communist Party (CCP). Hu Jintao, the newly elected CCP Party General Secretary and the President of the PRC, has quickly emerged from the shadow of his predecessor Jiang Zemin, and begun to present to the world with his new populist style and the new "three people's principles."[49] His focus is on strengthening the party's eudemonic appeal. The traditiononal *men ben* ideas have all of a sudden been revived.

The new leaders quickly launched what many have characterized as the Chinese version of "New Deal."[50] In a speech to a meeting celebrating the 20th anniversaries of the 1982 Constitution, Hu made it clear that all parties must live within the confines of the Constitution, and respect the authority of the Constitution. He acknowledged that the existing Constitution had not been observed adequately, and that the Constitution itself was also in need of amendment.[51] Under his influence, the NPC amended the Constitution which for the first time acknowledged that the citizen's human rights and property rights must be protected.

The new leadership has promised new leadership styles and new thinking. The annual informal meeting and gathering in *Beidaihe*, a beach resort in northern China, were cancelled in 2004. Laws and policies were modified to make them more humane and sensitive to people's needs. The Incident of Sun Zhigang, for example, led to the abolishment of the notorious detention system used to discriminate against rural migrants in the cities. Sun was a college student who was beaten to death by lawless public security personnel. When the news was reported on the Internet, the public was outraged over the brutality of the government employees, and the legitimacy of the arbitrary detention and abuse of the homeless people were questioned. The State Council acted very swiftly to issue a new decree. It abolished the system of detention for people who were homeless or without proper identification documents, and replaced it with a new system of homeless shelters and public assistance stations.

In addition to cultivating a populist image, attention has also been given to the growing concerns over the income disparities existing in various forms. Three types of income disparities exist in China today: the urban income disparity, the urban-rural income disparity, the regional income disparity. Income disparity between the rich and poor has reached an all time high. The richest 10% of urban residents own 50% of individual property.[52]

---

49 Hu Jintao, "Speech at the Graduation Ceremony of the Seminar on the Theory of the Three Represents," *People's Daily*, February. 18, 2003. The "Three People's Principles" are: "use my power for the people, link my feelings to the people, and focus my heart on the pursuit of public welfare."

50 Chen, L., "The 'New Deal': Politics and Policies of the Hu Administration," in T.Y. Yang ed., *China after the Sixteenth Party Congress* (Whitby, Canada: de Sitter Publication, 2005), p. 9.

51 Hu Jintao, "Speech at the Meeting Celebrating the 20th Anniversaries of the 1982 Constitution," *People's Daily*, December 4, 2002.

52 Lu Xueyi, Li Peilin eds., *The Blue Book of Chinese Society (2004)* (Beijing: CASS Press, 2004); Lu Xueyi, Li Peilin eds., *The Blue Book of Chinese Society (2005)* (Beijing:

Table 2.5 Regional Income Disparity in China (in Yuan)

Year	Eastern region	Central region	Western region	Inland region
1985	1,047	704	582	656
	(100.0)	(67.2)	(55.6)	(62.7)
1993	3,901	2,072	1,765	1,952
	(100.0)	(53.1)	(45.2)	(50.0)
2000	10,768	5,978	4,606	5,436
	(100.0)	(55.5)	(42.8)	(50.5)
2004	18,217	9,481	7,219	8,584
	(100.0)	(52.0)	(39.6)	(47.1)

Source: Chi Hung KWAN, "Regional Disparities Have Gone Beyond Acceptable Limits – The Path to an All-Round Well-Off Society Remains Distant," numbers in bracket show income level in regions concerns relative to that of east region, on-line: http://www.rieti.go.jp/en/china/05112901.html.

In its annual human development report, the United Nations Development Program (UNDP) warned China for possible instability resulting from its poor record of urban-rural income disparity.[53] Although both urban and rural incomes have increased, the urban areas have grown even faster, resulting in a 3.2:1 urban and rural income gap.[54] The Gini coefficient, a key measure of income disparities, has increased from 0.21 in 1978 to more than 0.46 in 2004, an alarming sign of growing inequality among its population.[55] Researches also show that the potential conflicts between the rich and the poor are number two of the top concerns to many people; second only to the conflicts over labor disputes with private business owners.[56]

Worried about the consequence of growing inequality, Beijing has set up a number of major programs to help reduce the gap. The Great Western Development

---

CASS Press, 2005).

53 United Nations Development Program (UNDP), *2005 Human Development Report* (New York: UNDP, 2005).

54 Ministry of Agriculture, P. R. China, *2005 Agricultural Development Report of China*, Table 22, available from: http://www.agri.gov.cn, accessed on December 28, 2005.

55 World Bank, *Sharing Rising Incomes: Disparities in China* (Washington: World Bank, 1997); Li Peilin, et al., *Social Conflicts and Class Consciousness in China Today* [Shehui chongtu yu jiejie yishi: dangdai zhongguo shehui maodun wenti yanjiu] (Beijing, Social Sciences Academy Press, 2005).

56 Li, et al., p. 166.

Program was initiated in 1999. So far over 850 billion RMB (U.S.$110) have been invested in the region, and over sixty major construction projects have been built.[57]

To reduce the urban-rural income disparity, a set of unprecedented new policy initiatives are now implemented: More funds are allocated to rural areas, and new subsidies are being proposed to improve conditions in rural education, agricultural productions, transportation, perversity-reduction, and health care.

Rebuilding of the rural cooperative health care system. China was once known for having a most-admired unique system of rural health care. Two thirds of its rural population were covered by the system supported by peasants and the People's Communes. However, with the abolishment of People's Communes and the introduction of the household responsibility system, the cooperative health care system vanished overnight. Peasants suddenly found themselves uninsured, and could not afford to get sick. In 1997, the central government proposed rebuilding the rural health insurance system, but little progress was made.

In 2002, a new effort was made to restore this cooperative health care system. Starting in 2003, a new financial scheme was put into place. The government is paying 2/3 of the health insurance premium for each participating peasant (20 yuan, and the amount will be increased again to 40 yuan or about $5 U.S. dollars in 2006). By the end of 2005, over 225 millions peasants enrolled in the system.[58] The government hopes the program will eventually cover all rural populations by 2010.

Elimination of agricultural tax. Excessive taxes are a major complaint peasants have registered with the government for years. Local governments have taxed people at will, and caused severe tensions between the government and peasants. Between the 1950s and 1990s, peasants paid 15.5% tax on their agricultural products. This rate was reduced to about 8.4% in 2000. At the meantime, the share of agriculture tax in the total government revenues has decreased from 40% to about 1%. In 2003, Premier Wen Jiabao proposed to eliminate agriculture tax in five years. By 2005, 28 provinces have already gotten away with the tax, a 50 billion yuan saving for peasants. In January 2006, the NPC voted to abolish the agricultural tax, three years ahead of the schedule.[59]

Fair treatment of migrant laborers. Economic development in the past two decades has drawn millions of farmers to cities in order to work as seasonal workers and day laborers. Discrimination against migrant laborers is widespread. To reduce discrimination, several measures have been taken.

First of all, the household registration is being relaxed to allow more free movement of peasants to urban areas. Efforts have been made to encourage peasants to settle in the city. It is expected the urbanization will absorb about 10 to 20 millions of peasants to cities each year in the next twenty years. Secondly, unpaid wages were another frustration migrant farmers have encountered. There were over 30 billion

---

57 Xinhua News Agency, February 11, 2005. Available from: http://www.xingua.com.cn, accessed on January 6, 2006.
58 China News Agency, December 26, 2005.
59 *People's Daily*, January 18, 2005.

yuan unpaid wages owed to farm laborers, according to a government estimate. Since 2004, Premier Wen has led the way to help farmer-laborers to get their unpaid wages. A new system of wage guarantee deposit is being set up in some provinces to prevent future occurrences.

These measures will certainly help reduce tensions and strengthen the utilitarian appeal of the government; they are after all a very popular undertaking. Beijing is currently drafting its 11th five-year plan. All indications suggest that the government will pay more attention to the issue of inequality and want to improve the well-being of the low income families. More social, health, and income securities programs will be established in the near future. These efforts may greatly enhance the government's legitimacy and avoid large scale popular uprisings that are so common in a transitional society.

Conclusion

The discussion so far reveals that in order to maintain its regime stability, Beijing has been constantly changing its system of legitimation. These efforts have several characteristics.

First, they are preemptive. There is no serious manifested crisis of legitimacy in sight, but the potential for a crisis is there. If left unaddressed, the CCP may soon face one. In this sense, the CCP has demonstrated its willingness to adapt itself according to the time. This certainly is one of the CCP's strengths since so many other communist parties have failed to do so.

Secondly, the CCP has demonstrated a good understanding of the traditional cognitive model of political legitimacy. The ancient *a priori* and *eudemonic* justifications are redefined several times to suit its own needs. Overall, the CCP has demonstrated high levels of adaptability.

Will all these translate into a more stable and peaceful regime in the long-run? The answer so far seems to be positive. First of all, the regime is no longer interested in spreading communist revolution worldwide; instead, it has become inward looking, and concerned more with its own domestic construction and economic development. As a gesture of the commitment to a peaceful international environment, the CCP has stopped exporting revolution and ceased providing financial and military aid to communist insurgents worldwide. China's successful bid for membership of the World Trade Organization (WTO) signaled her embracement of the economic globalization.

Secondly, it no longer treats class struggle as a key task; instead, it now emphasizes social harmony more. Social corporatism seems to be more appealing to the leaders in Beijing than ever. From class struggle to class cooperation, and from social antagonism to social harmony, a sea change has occurred in term of the party's ideological orientation.

To promote regime stability and sustain its peaceful development, further political modernization is needed to bring up to date the system of political legitimation. It appears that there are many limits to the way the CCP is legitimizing itself. Chinese governing theory focuses heavily on the notion of government for the people while undermining the notion of government of the people and by the people. This theory believes that the government can act as a trustee of the people as long as it can keep its "advance nature" and "virtuous ethics." This is simply no longer adequate in light of the development of an industrial and post-industrial society.

The traditional model relies too much on the tacit or inexplicit consent of the people without enticing any form of expressed consent. In ancient time, the tacit consent simply means there is no objection to the ruler and society and whoever accepts the benefits of the society shall therefore be obligated to accept the legitimacy of the authority. The use of divine right, hierarchical virtue, and paternalistic love makes the traditional theory of legitimacy inherently authoritarian. Ancient Chinese rulers found it practical to enshrine themselves as sons of Heaven or sons of God. This inevitably made them infallible and absolute. Confucian ideas of hierarchal virtues and paternalistic love justified political inequality between rulers and the people, which prevented people from participating equally in public affairs. Paternalism validates a state by claiming that the person interfered with by the state will be better off or be better protected from harm.[60] However, a "happy slave" is still a slave no matter how happy he or she is.[61]

Expressed consent in modern time is a totally different way to legitimize a government. What is missing in the current Chinese system of legitimation is the procedural legitimacy. In a modern rational-legal based system, authority is restrained by explicit rules and popular vote. Violation of procedure will lose legitimacy. According to Max Weber, the belief in the validity of legal statute and functional "competence" based on rationally created rules is the key to modern legitimacy.[62] Explicit consent manifested in the form of ballot, voting, and public opinion must be incorporated into the system. The inclusiveness of participation, transparency, political competition, and fairness must be upheld. A three-dimensional system of legitimation which includes the original, utilitarian and procedures justifications is what China needed to sustain its long-term stability and peaceful development.

---

60 Lei Guang, "Elusive Democracy: Conceptual Change and the Chinese Democracy Movement, 1978–1989," *Modern China*, vol. 22, no. 4, October–December 1996, p. 417.

61 Herzog, Don, *Happy Salves: A critique of Consent Theory* (Chicago: The University of Chicago Press, 1989).

62 Max Weber, " Politics as a Vocation," in *Max Weber: Essays in Sociology* (New York: Oxford University Press, 1946), pp. 77–128.

Chapter 3

Corruption, Economic Growth and Regime Stability in China's Peaceful Rise

Shawn Shieh

Corruption has long been seen as a cancer on the Chinese Communist Party even through the high growth years of the 1990s and into the 2000s. During those years, the problem of corruption was to some extent overshadowed by the economic and social revolution engendered by Deng's reforms. But the problem persisted and seems to have worsened in recent years. Those who have studied corruption in China most closely agree that corruption is a widespread and continuing problem.[1] There are reports of large-scale corruption in China's financial institutions, with stories of bank officials fleeing overseas with millions of yuan in bank deposits. We also hear about onerous taxes and fees and corrupt land deals that have sparked violent protests in the countryside.

According to a World Bank study that measures governance indicators for the world's countries over the last few years, China's performance has declined among all six indicators since 1996: voice/accountability; political stability; regulatory quality; rule of law; and control of corruption. The declines in regulatory quality and control of corruption, in particular, have fallen significantly (see Table 3.1).

These trends raise the central question of this chapter: does corruption in China pose a threat to the stability of the regime and ultimately to prospects for its peaceful development? This chapter seeks to address this question by focusing on the threat that corruption poses to regime stability via its impact on economic growth. To assess the extent of that threat, we draw on the experiences of Southeast and East Asian countries to identify the conditions under which corruption is most harmful to economic growth and thereby regime stability.

---

[1] Zengke He, "Corruption and anticorruption in reform China," *Communist and Post-Communist Studies*, vol. 33, 2000, pp. 243–270; Andrew Wedeman, "The instensification of corruption in China," *China Quarterly*, no. 186, December 2004, pp. 895–921; Yan Sun, *Corruption and market in contemporary China* (Cornell: Cornell University Press, 2004); Melanie Manion, *Corruption by design: building clean government in mainland China and Hong Kong* (Cambridge: Harvard University Press, 2004).

Table 3.1 Governance Indicators for China (1996–2004)

	1996	1998	2000	2002	2004
Voice and Accountability					
Estimate (-2.5 to +2.5)	-1.29	-1.51	-1.37	-1.38	-1.54
Percentile Rank	12.0	7.9	10.5	10.1	7.3
Political Stability					
Estimate (-2.5 to +2.5)	0.12	0.06	0.13	0.06	0.07
Percentile Rank	50.6	49.7	54.5	45.9	46.6
Government Effectiveness					
Estimate (-2.5 to +2.5)	+0.18	+0.17	+0.22	+0.20	+0.11
Percentile Rank	66.5	64.5	64.0	65.2	60.1
Regulatory Quality					
Estimate (-2.5 to +2.5)	-0.06	-0.07	-0.21	-0.43	-0.45
Percentile Rank	47.0	42.9	36.9	37.8	35.0
Rule of Law					
Estimate (-2.5 to +2.5)	-0.45	-0.22	-0.33	-0.26	-0.47
Percentile Rank	37.3	52.4	48.7	48.5	40.6
Control of Corruption					
Estimate (-2.5 to +2.5)	-0.01	-0.14	-0.34	-0.35	-0.51
Percentile Rank	58.7	60.7	44.6	44.4	39.9

Source: World Bank, Governance Indicators: 1996–2004, http://www.worldbank.org/wbi/governance/govdata/. For an explanation of data and methodology, see D. Kaufmann, A. Kraay, and M. Mastruzzi, "Governance Matters IV: Governance Indicators for 1996–2004" (Draft, May 9, 2005), http://www.worldbank.org/wbi/governance/pubs/govmatters4.html.

Note: The Estimate indicators are scaled from –2.5 (worst) to +2.5 (best). The Percentile Rank provides a measure of where China ranks on each measure relative to other countries included in the surveys.

The Argument: Why Focus on Economic Growth?

Regime stability is a broad term, but in political science parlance is generally used to refer to the stability of a particular system of government or administration. In the context of the PRC, the regime in question is the system of government established and supported by the Chinese Communist Party. The question is, how does one define stability? One way would be to view it as a continuum running from the status quo or gradual change on one end to violent upheaval and regime collapse on the other.[2] At one end of this continuum, major events and policy changes would not be seen as threats to stability as long as they did not threaten to upset the nature of the regime. Deng's reforms are a good example; they were gradual measures that over time had the cumulative effect of revolutionizing the economy and society but did little to change the nature of the regime.[3] At the more unstable end of this continuum, threats would come in forms that were not sanctioned by the CCP, such as violent demonstrations, protests, strikes, etc. The June 4th protests in 1989 would be the best example of such a threat. Regime instability in its more extreme forms, e.g. coups, revolutions, secessions, would lead to a change in the regime. Regime instability would generally involve violence not sanctioned by the CCP but could also include mass demonstrations and elite defections that resulted in the "velvet revolutions" in Eastern Europe in 1989 and the replacement of a authoritarian system with one committed to constitutional democracy. Regime instability then does not have to be seen as undesirable because it could refer to a nonviolent transition to democracy.

There are several ways that corruption could contribute to conditions that destabilize the regime in both a subjective and objective sense. In terms of political consequences, corruption can lower confidence and trust (a subjective measure) in the CCP and its governing apparatus to manage the pressures produced by social and economic development, and it can undermine the mission and quality of the party-state bureaucracy (an objective measure). In terms of societal consequences, corruption can worsen social inequality by creating the perception that those with power are gaining an unfair share of the wealth (a subjective measure) and by actually using political power to skew the distribution of wealth (an objective measure). Finally, corruption has important economic consequences: it can harm economic growth and stability, which is seen by many observers to be the main reason for regime stability and legitimacy today. Of course, there is overlap among these three areas. Threats to economic growth and stability, and widening social inequality, would further damage the public's confidence and trust in the CCP. And, as we will examine later on, corruption of the party and state elite can erode the state's capacity to promote and manage economic growth.[4]

---

2   See the chapters by Steven F. Jackson, "Introduction: a typology of stability and instability," and H. Lyman Miller, "How do we know if China is unstable?" in David Shambaugh, ed., *Is China Unstable: Assessing the Factors* (M.E. Sharpe, 2000).

3   In fact, some have argued that the reforms have allowed the regime to continue its authoritarian rule and delay democratization. See Mary Gallagher, "Reform and openness: why China's economic reforms have delayed democracy," *World Politics* vol. 54, April 2002, pp. 338–372.

4   All of these scenarios envision corruption as a contributing rather than precipitating factor setting the condition for a withdrawal of elite support or a proactive coup, and/or triggering mass protests against the regime that could lead to a revolution. But corruption could also be a precipitating factor that triggers an event or chain of events that destabilizes a regime. In the June 4th protests, corruption did play such a role because the protests were sparked in part by complaints about official corruption. One can also imagine a corruption

Of these three areas, the political and social ramifications are more obvious in the threat they pose to regime stability. For instance, there seems to be little doubt among academics and policymakers that corruption does harm people's confidence and trust in the CCP and its governing institutions.[5] Anecdotal measures such as reportage and other press reports about popular dissatisfaction with corruption and protests sparked by corrupt officials (witness the June 4th protests), surveys both within and outside of China,[6] and even a reading of the CCP's leadership's attitude toward corruption all support this relationship.

There also seems to be little ambivalence about the extent to which corruption contributes to inequality both subjectively and objectively. To take the subjective dimension, the very nature of corruption, which involves the transfer of wealth to those with power and influence, benefits the "haves" at the expense of the "have nots." One only has to look at press reports and reportage to see that popular attitudes connect corruption with the rise of a wealthy, politically-connected class such as the "princelings" who are the offspring of high-level party leaders. Objectively, there is also empirical evidence to suggest that corruption has benefited the "haves" disproportionately. For example, An Chen and Ding Xueliang both show that state enterprise reform has resulted in the privatization of state assets with state enterprise directors and party and state officials being the biggest beneficiaries. In stark contrast, enterprise workers who end up being laid off in this process are the biggest losers.[7]

In the economic realm, however, the threat posed by corruption on economic growth has been an ambiguous and even contentious issue. This may not be surprising to those familiar with the social science literature on corruption where economists have generally seen corruption as a drag on growth, while some political scientists (notably Samuel Huntington) have argued that corruption may serve as a "grease" to help businesses get around oppressive government regulations and red tape or

---

scandal that reached high into the party leadership, combining with other events (the anniversary of June 4th, protests in Hong Kong, a sudden outbreak of SARS, a sudden decline in the economy, a severe environmental problem), to precipitate a withdrawal of elite support and/or mass protests, thus setting the stage for a coup or revolution.

5 See Yan Sun's discussion of how this issue is viewed in Chinese writings in her article "The politics of conceptualizing corruption in reform China," *Crime, Law and Social Change*, vol. 35 (2001), pp. 262–263.

6 See Transparency International's annual reports, http://www.transparency.org/publications/annual_report, a People's Bank of China survey of financial sector corruption published in the January 10, 2005 issue of *Caijing*, and Lianjiang Li, "Support for anti-corruption campaigns in rural China," *Journal of Contemporary China* vol. 10, no. 29, 2001, pp. 573–586.

7 An Chen, "Socioeconomic polarization and political corruption in China: a study of a correlation," *Journal of Communist Studies and Transition Politics*, vol. 18, no. 2, 2000, pp. 53–74. X.L. Ding, "The Illicit Asset Stripping of Chinese State Firms," *The China Journal*, vol. 43, January 2000, pp. 1–28.

as a code word for the privatization of state assets.[8] Recent work by economists has marshaled some compelling evidence that corruption does slow growth.[9] But China's unparalleled growth over the last twenty-five years, combined with high levels of corruption, have resurrected this debate, with some arguing that China's corruption may be more "developmental" than "destructive," at least compared with other developing countries.[10]

As Yan Sun shows, the academic ambivalence over whether corruption has a harmful impact on growth is also reflected in subjective attitudes on this issue. Looking at the popular, policy and academic debates over corruption in China, Sun finds that while the dominant attitude is one that sees corruption as harmful to development, there are those who see corruption as functional to development or at the very least a necessary price to pay to make the transition to a market economy.[11] Interestingly, Sun notes a similar distinction in the Chinese debates to the distinction made above about subjective attitudes toward corruption's impact on regime legitimacy versus corruption's impact on economic growth. She finds that Chinese attitudes are much more impassioned and indignant about the political and social consequences of corruption than they are about the economic consequences.

If we accept the above claims that there is general consensus about corruption's corrosive effect on public trust and confidence in the regime and on social inequality, then it follows that the critical case that needs closer examination is the effect that corruption has on economic growth. This relationship is critical in two ways. One is because economic growth is the one area where corruption is seen by some to have a positive impact or at very least is not viewed as harmful. Second, economic growth is in itself an important source of the CCP regime's legitimacy and capacity. If we find that in fact corruption's impact on economic growth is more serious than previously acknowledged, then we have stronger grounds for being pessimistic about regime stability.

To assess the relationship between corruption and growth, this chapter uses a comparative approach that draws on insights from the larger literature on corruption (including the related topics of rent-seeking and clientelism) and state-business relations in the Asian region. This approach has surprisingly not been used in previous studies of corruption in China but we believe that placing China's corruption problem in a broader, comparative framework will lead to a more objective assessment of the

---

8   This ambivalence regarding corruption is apparent in Shambaugh's edited book, *Is China Unstable?* See the chapters by H. Lyman Miller, "How do we know if China is unstable?," pp. 24–25, and Bruce Dickson, "Political instability at the middle and lower levels: signs of a decaying CCP, corruption and political dissent," pp. 48–49.

9   Paolo Mauro, "Corruption and growth," *Quarterly Journal of Economics*, vol. 110, 1995, pp. 681–712.

10   Yan Sun,"Reform, state and corruption: is corruption less destructive in China than in Russia? *Comparative Politics*, vol. 32, no. 1, 2002, pp. 1–20. Andrew Wedeman, "Development and corruption: the East Asian paradox" in Edmund T. Gomez, *Political business in East Asia* (London: Routledge, 2002).

11   "The politics of conceptualizing corruption," 1999, pp. 257–263.

threat that corruption poses to regime stability in China. The comparability of China with other countries in the Asian region is, we feel, justified. China is increasingly compared with these countries when it comes to issues of development and state-business relations.[12] Unlike the China of the 1970s and 1980s, the China of the 1990s and 2000s, with its authoritarian bureaucratic state, growing nonstate sector, particularly a more visible private business class, and increasing marketization and openness to the global economy, make the East and Southeast Asian countries increasingly attractive as comparisons and as cautionary tales of the problems that China might encounter in the future.[13]

The underlying premise behind this approach is that corruption exists to a significant degree in all of these countries but that its impact on economic growth should not automatically be seen as negative. Because of its subjective nature, the term corruption as used in both the media and the academic literature all too often embraces a very wide, and imprecisely defined, range of activities that may or may not be harmful. To take an example from the academic literature, the term "rent-seeking" is often used synonymously to mean corrupt activities. This may be because the term was coined by neoclassical economists who used the term to describe the costs of state intervention in generating "abnormal" profits (i.e. rents) beyond what a competitive market would yield. Rent-seeking, in this context, carried with it a negative connotation of inefficiency, bureaucratic red tape and corruption.[14] But as Mushtaq Khan and K.S. Jomo point out, rent-seeking refers to a wide range of activities "which seek to create, maintain or change the rights and institutions on which particular rents are based."[15] These activities range from illegal acts involving bribery and coercion, to subsidies provided to infant industries, to legal activities such as lobbying or advertising. Understanding whether rent-seeking is harmful or not, then, requires understanding the larger political and institutional context in which rent-seeking occurs.

The same caveat can be made about corruption, which embraces an even wider range of activity than rent-seeking. Rather than assume that the effects of corruption are negative, this paper sees those effects, and the degree to which they are harmful, as dependent on a range of factors, in particular, conditions related to the broader state-society context such as the nature of the state apparatus and of state-

---

12 See Barrett L. McCormick and Jonathan Unger, eds., *China after Socialism: In the Footsteps of Eastern Europe or East Asia?* (Armonk, NY: M.E. Sharpe, 1996).

13 Margaret Pearson does make a case that China can be constructively compared with East and Southeast Asian countries in terms of state-business and state-society relations. See Ch. 6 in her book, *China's New Business Elite: the political consequences of economic reform* (Berkeley: University of California Press, 1997).

14 On the ideological bias behind the rent-seeking approach, see Paul Hutchcroft, "The politics of privilege: assessing the impact of rents, corruption, and clientelism on Third World development," *Political Studies* vol. XLV, 1997, pp. 639–658.

15 "Introduction" in Mushtaq Khan and Jomo K.S., *Rents, Rent-Seeking and Economic Development: Theory and Evidence in Asia* (Cambridge: Cambridge University Press, 2000), p. 5.

business relations, the form corruption and/or rent-seeking takes and its impact on specific political and economic institutions. The remainder of this chapter surveys the comparative literature on corruption, rent-seeking and state-business relations, with the primary focus on studies of East and Southeast Asia, and identifies those conditions in which clientelism and corruption are seen as harmful to economic growth and stability. The last section then looks at recent trends in corruption and state-business relations in the PRC to see whether those trends make corruption in China as much of a threat as some studies have claimed.

Corruption, Economic Growth and Regime Stability: Lessons from East and Southeast Asia

Over the last two decades a number of studies have emerged attempting to explain the factors behind the economic success (or lack of success) of the East and Southeast Asian countries. Earlier studies, such as Chalmers Johnson's *MITI and the Japanese Miracle*, pointed to the importance of a developmental state comprised of a technocratic bureaucratic class insulated from social demands. In this model, competent bureaucrats make industrial policies that selectively intervene in and provide assistance for promoting growth and competitiveness in certain industrial sectors. More recent scholarship, however, has recognized that a significant degree of clientelism and corruption has coexisted with economic growth in many of these economies, and sought to explain why these "neotraditional" or "patrimonial" features have been less harmful in some cases than in others. In doing so, the literature has produced a number of important observations on corruption and its effect on economic development. In this section, we summarize what we feel are the most important considerations: (1) the autonomy and coherence of the state apparatus; (2) balance of power between state and private actors; (3) the nature of the corruption in issue; and (4) anticorruption measures.

Autonomy and Coherence of the State Apparatus

One finding, continuing the line of thinking started by Johnson, is the importance of a strong state apparatus for promoting economic growth. This means in particular an economic bureaucracy that is cohesive, disciplined, and centrally coordinated, and that is insulated from rent-seeking social groups.[16] Generally, the existence of the latter has also been identified with an authoritarian, corporatist ideology and framework that controls business groups and prevents collective action on their part. In addition, a developmental state exercises its policy-making power selectively in intervening in markets to guide corporate behavior and ultimately the pattern of industrial development. This observation underlines the role of a strong economic

---

16 Andrew MacIntyre, "Business, government and development: Northeast and Southeast Asian comparisons," in Andrew Macintyre, ed., *Business and government in industrialising Asia* (Ithaca: Cornell University Press, 1994).

bureaucracy as an important constraint on clientelist pressures that threaten to overwhelm the policy-making process in any developing country.

Peter Evans largely concurs with this notion of a developmental state but adds to it an important insight when he cautions against seeing a developmental state as one that is completely autonomous from private business interests and solely intent on suppressing or policing the business class.[17] Instead, he argues that the classic developmental states (i.e. Japan, South Korea, Taiwan) possess a type of autonomy that he terms "embedded autonomy." Developmental states, in other words, were not simply autonomous in that they had the capacity to make policy decisions independent of private interests, but also "embedded" in that they were effective in building institutionalized links with the private business elites, and convincing them to support their policy initiatives.[18]

> This support came in the form of assisting private entrepreneurs and encouraging them to enter new sectors. Autonomous states completely insulated from society could turn into effective predators. Developmental states must be immersed in a dense network of ties that bind them to societal allies with transformational goals. Embedded autonomy, not just autonomy, gives the developmental state its efficacy.[19]

Instead of seeing distributional coalitions as interested purely in rent-seeking, detrimental to development, and thus something that the state needs to be insulated against, Evans sees the mobilization and organization of social groups as a necessary ingredient to preventing elite clientelism and predation. Evan's thesis is valuable because it distinguishes between networks and groups that contribute to the state's ability to make and implement economic policy and thus enhance the state's authority,[20] and networks and groups based on narrow, particularistic interests that seek to undermine or go against state economic goals.

Balance of Power Between State and Private Actors

A second important finding in the literature continues the line of thinking found in Evans by pointing out that it is not simply state strength and coherence that matters,

---

17 "Predatory, developmental and other apparatustes: a comparative political economy perspective on the Third World," *Sociological Forum*, vol. 4, no. 4, 1989, pp. 561–587; and *Embedded Autonomy: States and Industrial Transformation* (Princeton: Princeton University Press, 1995).

18 As Sylvia Maxfield and Ben Schneider point out, embeddedness also means good information flows between the state and private sector so that state actors can properly evaluate the impact of policy decisions, while business can obtain important information from state actors to improve their performance. See their edited volume, *Business and the State in Developing Countries* (Ithaca, NY: Cornell University Press, 1997), pp. 8–9.

19 Evans, *Embedded Autonomy*, 1995, p. 248.

20 One thinks of networks that bring together business associations and firms with bureaucratic agencies in Korea and Japan and the personal networks that allow for circulation of entrepreneurs into the bureaucracy and former bureaucrats into business associations.

but the nature of the state-business relationship, in particular the balance of power between the state and private entrepreneurs. This argument is developed at length in studies by David Kang[21] and Andrew Wedeman.[22] Both see the distribution of power between the state and private business as an important determinant of corruption's destructiveness. The most harmful types of corruption, what Wedeman calls degenerative corruption, occur when there is an imbalance of power between state and business. In the situation where the state is powerful and business weak and dispersed, the state tends to play a predatory role engaging in the looting of the state treasury, or the extortion of monies from private interests. A less egregious example of this imbalanced arrangement can also be found in Indonesia where Suharto controlled the bureaucracy and banks and distributed rent-generating opportunities to cronies and family.[23] Business remained weak or dependent on ties with Suharto. Kang argues that while this arrangement appeared stable and fostered economic growth, it quickly became unstable with the onset of the Asian financial crisis in 1997 which severely weakened Suharto's authority and legitimacy.[24] At the other extreme, where the state is weak and business powerful and concentrated, private business can overwhelm the state, as in the case of Marcos' "booty capitalism" in pre-martial law Philippines or the mafia in Russia.[25] Corruption becomes less destructive where the distribution of power between state and private business is more balanced. In this case, more harmful forms of corruption such as plundering and looting give way to what Wedeman calls "developmental corruption" involving collusion and mutual benefits between the state and private interests.

> What sets developmental corruption apart from degenerative corruption is that in the cases previously discussed corrupt officials channeled looted public resources to business which they either owned or had a considerable stake in and used their control over policy to create rents that these enterprises could easily scrape off, whereas in the case of East Asia corrupt politicians remained at arm's length and rather than arrogate public resources to themselves, they were more likely to sell them to private businesses.[26]

For Kang, there are two such situations where a balance of power occurs. One is where you have a weak state and a dispersed business sector, a situation approximated in the advanced industrial countries. The other is where you

---

21 *Crony Capitalism: Corruption and development in South Korea and the Phillipines* (Cambridge: Cambridge University Press, 2002).

22 See "Looters, rent-scrapers and dividend collectors," 1997, and "Development and corruption," 2002.

23 This arrangement was similar to the martial law period under Marcos.

24 "Transaction costs and crony capitalism in East Asia," *Comparative Politics*, July 2003, pp. 439–458.

25 On the Philippines, see Kang, *Crony Capitalism*, 2002. On Russia, see Joel S. Hellman, Geraint Jones and Daniel Kaufman, "Seize the state, seize the day: state capture, corruption and influence in transition," *Policy Research Working Paper* (Washington, D.C.: World Bank, 2000).

26 "Development and corruption," 2002, p. 46.

have a strong state and a concentrated business sector, a situation he refers to as "mutual hostages." One example of the latter is South Korea where the relationship between state and chaebols was one of mutual benefit and collusion. Corruption existed but was moderated by the ability of economic bureaucrats to make and implement policies promoting exports and to mobilize private business toward those ends. Kang argues that this cooperation arose not out of regard for the public or national interest but for more self-regarding reasons. He likens this situation to a classic Prisoner's Dilemma where neither side – state or private business – is powerful enough to take advantage of the other and realize that collusion is the better option. Corruption occurs but in the process so does economic growth.[27]

Still other studies by economists, taking a different approach informed by principal-agent models and public choice theory, have come up with similar conclusions about the importance of a disciplined, coherent state. In Andrei Schleifer and Robert Vishney's influential model, corruption is less destructive when there is a more centralized and disciplined state (what they call a unified or joint monopoly) that has a monopoly over the price of bribes for complementary goods and services and the capacity to coordinate and enforce collusion among its various agencies over the price of those bribes.[28] The less attractive alternative is a more decentralized and fragmented state where bureaucratic agencies become independent monopolists who set the price of bribes to maximize their own revenue. According to Schleifer and Vishney, corruption in a joint monopoly system does less damage to the economy because the state will set the price of bribes at a level that will bring in revenue but not drive down demand for their goods and services. The reason for this is that the concern of a joint monopolist is to maximize total revenue from bribes, whereas independent monopolists are content to raise the price of their bribes without considering the effect on demand for complementary goods and services. The system that best dampens the destructive edge of corruption, however, is neither joint nor independent monopoly, but competitive bureaucracy. This situation arises when the complementary goods or services can all be provided by more than one government agency and when there is competition rather than collusion between these agencies. In this situation, the price of a bribe will be driven to zero as more agencies enter the market for that good or service, and the impact of corruption on the demand side and thus on economic growth will be minimal.

---

[27] *Crony capitalism*, 2002, Chapter 1. The Asian financial crisis seems to vindicate Kang's thesis since South Korea was able to recover from the crisis more quickly than Indonesia where the downfall of Suharto had a more devastating impact on the economy and society.

[28] "Corruption," *The Quarterly Journal of Economics*, vol. 108, no. 3, 1993, pp. 599–617.

The Nature of Corruption: Form, Function and Effects

Another set of considerations has to do with the nature of corruption itself and its effects on the economy and state. These considerations can be grouped into three related areas: (1) the form that corruption takes, (2) the way corrupt monies are invested, and (3) the effect corruption has on state institutions and public policy.

The form that corruption takes is important for assessing corruption's destructiveness. This is important because in both scholarly and media accounts, the term corruption is used to refer to a wide range of activities that all conjure up negative connotations but, in reality, have very different effects on economic growth. Several studies have made a useful distinction between three types of corruption: looting; rent-generation; and profit-sharing. Looting refers to the theft of public funds and property and to the extortion of bribes by public officials who offer nothing in return. Rent-generation describes the manipulation of public policy or macroeconomic instruments to create rents (defined as a profit created by administratively raising prices for services above the market value) for officials and politicians. An example of rent-generation would be the creation of a state-owned monopoly selling goods or services at an above-market price and the diversion of that profit into the pockets of officials running the monopoly. Another example is the phenomenon of official profiteering in China (*guandao*) during the 1980s. In this case, officials sold goods acquired at low state-set prices for higher, "market" prices and pocketed the difference. In the third form of corruption, profit-sharing, private businesses pay bribes to officials in return for favorable policies and services. While there is some overlap between rent-generation and profit-sharing (and many scholars use the term rent-seeking to refer to both), the difference is in who is pocketing the profit made from the manipulation of policies. In rent-generating activities, the rents or profits are going to officials; in profit-sharing, they are going to private businesses that pay a bribe in return.[29]

How corrupt monies are disposed of is another consideration. If those monies are invested in productive activity, then corruption may not have a detrimental effect on development. If, however, those monies are spent on nonproductive activity, such as consumption of imported and luxury goods, or invested overseas, then corruption tends to be more destructive because it leads to a net loss of capital from that country.[30] Here, the calculus may differ depending on whose monies we are referring to. State actors' motivations differ. As Wedeman points out, political leaders who loot and plunder may be more inclined to plow that money back into building their

---

29 Hutchcroft makes a similar distinction but a different set of terms in rent-deployment (or generation) and rent-seeking. Rent deployment is similar to rent-scraping in that the initiative for the creation of the rent is coming from above by state officials and organizations seeking advantage. Rent-seeking is more like profit-sharing in that the initiative is coming from below by nonstate groups and individuals seeking an advantage. See "The politics of privilege," 1997, p. 649.

30 Wedeman, "Looters, rent-scrapers and dividend-collectors," 1997, p. 460.

own empires or those of their cronies, or to deposit the money into overseas bank accounts.[31] The degree of competition may also be a factor. As Richard Doner and Ansil Ramsay argue, competitive clientelism tends to encourage reinvestment in the country to build and sustain clientelist networks.[32] On the other hand, to return to the importance of the developmental state, the willingness of private interests to invest their profits from corrupt transactions in beneficial ways will depend on the capacity of the state to enforce or promote productivity criteria (as in South Korea), and the security of the domestic environment.[33]

When it comes to the effects of corruption, comparative studies have focused on two areas. One is corruption's impact on state institutions. For Hutchcroft, corruption based on clientelistic ties that overlap with formal authority structures is less destructive than corruption based on informal networks that compete with formal lines of authority.[34] This observation is in line with Evans' point that informal networks and groups can be beneficial to realizing state economic goals. One indicator of that overlap is whether or not social groups get services in return for their bribes. Hutchcroft cites Rose-Ackerman's notion of "disorganized bureaucracy" to describe a system where corrupt bureaucrats accept bribes but the bribers cannot be sure that those bureaucrats have the power to perform their side of the bargain.[35] He even proposes that corruption that involves a higher degree of overlap between formal lines of authority and informal networks "may occasionally promote state institutionalization."[36] Yan Sun employs a similar standard in pointing out that one reason corruption in Russia is more harmful is because it is more like outright extortion "with no guarantee of favors in return."[37]

Corruption's impact on public policy is also important, in particular, its impact on macroeconomic policy and the functioning of the market. While it has been a long-standing assumption that corruption can grease the wheels of the bureaucracy and make it more responsive to private business interests, more recent comparative studies have come to more nuanced and helpful conclusions. One is that corruption tends to be more harmful when it infiltrates agencies responsible for macroeconomic regulation, in particular regulation of the banking and financial sector. As some have pointed out, one reason Thailand has enjoyed growth in the face of high levels of corruption is because of the relative autonomy of its macroeconomic agencies at least until the late 1980s.[38] Echoing Schleifer and Vishney's argument, they note

---

31 "Development and corruption," 2002.

32 "Competitive clientelism and economic governance: the case of Thailand," in Sylvia Maxfield and Ben Ross Schneider, eds., *Business and the State in Developing Countries* (Ithaca, NY: Cornell University Press, 1997).

33 Hutchcroft, "The politics of privilege," 1997, p. 649.

34 "The politics of privilege," 1997, pp. 647–648.

35 Ibid., p. 648.

36 Ibid., p. 656.

37 "Reform, state and corruption," 1999, p. 11.

38 Anek Laothamos, "From clientelism to partnership: business-government relations in Thailand," in Andrew Macintyre, ed., *Business and government in industrialising Asia*

that corruption is more harmful when it dampens competition and obstructs the smooth functioning of the market. Doner and Ramsey argue that economic growth in Thailand occurred alongside substantial rent-seeking and corruption because at the micro level clientelism was competitive (due to intraelite competition among political-military patrons who opened access to commercial banks for their business clients) and allowed for entry of new clientelist factions into industrial sectors like textiles, but at the level of macroeconomic management, state agencies were staffed by technocrats who consulated closely with commercial banks and were shielded from clientelist pressures. They term this arrangement "competitive clientelism." Doner and Ramsey note that this competition avoided the "independent monopoly" arrangement described by Schleifer and Vishney because "essential government goods…could be 'supplied by at least two government agencies'."[39]

It is important to note that the above three areas are interrelated. That is, the form corruption assumes makes a difference in the way corrupt monies are extracted and invested and in the effects that corruption has on the economy and state institutions. Not surprisingly, looting is seen as the most destructive type of corruption in its effect on development. Looting does not necessarily plow monies back into the economy, and tends to be sent abroad, or if it is invested domestically, it does so in perverse ways such as the building of personalistic business empires and state monopolies, which is detrimental to a market economy. Looting, which includes the extortion of money from private interests without any type of service in return, is also more harmful because of its predatory and less predictable nature. State predation creates an uncertain environment for investment. Rent-scraping or rent-generation is also somewhat harmful because it is made possible by the creation of state monopolies, or by other activities initiated by officials such as the imposition of informal taxes and fees. Profit-sharing on the other hand tends to result in money invested in the nonstate sector, and thus may not be detrimental to business development, and may even have a beneficial effect.

Finally, corruption's destructiveness also depends on the will and capacity of the state to curb corruption through anticorruption measures. Yan Sun finds that one reason corruption is less destructive in China compared with Russia is because the former has been able to maintain discipline within the hierarchy and punish those accused of corruption, whereas in Russia, corrupt officials have more impunity.[40] But will and capacity alone are insufficient to successfully combat corruption; the type of anticorruption measure used is also important. For Jon S.T. Quah, an effective anticorruption strategy requires both (1) adequate anticorruption measures; and (2) commitment from the political leadership to enforce those measures. He argues that China's anticorruption falls in the "hopeless" category because the

---

(Ithaca: Cornell University Press, 1994); Tom Wingfield, "Democratization and economic crisis in Thailand: political business and the changing dynamic of the Thai state," in Edmund T. Gomez, ed., *Political business in East Asia* (London: Routledge, 2002).

39 "Competitive clientelism and economic governance," 1997, p. 450.

40 "Reform, state and corruption," 1999.

Communist Party has been unwilling to punish more senior leaders.[41] In contrast, in places like Singapore and Hong Kong, anticorruption measures have had an effective, measurable impact. Melanie Manion also finds that China's anticorruption efforts have focused more on selectively disciplining officials through periodic campaigns, rather than reducing institutional opportunities and incentives in the legal, administrative and constitutional system as Hong Kong did in cleaning up its government. Manion notes that the Chinese government has only recently shown the political will to address corruption through legal and administrative reforms, but has yet to address the larger issue of constitutional design.[42]

How Destructive is Corruption in China: Using Lessons from East and Southeast Asia

The above discussion provides us with some concrete comparative benchmarks by which to assess the state of corruption in reform China. As we stated earlier, an important assumption behind the use of these benchmarks is that useful lessons can be drawn by comparing China to other Asian countries on the relationship between corruption and development. If nothing else, these benchmarks force us to look at China's corruption problem using terms and analytical frameworks that permit cross-national comparisons, rather than describing those problems in terms that make China's corruption problems sound unique and distinctive. But we also believe that China's state and society are evolving in ways that make comparisons with other Asian countries increasingly valid, and that the experience of other Asian countries can shed valuable insights on the threat that corruption poses in China *by taking into account the changing state-society context in which corruption occurs*. In this section, we look at important trends in corruption and state-business relations in China during the last two decades, and use the benchmarks generated from our comparative analysis above to evaluate the danger that corruption poses to economic growth and regime stability in China. We examine first those areas where corruption does pose a serious threat, before discussing areas that offer a more optimistic or neutral assessment.

The Bad News: Weak Constraints on Corruption, and Signs of Destructive Corruption

On the pessimistic side, the Chinese state lacks certain features that are useful in limiting and suppressing corruption and there are certain trends associated with the more destructive forms of corruption. We focus first on areas where China falls short of effective constraints on destructive corruption: the absence of a "hard" developmental state; and the weakness of corporatist institutions. Here it

---

41 "Corruption in Asian countries: can it be minimized?" *Public Administration Review*, vol. 59, no. 6, 1999, pp. 483–494.

42 *Corruption By Design*, 2004, Ch. 6.

is assumed that these constraints do not prevent corruption altogether but that they limit and perhaps discourage more destructive forms of corruption. We then look at trends signaling more destructive forms of corruption: corruption in the areas of macroeconomic regulation, and the emergence of organized, collective corruption.

One crucial constraint that China clearly lacks is a disciplined, cohesive state along the lines of South Korea or Taiwan. MacIntyre points to two important elements of such a state: (i) one insulated from distributional societal pressures and willing to use coercion; and (ii) a centrally coordinated and organizationally cohesive bureaucracy.[43] The Chinese state may possess the first, but falls far short on the second criteria. Many scholars see the Chinese state as fragmented, decentralized and undisciplined. Despite numerous efforts to reform the civil service, personnel selection continues to be fraught with problems. Patronage, the use of criteria other than merit and expertise (e.g. family connections and political loyalty) continue to be important in hiring and promotion decisions, and the buying and selling of offices has been a new and growing problem since the 1990s. Lu Xiaobo shows that, despite reforms to streamline and professionalize the bureaucracy, the neotraditional, patrimonial character of the Maoist party-state continues to plague the post-Mao party and state bureaucracy and undermines its ability to be autonomous and disciplined. He acknowledges the establishment of a civil service exam and use of merit in hiring and promotion, but notes that this merit-based approach is still used on a limited basis. More importantly, he finds that cadres have interpreted many of the rationalizing reforms in neotraditional and particularlistic ways, thereby distorting the intent of the reforms. He shows how the bureaucracy has actually grown in the 1990s and details the emergence of new forms of cadre corruption and misconduct that have come about in response to the administrative reforms.[44] In another article, he terms the Chinese state a neotraditional administrative state that is market-distorting, as opposed to the market-promoting developmental states one finds in East Asia.[45] Margaret Pearson concurs, arguing that China's economic bureaucracy stands in stark contrast to those of South Korea and Taiwan. "Economic policymakers in the PRC often are well educated and extremely bright, but their training tends to be in engineering or in other production-related fields that are not best suited to policy-making."[46]

To be fair, the Chinese leadership has made a concerted push during the 1990s to further streamline and rationalize the bureaucracy, and to reduce incentives for official corruption and misconduct. Yang Dali has documented many of these reforms in his recent book, *Remaking the Chinese Leviathan*, and argued that the Chinese leadership has been successful in overcoming resistance and inertia within

---

43 "Business, government and development," 1994.

44 *Cadres and corruption: the organizational involution of the Chinese Communist Party* (Stanford: Stanford University Press, 2000).

45 "Booty socialism, bureau-preneurs, and the state in transition: organizational corruption in China," *Comparative Politics*, vol. 32, no. 3, 2000, pp. 273–294.

46 *China's New Business Elite*, 1997, p. 153.

the bureaucracy and made significant progress in rationalizing economic governance, including introducing a more merit-based civil service system. He admits though that civil service reform has been limited to the lower levels of the bureaucracy, and that "genuine improvement will take time and sustained political commitment from the central leadership."[47] Other studies also reveal that many problems remain and that China's goal of creating a disciplined, developmental bureaucracy is still a work in progress and years, perhaps decades, from accomplishing.[48]

A related constraint that China lacks is effective corporatist institutions. In the comparative literature, corporatist ideology and institutions are seen as another important element of the developmental state. Corporatist arrangements, such as business associations and industry conglomerates, are seen as a way to insulate the state from distributional coalitions seeking particularistic advantage, yet provide the embeddedness in society that states need to mobilize private interests to achieve developmental goals. For Maxfield and Schneider, business associations, especially encompassing, multisectoral associations, act as a disincentive against collusive behavior by providing a formal mechanism for promoting state-business collaboration in ways that serve the economy as a whole rather than particular sectors or firms.[49] A number of scholars have already noted the appearance of corporatist elements in reform China as the leadership seeks to recognize and control emerging social forces, harnessing them in pursuit of national goals without allowing them to become autonomous. But they also point out that corporatist arrangements in China, particularly those that are encompassing and national in scope, are in reality quite weak and undeveloped.[50]

In terms of trends associated with more destructive forms of corruption, several areas stand out. One particular area of concern for China is the emergence of widespread corruption in the financial sector. After all, corruption and cronyism in the financial sector was seen by many analysts as an important factor leading to the 1998 financial crisis in Thailand, Indonesia and South Korea. While China was insulated from the crisis because of the closed nature of its economy, some China scholars have pointed to corruption in China's financial sector as a problem that China shares with its East and Southeast Asian counterparts. Indeed, Nicholas Lardy writes, "financial losses caused by fraud, corruption, and other lending irregularities in Chinese banks seem greater than those associated with crony capitalism in Indonesia or by corrupt Korean bank lending practices that were used to channel hundreds of millions of U.S. dollars into the pockets of Korea's highest leaders."[51]

---

47 *Remaking the Chinese leviathan: market transition and the politics of governance in China* (Stanford: Stanford University Press, 2004), p. 183.

48 Manion, *Corruption by Design*, 2004; Yan Sun, *Corruption and market*, 2004.

49 *Business and the State in Developing Countries*, 1997, pp. 17–21.

50 Pearson, *China's New Business Elite*, 1997; Scott Kennedy, *The Business of Lobbying in China* (Cambridge: Harvard University Press, 2005).

51 "China and the Asian financial contagion," in Karl D. Jackson, ed., *Asian Contagion: the causes and consequences of a financial crisis* (Boulder, CO: Westview Press, 1999), p. 84.

There is strong evidence that corruption in China has spread to other areas of the bureaucracy, in particular new regulatory agencies concerned with macroeconomic management such as taxation, banking, state asset management, financial discipline inspection, customs, the stock market, real estate, international trade.[52] Corruption in areas of macroeconomic management should worry us because of the attention it has gotten from comparative studies of corruption in other areas of Asia, and because of evidence that corruption in this sector can have more destructive effects on economic development. The problems of excessive, politically motivated bank lending, for example, undermined investor confidence in places like Indonesia and South Korea in the months leading up to the 1998 Asian financial crisis. The problem of nonperforming loans in the state banking sector China is a well-known problem that has existed since at least 1990 when the Chinese government switched from budgetary subsidies to bank financing to cover the losses of state-owned enterprises (SOEs). Since then, it has been estimated that over a trillion yuan in loans have been channeled to SOEs.[53] While much of the increase in lending over the 1990s has gone to cover bank losses, there is evidence of substantial corruption in the financial system. The most publicized cases are those of bank employees who embezzled bank funds on a grand scale.[54] These highly publicized cases however are only one indication of widespread, systemic embezzlement in the state banking sector going back to the late 1980s. X.L. Ding's careful study of corruption in the financial sector notes that in the 1988–1990 years, the financial sector recorded 15,000 cases of "grave wrongdoings" (mostly embezzlement and kickbacks) involving at least 900 million yuan in bank funds. He also estimates that for the 1991–1997 period, about 5.5 billion yuan in bank funds were illegally diverted into the pockets of bank managers.[55]

Other areas of macroeconomic management that have been compromised by corruption include taxation, and the management of state assets and land. Tax evasion continues to be a major problem in all sectors of the economy, although more prevalent in the private and collective sectors than in the state-owned sectors, and often involves collusion between state tax officials and enterprise managers.[56] One highly publicized case in Guangdong province involved more than a thousand

---

52 See Lu, "Booty socialism, bureau-preneurs, and the state in transition," 2000; Ting Gong, "Forms and characteristics of China's corruption in the 1990s: change with continuity," *Communist and Post-Communist Studies* vol. 30, no. 3, 1997, pp. 277–288; and X.L. Ding, "The quasi-criminalization of a business sector in China: deconstructing the construction-sector syndrome," *Crime, Law and Social Change* vol. 35, 2001, pp. 177–201 and "Systemic irregularity and spontaneous property transformation in the Chinese financial system," *The China Quarterly*, vol. 163, September 2000, pp. 655–676.

53 Andrew Wedeman, "State predation and rapid growth: politicization of business in China," in Edmund T. Gomez, ed., *Political business in East Asia* (London: Routledge, 2002), p. 163.

54 See the cases in X.L. Ding, "Systemic irregularity and spontaneous property transformation," 2000.

55 "Systematic irregularity and spontaneous property transformation," 2000, p. 669.

56 Ting Gong, "Forms and characteristics of corruption," 1997.

companies in two cities that bribed taxation and other economic officials from 1998 to 2000 in return for falsified tax invoices. Overall, it was estimated that more than 172,000 fake invoices were produced amounting to 32.3 billion yuan, and leading to the evasion of 4.2 billion yuan in taxes.[57] Another area where taxation authority is being abused is the levying of various taxes and fees by a wide range of agencies that then go into their extrabudgetary funds or slush funds. This problem has especially serious ramifications for social unrest in the rural areas where levying of informal taxes and fees, and seizure of lands by local governments for development, have sparked numerous protests by farmers.[58]

The management of state assets has been another long-standing problem area. There has been a long history of state assets being diverted for use by public units and private individuals. But efforts to reform SOEs in the late 1980s and 1990s opened up unprecedented opportunities for misappropriation and misuse of state assets. One of these reforms begun in 1986 was the factory director responsibility system that gave more decision-making authority and responsibility to the factory manager. The other reform was to transform small and medium-sized SOEs into shareholding enterprises or sell them to private or foreign investors. As a number of scholars have shown, however, one of the unintended consequences of these reforms was the large-scale diversion of SOE assets into the hands of managers, officials, and private entrepreneurs.[59]

Another area of concern is the emergence of large-scale corrupt networks involving multiple officials and private actors such as entrepreneurs and criminal elements. This type of collective corruption has been on the rise since the 1990s and has come to light in high-profile cases like the Zhanjiang and Xiamen Yuanhua smuggling cases in 1997 and 1998, and the Shenyang case in 2000. These cases are destructive not only because of their scale and size but also because they create informal networks that compete with and undermine formal lines of authority. In some cases, collective corruption resulted in the capture of an entire state agency or locality and recalls similarities with corruption in post-Soviet Russia.[60] In many of these cases, the central-level supervisory groups that went into these areas to investigate the corruption encountered significant resistance from local authorities in their investigation. In the Xiamen Yuanhua case and others, the investigative team was threatened and reinforcements and direct involvement by the deputy head of the central Discipline and Inspection Commission were necessary to break the

---

57 Central Planning Commission Propaganda and Education office [Zhongyang jiwei xuanchuan jiaoyu shi], *An educational reader of an analysis of typical cases [Dianxing anjian pouxi jiaoyu duben]* (Zhongguo Fangzheng chubanshe, 2002), p. 208.

58 See Thomas Bernstein and Xiaobo Lu, *Taxation Without Representation in Contemporary Rural China* (Cambridge: Cambridge University Press, 2003).

59 An Chen, "Socioeconomic polarization and political corruption in China," 2002; X.L. Ding, "The Illicit Asset Stripping of Chinese State Firms," 2000.

60 Shawn Shieh, "The rise of collective corruption in China: the Xiamen smuggling case," *Journal of Contemporary China* vol. 13, no. 41, 2005. Yan Sun also surveys a number of these cases in Chapter 4 of her book, *Corruption and Market*, 2004.

corruption ring. In other cases, investigative teams had to be relocated to other areas in order to ensure their safety.[61]

The Good News: Signs of Developmental Corruption and Constraints on Destructive Corruption

Despite the negative developments summarized above, there are also encouraging signs of constraints on destructive corruption and "developmental" forms of corruption. In using the term "developmental," we do not mean that corruption is preferable to legal, productive transactions; rather that developmental forms of corruption are not seen as a serious threat to China's economic growth and, in some ways, may promote growth.

One important constraint on destructive corruption that China does possess is a strong, legitimate collective governing body – the CCP – that has the capacity to limit corruption and provide some protection for property rights, despite signs of predatory behavior on the part of the state.[62] While this seems to contradict our argument above about China lacking a strong, developmental state, the contradiction can be resolved if we distinguish between two different dimensions of state power. In pointing out that China lacks a cohesive, disciplined bureaucracy, we are saying that China is weak in terms of what Michael Mann calls "infrastructural power" or the power to selectively intervene in markets and civil society in ways that promote growth. But what China does have is "despotic power" which Mann defines as "the range of actions which the elite is empowered to undertake without routine, institutionalized negotiations with civil society groups."[63] That power is evident in the capacity and will of the Chinese leadership to launch anticorruption campaigns and round up high-level leaders on corruption charges. It is also evident in its ability to respond effectively to the Asian financial and the SARS crisis. Compared with post-Soviet Russia, Suharto's Indonesia, Marcos' Philippines, and Thailand under military rule, the CCP comes off as a stronger, legitimate, more stable ruling body.

In addition, it is encouraging that the Chinese state has recognized and taken steps to address its weaknesses in the area of infrastructural power. Dali Yang makes the case that the central government has taken steps to reduce incentives for corruption and strengthened its coherence and regulatory authority. As evidence, Yang notes the ability of the central government to divest enterprises owned by military and other party/state units, to restructure and downsize the bureaucracy, to put in place institutions to make governance more transparent and more regularized, to crackdown on smuggling, and to quickly negotiate China's entry into the

---

61 See Shieh, "The rise of collective corruption in China," 2005, pp. 84–87, and Sun, *Corruption and Market*, 2004, pp. 188–189.

62 See Yan Sun's discussion in "Reform, state and corruption," pp. 6–7.

63 "The autonomous power of the state: its origins, mechanisms and results," in John A. Hall, *States in History* (Oxford: Basil Blackwell, 1986), p. 113.

WTO.[64] From a comparative perspective, these steps are important in closing off opportunities where independent monopolies might emerge within the bureaucracy. There is also evidence that, while formal interest representation through corporatist and pluralist channels are weak and undeveloped, those channels are beginning to emerge in certain sectors and in some cases are playing a more important role than clientelism. Scott Kennedy's study of the steel, consumer electronics and software industry sectors suggest that business firms are developing multiple strategies and channels for shaping government policies and decisions that do not fall neatly in the clientelist category.[65]

Another reason for optimism is the shift from rent-generating, nontransaction forms of corruption to transaction forms of corruption that involve rent-seeking and profit-sharing.

Nontransaction forms of corruption are those that involve officials preying on public resources, rather than private ones, and generally do not involve two-way exchanges between officials and citizens. Transaction forms are those that involve a two-way exchange, such as bribery. There is an overlap between the two types and sometimes it is difficult to distinguish between the two, since nontransaction forms of corruption that involve looting or misappropriation of state assets may also have a transaction component. As a number of scholars have pointed out, much of what is called corruption in China, especially during the 1980s, fell in the nontransaction category. But since the 1990s, one major change in corruption trends has been the shift from rent-generation to rent-seeking or profit-sharing where the rent is sold to another unit or individual in return for a kickback or bribe.[66] In many cases, the briber is another state agency or SOE, which technically means it falls in the nontransaction category, but increasingly it is a nonstate actor. This shift is significant for two reasons. One is because the comparative literature indicates that transaction forms of corruption tend to be less destructive than nontransaction forms because there is a greater probability of the percentage of the proceeds in transaction cases going to nonstate actors and productive activities. True, the allocation of resources is not ideal and certainly not equitable or fair from a social welfare point of view, nor is it entirely efficient from an economic point of view since some of it may go into speculative or nonproductive activities such as the property market or buying imported luxury goods, but in terms of its impact on economic growth, these forms of corruption are less destructive than if those resources had been pocketed by bureaucrats and not invested at all in the domestic economy. There is even reason to believe that some cases of looting that fall in the nontransaction category actually share more in common with transaction type cases and are less harmful than the term "looting" or "asset-stripping" imply. For instance, Yan Sun cites a Chengdu survey showing that in 73 percent of cases involving official misappropriation, the funds in question were used as startup or working funds for the business activities of the

---

64 *Remaking the Chinese Leviathan*, 2004.
65 *The Business of Lobbying in China* (Cambridge: Harvard University Press, 2005).
66 Lu Xiaobo, *Cadres and Corruption*, 2000, Ch. 6.

corrupt officials, while the rest tended to go into business activities or relatives and friends or speculation in the stock market.[67] Also a close reading of corruption cases suggests that even those activities which appear to be looting on the surface, such as embezzlement of state funds and property, and asset stripping, actually come closer to rent-generation and profit-sharing.[68]

The other reason this shift is significant is because it shows that organizational and individual corruption in the state sector is no longer the sole or even dominant locus of corruption. Instead, nonstate actors, in particular private entrepreneurs and other social actors and organizations and organized crime, are playing an increasingly assertive role in initiating corrupt exchanges. Patterns of corruption, and state-business, relations, in other words are beginning to resemble those found in other East and Southeast Asian countries where the relationship between the state and private business is an important determinant shaping economic growth. David Wank has noted that this trend has led to an important change in the nature of clientelist ties between state and business from "dependent clientelism" to "symbiotic clientelism."[69] In dependent clientelism, official patrons provided material advantages to clients who cultivated ties (*guanxi*) with them. These ties had an affective component, involving personal trust, and were stable over time. In symbiotic clientelism, it is the private entrepreneurs who are providing material advantages to official patrons. Because private entrepreneurs have more leverage, they have more choice of official patrons. In contrast to dependent clientelism, then, symbiotic clientelist ties tend to be more open-ended, commercialized, and less stable over time. The downside of symbiotic clientelism is that, in comparison with dependent clientelism, it undermines formal lines of authority by holding out rewards and opportunities that lie outside of the bureaucracy and entices officials at the local level to deviate from central policies. Symbiotic clientelism was, for example, evident in the Zhanjiang, Xiamen and Shenyang corruption cases where private entrepreneurs, and organized crime, played a central role not only as rent-seekers but as organizers of rent-seeking networks.

One final trend related to the shift to transaction forms of corruption has to do with the balance of power between the state and private interests. In the 1980s, the state easily dominated this relationship, and nontransaction types of corruption was the game of the day. One encouraging trend is that since the 1990s the balance of power has been shifting to a more equal relationship between the state and private business, at least at the local level in coastal regions where private firms are more

---

67 *Corruption and Market*, 2004, p. 114.

68 See the cases discussed in X.L. Ding, "The illicit asset stripping of Chinese state firms," 2000, and An Chen, "Socioeconomic polarization and political corruption in China," 2000.

69 "Bureaucratic patronage and private business: changing networks of power in urban China," in Andrew Walder, ed., *The waning of the communist state: economic origins of political decline in China and Hungary* (Berkeley: University of California Press, 1995), pp. 153–183.

numerous and carry more weight vis-à-vis local government agencies.[70] As a result, transaction type cases have been on the rise. This change in balance of power is not in and of itself a good thing. As our review of the comparative literature reminds us, a coherent, disciplined bureaucratic elite with a prodevelopmental ideology and institutionalized links with the private sector are also important factors. But a balance of power does serve to constrain predatory behavior by the state, and encourage more of a symbiotic relationship between bureaucrats and private entrepreneurs.

The Grey Area: Neither Good Nor Bad News

In this section, we discuss those areas where corruption's effect on economic growth and stability is either neutral or unclear. One grey area is the competitive nature of corruption in China where there is widespread competition on both the demand side (among bribers) and on the supply side (among officials accepting bribes). In her recent book-length study of corruption in China, Yan Sun concludes that corruption in China aligns most closely with the Rose-Ackerman's competitive bribery model in which "rent extraction is shared among multiple officials and private interests... ."[71] What you do not have is a situation of joint monopoly or kleptocracy where one ruler or group (such as Indonesia's Suharto or Zaire's Mobutu) holds a monopoly over rent-seeking opportunities and can enforce that monopoly through the hierarchy (see Table 3.2). Nor do you have a situation of a bilateral monopoly, as you might find in post-Soviet Russia or the Philippines under Marcos during the period of martial law, where rents are shared between the ruler and a few powerful private interests. At the same time, you do not have the other extreme of independent monopolies where each subordinate office in the bureaucracy enjoys a monopoly over a particular good or service. Corruption in China best approaches a situation of competitive bribery where there is competition among both private actors and officials for rents and other state resources, and competition among rent-generating officials.

The upside of competitive bribery is that it is more inclusive than the monopolistic types of bribery. The proceeds of rent-seeking are not monopolized by a few officials or entrepreneurs, and barriers to entry are kept low. Thus there is not the appearance that only a very small group is benefiting from corruption, in contrast to a joint monopoly or bilateral monopoly situation where bribery and its benefits are highly centralized. Also, competition among officials for bribes can have the effect of suppressing the price of bribes, unless there is also similar competition on the demand side. The downside to competitive bribery is that it brings new entrants into the rent-seeking arena on both the supply and demand side thus inducing what

---

70 Yan Sun shows that there is regional variation in this balance of power and thus the type of corruption that emerges in those regions. She distinguishes between top-down corruption chains in poorer, less commercialized areas where the local state is dominant, and a bottom-up dynamic in coastal areas where commercial opportunities are plentiful and competition for rent-seeking is intense. See *Corruption and Market*, 2004, Ch. 4.

71 Ibid., p. 194.

Table 3.2 Typologies of State-Society Structures and Their Effect on Corruption

Type	Characteristics	Effect on Growth	Examples
independent monopoly	fragmented, disorganized bureaucracy bribes ineffective	highest bribes lowest overall revenue most harmful to growth	post-Soviet Russia
joint monopoly	unified, coordinated bureaucracy bribes effective	moderate bribes highest overall revenue less harmful to growth	Soviet Union Suharto's Indonesia
competitive bureaucracy	bureaucratic agencies lack monopoly over goods and services bribes effective	lowest bribes least harmful to growth	Thailand China
kleptocracy	one ruler, multiple bribers, ruler has monopoly power, rents go to the ruler		Zaire under Mobutu Haiti under Duvalier
bilateral monopoly (I)	one ruler, few bribers, both have monopoly power, balance of power between ruler and bribers, rents shared between ruler and bribers		mafia-dominated states post-Soviet Russia Philippines under Marcos Indonesia under Suharto
bilateral monopoly (II)	multiple officials, few bribers, bribers have monopoly power, bribers more powerful than state		pre-martial law Philippines post-Soviet Russia
competitive bribery	multiple officials, multiple bribers		Thailand China
monopoly clientelism	patron-client ties used to raise barriers to entry and reduce competition	market-repressing exclusionary	Indonesia under Suharto Philippines under Marcos
competitive clientelism	patron-client ties used to lower barriers to entry	market-promoting inclusionary	Thailand China

Sources: Andrei Schleifer and Robert W. Vishney, "Corruption," *The Quarterly Journal of Economics* vol. 108, no. 3, 1993, pp. 599–617; Rose-Ackerman, *Corruption and Government: Causes, Consequences and Reform* (Cambridge: Cambridge University Press, 1999), Chapter 7; Richard Doner and Ansil Ramsay, "Competitive clientelism and economic governance," in Sylvia Maxfield and Ben Ross Schneider, eds., *Business and the State in Developing Countries* (Ithaca, NY: Cornell University Press, 1997).

Rose-Ackerman calls an "upward spiral of corruption."[72] This is particularly so if the profitability of bribery rises. According to a number of Chinese and Western scholars, this is what seems to be happening in China with corruption seeping into new sectors like law enforcement and the judiciary, and the rise of large-scale cases involving senior cadres.[73] Wedeman confirms this trend in noting an "intensification of corruption" in China with a qualitative shift toward major cases involving high-level, high-stakes corruption during the 1990s.[74] As Manion and others point out, this upward spiral makes corruption less easy to identify and punish, because "everyone is doing it," and thus more profitable.[75]

One trend that might serve to limit this upward spiral is the regime's commitment to anti-corruption reforms. We place this in the grey area because while the Chinese leadership has shown a willingness to curb corruption through the use of disciplinary and law enforcement agencies, institutional incentives and anticorruption campaigns, the evidence regarding the effectiveness of these measures is mixed and preliminary. Certainly, China's anticorruption campaigns are not "hopeless" as Quah describes them. The Chinese leadership has strengthened party and state disciplinary agencies, promulgated numerous regulations and laws against corrupt behavior, and shown the will and ability at various times during the reform period to launch campaigns cracking down on corruption and discipline its cadres. However, it is also becoming evident that these measures have not had the effect of reducing corruption in China. Studies show that disciplinary and law enforcement agencies have acted to shield officials, especially more senior officials, from harsh punishment.[76] Likewise, anticorruption campaigns do play an important function in signaling to the public the regime's resolve to combat corruption and they do catch large numbers of corrupt cadres. But analyses show that campaigns at best may deter petty acts of corruption but have been ineffective in deterring high-level, high-stakes corruption involving larger sums of money and senior officials.[77] In other words, China's anticorruption strategy has at best only kept up with the growing opportunities for corruption that have emerged in China's marketized economy, and kept the problem from spiraling out of control. At worst, it has maintained the equilibrium of widespread corruption and made little progress toward reaching a new equilibrium point of clean government. Drawing on studies of successful anti-corruption experiences in Hong Kong and Singapore, a number of Chinese and Western scholars have argued that making the shift to a new equilibrium would require greater attention to redesigning and

---

72 *Corruption and Government: Causes, Consequences and Reform* (Cambridge: Cambridge University Press, 1999), p. 124.

73 Yan Sun, *Corruption and Market*, 2004, pp. 194–195; He Zengke, "Corruption and anticorruption in reform China," 2000.

74 "The intensification of corruption in China," 2004.

75 *Corruption By Design*, 2004, pp. 12–13.

76 Melanie Manion, *Corruption By Design*, 2004, ch. 4; Yan Sun, *Corruption and Market*, 2004, ch. 5.

77 Andrew Wedeman, "Anticorruption campaigns and the intensification of corruption in China," *Journal of Contemporary China*, vol. 14, no. 42, February 2005, pp. 93–116.

strengthening disciplinary agencies, putting in place a set of institutional incentives to deter corruption, and constitutional design.[78]

The picture is also mixed in terms of where corrupt monies go. Monies from rent-generating and profit-sharing activities have generally stayed in the country. But there is no doubt that some of it is invested in speculative areas that can generate a quick and high rate of return, such as real estate, the stock market, or illegal activities such as smuggling.[79] There have also been reports of large amounts of embezzled money leaving the country. Capital flight is a substantial and possibly a serious problem although it is difficult to know just how much of the money leaving China is made through corrupt means.[80] What is clear is that the number of cases of officials absconding with money abroad, and the amounts involved, have risen sharply since the mid-1990s and they involve mostly banking officials and managers of state-owned companies. Estimates of the number of officials and amount of money vary depending on the source but run in the neighborhood of thousands of officials and tens of billions of U.S. dollars every year.[81] It is also unclear how much of this money stays abroad and how much is reinvested into the Chinese economy since significant amounts are said to be transferred to offshore finance centers in the British Virgin Islands and the Bahamas which are then reinvested back into China.[82]

Conclusion

What should we make of these trends in light of what we know about corruption and its effects on economic growth and stability in East and Southeast Asia? Unlike recent studies of corruption in China, our comparative assessment brings us to a more optimistic conclusion that sees China's corruption leaning more to the developmental than the destructive end of the spectrum. Corruption is not of the predatory type found in Mobutu's Zaire where leaders looted the national treasury. Nor has it manifested itself in the capture of regulatory agencies, or monopolies, by private and criminal interests as we have seen in Russia or the Philippines, although several cases have emerged at the local level in places like Xiamen. The existence of a relatively stable and autonomous Leninist state during most of the Communist Party's rule has played an important part in limiting outright predation by a powerful bureaucratic elite on a weak society up to the early 1990s. It has also prevented powerful private interests

---

78 Zengke He, "Corruption and anticorruption in reform China," 2000; Melanie Manion, *Corruption By Design*, 2004.

79 X.L. Ding, "Systemic irregularities and spontaneous property transformation," 2000.

80 See Frank R. Gunter, "Capital flight from China: 1984–2001," *China Economic Review*, vol. 15, 2004, pp. 63–85.

81 "4,000 officials flee overseas with U.S.$50 billion of illicit money," *Xinhua News Agency*, August 10, 2005; "Capital flight: capture of corrupt officials a long drive, *China Daily*, August 13, 2004 (accessed from China Internet Information Center, www.china.org.cn).

82 Jonathan Watts, "Corrupt officials have cost China," *The Guardian*, August 20, 2004.

or societal coalitions from undermining or distorting state policies during the last decade as the influence of private interests has grown and the bureaucratic elite has become less disciplined. At the same time, China has a long way to go before it can draw parallels with the developmental states of South Korea and Taiwan. It lacks a cohesive, meritocratic and disciplined bureaucracy with a strong corporatist ideology, and formal corporatist and/or pluralist channels of interest representation remain undeveloped. As a result, clientelism remains an important mechanism for many facets of state-business interaction. China then remains somewhere in the middle of the spectrum between destructive and developmental corruption, although closer to the developmental than the destructive end (see Table 3.2).

China has drawn some parallels with Indonesia under Suharto with good reason. Writing just after Indonesia's collapse in the 1998 Asian financial crisis, Minxin Pei argued that like Suharto's regime, China suffered from "weak banks, a real estate glut, decrepit financial regulatory regimes and crony capitalism...and uncontrolled, systemic corruption... ."[83] Pei drew the parallel as a warning to China that if it did not address these weaknesses, it could undergo a similar fate. Interestingly, however, the parallel with Indonesia could also be given a positive spin because under Suharto, rampant crony capitalism and corruption occurred alongside rapid economic growth, much as we see in China. However there are some important differences between the two countries. One is that in Indonesia, Suharto and his family and close friends enjoyed a near monopoly over rent-seeking opportunities. Indonesia, in this regard, approximated a joint monopoly situation, whereas corruption and cronyism in China resembles more a situation of competitive bribery and clientelism where control over rent-seeking opportunities is much more decentralized and fragmented. Secondly, the CCP is a more stable, organized, and effective institution than Suharto's regime and has responded to the Asian financial crisis with reforms to deal with the very problems Pei mentions. Both these differences suggest that China is in a better situation than Indonesia, not to mention other differences that make China's economy less susceptible to external economic shocks.[84]

Perhaps the one Asian country that most closely approximates the Chinese experience is Thailand prior to democratization in the 1990s. Their similarities include: widespread clientelism and corruption; the rise of business associations and other formal channels for business influence in the policy-making process; limited organizational coherence and discipline in many parts of the Thai bureaucracy; and rapid economic growth.[85] The system of competitive bribery that we see in China is also quite similar to the Thai experience. In explaining why Thailand's economy grew despite high levels of corruption, scholars pointed to the fluid nature of Thai politics where no sector, group or personal faction enjoyed a prolonged or exclusive grip on power and how this fragmented, decentralized arrangement led to a form

---

83 "Will China become another Indonesia?" *Foreign Policy* vol. 163, Fall 1999, p. 94.

84 For a discussion of these differences, see Nicholas Lardy, "China and the Asian financial contagion," 1999.

85 Laothamatas, "From clientelism to partnership," 1994, p. 208.

of "competitive clientelism" whereby patrons in the military and bureaucracy competed for clients in the private sector, and vice versa. According to Doner and Ramsay, competive clientelism was less harmful to growth because it compelled patrons to keep their corrupt monies in Thailand to build their patronage networks, and prevented monopolization of economic sectors by a small number of rent-seekers. As a result, entry barriers were kept low unlike in monopoly clientelism wherein entrepreneurs use their access to the state to keep entry barriers high thereby suppressing competition.[86] While the Thai situation is similar to China's, there is one important difference. Unlike China where corruption has infected the fiscal and financial systems, the Thai state seems to have enjoyed greater autonomy and professionalism in its macroeconomic agencies such as the finance ministry, the central bank and the Economic and Social Development Board.[87] If China is able to strengthen and insulate its macroeconomic agencies from business pressures, then Thailand may represent China's future.

To sum up, our comparative approach using benchmarks from the East and Southeast Asian experience to evaluate China's corruption problem yields a mixed but somewhat more optimistic assessment than if we had looked at China's corruption problem in isolation. As we discussed in the introduction to this chapter, corruption in China is widespread and may threaten regime stability by undermining public trust and confidence in the regime and contributing to both the perception and reality of widening social inequality. But at this point, corruption does not have debilitating consequences for economic growth. There are a number of trends in China that push corruption away from the destructive end of the spectrum and more towards the developmental end: the existence of a stable, collective ruling body which has taken steps toward strengthening coherence and discipline within the bureaucracy; the dominance of rent-seeking and profit-sharing over more harmful forms of corruption; a decentralized, fragmented system of competitive corruption that keeps barriers to entry low; and an emerging balance of power between the state and private business. In this regard, we place China's corruption problem closer to the developmental side of the spectrum in the neighborhood of Thailand and South Korea (see Figure 3.1).

But there are a number of areas of concern. One is the way in which corrupt monies are invested in areas of speculative activity rather than productive activity, and the continuation of capital flight. More serious is the spread of corruption to areas of the bureaucracy concerned with macroeconomic management, and the emergence of corrupt networks that directly undermine and compete with the formal

---

86 "Competitive clientelism and economic governance," 1997.

87 Just how insulated these agencies were, however, is a point of debate, and many scholars point out that these agencies became more politicized and susceptible to corruption as Thailand democratized and relatively insulated technocrats were replaced with political appointees and promotions in the civil service became based more on connections with political parties than on merit. See Tom Wingfield, "Democratization and economic crisis in Thailand," 2002.

Figure 3.1   Spectrum of Destructive and Development Corruption

DESTRUCTIVE   DEVELOPMENTAL
←--→

Zaire   Russia   Philippines   Indonesia   Thailand   South   Korea   Taiwan
                   under   under
                   Marcos   Suharto

CHINA

state hierarchy. If these trends continue, then there will be good reason to worry about economic growth and regime stability in China because it will be moving in the direction of an Indonesia rather than a Thailand or South Korea. In this scenario, corruption might disrupt economic growth and undermine regime stability which are vital for China's "peaceful development."

Perhaps the more important question is not whether or when corruption will destabilize growth in China, but whether China can carry out governance reforms that will move China away from an equilibrium situation of widespread corruption. The competitive nature of clientelism and corruption in China is a double-edged sword in this regard. It keeps the political and economic cost of corruption down and brings more players into the game, but ultimately encourages more corruption in the system and makes widespread corruption more difficult to deal with. While widespread corruption may not pose an immediate danger to economic growth, it does threaten regime stability by lowering public trust in the regime, undermining the competence of the bureaucracy, and aggravating social inequality. Abolishing widespread corruption then is critical but will require more thorough-going reforms: creating institutional disincentives, streamlining the bureaucracy, strengthening legal punishments and improving transparency in the legal and political system. Whether China's leaders have the political will and authority to carry out reforms in these areas, however, remains an open question.

Chapter 4

Strategic Repression and Regime Stability in China's Peaceful Development

Andrew Wedeman

Introduction

Over the past decade, China has apparently experienced a marked increase in unrest. According to official statistics, the number of "mass incidents" increased from 8,700 in 1993 to 40,000 in 2000, 58,000 in 2003 and 74,000 in 2004.[1] The number of protestors involved reportedly increased from 860,000 in 1993, to 3 million in 2003, and 3.7 million in 2004.[2] During the first ten months of 2004, protests were reported in 337 cities and 1,955 counties.[3] Anecdotal evidence from press reports also suggests a rise in the number of violent clashes between police and demonstrators.[4] The increasing mass unrest could undermine the regime stability, which is vital to China's "peaceful development," particularly when rapid industrialization and social changes have created many problems that the government cannot resolve effectively and quickly.

On the surface, evidence of rising unrest would suggest a future of instability and hence uncertainty about the long-term survival of the current regime. It would, however, be wrong to jump to such a conclusion without knowing in more detail

---

1 The Ministry of Public Security defines a wide range of activities including groups submitting petitions, sit down protests, strikes, demonstrations, and riots under the general rubric of mass incidents. See Murry Scot Tanner, "China Rethinks Unrest," *The Washington Quarterly*, vol. 27, no. 3, 2004, pp. 137–156; Murray Scot Tanner, "Chinese Government Responses to Rising Social Unrest," Testimony presented to the U.S.-China Economic and Security Review Commission, April 14, 2005 available at http://www.rand.org; Minxin Pei, "China is paying the price of rising social unrest," Financial Times (London), 11/7/05; and South China Morning Post 7/7/05.

2 It is unclear how the Ministry of Public Security calculates their numbers. If they are correct, they show, paradoxically, a rather sharp decline in the average size of protests from roughly 100 persons per mass incident to 50. Murray Scot Tanner, "Protests now flourish in China," *International Herald Tribune*, 6/2/04.

3 "A Rise in Mass Action Worries China's Communist Party," *The Economist*, 10/1/05.

4 In December 2005, for example, police opened fire on Molotov cocktails and homemade bomb-throwing demonstrators in Dongzhou, Guangdong, killing 20. Six months earlier, "security men" killed six in a protest in Zhejiang. Howard W. French, "China Used Bribes and Threat to Silence Village," *New York Times* 12/17/05: A1 and A6.

the nature of the mass unrest. China is, after all, a huge, unevenly governed country and hence some level of unrest is "natural." In fact, most protests are rooted in purely local issues and few pose a tangible threat to regime survival.[5] Moreover, some considerable portion of what the Ministry of Public Security defines as "mass incidents" would be considered "normal" local political actions in the west.[6] In fact, a rise in mass incidents can be interpreted as either evidence of decreasing regime stability or a transition from a tightly controlled and repressed society to a more open one in which citizens have greater freedom to assemble and make their voices heard. By the same token, increased reporting on such incidents can be taken as evidence of increasing transparency. Thus, while it is tempting to interpret evidence of rising unrest as proof of the impending failure of Hu Jintao's "peaceful development" strategy, it is more appropriate to recognize that the loosening of restrictions inherent in the "peaceful development" strategy is likely to cause increased "instability" because most of what are considered "mass incidents" are in fact manifestations of an increasingly assertive civil society. The key to regime stability and survival may, therefore, lie less in the level of unrest, than its response to the proliferation of challenges. In fact, regime stability and the chances for "peaceful development" likely depend in large measure on the regime's willingness to recognize that not only can it no longer hope to crush all manifestations of dissent but must instead live with the "turmoil" that is inherent in a more open society.

According to Tanner, as the level of unrest has increased the authorities have come to accept that unrest is inevitable and have stopped trying to repress all protests and have instead adopted tactics designed to contain and manage unrest.[7] Managing unrest is not, however, simply a matter of changing police tactics. Managing protest also implies a shift from "reflexive repression" to "strategic repression." Repression tends to be viewed as a pathology born out of a regime's fear, paranoia, brutality, and unwillingness to tolerate any form of heterodoxy that challenges its claim to political hegemony.[8] In some extreme cases, it may be true that any manifestation of

---

5   At the same time, however, it must be recognized that many times local problems mushroom into open protests because of imperfections in the Chinese legal and administrative system, imperfections created in part by the ad-hoc nature of reforms and in part by the CCP's continued monopoly on political power. Thus, for example, in a case involving the confiscation of land by authorities in Shiqiao, Hebei, 15 villagers were arrested after the local court's summary refusal to hear a suit against the local government triggered a demonstration and that then erupted into "riot." Joseph Kahn, "When Chinese Sue the State, Cases Are Often Smothered," *New York Times* 12/28/05.

6   Many of the clashes between local governments and peasants are analogous to fights over zoning in American communities, some of which lead to public protests. But whereas public protests in China often receive considerable attention in the western media, most zoning protests in the U.S. go unreported in the national media and may merit only a few lines in the local press.

7   Tanner, "China Rethinks Unrest," p. 152.

8   In official rhetoric, heterodoxy (*xia* 邪), which also means "evil," refers to any group not officially registered and recognized by the state. See Freedom House, "Report Analyzing Seven Secret Chinese Government Documents" (Washington DC, February 11, 2002,

deviance, real or imaginary, is dealt with swiftly and harshly. Most regimes, however, outlaw and repress certain forms of dissent (e.g., "armed subversion,") but ignore or tolerate many others. Even an authoritarian regime can abide some degree of dissent because, after all, not all heterodoxies are equally dangerous. Some dissidents may call for the violent overthrow of the regime or espouse ethnic separatism. Others may demand greater academic and artistic freedom. Still others may object to state interference in their personal lives or may have become "infected" by any number of strains of "spiritual pollution" that lead them to grow their hair long, get perms, and wear bell bottoms. There is, obviously, a significant difference between bomb-throwing subversives and those who only want to rock and roll. While the latter may be "deviant" and politically suspect, and punk rockers may deeply offend officials' sensibilities, purple Mohawks and loud music are unlikely to truly threaten the regime's grip on power. Between the extremes of the ill mannered punk and the armed subversive are arrayed a wide and varied range of ambiguous challengers, some of whom may be a real threat and others little more than political nuances.

Because repression can be politically costly and is never entirely risk free, a regime – even a repressive regime – needs to strategically differentiate among these various challengers.[9] It needs to decide which require immediate suppression, which should be placed under surveillance to determine if they are likely to become threats, and which can be safely ignored for the time being. In the process, the regime also needs to determine how it will respond to what it believes are emerging threats. In

---

available at www.freedomhouse.org). In the text, however, I use hegemony and heterodoxy in a rather loose Gramcian sense to mean, on the one hand, a dominant ideational construct and its subaltern rivals. In more concrete terms, I take hegemony to mean the state's claim to the right to define, construct, and regulate social discourse in ways that allow it to determine the bounds of political, social, and cultural acceptability whereas heterodoxy refers to those groups that reject the state's right to set the agenda and instead advance rival claims.

9 On the strategic nature of repression see Scott Sigmond Gartner, "The Non-Linear Relationship Between Government and Opposition Violence," *Journal of Peace Research*, vol. 33, no. 3, 1996, pp. 273–87; Will H. Moore, "The Repression of Dissent: A Substitution Model of Government Coercion," *The Journal of Conflict Resolution*, vol. 44, no. 1, 2000, pp. 107–27; Will H. Moore, "Repression and Dissent: Substitution, Context, and Timing," *American Journal of Political Science*, vol. 42, no. 3, 1998, pp. 851–73; Mark Lichbach, "Deterrence or Escalation? The Puzzle of Studies of Repression and Dissent," *The Journal of Conflict Revolution*, vol. 31, no. 2, 1987, pp. 266–97; Christian Davenport, "Multi-Dimensional Threat Perception and State Repression: An Inquiry into Why States Apply Negative Sanctions," *American Journal of Political Science*, vol. 39, no. 3, 1995, pp. 683–713; Dipak K. Gupta, Harinder Singh, and Tom Sprague, "Government Coercion of Dissidents: Deterrence or Provocation?" *Journal of Conflict Resolution*, vol. 37, no. 2, 1993, pp. 301–39; Conway W. Henderson, "Conditions Affecting the Use of Political Repression," *The Journal of Conflict Resolution*, vol. 35, no. 1, 1991, pp. 120–42; Dean Hoover and David Kowalewski, "Dynamic Models of Dissent and Repression," *The Journal of Conflict Resolution*, vol. 36, no. 1, 1992, pp. 150–82; and Steven Jackson, Bruce Russet, Duncan Snidal, and David Sylvan, "Conflict and Coercion in Dependent States," *The Journal of Conflict Resolution*, vol. 22, no. 4, 1978, pp. 627–57.

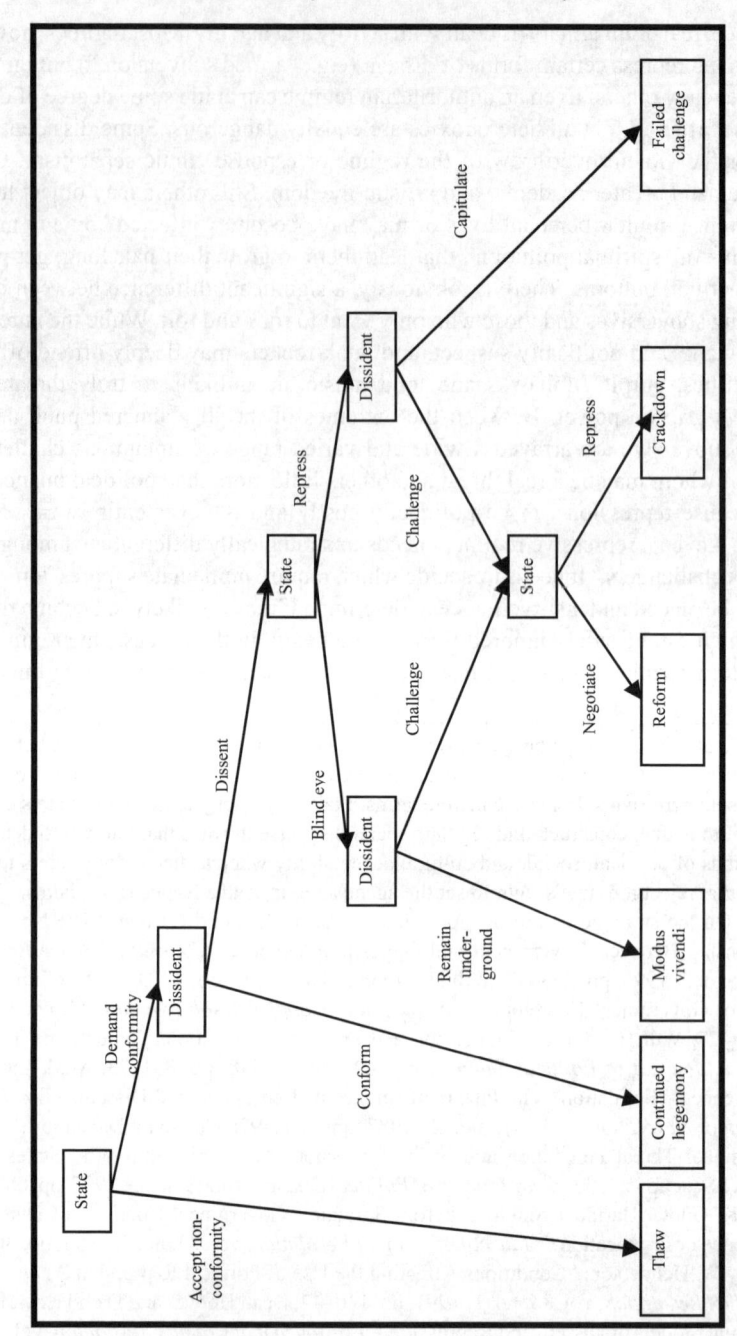

Figure 4.1 Strategic Repression

some cases, it may determine that a threat is so serious that preemptive repression is necessary. In other cases, it may decide that while the threat is minimal at present, if not nipped in the bud it could mushroom into a serious challenge and hence requires preemptive repression.[10] The regime may also decide that a preemptive strike will deter further dissent by "killing the chickens," to borrow a Chinese idiom, to "scare the monkeys." The regime may, finally, decide some forms of heterodoxy are sufficiently benign that they are best given a "blind eye" and simply ignored.[11]

Dissent and resistance are also strategic. When the state cracks down, dissidents – those who escape arrest in the initial round up – must decide whether to fight, run for cover, or capitulate. Even if the state does not crackdown and turns a blind eye to heterodoxy, dissidents have the option of lying low and remaining below the regime's radar, in which case they accept the regime's tacit offer of a blind eye by not openly challenging the state's now fictive claim to hegemony. Dissidents may, however, view the blind eye as a sign of weakness and decide to escalate by repeating or intensifying their challenge, thus confronting the state with the choice between fighting and capitulating. The repression-dissident dynamic can thus be conceptualized as an extensive forms game (see Figure 4.1).[12]

The precise structure of the game and its outcomes are of secondary importance. The key point is to recognize that if the authorities in China have responded to the rising tide of unrest by adopting a strategy of unrest management, then we ought to see variation in how the regime responds to different heterodoxies. Measuring variations in the harshness with which the regime responds to different challenges is, of course, difficult. First, we are much more likely to detect when the regime drops the hammer on dissent than when it turns a blind eye and does not drop the hammer. In instances where the regime adopts a tacit "live and let live" attitude toward heterodoxy, both sides have little incentive to admit that they have cut a deal with the "devil" that allows for the parallel existence of hegemony and heterodoxy. Thus the state is unlikely to publicize the existence of such heterodoxy. Nor are heterodox groups likely to advertise the state's decision to turn a blind eye. Second, neither the regime nor its critics can be assumed to provide unbiased information about the extent and severity of repression. Repressive states are, of course, highly unlikely to publicize the extent of dissent.

---

10 Preemptive repression is, in fact, the preferred option for a state seeking to crush challengers because it allows that state to strike before dissent reaches some critical level and dissident groups have had an opportunity to organize and expand.

11 The term blind eye, meaning to consciously and conspicuously ignore something that one is obviously aware of, originates with Lord Horatio Nelson, who when ordered to disengage at the Battle of Copenhagen (1801), reportedly placed his spyglass to the eye he had lost at the siege of Calvi in 1794 and announced that he could not see the signal. See "The Battle of Copenhagen, 1st April 1801," nelson-society.org.uk.

12 Although depicted as a one-shot game, the game can be an infinitely iterated sparring match between the regime and its opponents. The game is also one characterized by significant information asymmetries that force both the state and dissidents (and those the state thinks might be dissident) in a state of highly imperfect information.

Nor are they likely to provide systematic information on repression. Dissents, on other hand, are likely to be forthcoming with information on abuses of human rights but may exaggerate or report incomplete and unverified information that paints the regime in the worst possible light. Many instances of repression may also go unreported.

Various advocacy groups publish extensive data detailing names, dates, locations, and circumstances of individual arrests, sentencing, and deaths. These data, in fact, are the major source of information on the unfolding struggle between hegemony and heterodoxy in China. Because of reporting bias, I treat these data not as pure fact per se, but rather as a form of narrative in which a selective disclosure of fact is used to describe different groups' relationship with the state. Herein I do not wish to imply that these groups' claims are false or that the data have been faked. In a similar manner, I do not treat the state's account of its actions and those of its challengers as fact but rather as its rendering of its interplay with its rivals. In reading these narratives it is, of course, necessary to pay attention not only to what is said, but also to what is left out because what is omitted from the story is the story of the blind eye. Understanding the struggle between hegemony and heterodoxy, in short, requires a nuanced reading not only of the lines of the story but of what is between the lines.

The near impossibility of trying to "prove a negative" – determining when repression does not happen – can be partially overcome by a comparative approach that contrasts the state's response to different heterodox groups. Some conflicts may be cast in stark Manichean terms – a life and death struggle between good and evil in which one side must prevail over the other. Other conflicts may be cast in terms of a moral trial in which dissidents endure oppression as a way of proving the moral and political bankruptcy of the state. Assuming that the tone and tenor of each narrative likely reflects the intensity of each conflict, in this chapter I examine the intensity of conflict between the state and variety of heterodox groups focusing on reported arrests and sentences. I propose that the state responds most harshly to those groups whose beliefs reject the possibility of the coexistence of hegemony and heterodoxy and who openly challenge the state. The state is, on the other hand, more likely to turn a blind eye to those groups whose beliefs are not antagonistic to its claim of hegemony and who avoid open challenges. I further propose that the probability of regime survival and hence the success of "peaceful development" will be dependent on the extent to which the regime is able and willing to turn a blind eye toward more benign heterodoxies.

The State and Its Challengers

Determining the long-term trend in the intensity of conflict between the state and dissident groups is difficult. According to official Chinese sources, the number of political prisoners has declined from 2,678 individuals serving prison sentences for counterrevolutionary crimes as of late 1994 to 2,026 in May 1997.[13] As of the following September, the official figure had fallen to 1,946.[14] In early 2000, the number was put at about 1,600.[15] By late 2002, the official number had fallen further, dropping to 1,300.[16] In 2003, various non-governmental organizations estimated that approximately 500 to 600 individuals remained in prison for "counter-revolutionary" offenses, while several thousand were serving time for violations of the new national security law.[17] Between 1998 and 2002, the Supreme People's Procuratorate reportedly approved 3,402 arrest warrants and prosecuted 3,550 individuals for "threats to national security," an average of about 700 a year.[18] The number of individuals under detention, however, only includes those who have been formally tried for specific offenses. It does not include those detained without trial or those detained for political reasons but convicted on non-political charges.

Given such "omissions," human rights groups have consistently described China as becoming more, not less, repressive (see Table 4.1). U.S. State Department reports on religious freedom issued in 2001 and 2002, for example, sharply criticized China, stating that in 2001 "the Government's respect for freedom of religion and freedom of conscience worsened" and "remained poor" in 2002.[19] Freedom House, meanwhile, which has given China its worst score for political rights (7 out of a possible 7) since 1989, describes it as "one of the most authoritarian states in the world."[20] In 2003, the U.S. Commission on International Religious Freedom described China as a "particularly severe violator of religious freedom. Persons continue to be confined, tortured, imprisoned, and subject to other forms of ill treatment on account of their religion or belief."[21] Two years later the commission declared that China "continues to engage in systematic and egregious violations of religious freedom."[22] The U.S. State Department's Bureau of Democracy, Human Rights, and Labor asserted that the authorities were "…quick to suppress any person or group, whether religious, political, or social, that they perceived to be a threat to government power, or to

---

13 U.S. Department of State, "China Country Report on Human Rights Practices for 1996" and U.S. Department of State, "China Country Report on Human Rights Practices for 1997."

14 U.S. Department of State, "China Country Report on Human Rights Practices for 1999."

15 U.S. Department of State, "China Country Report on Human Rights Practices for 2000."

16 U.S. Department of State, "China Country Report on Human Rights Practices for 2002."

17 U.S. Department of State, "China Country Report on Human Rights Practices for 2004."

18 Congressional-Executive Committee on China, "Annual Report 2003."

19 U.S. Department of State, "International Religious Freedom Report," October 2001 and October 2002.

20 Freedom House, "Freedom in the World Country Ratings 1972–1973 to 2001–2002" and Freedom House, "2003 Annual Report." Freedom House did raise China score for civil rights from 7 to 6 in 2000.

21 "Annual Report of the United States Commission on International Religious Freedom," May 2003.

22 "Annual Report of the United States Commission on International Religious Freedom," May 2005.

Table 4.1 Assessments of China's Human Rights Record

	Human Rights Watch	U.S. State Department	Amnesty International
1990	Intensified and institutionalized repression		
1991	Undiminished hard-line stance		
1992	Maintained hard stance		
1993	Continued abuse	Some positive steps, but continued to repress and failed to control abuses	
1994	Deteriorated	Continued widespread abuse	
1995	Continued to demonstrate disdain for human rights	Stepped up repression of dissent	
1996	Stepped up and tightened controls	Continued widespread human rights abuses	Political repression remains systemic
1997	Changed little in terms of the overall human rights situation	Positive steps, although serious problems remain	Serious human rights violations continued
1998	Some encouraging developments but strict controls remained	Human rights record deteriorated sharply	Continuing violations
1999	Controls on basic freedoms were tightened	Poor human rights record deteriorated markedly	Most serious and wide-ranging crackdown in a decade
2000	No signs of easing stringent curbs on basic freedoms	Poor record worsened	Continued repression
2001	Increased human rights violations	Remained poor, continued numerous and serious abuses	Serious human rights violations increased
2002	Calculates carefully when to tread lightly and when to crack down hard	Remained poor, some positive developments but quick to suppress	Serious human rights violations continued and the situation deteriorated
2003	Mixed, minimal response to some while seeking to eliminate and destroy others	Backsliding	
2004	Some progress but remains highly repressive	Remained poor, numerous and serious abuses	

Sources: U.S. Department of State, "China Country Report on Human Rights Practices," various years; Amnesty International, "Annual Report" various years; Amnesty International, "China: No One is Safe: *Political repression and abuse of power in the 1990s*," AI Index ASA 17/001/96, March 1 1996; and Human Rights Watch, "World Report," various years.

national stability."[23] The bureau argued that the worsening of human rights abuses stems "from the authorities' extremely limited tolerance of public dissent aimed at the Government, fear of unrest, and the limited scope or inadequate implementation of laws protecting basic freedoms."[24]

Conventional wisdom thus suggests that the regime responds reflexively whenever it feels threatened by heterodoxy. It is recognized, of course, that not all abuses are the result of conscious government policy.[25] Some abuses are committed by local authorities and even individual cadres acting contrary to government policy and in violation of Chinese law. Others are abuses in the eyes of international observers but not in the view of the Chinese government.[26]

Data on arrests and detentions reported by the Dui Hua Foundation in its "Occasional Papers" series make it clear that the regime is engaged in ongoing conflicts with a number of specific groups (see Table 4.2).[27] According to the Dui Hua Foundation, these data are a fraction of the number of actual detainees and arrests. These data nevertheless shed light on the "battle lines" in the fight between hegemony and heterodoxy. They show, for example, that the number of "political" detainees increased in the wake of the 1989 anti-government demonstrations. Similarly, the crackdown on cults begun in 1999 produced a surge in the number of persons detained for involvement in "sectarian" movements, including most prominent Falun Gong. Other prominent heterodox groups include the underground Catholic and Protestant churches, as well as a diverse set of evangelical sects. Tibetan and Uighur separatists constitute a fourth major group among the known detainees. During earlier years a fairly significant number of detainees were what I have coded as "subversives." These were primarily members of groups allegedly plotting armed uprisings or other forms of violence and hence differ from what I have classified

---

23 U.S. Department of State, "China Country Report on Human Rights Practices for 2000."

24 U.S. Department of State, "China Country Report on Human Rights Practices for 2001."

25 Amnesty International, "China: Nobody is Safe," AI Index ASA 17/001/96, March 1 1996.

26 For instance, Amnesty International routinely denounces China's use of the death penalty as an abuse of human rights, even though Chinese law establishes capital punishment as the legal penalty for certain crimes and lays down procedures for imposing death sentences and an appeals procedure. In the Chinese view, therefore, executions are conducted legally and in accordance with its sovereign rights. Amnesty objects, however, on the grounds that sentences are often imposed arbitrarily and the automatic one week appeal to the Supreme People's Court does not provide a meaningful hedge against possible miscarriage of justice. Moreover, Amnesty objects to the large number of death sentences handed down each year and the manner in which executions are generally carried out.

27 I used the two series because the Occasional Paper data allowed me to directly code based on relatively detailed summaries of individual cases, whereas the Database series allowed for less leeway in codes because it provided very short comments on each case. Moreover, the two data sets only partially overlapped but could not be combined into a single data set.

Table 4.2 Dui Hua Foundation Documented Detainees and Arrests

	Prior to 1984	1985–1988	1989–1992	1992–1998	1999 and after	Total	
Christian	34	15	18	97	79	243	19.00%
Labor					3	3	0.23%
Political	31	25	181	33	56	326	25.49%
Protester				2	54	56	4.38%
Sectarian	56	60	72	29	145	362	28.30%
Separatism	1	1	37	38	18	95	7.43%
Spying	6	5	7	2	25	45	3.52%
Subversive	53	21	33	24	10	141	11.02%
Other			2		6	8	0.63%
Total	181	127	350	225	396	1,279	

Source: Based on data in Dui Hua Foundation, "Occasional Papers" no. 1–18.

as "political" detainees, most of whom were involved with groups that advocated political change but not violence. Interestingly, the number of persons alleged to be involved in violent subversion has fallen off in recent years. In these same years, however, a new type of dissidence has appeared. This new type consists of that I have classified as "protestors:" individuals detained for organizing anti-government demonstrations and protests whose target is not the political system as a whole, but rather respond to local issues typically involving an allegation of misconduct on the part of local government officials. Individuals charged with espionage – almost invariable spying for Taiwan – constitute a final cluster.

Surprisingly, only a small number of detainees (52) were held on labor-unrest related charges. This is noteworthy because the restructuring of state-owned enterprises after 1997 precipitated a wave of layoffs, plant closings, and bankruptcies. Rising wage, benefit, and pension arrears have exacerbated the situation leading to a rising tide of strikes, demonstrations, and militancy in the once privileged state sector. The number of strikes and demonstrations increased, according to some estimates, from 60,000 in 1998 to 100,000 in 1999.[28]

Little is currently known about the overwhelming majority of these protests. Based on those cases in which some details are available (a mere 173), it would appear that a significant number (40 percent) involved in blockages of road and railroads or the occupation of factories and government offices. More than a quarter (27 percent) resulted in clashes between demonstrators and police, while over 20 percent led to arrests. Injuries were reported in 15 percent.[29] A number involved

---

28 Information Centre for Human Rights and Democracy, 4/28/03 in *BBC* 4/28/03.
29 Data were drawn from both the China Labour Bulletin website and from a Lexis-Nexis search.

sizable numbers of demonstrators.[30] Yet, labor unrest accounts for less than 3 percent of the known detainees. The low number of detained labor leaders reported by the Dui Hua Foundation is not out of line with reports by other groups. Data gathered from the China Labour Bulletin suggest that some 55 individuals have been detained on labor protest-related charges in recent years.[31] Data gleaned from annual surveys by the International Confederation of Free Trade Unions (ICFTU) imply a higher number (123). The ICFTU data, however, includes 27 individuals arrested in the wake of the 1989 anti-government demonstrations, who I coded as "political" in my reading of the Dui Hua data.

Differences in the numbers obtained from these two sources notwithstanding and allowing that the real number of arrests may be significantly higher (albeit by some unknown factor), the fact remains that if 2–3 million workers demonstrate annually and a significant percentage of demonstrations end up in some sort of clash with police, that only 50–100 arrests have been documented over the past decade (or roughly a half dozen annually) is we believe noteworthy. The assertion by the State Department and others that the regime is hypersensitive to challenges and "quick to suppress" implies that a surge in labor militancy should precipitate a harsh crackdown. Yet the regime's response has been muted. In most cases, the authorities appear willing to tolerate demonstrations – at least so long as they do not turn into riots. Local officials when queried about demonstrations by Hong Kong-based researchers replied that they had become a routine fact of life, particularly in areas hit by widespread layoffs and plant closures.[32] According to the ICFTU:

> The Chinese government is keenly aware that labor protests are a potential threat to its ability to remain in power and as such has continued to implement a carrot and stick response aimed at avoiding escalations. In practice, this has meant arresting and imprisoning organizers and making minor concessions to the main body of protestors.[33]

---

30 In 1997, 100,000 workers reportedly demonstrated in Mianyang (Sichuan). In 2002, 50,000 were said to have demonstrated in the Daqing oilfields (Heilongjiang) at the same time that 30,000 workers were demonstrating in Liaoyang (Liaoning). *AP*, 7/17/97; *NYT* 7/18/97; *Toronto Star*, 7/18/97; *AFP*, 3/1/3/02; and *AFX*, 3/21/02.

31 My data on labor protests suggests that the number of arrests is much higher. In the 173 protests I examined, at least 340 were reportedly detained by police. These reports, however, suggest that many of those detained during demonstrations were quickly released, which implies that most were not charged with criminal wrongdoing. In a strike against Stella International in Dongguan (Guangdong), for example, police initially detained 75 workers but only charged 10 with destruction of property. U.S. Department of State, "China Country Report on Human Rights Practices for 2004."

32 Hong Kong interview, May 2004. According to my informant, when his organization contacted a particular municipality regarding a reported demonstration, the official they reached replied "which demonstration? We have five going on today."

33 ICFTU, "Annual Survey of Violations of Trade Union Rights (2004)," 6/1/04.

In a similar vein, Human Rights Watch concludes:

> In comparison to aggressive campaigns waged against individuals who tried to form independent political parties and against Falungong adherents, the government's response [to labor unrest] was relatively restrained. In part, this may have been because labor unrest threatens the legitimacy of the Chinese Communist Party in a way that other challenges do not: Article 1 of the Chinese constitution claims that China "is a socialist state under the people's democratic dictatorship, *led by the working class…*" (emphasis added). The government's response also suggests that authorities recognize the depth of dissatisfaction among laid-off workers and the popular support the cause might attract: authorities may fear an even greater backlash were they to be viewed as cracking down too hard on workers.[34]

The lack of a harsh response to labor unrest reflects the regime's dilemma. On the one hand demonstrations against layoffs, unpaid wages, meager pensions, and poor working conditions could morph into anti-government demonstrations. This creates incentives for the state to nip the movement in the bud. At the same time, however, the size of the demonstrations and the political cost that would accrue to a communist party-led crackdown on its nominal proletarian class base create disincentives for a crackdown.[35] Given these competing pressures, a strategy that combines tolerance for demonstrations with selective repression of individual militants is preferable to an open attack on labor. Moreover, the regime faces the reality that repression would not solve the underlying problem of unemployment, unpaid wages, and lost benefits. To cope with these problems the regime has few better alternatives but to try to placate disgruntled workers with cash payments and promises.

The tenor of the state's strategy in dealing with labor unrest is evident in its response to large scale demonstrations in Liaoyang and Daqing during 2002. In both instances, workers faced with layoffs, unpaid wages, and the loss of retirement and severance benefits, which they believed to be linked to corruption and malfeasance, mounted a series of protests, culminating in large marches (35,000 in Liaoyang on March 11, 2002 and 50,000 in Daqing on March 4, 2002). Local authorities responded by promising to look into the protesters' grievances and paid part of the disputed wages and benefits. Thereafter, the number of protesters began to diminish. Once the protest lost momentum, the police first arrested a small number (four in the case of the Liaoyang protest and perhaps even fewer in Daqing) of the "organizers" and then made a show of force when new protests erupted. According to Human Rights Watch, in both instances, local authorities "managed" the protests out of fear that suppression and mass arrests would only fan further discontent and could trigger more serious agitation.[36]

---

34 Human Rights Watch, "Paying the Price: Worker Unrest in Northeast China," 6 (August 2002).

35 Tanner's reading of internal police documents leads him to believe that some within the police apparatus sympathize with the laid off workers and are thus reluctant to deny them the right to protest. Tanner, "China Rethinks Unrest," pp. 143–44.

36 Human Rights Watch, "Paying the Price," p. 35.

To an extent, the demonstrators also appear to understand that there are limits to how far they can push the state.[37] In most cases, protesters seem to accept government promises of cash payments as sufficient grounds to call off demonstrations. More critically, the overwhelming majority of laid off workers have not demonstrated and have instead "accepted" their plight.[38] Thus, even though the recent wave of labor unrest may appear to threatened the communist party's political monopoly, in reality the threat has been contained without recourse to systematic repression. So long as carrots are sufficient to placate the majority of disgruntled workers, the state need only applied the stick to a select few – those who engage in violence and, more critically, those who might emerge as leaders and organizers. Successful repression, in fact, selects out the "trouble makers" from the mass of protesters, creates separation between the mass and potential leaders, and uses the individualized repression of a few to cow the many.

The Variability of Repression

The strategic nature of repression in China is also evidenced by its variability. As noted earlier, members of underground Christian churches and various homegrown sectarian groups constitute two of the largest groups of detainees. Both groups have faced repression since the early 1950s when the state imposed controls over religious activity and cracked down on what it considered "feudal superstition." Despite harsh repression during the Cultural Revolution, the state never wiped out either group. With the advent of reform and post-Mao relaxation, both quickly reemerged and began to expand rapidly.

According to supporters of the underground church movement, the number of Protestants has jumped from 834,000 in 1949 to 63 million in 1987 and to perhaps as many as 80 million by 2000. Of these, only 15 million were formally registered with the official state church, the Three Self Patriotic Movement.[39] Other estimates of the number of Protestants put the total around 45–50 million, including approximately 30 million members affiliated with the underground house church.[40] The underground Protestant church is, however, split between unregistered "mainstream" congregations and a range of evangelical and fundamentalist groups, some of which espouse more radical theologies.[41] The number of Catholics is believed to be around 10 million

---

37 *NYT*, 3/10/03.

38 Marc J. Blecher, "Hegemony and Workers' Politics in China," *The China Quarterly*, no. 170, 2002, pp. 285–86 and Dorothy J. Solinger, "Labour Market Reform and the Plight of the Laid-off Proletariat," *China Quarterly*, no. 170, 2002, pp. 304–25.

39 Bob Fu, "Persecution and Christian Apologetics: The Dynamic Growth of the Chinese Church," talk delivered March 19, 2003. Copy of text provided by Reverend Fu.

40 U.S. State Department, "International Religious Freedom Report, 2001."

41 The number of sects is unknown and designation of a sect as a "cult" or "heretical" is obviously controversial. About a quarter of the individual cases I culled, the China 21 data were identified as members of specific sects or congregations.

Figure 4.2   Arrests of Protestants

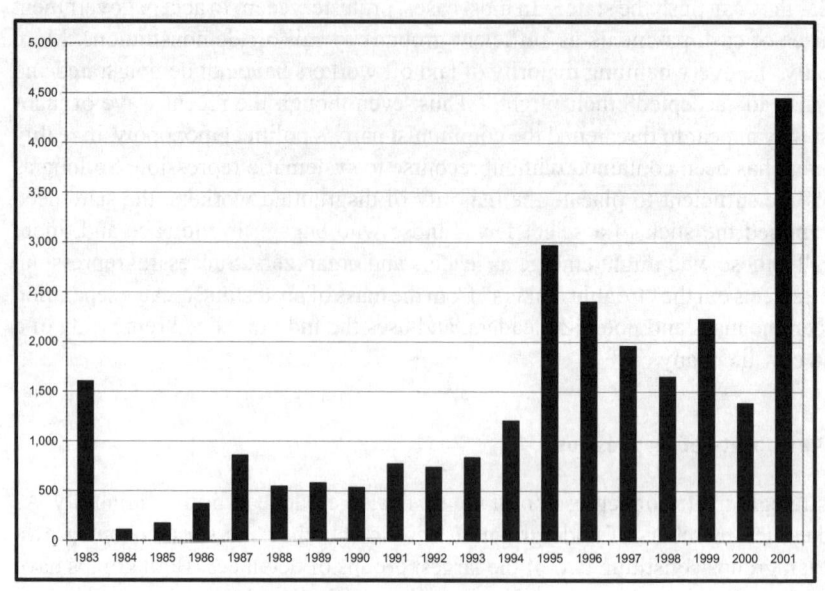

Source: Religious Freedom for China, "Some Statistics of the Continuous Persecution on House Churches by the Chinese Government (up to December 30th, 2001)," available at: http://www.china21.org/English/News/0423li_truth_table.htm.

Figure 4.3   Arrests of Catholics

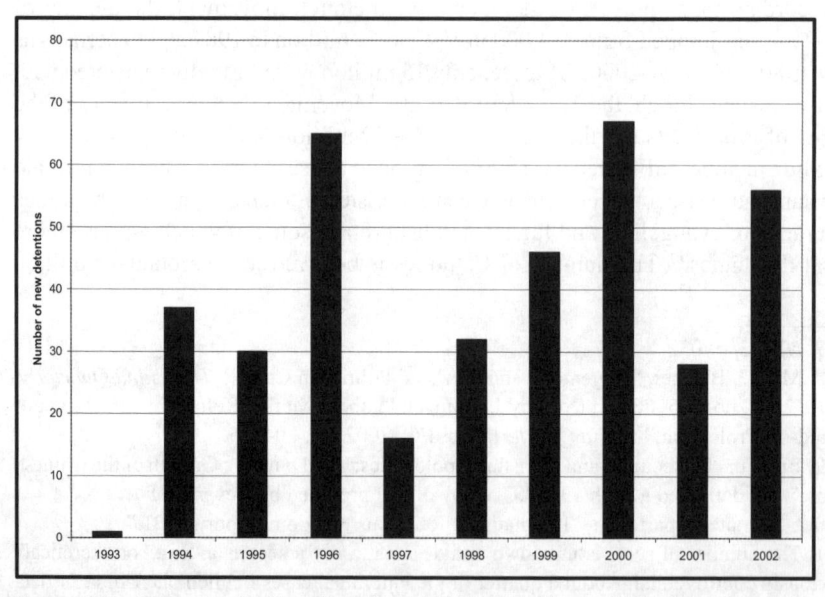

Source: Press Releases: Cardinal Kung Foundation, available at: cardinalkungfoundation.org.

with about half affiliated with the official church and half attending underground services.[42]

According to the New York-based Committee for the Investigation of Persecution of Religion in China (CIPRC), since the early 1980s, 2.7 million Protestants have been arrested or detained, 440,000 jailed, 10,000 tortured to death, 20,000 crippled by torture, and 1.13 million individuals fined. In addition, 200,000 individuals have either gone underground or are missing, including 750 for whom arrest warrants have been issued.[43] Other data published by the Committee breaking down arrests by year and status, detail a more modest 25,000 arrests, 4,000 imprisonments, 130 deaths, and over 10,000 fines issued (see Figure 4.2). These data show spikes in 1983, 1996, and 2001. Systematic data on arrests of Catholics are not available. The Cardinal Kung Foundation, a New York-based Catholic group, documents approximately 550 arrests of Catholics between 1994 and 2003, but states that many more have been detained, arrested, or imprisoned. The number of documented arrests spiked in 1996, when 109 cases were reported (see Figure 4.3). In most years, approximately 50 arrests were reported.

Documenting the growth of homegrown sectarian groups is much more difficult because most are small and localized. There are believed to be over 100 million Buddhists in China but the number of people involved in sectarian cults is unknown. The largest sectarian group, Falun Gong, claimed to have upwards of 100 million practitioners at the time it was outlawed in 1999 but that claim is believed to be inflated. Other estimates put the number at about 40 million. Most of those involved with Falun Gong were, however, casual followers and the number of hard core members is believed to be around 2 million.[44]

The number of individuals detained for sectarian activities is unknown. According to Dui Hua, 1,150 individuals had been detained for sectarian activities as of the summer of 2004.[45] Of these 1,103 were identified as members of Falun Gong. Data drawn from the foundation's "Occasional Paper" series which covers the 1980s and early 1990s reveal a total of 381 individuals detained for sectarianism,

---

42 U.S. State Department, Bureau of Democracy, Human Rights, and Labor, "International Religious Freedom Report 2004."

43 Committee for the Investigation of Persecution of Religion in China website: http://www.china21.org/English/docs/state-final.htm.

44 Julia China, "The Falun Gong: Religious and Political Implications," *American Asian Review*, vol. 19, no. 4, 2001, pp. 1–18; Benoit Vermander, "Looking at China Through the Mirror of Falun Gong," *China Perspectives*, no. 35, 2001, p. 4; Cheris Shun-ching Chan, "The *Falun Gong* in China: A Sociological Perspective," *China Quarterly*, no. 179, 2004, pp. 665–83; Ronald C. Keith and Zhiqiu Lin, "The '*Falun Gong* Problem:' Politics and the Struggle for Rule of Law in China," *China Quarterly*, no. 175, 2003, pp. 623–42; Nancy N. Chen, "Healing Sects and Anti-Cult Campaigns," *China Quarterly*, no. 174, 2003, pp. 505–520; and Hongyan Xiao, "Falun Gong and the Ideological Crisis of the Chinese Communist party: Marxist Atheism vs. Vulgar Theism, *East Asia*, Spring-Summer 2001: pp. 123–143.

45 Dui Hua data provided to the author April 2004.

Figure 4.4 Arrests for Sectarian Activity

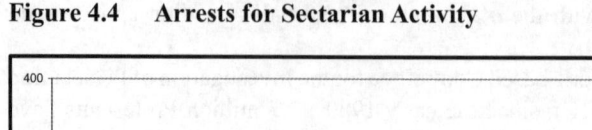

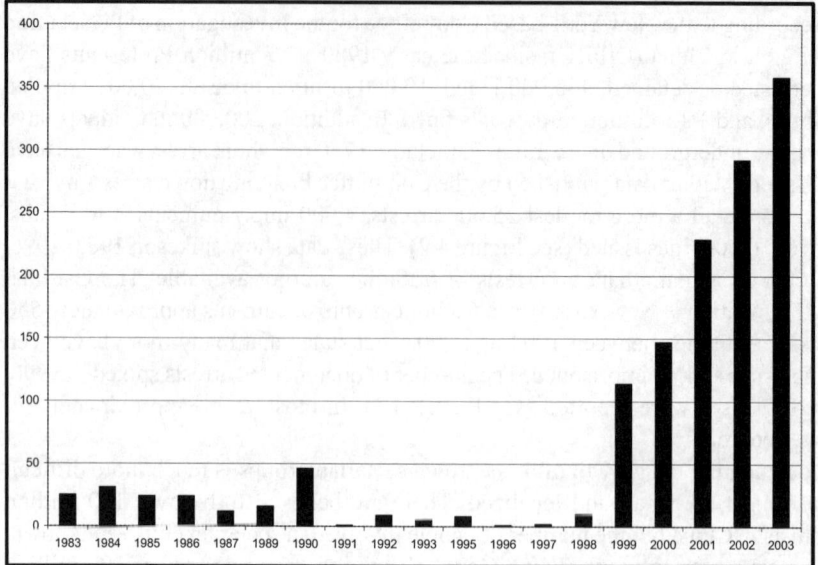

Source: Data for 1983–1997 from Dui Hua Foundation, "Occasional Paper" no. 1–18. Data for 1998–2003 from Dui Hua Foundation data provided to the author April 2004.

of which 120 were members of Falun Gong.[46] The remaining 261 were linked to a wide range of smaller groups. Juxtaposing these two sets of data suggests that there has, not surprisingly, been a marked surge in detentions for sectarian activity since the crackdown on cults in 1999 (see Figure 4.4). Falun Gong, for its part, claims that over 100,000 of its followers have been sent to reform through labor (*laogai*) camps or imprisoned but provides little documentation to support its claim.[47]

Data on the suppression of the underground church movement and sectarian groups reveal considerable variation in the intensity of repression. Among 1,453 Protestants reported detained and for whom data were available on the length of detention, over half were released the same day. Only 11.5 percent were sentenced to prison for a year or more, including 106 who were sentenced to terms in excess of 10 years and 5 sentenced to life or death (see Table 4.3).[48] Nearly two-thirds

---

46 Dui Hua Foundation, "Occasional Papers" no. 1–18.

47 "The Falun Gong Report, 2005:" p. VII. Falun Gong's running list of those it claims have died as a result of prosecution can be found at http://www.clearwisdom.net/. Falun Gong initially published the names of detainees but halted the practice in favor of publishing reports on deaths of its practitioners either while in police custody or as a result of mistreatment while in detention.

48 The data also included 186 cases in which individuals were reportedly "detained" but it was not clear for how long.

Table 4.3 Length of Detention

	One day or less	1 to 15 days	Six months or less	1 to 3 years	4 to 10 years	Over 10 years	Life or Death	Total
Protestant	758	419	109	13	43	106	5	1,453
Catholic	282	76	33	51	4			446
Tibetan		78	225	20	456	465	93	1,337

Source: Based on data from The Committee for the Investigation of Persecution of Religion in China (CIPRC) available at: http://www.china21.org/English/News/04231i_truth_table.htm.; Steven D. Marshall, *Suppressing Dissent: Hostile Elements II – Political Imprisonment in Tibet*, 1987-2000 (London: Tibet Information Network, 2001); and The Cardinal Kung Foundation, available at: cardinalkungfoundation.org.

of 446 Catholics arrested were similarly let go within a day and only 12 percent (55) were sentenced for a year or more. By contrast, 77.3 percent of Tibetans detained on political charges were sentenced to over a year in prison, including large numbers (42 percent) who were sentenced to 10 years or more. When short-term detentions are factored out, however, the differences in severity are somewhat less obvious (see Table 4.4).

Other data also suggest that the regime was particularly harsh in dealing with suspected Uighur separatists. Out of 212 individuals Amnesty International reported as sentenced to death for overtly political offenses between 1995 and 2000, 209 were sentenced in Xinjiang on charges related to separatism, splittism, subversion, or terrorism.[49] Data from Uighur nationalist sources show almost 98 percent of those charged with political offenses in Xinjiang went to prison for a year or more and that close to half of those for whom the sentence was known were sentenced to death (see Table 4.5).[50]

---

49 Based on data reported in Amnesty International, "China Death Penalty Log," 1995–2000. The other three were sentenced in Beijing on espionage charges.

50 Approximately a dozen ethnic Mongols were arrested during early 1995 on charges relating to separatist activity. Data on these individuals were, however, too sketchy to make even preliminary inferences.

Table 4.4 Variations in Sentencing

	Less than a Year	1-3 Years	3-5 Years	5-10 Years	Over 10 Years	Death	Total (n)
Christians	1.37	42.47	17.81	20.55	8.22	9.59	73
Labor	3.85	42.31	11.54	42.31			26
Political	0.00	36.13	19.33	25.21	17.65	1.68	119
Protestor	3.70	40.74	37.04	18.52			27
Sectarian	0.00	36.73	18.00	29.27	16.00		550
Separatism	0.00	34.78	43.48	21.74			23
Espionage	5.88	14.71	14.71	26.47	35.29	2.94	34
Total	5	311	163	236	127	10	852

Source: Dui Hua Foundation data provided to author April 2004.

Differences in the severity with which the state has responded to the underground Christian movement and separatists in Tibet and Xinjiang likely reflect differences in the nature of the group's challenge to its claim of hegemony. Whereas the underground Christian churches reject the state's right to regulate religious activity, there is nothing overtly political in their embrace of heterodoxy. It is quite possible, to borrow a classic phrase, for dissenting Christians to render formalistic obedience unto the state while denying the states claims to hegemony. Moreover, religion can be practiced in private. It is therefore possible for the underground churches and the state to exist in parallel, each in effect ignoring the other. At times, of course, the two may find themselves forced to interact and the state may find itself "provoked" into repression when underground Christians go "public" either by openly proselytizing or by holding large or highly visible services. At other times, the state may seek confrontation. In the case of the underground church, heterodoxy and hegemony, therefore, can coexist but only if both choose coexistence. Coexistence is, of course, facilitated in this instance by the fact that religion per se is not proscribed and hence it

Table 4.5 Sentences Handed Down for Separatism in Xinjiang

Sentence	Number Sentenced	Percentage Total	Percentage Known
Less than 1 year	3	1.12	2.14
1 to 3 years	2	0.75	1.43
3 to 5 years	30	11.24	21.43
more than 5 years	39	14.60	27.85
Death Sentence	66	24.72	47.14
Subtotal	140	52.43	
Unknown	127	47.57	
Total	267	100	

Source: Based on data gathered from East Turkistan information Centre, available at: http://www.uygur.org/english.htm.

is not the belief that the state finds offensive. Instead, the state demands that believers formally recognize its hegemony by submitting to its regulation and oversight. In addition, supporters of the underground church movement admit that there are not large theological differences between the above and the mainstream underground churches.[51] There are, however, serious splits between these mainstream groups and radical groups, some of whom both the state and members of the mainstream underground churches consider "heretical cults."[52]

---

51 See David Aikman, *Jesus in Beijing: How Christianity is Transforming China and Changing the Global Balance of Power* (Washington, DC: Regnery, 2003), pp. 136–37; Xu Mei, "China's Anti-Cult Campaign in Context: Difficulties Abound in Sorting Out a Confusing Situation," *Compass News Direct*, 2002; Deng Zhaoming, "Recent Millennial Movements on Mainland China: Three Cases," *INTER-RELIGIO*, no. 34, 1998, pp. 47–57; William T. Liu and Beatrice Leung, "Organizational Revivalism: Explaining Metamorphosis of China's Catholic Church," *Journal for the Scientific Study of Religion*, vol. 41, no. 1, 2002, pp. 121–138; and UK Home Office, Immigration and Nationality Directorate, "Minor Christian-influenced Groups in PRC" http://www.ind.homeoffice.gov.uk.

52 The group "Lighting from the East" (aka Eastern Lighting), for example, embraces a "third gospel" composed by its leader, a 30-year-old woman named Deng. According to various other Protestant groups, Eastern Lighting has abducted, beat, and tried to brainwash those who have questioned "the heresies of the female Christ." Moreover they charge, "The group teaches its followers to abandon their families and jobs. It exerts control over its followers by using drugs and sexual entrapment. Absolute obedience is demanded and those who oppose the group are punished with beatings, bribery, kidnap and murder." *South China Morning Post*, 6/22/02. Also see Matthew Forney, "Jesus is Back, and She's Chinese," *Time*

Repression of such cults was, in fact, considerably harsher than that of the more mainstream underground church movements because the state often views them as criminal organizations disguised as shame religious organizations.[53] Thus, for example, in suppressing the Shouters, the state designated it a "counter-revolutionary" organization and charged that its Taiwanese founders had used the cult to engage in criminal activity.[54] "Cult leaders" have also been charged with rape, theft, and other crimes.[55] Many have also been prosecuted for "cult activities," the same charge that has been leveled against members of groups like Falun Gong.[56]

11/5/01 and Tony Lambert, "Lighting from the East: A Satanic Cult Exposed," *China Insight*, October 2001, available at http://www.us.omf.org/content.asp?id=13682. The founder of the Lingling sect, on the other hand, proclaimed himself the "second Jesus" while the head of the Lord God sect claimed to be god. Xu Mei, "China's Anti-Cult Campaign in Context: Difficulties Abound in Sorting Out a Confusing Situation," *Compass News Direct*, 2002.

53 Center for Religious Freedom, a Division of Freedom House, "List of the 63 Christians from South China Church who were arrested recently," http://freedomhouse.org/religion/china, 5/5/2003. Classified public security documents focused primarily on charges of rape, fraud, and violent retaliation in their summary of the case against the church. See Beijing Municipal Public Security Bureau, "General Notice on the Activities of the South China Church Cult Organization," 2001 reproduced in *Chinese Law and Government,*, 36, no. 2, 2003, pp. 81–87. The indictment of the Eastern Lighting Cult, on the other hand, stressed its attempts to infiltrate the party, state, and official church; ties with outside groups; its "glaring political color and purpose;" its "tight organization;" and secrecy, not the violence and kidnappings that members of the mainstream underground church have accused the group of committing. See "Announcement of the First Division of the Shijiazhuang Public Security Bureau," September 2001 reproduced in *Chinese Law and Government*, vol. 36, no. 2, 2003, pp. 65–73.

54 *UPI*, 6/21/94; *AFP*, 6/21/94; and *South China Morning Post*, 7/23/95.

55 In 1996, for example, Wu Yangming, a peasant who founded the "Holy Emperor" sect and proclaimed himself the reincarnation of Christ, was executed for multiple rapes in 1996. *Xinhua*, 3/28/96 and *The Guardian* 5/1/96. Three years later, the leader of the "Principal God" sect Liu Jiaguo was also executed for rape. *Xinhua*, 10/30/99. Several leaders of the South China Gospel Church were sentenced to death in 2001 on charges of rape, assault, and sabotage.

56 The state defines a cult as an illegal religious organization that deifies its leaders, "spreads superstitions and heterodox beliefs," excites "doubt," deceives, and disturbs "social order in an organized manner that brings injury to the lives and property of the citizens. Ministry of Public Security, "Notice On Various Issues Regarding Identifying and Banning of Cultic Organizations" 2000, reproduced in Freedom House, "Report Analyzing Seven Secret Documents." Members of illegal cults can also be prosecuted for:

> Holding illegal assembly or demonstrations to incite or deceive, or organizing their members or others to besiege, charge, seize, disrupt public places or places for religious activities, or disrupt social order. Resisting departments involved with banning their groups, or resuming the banned groups, or establishing other sects, or continuing their activities. Instigating, deceiving, or organizing their members or others to refuse fulfilling their legal obligations, and the case is serious. Publishing, printing, duplicating, or distributing publications spreading malicious fallacies and printing symbols of their sects.

The state and separatists, on the other hand, cannot peacefully coexist because separatism by its very nature denies the legitimacy of the state's hegemony. Even when ethnic nationalists do not seek independence but instead demand greater regional autonomy, the nature of their political demands are a direct challenge to the state and hence coexistence can only occur if the state accepts the legitimacy of its challengers and seeks compromise. In a sense, therefore, these challenges create a zero-sum game quite different from that created by the mainstream underground churches. It would be difficult to see how Beijing could, therefore, turn a blind eye toward separatism but it is possible to see how it could ignore unauthorized religious activity. Finally, it seems clear that the state has responded harshly in Xinjiang because it believes that the separatist movement there has adopted a strategy of violent resistance. In Tibet, on the other hand, the separatist movement has generally rejected violence and the number of death sentences handed down has been slight.[57]

Similarly, the harsh state response to Falun Gong can be linked to the nature of its challenge. As argued in abstract earlier, hegemony and heterodoxy may coexist if each elects to blind eye the other. After tolerating Falun Gong's growing presence during the mid-1990s, the regime turned against it in the late 1990s, first charging it with engaging in cult-like activities and then actively suppressing it after 10,000 practitioners staged a silent protest in central Beijing on April 19, 1999 and a smaller group demonstrated a second time on June 6.[58] After an initial wave of arrests and detentions during which practitioners were pressured to renounce the group and stop engaging in its practice, a hardcore of practitioners responded by coming back at the state. According to official sources, members of Falun Gong "besieged" government offices in some 300 cities during the summer of 1999.[59] Even as the crackdown intensified, individual practitioners and small groups of believers traveled to Beijing to protest and submit petitions. Many were arrested, deported back home, detained, beaten, "brainwashed," and then released, only to then head back to Beijing to protest

---

Prosecutors were specifically enjoined to severely prosecute those cult leaders who seduced, raped, or sexually exploited women and underage girls; who advocate violence or the refusal of medical treatment; whose sectarian beliefs advocated "splitting China, endangering the reunification of China or subverting the country's socialist system; and those use engaged in criminal activity." Supreme People's Court and the Supreme People's Procuratorate, "Judicial Explanations on Crimes by Cults," 10/9/99 reproduced in *China Law and Government* vol. 36, no. 6, 2003, pp. 87–89.

57 Tibetan separatism, of course, did experience periods of violence resistance, particularly during the 1950s when the U.S. CIA and Indian intelligence supported a low-level guerrilla war. See John K. Knaus, *Orphans of the Cold War: America and the Tibetan Struggle for Survival* (New York: Public Affairs, 1999) and Mikel Dunham, *Buddha's Warriors* (New York: Jeremy P. Tarcher, 2004).

58 Vermander, "Looking at China," p. 4.

59 "The Political Motive Behind the More Than Three Hundred Sieges," cited in *Chinese Law and Government*, vol. 3, no. 5, 1999, pp. 87–90.

again.[60] Far from backing away, members of Falun Gong seem to court confrontation with the state, with the result that the confrontation actually escalated after the initial crackdown when Falun Gong refused to go quietly underground. As a result, the level of violence quickly reached, according to Falun Gong, unprecedented levels. As of late 2005, the group claimed that nearly 2,800 of its members had died while in police custody, as a result of police brutality, or had committed suicide to escape persecution.[61]

The intensity of repression not only varies between groups but can also vary across localities. In his field work on Catholics in Hebei, for example, Madsen found that heterodox groups and communities frequent adopt strategies of conflict avoidance or engage in passive resistance that allows them to coexist with the state even though they reject its claims of hegemony.[62] In other villages, the underground movement had become so strong that the state simply opted to look the other way.[63] In other areas, however, intense conflicts existed not only between the state and the underground church, but also between the above and underground church.

The data on arrests of Protestants and Catholics, for instance, suggest significant regional variations in the intensity of repression. In the case of Protestants, a disproportionate number of arrests were reported in Liaoning, Hubei, Nei Menggu, and Jiangsu (see Table 4.6). Henan, where just under a third of Chinese Protestants lived, accounted for roughly the same percentage of arrests. Anhui, on the other hand, which also had a large Protestant population reported a disproportionately few number of arrests, while in Zhejiang, which was home to a particularly visible Protestant population in and around Wenzhou, only a small number of arrests were reported. A highly disproportionate number of Catholics were reported arrested in Jiangxi (see Table 4.7). This is not necessarily surprising because Jiangxi is the site of a major Marian shrine, Yujiashan, which attracts large numbers of pilgrims each Easter and has been the site of several major confrontations with the police. Hebei, where over 40 percent of the reported arrests occurred, is also home to a major Marian shrine, Donglu near Baoding, and many of the arrests reported were linked to the Easter pilgrimage.[64] The number of arrests in Fujian was also high relative to the estimated size of the Catholic population.

---

60 This theme of arrest, deportation, and return to Beijing is repeated over and over in the accounts of the death of Falun Gong members. See http://www.clearwisdom.net/emh/special_column/ death_cases/death_list.html.

61 Data available at http://www.clearwisdom.net/emh/special_column/death_cases/death_list.html.

62 See Richard Madsen, *China's Catholics: Tragedy and Hope in an Emerging Civil Society* (Berkeley, CA: University of California Press, 1998).

63 U.S. Department of State, Bureau of Democracy, Human Rights, and Labor, "International Religious Freedom Report 2002."

64 In 1996, for example, between 80 and 120 Catholics were arrested in an attempt to prevent Christmas services on Yujia, while other Catholics were ordered to remain in their villages and placed under surveillance. Human Rights Watch, "State Control of Religion."

Strategic Repression and Regime Stability in China's Peaceful Development   111

Table 4.6 Spatial Distribution of Arrests of Protestants, 2001–2003

	Reported Arrests	Percentage Reported Arrests	Protestants, estimated 1997–1998	Percent Protestants
Beijing	2	0.10	20,000	0.12
Tianjin			15,000	0.09
Hebei	27	1.42	300,000	1.77
Shanxi	49	2.57	200,000	1.18
NeiMenggu	75	3.93	150,000	0.88
Liaoning	257	13.48	400,000	2.35
Jilin	3	0.16	200,000	1.18
Heilongjiang	70	3.67	600,000	3.53
Shanghai	2	0.10	140,000	0.82
Jiangsu	413	21.66	1,000,000	5.89
Zhejiang	18	0.94	1,300,000	7.65
Anhui	102	5.35	3,000,000	17.66
Fujian	4	0.21	630,000	3.71
Jiangxi	6	0.31	300,000	1.77
Shandong	48	2.52	800,000	4.71
Henan	604	31.67	5,000,000	29.43
Hubei	95	4.98	150,000	0.88
Hunan	6	0.31	200,000	1.18
Guangdong	6	0.31	200,000	1.18
Guangxi	22	1.15	90,000	0.53
Hainan			37,000	0.22
Chongqing	47	2.46	200,000	1.18
Sichuan	40	2.10	400,000	2.35
Guizhou			360,000	2.12
Yunnan			800,000	4.71
Xizang				
Shaanxi	10	0.52	350,000	2.06
Gansu			69,000	0.41
Qinghai			30,000	0.18
Ningxia			10,000	0.06
Xinjiang	1	0.05	40,000	0.24
Total	1,907		16,991,000	

Source: Based on data from The Committee for the Investigation of Persecution of Religion in China (CIPRC) available at: http://www.china21.org/English/News/0423li_truth_table.htm.

Table 4.7 Spatial Distribution of Arrests of Catholics, 1994–2003

	Province Arrested In	Percent Arrests	Registered Catholics, 1988–1989	Percent Registered Catholics
Beijing	3	0.55	40,000	1.55
Tianjin	1	0.18	90,000	3.50
Hebei	226	41.47	800,000	31.09
Shanxi				
NeiMenggu	3	0.55	200,000	7.77
Liaoning				
Jilin	1	0.18	40,000	1.55
Heilongjiang	1	0.18	35,000	1.36
Shanghai	5	0.92	120,000	4.66
Jiangsu			170,000	6.61
Zhejiang	6	1.10		
Anhui				
Fujian	92	16.88	210,000	8.16
Jiangxi	159	29.17	10,000	0.39
Shandong	4	0.73	130,000	5.05
Henan	34	6.24		
Hubei			50,000	1.94
Hunan				
Guangdong			110,000	4.27
Guangxi			30,000	1.17
Hainan			3,000	0.12
Chongqing				
Sichuan			300,000	11.66
Guizhou				
Yunnan				
Xizang				
Shaanxi	4	0.73	180,000	6.99
Gansu			50,000	1.94
Qinghai	4	0.73		
Ningxia			5,500	0.21
Xinjiang	2	0.37		
Total	545		2,573,500	

Source: Based on data from The Cardinal Kung Foundation, available at: cardinalkungfoundation.org.

As noted earlier, arrest and sentencing data are inherently suspect because of reporting bias. Quite frankly we cannot be sure that disproportionately largely numbers of reported arrests in particular localities are necessarily the result of more intense conflict in that area or a mathematical artifact created by the lack of full reporting in other localities. Similarly, self reported data cannot be viewed as unbiased. Problems of reliability notwithstanding, the data strongly suggest that the intensity of conflict between heterodoxy and hegemony varies considerably between groups. The data also show that the intensity of conflict varies across time. In the case of Falun Gong, for example, the movement developed for a number of years before the state branded it heterodox and banned it. In the case of Protestants and Catholics, religious activity was subjected to intensifying repression after the communist takeover in 1949, but it was not until the Cultural Revolution that most activity was either forced underground or suspended.[65] With the advent of reform, official tolerance increased. Greater official tolerance was, however, interspersed with periodic crackdowns, some of which targeted specific groups (e.g., the the Beili Wang (Established King Sect), the Mentu Hui (Disciples), Shouters, the South China Morning Church, etc.). Non-Christian sects, some of which resembled traditional secret societies, were also subject to periodic repression. Ethnic separatists, on the other hand, faced consistent and often harsher repression.

Conclusions

The U.S. State Department describes the Chinese government as "…quick to suppress any person or group, whether religious, political, or social, that they [perceive] to be a threat to government power, or to national stability."[66] The first part of this description implies that the regime will reflexively repress heterodoxy. But key to understanding the interplay between hegemony and heterodoxy – and hence Beijing's response to increasing unrest – actually lies in the final part of the statement. The regime's response to different heterodoxy groups suggest that while the regime will respond harshly to heterodoxy when it believes that heterodoxy is a "threat," it recognizes that not all heterodoxies are threatening to the same degree. Heterodoxy in the form of separatism and subversion is considered a clear and present danger to which the state will respond with harsh repression.

Its attitude toward other forms of heterodoxy varies from intolerance to tacit acceptance. Today, individual nonconformity, which in the early 1980s triggered campaigns against "spiritual pollution," rarely evokes repression. The state's response toward other forms of heterodoxy varies in part because while policy is set in Beijing, tolerance is often determined locally. In some localities cadres may zealously and rigidly enforce prohibitions that cadres in other localities may ignore or laxly enforce. The intensity of repression is also determined by heterodox groups'

---

65 See Liu and Leung, "Organizational Revivalism," pp. 121–38.
66 U.S. Department of State, "China Country Report on Human Rights Practices for 2000."

response to the state. In the case of labor, disgruntled workers have adopted a strategy of "probe and retreat," mounting highly visible public protests to bring attention to "injustice" but quickly backing down when the state signals that it will stand and fight. Similarly, the mainstream underground church movement has relied on a strategy of strategic defense, refusing to abide by the states rules but avoiding direct confrontation. Falun Gong's response stands in stark contrast. Instead of backing down when the state denounced it, the group launched a massive counteroffensive that first brought 10,000 protestors to Beijing and was then sustained by successive waves of smaller protests in Beijing and open defiance elsewhere. By fighting back, Falun Gong gave the state a black eye and triggered a cycle of intensified violence. Other groups have also found that there is a line beyond which they pass at grave danger and yet willingly cross that line.

It is evident today that the Chinese state will have to become more strategic in dealing with heterodoxy if for no other reason than politically it simply cannot afford to reflexively crush every heterodox "weed." In the current environment, attempting to suppress all dissent would likely overextend the state's resources. It seems prudent, therefore, to conclude that the regime will rely ever more on the blind eye as a way to manage heterodoxy by sorting out those challenges that are imminent threats to the CCP's political monopoly from those that merely fail to adequately acknowledge its hegemonic claims. When the state tacitly compromises the scope of its claimed hegemony, however, it implicitly retreats and hence opens up of greater space for civil society and thus cedes greater autonomy to heterodoxy groups. Tolerance of certain heterodoxies and even recognition that suppression is not politically efficient in some instances does not, of course, imply that the state will renounce its claimed right to set the rules. A shift toward strategic repression and the blind eye is thus not capitulation but rather an integral part of the shift away from a strategy of comprehensive control to one of unrest management.

At this early juncture, it would be difficult to determine whether unrest management and strategic repression will enable the regime to survive and peacefully evolve toward a new political order. To an extent, the regime's response to Falun Gong suggests that it remain inflexible and wedded to the harsh methods of the past. Its response to the spread of the underground Christian churches and rising labor unrest, on the other hand, suggest that the regime is increasingly willing to make the sorts of concessions necessary to avert sustained and politically damaging conflict between state and society. The outlook is further clouded by the gulf that separates what Beijing intends from what local officials do. As is clear in cases such as the recent shooting in Dongzhou and violence in places such as Taishi and Huankantou, the most volatile situations tend to be those in which local authorities, often in league with local thugs, take the law into their own hands and use their power to repress "legitimate" protests because it is the repression "legitimate" grievances that is apt to mushroom into larger scale anti-regime protest movements.[67] Regime survival thus

---

67 See Kevin O'Brien, "Rightful Resistance," *World Politics*, vol. 49, no. 1, 1996, pp. 31–54 and Li Lianjiang and Kevin O'Brien, "Popular Contention and Its Impact in Rural

depends not only on Beijing's willingness to adopt more flexible policies toward "normal" unrest, but perhaps even more critically on its ability to exert effective control over local officials. Movement toward a less rigid and doctrinaire policy of political control could, in fact, be thwarted by criminalization of local authority. In a fundamental sense, therefore, regime survival and hence the chances of peaceful development hinge not only on Beijing moving away from a policy of reflective repression and toward a policy of strategic repression but also on its ability to effectively control the state apparatus.

China," *Comparative Political Studies*, vol. 38, no. 3, 2005, pp. 235–59.

Chapter 5

Hybrid Regime and Peaceful Development in China

Zhengxu Wang

The most formidable challenge China faces is the regime question. Will China become a democracy, or will it remain a one-party authoritarian system? This affects China's "peaceful rise" in two ways. Externally, a democratic China will assure its neighbors and other international players of its peaceful intention, as the openness and transparency of its government will have the ability to do so. Moreover, other countries will certainly be more willing to live with a democratic China. Internally, China's development cannot sustain under a rigid political system. In face of the more and more diverse and modern economy and society, a rigid political system cannot meet the needs of governance. Either socioeconomic development will be suppressed, or disruptive changes in the political system will occur. Both, however, will likely discontinue China's economic development and social modernization. Hence, although most observers are concerned with how regime change or non-change in China will affect its external relations, it is its internal effects that will determine whether the goal of "peaceful development" is attainable for China.

How will the Chinese political system evolve in the coming decades, then? This chapter identifies important trends of recent sociopolitical developments in China, and proposes a framework for understanding changes that are to come. I argue that China is becoming a hybrid regime, which will be the intermediary regime type before China becomes a full democracy. I first introduce the "hybrid regime" type as conceived by scholarship in democratization. Then I identify recent political changes in China, arguing that these changes are moving the China polity toward a "hybrid regime." I focus on changes in two important areas: the trend toward constitutionalism and rule of law, and the changing state-society relationship. Next, I examine the general direction of political development in China, arguing that future changes will amount to a transition of China's polity beyond a hybrid regime and toward a fully democratic one. I conclude with a discussion of how these changes will interact with China's "peaceful rise" strategy.

The Regime Question

The concept of "hybrid regime" is a recent development in the empirical studies of democracy.[1] At the end of the Cold War, the collapse of the Communist rule was followed by some kind of electoral political systems in a big number of countries. At about the same time, many third world countries, especially those in Africa, also saw the transition from one-party systems to multi-party electoral systems. Such bamboo-shoots-following-a-Spring-rain growth of elections around the world resulted in many believing that democracies are established in these countries.[2]

But scholars soon realized that the end of authoritarianism does not necessarily mean the establishment of democracy. In many places, it is true that some kind of electoral system has replaced the earlier one-party rule, dictatorship, autocracy, or oligarchy. But behind the façade of elections, what really rules is still either individual dictatorship or one-party control. Indeed, many regimes in the world became neither democratic nor strictly authoritarian. Scholars start to call these regimes semi-authoritarianism, competitive authoritarianism, electoral authoritarianism, liberalized autocracy, semidemocracy, pseudodemocracy, partial democracy, illiberal democracy, electoral democracy, and election without democracy. They are "democracies with adjectives" or "adjective authoritarianism." This is how the term "hybrid regime" came about. It was intended to be a correction of earlier optimism (or indeed buoyancy): scholars realized that countries can remain "hybrid" for a long time without consolidating as liberal democracies while some may even reverse to authoritarianism.[3]

---

1   See Larry Jay Diamond, "Thinking About Hybrid Regimes," *Journal of Democracy* 13, no. 2 (2002). Also see the symposium on "Election without Democracy" in the same issue of *Journal of Democracy*.

2   Huntington had earlier called the emergence of democracies from late 1970s through the 1980s as the Third Wave. Later, scholars call this post-1989 democratization the Fourth Wave while many other scholars tend to lump all recent democratizations into the "Third Wave," including those of Mexico, South Korea, Taiwan, Thailand, Indonesia that clearly took place after the writing of Huntington's book. Others have seriously challenged the notion of waves in global history of democratization. For "Wave," see Samuel P. Huntington, *The Third Wave: Democratization in the Late Twentieth Century* (Norman, OK: University of Oklahoma Press, 1991); Larry Jay Diamond, "Is the Third Wave Over?," *Journal of Democracy* 7, no. 3 (1996); Larry Jay Diamond, ed., *Consolidating the Third Wave Democracies, A Journal of Democracy Book* (Baltimore: Johns Hopkins University Press, 1997); Michael McFaul, "The Fourth Wave of Democracy and Dictatorship: Noncooperative Transitions in the Postcommunist World," *World Politics* 54, no. 2 (2002). For an assessment and challenge of the "waves" conception, see Renske Doorenspleet, "Reassessing the Three Waves of Democratization," *World Politics*, no. 52 (2000).

3   This intellectual discovery is not new, of course. As Diamond points out, from very early, scholars have warned about the "uncertainty of transition" following the end of dictatorship. The caution against equating election with democracy was also voiced a long time ago, despite Schumpeter's classical definition of democracy as a procedure through which leaders are chosen on a competitive basis. See Diamond, "Thinking About Hybrid

This realization should not necessarily lead to pessimism, however. The moving of a regime from authoritarianism into a hybrid type is at least one step forward. It is true the end of authoritarianism does not mean democracy, but at least the regime has transitioned *out of* authoritarianism. Although a hybrid regime is not fully democratic, and may reverse to authoritarianism, it is still more democratic than a purely authoritarian one. More importantly, many hybrid regimes do make further progress toward full democracy. Several important cases of successful democratization, indeed, went through the authoritarian-hybrid-democratic stages.[4] More systematic research shows that given right conditions over time, hybrid regimes do become more democratic.[5] If political changes in China amass to the extent that the regime becomes a hybrid one, then the likelihood of China becoming a democracy has increased significantly. Hence, once China becomes a hybrid regime, the question becomes, will China *continue to* move away from authoritarianism and toward democracy.

From another point of view, the ruling Communist Party in China has set a goal of gradual and incremental democratization.[6] Of course, building "socialist democracy" or "people's democracy" has always been the official rhetoric. But recently, this rhetoric is supplemented by some serious efforts of searching for concrete plans of implementation. Such efforts include a conscious acceptance if not encouragement of academic studies of political transition,[7] and incremental experiments of reforms

---

Regimes." For the earlier scholarship mentioned in this article, see Guillermo O'Donnell, Philippe C. Schmitter, and Laurence Whitehead, eds., *Transitions from Authoritarian Rule: Prospect for Democracy* (Baltimore, MD: The Johns Hopkins University Press, 1986). For an earlier discussion of "semi-democracy," see Diamond, ed., *Consolidating the Third Wave Democracies*.

4   Taiwan is a textbook example. Although it remains a one-party authoritarian polity through the mid-1980s, starting from the 1960s it had allowed limited elections, first at the grassroots level but eventually up to the national level. Hence, at least as early as the 1970s, Taiwan had qualified as a hybrid regime.

5   See two most recent works that offer evidences of hybrid regimes transitioning into democracies: David Epstein, Robert Bates, and Sharyn O'Halloran, "Democratic Transitions: The Key Role of Partial Democracies," in *Annual Meeting of the American Political Science Association* (Washington, DC: 2005); Staffan Lindberg, "Long Live the Transition Paradigm: The Power of Elections," in *Annual Meeting of the American Political Science Association* (Washington, DC: 2005).

6   In October, 2005, the Chinese government released a white paper on building democracy. It states that China is committed to building a "socialist democratic political system," but it will be done under Party leadership and in a gradualist way.

7   An example is the emergence of a group of Western-trained, pro-political reform scholars and policy thinkers within the regime, such as Yu Keping, who is a major advisor to the top leadership in political reform. For the conception of democratization of this group of scholars *cum* policy formulators, see Keping Yu, "Toward an Incremental Democracy and Governance: Chinese Theories and Assessment Criteria," *New Political Science* 24, no. 2 (2002). Academic discussion of political reform and political transition has been largely tolerated if not encouraged. See an example in Wang Guixiu, *Zhongguo zhengzhi tizhi gaige*

on the party-state.[8] If the regime itself is searching for ways to resolve the mismatch between a one-party regime and a more and more diverse and dynamic economy and society, then we can expect political reforms to continuingly reduce the authoritarian nature of the regime.

Categorizing the Chinese Regime

First let us examine the existing literature, to see whether the Chinese regime as it is today can be categorized as hybrid. In a rough sense, hybrid regimes are either semi-democracy or semi-authoritarian. Clearly, a semi-democracy is more democratic than a semi-authoritarian regime. The problem is, it is hard to distinguish them: for a given non-democracy and non-authoritarian regime, generally there is no specific criteria to categorize it as semi-democratic or semi-authoritarian. Larry Diamond proposes a six-type categorization for the various forms of regimes.[9] From the most democratic to the most undemocratic:

(1) Liberal Democracy
(2) Electoral Democracy
(3) Ambiguous Regime
(4) Competitive Authoritarian
(5) Hegemonic Electoral Authoritarian
(6) Politically Closed Authoritarian

According to him, types (1) and (2) are democracy, while (4) through (6) are non-democracy. Type (3) countries are hard to classify due to limited information, but they are either electoral democracy or competitive authoritarian (that is, given enough information, they can be categorized either as type 2 or type 4). Using this topology, (4), (5), and some or all of (3), are hybrid regimes – that is, except for democracies and what can be considered "truly closed" regimes (type 6), all regimes are "hybrid."

Now the question is which does China belong to? China certainly is not type 1 or 2. Most people would categorize China as a type 6, a fully closed system. My focus here is to see, using Diamond's criteria, whether China qualifies as either type 4 or

---

zhi lu [The Path of China's Political Reform]. Zhengzhou, Henan: Henan Renmin Chubanshe (2004). Similar academic works abound now in China.

8 Such as village elections and the experimental elections at township and county government levels, see Lai Hairong, "Development of Competitive Election at the Township Level in Sichuan [Jinzheng xing xuanju zai Sichuan Sheng xiangzheng yi ji de fazhan]," *Strategy and Management*, 2003 (2). Similar studies of elections in China can be found at China Elections and Governance (http://www.chinaelections.org). Other experiments of election include intra-party election of important party posts.

9 Diamond, "Thinking About Hybrid Regimes."

type 5, instead of type 6. If so, China should be called a hybrid regime, not a strictly authoritarian one.

Types 4 and 5 are both competitive authoritarian regimes. In both types, there exists "multi-party electoral competition of some kind."[10] The difference lies in the competitiveness of the election. In a type 4 polity, there are formally recognized democratic institutions, and such institutions are "widely viewed as the principal means of obtaining and exercising political authority." What disqualifies such regimes from being truly democratic is the violation of rules by incumbents, making the system undemocratic.[11] Such is a "competitive authoritarian" regime. In contrast, a hegemonic electoral authoritarian regime (type 5) exhibits even lower degrees and forms of competitiveness. The ruling party or dictator more or less has firm control over political power. Some also call such kind of regime "electoral dictatorship." Still, they provide some sort of election, and, according to Diamond's criteria, "some space" for political opposition.[12] Put simply, a competitive authoritarian regime is democratic in form but authoritarian in nature, while a hegemonic electoral authoritarian regime is authoritarian with some rudimentary democratic elements.

In its current form, China is clearly a one-party dominated, authoritarian regime. But does China meet the criteria to be either a "competitive authoritarian" or a "hegemonic electoral authoritarian" regime? The most critical criterion is whether electoral institutions exist and how open and competitive the elections are. Some form of meaningful elections will distinguish China from the type 6, politically closed regimes, while the openness and competitiveness of the elections will determine whether China is a type 5 (hegemonic electoral authoritarian) or a type 4 (competitive authoritarian). Now truth is China does have a fairly sophisticated electoral system. Nominally, all the important government offices are elected: members of Chinese legislatures (people's congresses) at the national, provincial, and county levels are all directly or indirectly elected; at each level of the government, the legislature votes for head of state and of governments and confer the appointment of cabinets. The elections, however, are not competitive above the village level. This fact should disqualify China as a type 4, a competitive authoritarian regime.

Nevertheless, if these elections are somewhat meaningful, or in Diamond's words, provide "some space" for political opposition, then China should qualify as a type 5, instead of type 6 (totally closed system such as North Korea and Iraq under Saddam). In recent years, elections in China are becoming more and more open, competitive, and meaningful. At the village level, where direct election was first introduced, election is totally competitive, and fairly free, open, and fair.[13] Starting

---

10 Ibid., p. 25.

11 Steven Levitsky and Lucan A. Way, "The Rise of Competitive Authoritarianism," *Journal of Democracy* 13, no. 2 (2002). Quote is from p. 52.

12 Diamond, "Thinking About Hybrid Regimes."

13 Studies of village elections in China abound. See Suzanne Ogden, *Inklings of Democracy in China* (Cambridge, MA: Havard University Press, 2002); Lai Hairong, "Development of Competitive Election at the Township Level in Sichuan."

from the year 2000 or so, direct and open elections are gradually expanded to township governments in several provinces. In some places, open elections of county magistrates have been experimented.[14] It is clear such elections at the lower levels of government (mostly township and county levels) will expand to other provinces in the coming few years. Hence, if we apply Diamond's standard in a minimalist way, the existence of open election, although at the grassroots levels, means China now qualifies as a type 5 regime. That is, China should not be categorized as a totally closed political system (type 6), but as a hybrid regime.[15]

Beyong Election: Liberalization in China's Politics

There are other criteria to meet besides the existence of elections for a regime to be qualified as "hybrid." Among them, Diamond mentions "some space" for political opposition, independent media, and social organizations that "do not seriously criticize or challenge the regime."[16] These criteria, despite their imprecision, are meant to emphasize political rights and civil liberties besides the formal existence of elections.[17] A hybrid regime, in contrast to a politically closed one, allows certain space for political initiative and influences by citizens. Moreover, in a hybrid regime, citizens enjoy a certain amount of civil liberties that are not available under a politically closed regime. In this regard, China is clearly moving away from a strict authoritarian government to a more mixed and hybrid system.

Two areas see most important developments: the changing nature of the political system toward constitutionalism and rule of law, and the rise of civil society. In both areas, we see increasing gain of civil liberties, political rights, and social space of

---

14 Most notably are the provinces of Sichuan, Yunnan, and Jiangsu. See *China Elections and Governance* (http://www.chinaelections.org). Furthermore, elections are being introduced or strengthened for within-party positions.

15 In fact, Taiwan before 1987 was considered by Diamond as a hybrid regime by the fact that local elections were held since the 1960s. That is, when Taiwan was still dominated by the KMT's Leninist state, the elections at the village and county level qualified it as a Type 5 regime. By the same standard, China now should be considered a Type 5 also. But instead, Diamond relies on Freedom House rating of the political rights condition in a given country. China is rated "7," the highest rating by Freedom House. Hence China is categorized with countries such as Cuba, North Korea, and the Iraq under Saddam as the least politically free. By my discussion, this rating of China is biased. China's situation of political rights should be rated as at least 6. This change of rating will move China into Type 5 of Diamond's category.

16 These criteria are again imprecise. What makes up "some space" for political opposition? What does it mean when it says that a social organization does or does not "seriously" criticize or challenge the regime? Furthermore, these two criteria seem conflicting. If social groups can only exist when they do not seriously challenge the regime, how can there be true political opposition?

17 The focus on election, however, has a point. The existence and good functioning of elections can be an indicator of the "democraticness" of a given polity. Elections of good quality generally means political and civil rights are also in good conditions.

the citizens on the one hand, and increasing openness, transparency, responsiveness, and accountability of the government on the other. The next section focuses on the development of constitutionalism and rule of law, while the following section examines the rising civil society. Both areas, as will be shown, see a dynamic relationship between the citizens and the state.

Rule of Law and Constitutionalism: Citizen and State Factors

The importance of rule of law to China's economic and social developments was recognized by the regime from the 1980s, when the government realized that a quality legal system is indispensable to the marketizing economy. For a while, legislations focused on economic and business regulations. But soon the government realized that legislations cannot be confined to the economic sphere, but must instead cover social and political spheres too. Especially after the 1990s, changing social relationships, changing roles between government and society, differentiation of social interests, the need for clean, limited, and competent government, citizens' struggles for social equality and justice, all demand for new rules and laws and their effective enforcement.

Indeed, two forces are driving political changes toward rule of law and constitutionalism, one from without and the other from within the regime. From without the regime, it is the citizens' demand and struggle for rights, justice, and fairness. This has a circling effect: on the one hand, rising citizens' awareness of rights and justice translates into demand for fair laws and policies and judicial justice; on the other, legislation and litigation of such laws further improve citizens' awareness of rights, liberties, justice, due process, limited government, and other ideas of constitutionalism – a self-enhancing process. From within the regime, rule of law has become an option for the Party as it searches for good governance. These two forces are discussed below.

Citizen Rights Movement I start with some examples related to how rising awareness of citizen rights and justice is driving the advancement of constitutionalism and rule of law. A most notable one is the Sun Zhigang case. Sun is a young college-trained artist who went to Guangzhou in South China to look for work. While walking on the street one evening, he was caught by the city police for not being able to produce the right identity documents. He was then taken into custody under a government regulation which prevents homeless and jobless individuals from roaming around the country (the regulation was made more than 20 years ago, when the economic reform was barely starting, to prevent people from illegal traveling). While in custody he was beaten to death by several people who were also in custody. When the story was carried by Nanfang Dushi Bao (Southern Metropolitan Newspaper), it generated a huge wave of public criticism of the outdated government regulation and how government agencies mistreat citizens. Citizens, journalists, public intellectuals, and legal scholars rebuked the government for the unreasonable policy and its inability to correct misdeeds. Three law PhD students of Peking University petitioned the

National People's Congress, China's legislature and the only institution with the authority to interpret the constitution, to call for a constitutional review of the regulation in question. From a legal point of view, their petition presented a strong case, as the regulation in question aims at limiting citizen liberty and rights provided by the Constitution, hence is utterly unconstitutional. To make the story short, the government abolished the regulation and punished the government officials whose incompetence and mistakes contributed to Sun's death.[18]

A second notable case is related to anti-discrimination. Many government regulations in China discriminate against citizens on the basis of gender, health, physique, and other factors. For example, in some government recruitment drives, applicants shorter than 1.70m are not eligible. Another example is the different retiring ages for male and female civil servants: 65 for male and 60 for female. Some of these requirements were set up in the past, and had their rationale. For example, the age difference for retirement was intended for female employees' welfare: women were given the advantage of retiring early, and receiving all the retirement benefits that men could only receive five years later. But such kinds of different treatments become discrimination, as more and more women like to work longer than before. So recently the call for removing such different standards has become strong.

The discriminatory nature of other job requirements is much more problematic, and they become targets of more intense public attack. The most notable is the hepatitis B discrimination case. Most provincial governments require health examination when recruiting civil servants (as do school and university admission processes). Among the discriminations based on physical or health reasons is one against hepatitis B virus (HBV) carriers. In January 2003, when a university graduate in Zhejiang Province was rejected for a government position because he was found to carry HBV, he killed two recruiting officers for suspicion of unjust manipulation by them. The student received the death penalty, but the case became well-known across the country. In September the same year, when an HBV carrier in Anhui Province was rejected for a government position, he brought the government to court. He won the lawsuit, although when the lawsuit ended the recruitment drive had already ended and he was not compensated. Nonetheless, soon 1161 petitioners joined him in his petition to the NPC for a constitutional review of the government's hiring policies across the country. As a result, at the end of 2003, the national government abolished this and other similar discriminatory policies across all the 30 plus provinces, at least on paper.[19]

---

18 Coverage and discussion of Sun Zhigang's case can be easily found on the internet. For a good synthesis, see Chapter 9, "Sun Zhigang Shijian": Shehui wenti yinfa de Zhengzhi Xiaoying ["Sun Zhigang Case": The political effects caused by a social problem], in Jie Liu, ed., *Zhongguo Zhengzhi Fazhan Jincheng, 2004 [China's Political Development, 2004]* (Beijing: Shishi Chubanshe, 2004), pp. 292–309.

19 The story of the hepatitis B carriers was also widely covered by the media. China's HBV carriers are reported to be 120 millions. For the story on an applicant killing two government officials, and the story about an applicant suing the government, see "Fan yigan qishi: Bu jinjin shi 1.2 yi ren de shenli [Anti hepatitis discrimination: Not just a victory for the 120 millions]"

Other related cases of citizens challenging state power for political and civil rights included the case of Yu Huafeng, an editor of an influential newspaper (*Nanfang Dushi Bao*). Yu was unjustly persecuted because his paper revealed several important cases of provincial government failure, including the Sun Zhigang Case mentioned aforesaid. Journalists, lawyers, public intellectuals, and legal scholars joined forces to demand justice for his case, resulting in a higher-level court re-issuing a ruling.[20] The Sun Dawu Case was similar. Sun Dawu is a peasant-turned entrepreneur who criticizes government policies that discriminate against peasants and rural industries. When his criticism became too harsh, the government detained him. This aroused a big wave of appeals and petitions from university students, professors, journalists, and public intellectuals, challenging the legal bases of his detainment. Eventually the government had to water down the case and find a face-saving excuse to issue a relatively light punishment on Sun.[21]

Of course, in all these cases the success in limiting government power or requesting remedy was partial. And many other cases of government abuse are left unchallenged.[22] Nevertheless, these and other cases do show the Chinese polity has

---

in *Nanfang Zhoumuo [Southern Weekend]*, August 5, 2004. Two recent articles can be found in Chinese newspapers: "Kao le diyimin que luoxuan gongwuyuan, yimin daxuesheng zhiyi Tonglinshi Renshiju [Ranked No 1 in the examination but disqualified for civil service; University graduate questions the Personnel Bureau of Tonglin City Government]" in *Xin'an Evening News*, October 28, 2005; and "1.2 Yi bingdu xiedaizhe ren xian weiquan kunjing [120 million HBV carriers still trapped in defending their rights]" in *Southern Weekend*, Oct 27, 2005. Activists have set up a website as the platform for information exchange and action coordination. All the reports can be found on the website "gan dan xiang zhao" (this is a Chinese idiom, which uses the inseparable closeness between the liver and the gallbladder to convey the idea of loyalty and mutual support between true friends.) URL: http://www.hbvhbv.com/.

20 The ruling in the verdict is still considered flawed by many legal scholars, who argue that Yu should be judged innocent in face of the evidences that were presented, see Ji Weidong, "Fali Tuiqiao 'Nandu An' [Legal Analysis of the Nandu Case]" in *Caijing*, no. 113, August 5, 2004. For news coverage of this case, see "Nandu An Chuxian Xianzhu Bianshu [Significant Uncertainties Emerged in Nandu Case]" *Caijing*, no. 109, June 5, 2004.

21 The excuse the government used was the illegality of some of Sun's business practices. This is of course not well-founded, because almost every firm in China is involved in some kind of activities that are short of being legal, partly due to the fact that economic laws are terribly lagging behind economic realities. Nevertheless, this ruling was seen as a compromise of the government, who might have feared a harsh persecution on Sun on the bases of criticizing government may lead to popular discontent. For the case of Sun Dawu, see "Yiwanfuweng Sun Dawu Beibu: Shi Jingji Fanzui Haishi Yinyan Huozui? [Billionaire Arrested: Economic Crime or Crime of Words?" *Nanfang Dushi Ba*o, July 11, 2003.

22 Most notable government abuses seem to be in land appropriation. Many local governments evicted peasants' land without offering sufficient compensation. These have led to hundreds if not thousands of peasant protests, including the recent incident in Guangzhou in which police opened fire on the protests and killed some villagers; See "Villagers Tell of Lethal Attack by Chinese Forces on Protesters," *New York Times*, December 11, 2005. In the

moved some small steps toward constitutionalism and rule of law. As many scholars point out, for the first time, government is legally being challenged and curbed by the citizens. And in all these cases the issue of constitutionality became a focal point in the debate, and the Constitution became the final source of legitimacy for citizens' grievances.[23] It appears, hence, that citizens, especially those educated and versed in legal languages, are able to fight for rights and justice in face of government power. What is also important is the emergence of attorneys and social activists who advocate for the wronged, who may not have the knowledge or skills to defend their rights.[24] The learning is still going on, but citizen demands and struggle will continue to advance constitutionalism and rule of law in China.

Searching for Good Governance   Another driving force toward rule of law and constitutionalism is, ironically, the ruling Chinese Communist Party (CCP)'s search for good governance. No doubt the Party is going through tremendous ideological and organizational transformation.[25] Especially, the top leadership seems seriously committed to building a good government. This may come out of the desire to maintain regime legitimacy, prolong CCP rule, or out of a sincere belief in good governance, or both. Regardless, to build good governance, the Party seems to rely on three major efforts: restructure government organizations and processes, improve competence of government officials, and prevent power abuse by promoting rule of law.[26]

One important issue for good government is to build a clean government and prevent power abuse. To do this, besides searching for better ways of party discipline,

---

cities, city government or real estate developers also use force to relocate residents, resulting in similar protests.

23 See a discussion of this in Dingjian Cai, "The Development of Constitutionalism in the Transition of Chinese Society," *Journal of Asian Law* (2005).

24 See a recent issue of *Yazhou Zhoukan* (Asia Weekly) published in Hong Kong, which carries a special symposium of lawyers and other activists of citizen rights that made the headlines in 2005: "2005 Fengyun Renwu: Zhongguo Weiquan Lushi [Headline Makers in 2005: China's Citizen Right Lawyers], *Yazhou Zhoukan*, December 25, 2005, pp. 12–21. For a scholarly discussion, see David Kelly, "Public Intellectuals and Citizen Movements in China in the Hu-Wen Era," *Pacific Affairs* (forthcoming).

25 For changes in party ideology, party rejuvenation, and the search for governing capacity, see chapters in Yun-han Chu, Chih-cheng Lo, and Ramon Hawley Myers, eds., *The New Chinese Leadership: Challenges and Opportunities after the 16th Party Congress, The China Quarterly Special Issues New Series* (Cambridge, UK: Cambridge University Press, 2004); John Wong and Yongnian Zheng, eds., *China's Post-Jiang Leadership Succession* (Singapore: World Scientific and National University Press, 2002); Guoguang Wu, *The Anatomy of Political Power in China* (Singapore: East Asian Institute and Marshall Cavendish Academic, 2005).

26 A good example of elite thinking on good governance can be found in Keping Yu, "Lun Zhengfu Chuangxin De Ruogan Jiben Wenti [on Several Fundamental Questions in Government Innovations]," *Wen Shi Zhe [Literary, Historical, and Philosophical Studies]*, no. 4 (2005). Yu is considered a major political advisor for the Party leader Hu Jintao.

the Party is looking to put government authority within legal constraints. To have an effective legal system to check government officials appears to be a consensus between the public and elite. The impersonal, generalist rule of law should replace the case-by-case handling of corruption, or ideological campaign, two methods which the Party heavily relied upon until now.[27] In early 2004, the government issued a blueprint for building a "government based on rule of law." The title Quanmian Tuijin Yifa Xingzheng Shishigangyao literarily translates as "A Blueprint for Comprehensively Advancing A Government According to Law." It emphasizes "using legal means in the administration of state affairs, economic, cultural, and social affairs." Most notably, it puts forward concepts such as constitutionality (he hu xianzheng yaoqiu), due process (chenxu zhengdang), openness (gongkai), public's right to government information (zhiqingquan), public's right to participate in policy decisions (canyuquan), and citizen's right to legal remedy (huode sifa jiuji quan). To achieve these goals, two kinds of legal constraints on government are put forward. The first is called legislative check (lifa jiandu), that is, any law or regulations made by government agencies are subject to review by the legislature. The second is judicial check (sifa jiandu), that is, government policies and behaviors are subjected to litigation: citizens can sue government agencies and request remedy for government misdeeds.[28]

These concepts may sound stunningly liberal for someone who is used to seeing the Chinese state as a tool of the Party to rule the public at its will. Yes, even by the late 1980s, there was still a debate among CCP elite whether the Party or the law should be the higher authority. Government power will be seriously constrained if all these institutions are put into place. The party has announced that any individual, agency, and group (i.e. including the CCP itself), should function within the constitutional framework.[29] Indeed, legal scholars who participated in the drafting of the document emphasize the intention of the plan "to curb power and officials."[30]

---

27 The Rule by Virtue (yide zhiguo) campaign and Three Stresses Campaign under Jiang Zemin are recent examples of the failure of using educative party campaign to achieve the goal of good governance, so is the "Maintaining Advancedness" (baoxian) campaign that was still going on as of late 2005. Nevertheless, these educative campaigns can be seen as a second-best choice at a time the building of rule of law is still far from completion. In the long run, an impersonal, generalist rule of law must be in place.

28 In 2005, a famous case of legal remedy involving She Xianglin happened, who was mistakenly convicted of murder and served in prison for many years before the person he supposedly "murdered" was found still alive. He received 900 thousand Chinese yuan as state compensation. See "She Xianglin zai huo 45 wan peichangjin [She Xianlin received another 450 thousand yuan of compensation]," in *Nanfang Dushi Bao*, October 28, 2005.

29 See Hu Jintao's speech on the 20th anniversary of the new Constitution, *Xinhua News Agency*, December 2004, 2002.

30 "Qicao Zhuanjia Tan 'Gangyao': Yifa Xingzheng Zhongzai Zhiguan Zhiquan [Legal Experts On 'Gangyao': The Emphasis Of 'Goverment According Law' Is on Curbing Officials and Curbing Power]," *China Youth Daily* 2004.

One may suspect the Party is only paying lip service to rule of law and having a blueprint does not mean anything if it is not actualized. In fact, concrete actions are being taken to achieve the proposed goals. One example is the promulgation of the Law on Legislation (Lifa Fa). The main idea for this law is the "legislative check" on lawmaking. Any government law, stature, or regulation contradictory to the Constitution will be nullified. Furthermore, this Law stipulates that any legislature curbing civil liberty can only be made by the National People's Congress (NPC). In fact, it is on the basis of this law that several regulations mentioned in the aforesaid discussion of citizen rights movement were found unconstitutional, and the concept of constitutional review was promoted.[31] Another example is the legislation of Government Force Law (Xingzheng Qiangzhi Fa). Aiming at preventing power abuse, this law stipulates the conditions under which the government agencies can use force on citizens. This and two laws promulgated earlier: Government Permission Law (Xingzheng Xuke Fa, 2003) and Government Punishment Law (Xingzheng Chufa Fa, 1996) form a relatively comprehensive legal framework to limit government power.[32] In any case, these developments are viewed with optimism and the advancement toward rule of law and constitutionalism will continue.[33]

Besides limiting government power through legal means, the regime's interest in transparency, openness, and accountability of government will also lead to rule of law and constitutionalism. This may sound surprising: why does a non-democratic regime want transparency or openness? This might be explained by two factors. First is that the top leadership is, as stated earlier, committed to good government.[34] Despite striking cases of corruption, many among the political elites share the ideal of benevolent, clean, modern, professional, and effective government.[35] Such beliefs and visions may come from the Confucian tradition of government responsibility, from the long-term influence of Party's discourse and education, or from recently acquired understanding of the modern governments in countries such as the U.S. and

---

31 See a discussion of this in Cai, "The Development of Constitutionalism in the Transition of Chinese Society."

32 The promulgation of these laws seems insufficiently studied by scholars. See a news analysis: "Jujiao Fenzu Shenyi: Xinzheng Qiangzhi Ruhe Zuzhi Quanli Lanyong [Focusing on Group Discussion: How can the Government Force Law Prevent Power Abuse], *People's Daily*, December 27, 2005, p. 10.

33 See a good discussion by a first-rate legal scholar based in Tokyo: Weidong Ji, "Cong Fazhi Dao Minzhu De Lichengbei: Jiedu "Quanmian Tuijin Yifa Xingzheng Shishigangyao" De Neihan He Tizhi Gaige De Qiji [a Milestone from Rule of Law to Democracy]," *Caijing*, April 20, 2004.

34 See, for example, the top leadership's decision to improve CCP's capacity to govern the country, released on the Fourth Plenum of the Sixteenth CCP Central Committee, 16–19 September 2004.

35 See a discussion in Kishore Mahbubani, "Understanding China," *Foreign Affairs* 84, no. 5 (2005).

Europe in the West, and countries such as Singapore in Asia.[36] That such beliefs are sincere is not doubted by people who have interacted with government officials in China,[37] and those who understand this seem to be optimistic that good government in China is an attainable goal.[38]

A second and probably more important cause to this urgent sense of government building is crisis of governance. In recent years, China sees more and more frequent social, economic, industrial, environmental, and public health crises. In dealing with these increasingly explosive crises, leaders as well as the public realize that openness, transparency and a system of accountability are the only choice. Take two among the most notable examples. The SARS epidemic in early 2003 taught a costly lesson on the importance of transparency. The central leadership realized that holding back information by government offices may have disastrous consequences. Through such lessons, the government realizes openness will improve governance instead of weaken its grid on power.[39] Recent lessons of transparency include the terrible coal mine accidents and cases such as the Songhua River contamination due to the explosion of a chemical plant. All cases involved damages resulting from government attempts to cover up.[40]

Another example is the Party's war against corruption. The Party now understands that information asymmetry is a major cause to its being unsuccessful in this war.

---

36 Many mid- to upper-level officials in China today are well-traveled, and many have enrolled in training programs in first-rate institutions such as the JFK School of Government in Harvard.

37 See an early study that shows good understanding of the quality of government officials in China in Kenneth Lieberthal and Michel Oksenberg, *Policy Making in China: Leaders, Structures, and Processes* (Princeton, NJ: Princeton University Press, 1988). For more recent studies, see, for example, Cheng Li, *China's Leaders: The New Generation* (Lanham, MD: Rowman & Littlefield Publishers, 2001); Cheng Li, "Jiang Zemin's Successors: The Rise of the Fourth Generation of Leaders in the Prc," *The China Quarterly* 161 (2000); Xiaowei Zang, *Elite Dualism and Leadership Selection in China* (London and New York: Routledge Curzon, 2004).

38 See a good though brief discussion in Mahbubani, "Understanding China."

39 On how the SARS crisis transform government thinking on transparency, see Chapter 10, "Feidian chongji bo": duiyu zhengfu gonggong guanli de jinshi [SARS shock: Implications to government's public administration] in Liu, ed., *Zhongguo Zhengzhi Fazhan Jincheng, 2004 [China's Political Development, 2004]*; John Wong and Yongnian Zheng, eds., *The Sars Epidemic: Challenges to China's Crisis Management* (Singapore and River Edge, NJ: World Scientific Publishing, 2004).

40 The Songhuajiang River contamination accident even became an international issue as downstream of the river goes into Russia, where cities also depends on the river for drinking water. See "China: Chemical blast polluted river," *Sunday Times*, November 23, 2005. Coal mine collapses or explosions are more publicized industrial accidents that caused deaths as well as social, economic, and environmental damages. In 2005 alone, there were 69 coal mine accidents, resulting in a total death toll of 2671. See, for example, "2005: Kuangnan Yinying xia de Zhongguo Meitanye [2005: China's Coal Industry under the Shadow of Mine Disasters]," *China Economics Times*, December 22, 2005.

Hence it has decided to build a system of financial disclosure for officials,[41] as well as allowing its national auditing agency to check (and release) financial records of government agencies. In 2004 alone, the National Auditing Authority revealed illegal financial practices in 38 Central Government agencies, involving a total amount of nine billion RMB. The illegal financial maneuvers revealed by the National Auditing Authority resulted in 222 cases filed with legal and disciplinary authorities, and 762 government officials charged with mal- or illegal practices.[42] Another practice of openness is to solicit information from the public. For example, major government appointments are announced for public scrutiny and testimony sessions are held for some major policy decisions. It appears the government is still learning how to achieve openness, transparency, and public accountability without threatening government's power. It has contemplated the idea of media exposure as a way to check government corruption and enhance accountability. Now it seems to be experimenting with limited election, especially inner-party election, as a way to achieve these goals.

Such efforts in checking government power and achieving openness, transparency, and accountability will materialize in a system of laws, regulations, and institutions. Hence, the search for good governance will push the government toward rule of law and constitutionalism, as will citizens' struggles for rights and justice. The two forces, the citizenry and the government, may have different motivations, but their goals are similar. For this reason, we can be optimistic that political changes in China will be toward the democratic direction.

Citizen Politics: The Radical and Moderate Face

As discussed in the last section, for China's improvement in constitutionalism and rule of law, citizens' struggle for rights and justice, together with the regime's search for good governance, are the two major driving forces. To further discuss

---

[41] In 1995, the State and the Party issued the regulation regarding financial discourse of government officials. Into the 2000s, the discussion to legalize this requirement has gained momentum. At the National People's Congress of 2005, it was made explicit that the Civil Service Law (Gongwuyuan Fa) will soon be revised to include such requirements. As an exemplar, all the party and state leaders (that is, politburo members and those above the level of vice premier) have made public their individual financial information, as reported by the June 2005 issue of the Hong Kong magazine Zheng Ming.

[42] See "Li Jinhua: 38 Ge Zhongyang Bumen Yusuan Zhixin Weigui Jin'e 90.6 Yi Yuan [Li Jinhua: 38 Central Government Agencies Illegal Fianacial Practices Involve Nine Billion Yuan]" and "Li Jinhua: Qunian Shenji Faxian Wentizhong you 762 Ren (Ci) Shou Chuli [Li Jinhua: 762 Officials Punished Due to Problems Found in Last Year's Auditing]" in *Zhongguo Xinwen Wang* (China News Net), http://www.chinanews.com.cn. For auditing of government agencies, do a Google search of the term Shenji Fengbao [Auditing Storm], or visit websites such as the "2004 Auditing Storm" of Nanfang Wang (South Web) at http://www.southcn.com/news/china/china05/sjfb/. Also see a discussion in Cai, "The Development of Constitutionalism in the Transition of Chinese Society."

the changing nature of the Chinese political system, in this section we will look at citizen politics from another perspective. Using a state-society relation perspective, in this section I argue that the rising power of civil society is in itself an aspect of the increasingly hybrid nature of the Chinese regime. In recent years, Chinese citizens demonstrate tremendous mobilizing power when a salient course emerges. In several notable cases, petitions and protests decisively resulted in changes in government policies and actions. These cases show that the power balance between the state and civil society has significantly shifted toward the latter. Of course, it is still not the case that the society has dominated the state. But, compared with the closed system China had in the past, today the civil society has acquired tremendous autonomy and influence. I relate a few cases here.

The Radical Face of Citizen Politics In the BMW case (Baoma An) in northeast China's Heilongjiang Province, a poor peasant was hit by a BMW, but the provincial government only punished the BMW owner lightly. Public opinion on the internet (which also spilled over to newspapers and magazines) led to central government's intervention into the case. In the Japanese High-Speed Train Case, a large-scale petition (also started from the internet) also led to government change of course. Activists also succeeded in bringing central government's attention to the potential environmental damage that a proposed dam project may have on the Nujiang River in Yunnan Province. Public opinion again led to the Supreme Court reviewing the case of a Shenyang (capital city of Liaoning Province) gangster, who was given a lighter punishment than what the public believed him to deserve.[43] Most recently, in the April 2005 Anti-Japan demonstration, citizens organized large-scale protests across dozens of cities in China. Because of the citizens' nationalism demonstrated in these protests, the Chinese government has to take a stronger stance when handling the Sino-Japan relationship.[44]

The state must have viewed these developments with ambivalence if not apprehension. In all cases, the citizens mobilized themselves for non-regime-challenging purposes. Their enthusiasm for justice, equality, or general good causes (such as environmental protection) shows that the regime has nothing to fear from the civil society. On the contrary, such citizen expression indeed helps the Central

---

43 For the BMW case, see "Jujiao Haerbing 'Baoma Zhuangren An' [Focusing on Haerbin's BMW-Hits-People Case]" at Dayang Web http://zhuanti.dayoo.com/gb/node/node_4339.shtml; For the High-Speed Train case, see China 9-18 Patriot Web: http://www.china918.net/; On the Nujiang River dam case, see Heart With Nujiang Web: http://www.nujiang.ngo.cn/. For the Shangyang Gangster case, see a collection of news reports and citizen discussion at sina.com: http://news.sina.com.cn/z/liuyongsy/index.shtml. Regarding how the use of internet and cell phone SMS has allowed tremendous mobilizing ability to citizen actions, see Yongnian Zheng and Guoguang Wu, "Information Technology, Public Space, and Collective Action in China," *Comparative Political Studies* 38, no. 5 (2005).

44 For anti-Japan demonstrations that took place from April–May 2005, and how this puts pressure on government policy making, see Peter Hays Gries, "Chinese Nationalism: Challenging the State?," *Current History* 104, no. 684 (2005).

Government to understand public opinion better, and to keep the government agencies (such as the Ministry of Railway in the High-Speed Train case and the energy authority in the Nujiang River case) in check. But on the other hand, the outburst of citizen movements did show that once mobilized, citizens can be extremely powerful, to the extent the state will be handicapped or even destabilized.

Clearly, today in China, the urban and educated young people have acquired interest in political and social issues, and the desire to express one's preferences is very strong among these people. The right response of the government should be opening formal channels for citizen participation and expression. Such channels, however, are terribly under-developed, or purposively contained. Without formal channels to absorb and direct citizens' expression and participation, internet chat rooms and cell phone SMS become the natural outlet. Internet and SMS are also the platforms for information exchange and instrument for action coordination, while large-scale petitions and street demonstrations are the available means for collective expression. Though the regime finds such citizen movements helpful (as they can enhance the regime's legitimacy), it has to curb them for fear of escalation.[45] As the government cannot afford to openly suppress citizens' passion and energy, the only workable solution is to open channels for political participation. The party rhetoric of "expanding political participation of the citizens in an orderly manner" is never more relevant here.[46] The bottom line is, rising civil society is pressing the government to open more channels of political participation, resulting in the democratization of the state.

The Moderate Face We also see the emergence of another form of citizen politics. This is the rise of interest-based civil organizations. Especially in the cities, many social groups are being formed: urban home owner associations (yezhu weiyuanhui), trade associations (shanghui), neighborhood and community associations (shequ weiyuanhui), rural development groups, and environmental groups.[47] These groups are not interested in national policies, but local issues. They seek self-governance to fill the space state power did not reach. They do not challenge, but negotiate and collaborate with the state in providing public goods. They are seldom origins of

---

45 Mary Gallagher called this dynamic "Authoritarian Populism." See Mary Gallagher, "China in 2004: Stability above All," *Asian Survey* 45, no. 1 (2005).

46 The Party's official line of political reform is to expand political participation of the citizens in an orderly manner. See the political report delivered by Jiang Zemin on the 16th Party Congress, November 18, 2002. For discussion of expanding political participation through election and other forms, see Zengke He, "Jianjin Zhengzhi Gaige Yu Minzhu Zhuanxing [Incremental Political Reform and Democratic Transition]," *Journal of Beijing Institute of Administration*, no. 3–4 (2004).

47 See studies such as Keping Yu et al., *Zhongguo Gongminshehui De Xingqi Yu Zhili De Bianqian [the Emerging of Civil Society and Changes in Its Governance in China]* (Beijing Shehui Kexue Wenxian Chubanshe, 2002). Lizhu Fan, ed., *Quanqiuhua Xia De Shehui Bianqian Yu Feizhengfuzuzhi [Social Transition and Nongovernmental Organizations under Globalization]* (Shanghai: Renmin Chubanshe, 2003).

radical actions, such as protests and street demonstrations, but the "social capital" in the classical way as identified by social scientists.[48]

The rise of such moderate, middle class-centered, and self-governance-oriented groups promises collaboration between the state and the civil society in generating public goods as well as state transformation. Such a collaborative state-society interaction will lead to the willing retreat of state. Indeed, today in China, state retreat from intervention and control of the social spheres is resulting in a more vibrant and pluralist society. Most notably, institutional innovations by the civil groups are likely to be recognized by the regime. Back in the late 1970s, many of the rural reform policies were simply acknowledgement of practices initiated by peasants. Once the Party recognized such practices, they were transported nationwide. Such a process is happening again as many of the self-government developments within civil society are tolerated, accepted, and encouraged by the state. The linkage between civil initiatives and state is the desire of both sides for better governance and public goods, and collaboration between the two is certainly generating positive outcomes in this regard. When the development of civil groups does not challenge state power but helps to generate better social and public goods, the collaborative transformation of state-society relationship is achieved.[49]

But such collaborations do not only result in changed state-society relationship. Civil society initiatives are also transferring government structure and processes. This is especially the case at the local levels – township, county, and city. In Fengqiao Township of Zhejiang, the township government works closely with villager groups on social issues such as public security and environmental protection. In Wenling city of Zhejiang, a form of consultative democracy is already in place, where the township government relies heavily on a system of "minzhu kengtan" (democratic consultation) to exchange ideas with citizens and make public policies.[50] In both

---

48 For the concept of social capital as associations and civic networks, see Robert D. Putnam, *Bowling Alone: The Collapse and Revival of American Community* (New York: Simon & Schuster, 2000); Robert D. Putnam, Robert Leonardi, and Raffaella Nanetti, *Making Democracy Work: Civic Traditions in Modern Italy* (Princeton, NJ: Princeton University Press, 1993). For an example of how civil association in China contributes to local governance and public goods such as public safety, economic development, services, and environmental protection, see Xunda Yu and Chengsin Chen, "Gongminshehui Yu Zhili: Yi "Fengqiao Jingyan" Wei Li [Civil Society and Governance: The "Fengqiao" Case," in *The International Conference on Civil Society Development in Transitional China* (Beijing: 2005).

49 For a detailed case study, see Shenyong Chen, Jinjun Wang, and Bin Ma, *Zuzhihua, Zizhu Zhili Yu Minzhu: Zhejiang Wenzhou Minjian Shanghui Yanjiu [Organizationalization, Self-Governance, and Democracy: A Study of Non-Governmental Trade Associations in Wenzhou, Zhejiang]* (Beijing: Zhongguo Shehuihexue Chubanshe, 2004).

50 For the Fengqiao case, see Yu and Chen, "Gongminshehui Yu Zhili: Yi "Fengqiao Jingyan" Wei Li [Civil Society and Governance: The "Fengqiao" Case." For the Wenling case, see Joseph Fewsmith, "Hu Jintao's Approach to Governance," in *China into the Hu-Wen Era: Policy Initiatives and Challenges*, ed. John Wong and Hongyi Lai (Singapore: World Scientific: 2005). For a comprehensive discussion of how civil society is changing government

cases, collaboration between the state and civil society has resulted in innovative government processes. As such, practices at the local level are inspirational to higher level governments where similar changes in government processes also take place. For example, some agencies now hold public consultation sessions when making important policies, and public consultation is required when the People's Congresses of various levels are drafting new laws.[51]

Civil society's interaction with the state, hence, takes both a radical and a moderate face. The radical citizen movements are more visible and more powerful, but are also viewed with apprehension by the government. The challenge is on the government to open formal channels of political participation and public expression, so that radical and explosive movements will be minimized. On the other hand, the state seems willing to work with moderate forms of citizen organization and expression, especially when such civil actions can lead to better governance at the local level. In both spheres, however, the society is actively changing the state, making it more responsive and perceptive. In this regard, civil society is changing the state into a hybrid system, and will continue to democratize it.

Hybrid Regime as Pathway to Democracy

To sum up the discussion so far, one has to point to the democratizing trend of Chinese politics. Elections are expanding in China: legislature elections at the county level are becoming more and more competitive, while elections of chief officials of villages, townships, and city communities are competitive and of decent quality. Furthermore, it is clear the Party is serious about within-party elections for the selection of better government officials and for more accountability. In this sense, China is clearly different from the "politically closed systems" such as North Korea and Iraq under Saddam. What is more important but less noticed by Western observers is the complex changes that are taking place within China. Citizen rights movements, the search for good governance, and the interaction between the civil society and the state all have important democratizing effects. More and more, Chinese politics is bringing itself closer to constitutionalism, rule of law, transparency, openness, societal autonomy, and civil liberties.

---

at the local levels, see Fan Li, "Zhongguo Jiceng Minzhu De Fazhan He Zhengzhi Gaige [Grassroots Democratic Developments and Political Reform in China]," (World and China Institute, 2004), Fan Li, ed., *Zhongguo Jiceng Minzhu Fazhan Baogao 2004* (Beijing: Zhishi Chanquan Chubanshe, 2005).

51 The most notable example in public consultation in policy making is the "Pricing Testimony" (jiage tingzheng) sessions. Starting from about 2001, the Central Government requires governmental agencies to hold testimony sessions before pricing major government services or goods of government-owned firms, such as electricity or train tickets. For consultation in law making, see an example: "Geshui tingzheng: Zhongguo zuigao lifa jiguan shouci quxing lifa tingzhenghui [Individual tax testimony: The highest lawmaking body of China holds the first legislative testimony session]," Xinhua News, September 28, 2005.

In fact, in the light of these changes in China's political system since the 1980s, people have debated on the nature of the Chinese regime. Categories such as post-totalitarianism, authoritarianism, neo-authoritarianism,[52] soft authoritarianism,[53] social democracy, consultative polity,[54] collaborate regime,[55] compound democratic regime,[56] have been proposed. Some of these terms are proposed to characterize the current Chinese polity; others are used to project what the Chinese polity will be like if the current trends continue. At the least, there clearly has emerged a consensus that China is already different from a purely authoritarian regime. Furthermore, all the proposals carry some optimism: China is moving out of authoritarianism and toward the more democratic end.

In this chapter, I have sorted these changes into several areas, and argued that China should be categorized as a "hybrid" regime. The usefulness of calling China a "hybrid" regime does not lie in the name itself, of course. That China is hybrid instead of purely authoritarian means that political change is taking place in China, and the upcoming changes are likely to be toward the democratic direction instead of a reversal to more political control and less democracy. In this sense, as I argued at the beginning of this chapter, although a "hybrid" China is still short of a democratic China, it is still more welcome than a purely authoritarian China.

Will China, as a hybrid regime, continue to move away from authoritarianism and toward democracy? According to scholars of regime changes, when public demand for democracy is high, a hybrid regime will move toward democracy. Scholarly findings show that the establishment and consolidation of democracy depends on the relative balance between the *demand for* and *supply of* democratic institutions. For example, in the post-communist Eastern Europe and Central Asia, countries with high public demand for democracy have seen democracy consolidated, while those with low demand have seen the reversal to authoritarianism.[57]

In modernizing societies, such as China, South Korea, and Taiwan, public demand for democratization increases as people's values become more and more pro-democracy, pro-equality, and pro-pluralism.[58] The story of South Korea and Taiwan has shown that once the authoritarian regime introduced

---

52 Public intellectual Xiao Gongqin was among the earlier people to introduce this idea to the Chinese audience.

53 Baum, Richard, 2004.

54 Kang Xiaoguang, 2003a.

55 Kang Xiaoguang, 2003b.

56 He Zengke, 2004.

57 See Richard Rose and Doh Chull Shin, "Democratization Backwards: The Problem of Third-Wave Democracies," *British Journal of Political Science* 31 (2001). For an analysis of demand and supply for democracy around the globe, see Ronald Inglehart and Christian Welzel, *Modernization, Cultural Change, and Democracy: The Human Development Sequence* (2005).

58 The argument is that socioeconomic modernization will give rise to a public that is pro-liberty, pro-equality, and pro-democratic forms of government. See Zheng-Xu Wang, "Changing Social Values and Democratization in China and East Asia: The Self-Expression

democratic elements (such as local or limited election, as well as opening up of some governmental processes), public demand will continue to pressure for more opening and relaxation. This can be attributed to continued interest differentiation as social relations diversify and become more complex, freedom of information, new awareness of individual rights and other constitutionalist ideas. Scholars have argued that socioeconomic modernization, such as that which is taking place in China amidst the fast economic growth of the 1980s, 1990s, and present, will give rise to a public that is more and more toward a liberalist, pro-democratic outlook. Such changes in citizens' attitudes will lead to higher demand for political opening, resulting in pressure for democratization.[59] Now, the increasing demand for changes toward democratic forms of government is clearly what we see in China. This chapter has shown that citizens are more and more assertive in demanding political and civil rights, limited government, government accountability, transparency, and participation in policy making, and they have succeeded in many significant ways.

For the "supply" side of this equation, as discussed aforesaid, the Chinese government is seriously committed to the search for good governance. This effort focuses on the building of transparent, accountable, efficient, and clean government. Basic efforts include improving professional competence of civil servants and re-engineering government processes (such as restructuring and introducing e-government), but more fundamental efforts include building rule of law and expanding inner-party democracy. These will incrementally change the party and the state in the coming years. At the same time, a discussion on full-scale political transition toward democracy is well under way.[60] Furthermore, the Party is also willing to retreat from spheres that either the market or civil society can take care of themselves, if only for the sake of reducing the fiscal burden of running a big government.

Hence we have a case of demand for political opening and potential supply that are likely to meet on a middle ground. That is why scholars argue for the likelihood

---

Phenomenon and Citizen Politics in Six Confucian Societies, 1981–2001" (Ann Arbor, MI: University of Michigan, 2005).

59 For this human development approach toward democratization, see Scott Flanagan and Aie-Rie Lee, "Value Change and Democratic Reform in Japan and Korea," *Comparative Political Studies* 33, no. 5 (2000); Ronald Inglehart and Wayen E. Baker, "Modernization, Culture Change, and the Persistence of Traditional Values," *American Sociological Review* 65 (2000); Inglehart and Welzel, *Modernization, Cultural Change, and Democracy: The Human Development Sequence*.

60 See important proposals such as He, "Jianjin Zhengzhi Gaige Yu Minzhu Zhuanxing [Incremental Political Reform and Democratic Transition]," Yu, "Lun Zhengfu Chuangxin De Ruogan Jiben Wenti [on Several Fundamental Questions in Government Innovations]." Tangbiao Xiao, "Zhongguo Zhengzhi Gaige De Tizhinei Ziyuan: Dui Difang Guanyuan Zhengzhi Taidu De Diaocha Yu Fenxi [within-Regime Resource of Political Reform in China: A Survey and Analysis of Politial Attitudes of Local Officials]," *Dangdan Zhongguo Yanjiu [Contemporary China Studies]*, no. 3 (2005).

of collaboration between the state and the society for political transition in China.[61] China is just turning into a hybrid regime at this point in time. In the coming 10 to 20 years, its political system is likely to become more open, with more and more competitive elements. In other words, the hybrid Chinese regime will acquire new features that will move it closer to a democratic one. Hybrid regime will eventually be a pathway toward China's democracy.

Conclusion: Hybrid China's Peaceful Rise

Returning to the six categories of regime mentioned previously, clearly, with its preliminary elections at the local level, the growing features of constitutionalism, rule of law, and a rising civil society, China should be categorized as a Type 5 regime – one of the three types of hybrid regimes proposed by Diamond. We should move beyond the old way of looking at China as a closed authoritarian regime. Although it is still dominated by one single party, as a hybrid regime it is a dynamic system and is transforming rapidly toward the direction of being more pluralist, competitive, and open. Hence, when we contemplate China's peaceful rise in the coming two decades, we should keep in mind that the trend of democratization and liberalization is neither stoppable nor reversible.

But nevertheless, we should not expect a quick transition to multiparty democracy. One major argument of the "hybrid regime" theory is that hybrid regimes can be relatively stable. In other words, China's can remain a one-party dominated regime for a long time, despite the tendency for liberalization and democratization.[62] In the case of Taiwan, after the introduction of limited elections, the KMT regime remained in power for several decades before it allowed for competitive multi-party elections. In the foreseeable future, the Communist Party of China will not tolerate organized opposition movements. As a result, no genuine multi-party competition will emerge in the short run.

But still, the Party will need to introduce more meaningful elections, such as the election to provincial assemblies, as well as inner-party elections for important appointment decisions. Other reforms are also needed to put checks on the

---

61 See Cai, "The Development of Constitutionalism in the Transition of Chinese Society," Xiaoguang Kang, "Lun Hezuo Zhuyi Guojia [on Collaborative State]," *Zhanlue Yu Guanli [Strategies and Management]*, no. 5 (1999).

62 For discussions of the relative robustness of the Chinese system under the CCP rule, see Richard Baum, "Systemic Stresses and Political Choices: The Road Ahead," in *The New Chinese Leadership: Challenges and Opportunities after the 16th Party Congress*, ed. Yun-han Chu, Chih-cheng lo, and James T. ed Myers (Cambridge, UK: Cambridge University Press, 2004); Xiaoguan Kang, "Zailun "Xinzheng Xina Zhengzhi": 90 Niandai Zhongguo Dalu Zhengzhi Fazhan Yu Zhengzhi Wending Yanjiu [a Second Examination Of "Administration Absorbing Politics": Studying the Political Development and Political Stability of China in the 1990s]," *Confucius 2000* (2002); Andrew J. Nathan, "Authoritarian Resilience," *Journal of Democracy* 14, no. 1 (2003).

government power, as well as reforms to allow for more citizen participation and openness and transparency of government. Once such steps are taken, this one-party dominated framework, although far from a full-fledged democracy, will be capable of delivering governance as good and competent as the United States or other advanced democracies.[63] It is with this prospect that the peaceful rise of China becomes attainable.

---

63 Mahbubani, "Understanding China."

PART 2
International Conditions of China's Peaceful Rise

Chapter 6

The International Conditions of China's Peaceful Rise: Challenges and Opportunities

Li Qingsi*

Introduction

Along with China's rapid economic development, China's rise has received a worldwide attention in the early 21st century. Though a country's development is primarily due to domestic rather than foreign factors, favorable or unfavorable international conditions could affect the process significantly, particularly in an era of economic interdependence and globalization. As the sole superpower, the United States will have a prevailing influence over China's development environment, through various international forces organized by and around it. However, the competition between China and the United States is mainly in low politics. Confrontation and war between big powers can only result in mutual destruction. This is particularly true for China and the U.S. if they are fighting against each other. If China has to break up the chains of the constraints set up by the U.S., China would have to develop ingenious diplomatic solutions and try to create favorable conditions for its peaceful development.

Based on idealism and interdependency theories, this chapter will examine the external conditions within which China's rise will take place. There is no perfect theory for interpreting the complex conditions of the modern world. Although idealism has undergone changes from time to time, covering a fairly broad perspective ranging from Wilsonian idealism through to contemporary neoliberal theories, the core of idealism that emphasizes the common goals and mutual interests of nations remains the same, which is particularly true in the highly interdependent world in the post-Cold war era when nations have to engage in win-win games instead of absolute gains and losses. Idealism informs us that cooperation and peace are possible when nations concentrate on mutual interests and common goals and open up the options of solving problems and conflicts at lower costs for all actors involved. China-U.S. relations would be a prominent example of interdependence of nations in the age of

---

* The author owes special thanks to Sujian Guo for his final revision of this chapter and Patrick Morgan for his proofreading of an earlier draft.

economic globalization and integration. Both have recognized the value of working together to achieve mutual interests and goals in many areas of regional and world affairs, ranging from the nuclear crisis on the Korean peninsula, to fighting global terrorism, and to the world public health, as we all recognize that we cannot succeed in fighting the political, economic, and social roots of these problems with military power and force. China-U.S. cooperation in regional and world affairs based on common goals and mutual interests would continue to contribute to the international solutions of many problems, conflicts, and crises that lack national solutions. In terms of China's "peaceful development" foreign policy, the Chinese leaders have recognized that it is in the fundamental interest of China to concentrate on the common interests, find common solutions to problems and frictions, and promote international stability and prosperity, in order to maintain a peaceful international environment for China's economic modernization.[1] In this chapter, using idealism and interdependence theories, the author will sort out the favorable and unfavorable factors i.e. the opportunities and challenges that will affect the process of China's rise, and explore the influence of other international actors. Great power relations in a billiard ball system of interaction will significantly shape China's external conditions. The author believes that the sole superpower's influence over China's further development is one key to its rise, and dealing with it must be a core part of its foreign policy. Finally, the chapter will lay out several points that China's foreign policy makers should pay attention to in interacting with the outside world in general, and the United States in particular.

China's Rise and the External Conditions

In 2004, the whole world sensed the implications of China's rapid economic growth, and the most frequent topic of discussions among global economic elites was about China. In 2005, China is the focal point of the world media, and some have even claimed that there is nothing to report without China.[2] Almost all important international conferences were discussing this booming Asian country one way or another. Asia is gradually forming an economic zone, with China as a new center (different from that of Japan), which amazingly resembles the early stages of the European integration.[3] Some media vividly describe China's low cost economy as an express train roaring by, leaving many countries on the platform. Whether it is the massive American deficit, or the declining U.S. dollar, or increasingly rising crude oil prices, or the future world economy, the eyes of the world seem to be on China.

---

[1] Robert G. Sutter, *China's Rise in Asia: Promises and Perils* (Lanham, MD: Rowman & Littlefield Publishers, 2005), pp. 4–5.

[2] Huang Lin, "The world media focus on China, with nothing to report without China" [Shijie Meiti Baodao Zhongguo Huoli Jizhong,Likai Zhongguo Wu Huati Ke Tan] http://news.sohu.com/20050602/n225793673.shtml.

[3] "Without much voice – Beijing becomes 'Asia Leader' by resorting to RMB," *The Voice of Germany*, http://www.BackChina.com 12/30/04.

Though "China collapse allegations" based on domestic problems still resound today,[4] China has managed to achieve such prominent growth while, at the same time, tackling such difficult domestic problems. What is paradoxically noticeable is that many critics abroad are optimistic about China's economy, believing that it would overtake that of the United States in about 30 years.[5] All in all, optimism about China's future outweighs pessimism.

Though many countries are rising today, it is obvious that China attracts most of the world attention. China's GDP in 2003 was 1,447 billion dollars, far behind that of the U.S. (11,004 billion) and Europe (11,025 billion). But in per purchase power (PPP), China's figure is 6719 billion dollars, about 1/6 of the world total, ranking it number two in the world by national PPP already.[6] Along with its remarkable economic development, China has other special traits, such as its Confucianism, which differs from the mainstream Western culture; a long and ancient civilization some 2000 years of history; the largest population and a seemingly endless supply of cheap labor; significant continental and oceanic geopolitical locations; a non-stop tidal wave of growth due to its uneven regional development; and its Communist party ruling system which is out of tune with the Western world. These features have provoked the superpower to resist its rise, using every means to prepare for such a challenge. It appears that the special features of China could influence the world through self-reforming and developing.[7] China's decline during the last few centuries, along with its resulting humiliation, has made the Chinese people realize that only by virtue of being strong and powerful may they enjoy decent living conditions. National comprehensive strength would be the fundamental guarantee for securing the national interests,[8] and therefore their conclusion is that China must rise. Though some still discuss how to understand the word "rise," the general belief is that "China is no longer happy free-riding on the U.S. in Asia" today.[9]

---

4 For instance the book *China is going to collapse* by Zhang Jiadun, an American Chinese Lawyer, talked about China's collapse from bad bank debts. Besides this, there are also all kinds of "collapses allegations" such as population, environment and political governance. Of course each of them is serious enough to cause a collapse, but none of them is isolated from the rest.

5 Ibid.

6 "Europe will lag behind China and the U.S. soon" [Ouzhou Bujiu Jiang Luohou Yu Zhongguo He Meiguo], Sichuan News Network, http://www.newssc.org/gb/Newssc/llzx/zjps/userobject1ai361041.html.

7 See Zhang Baijia,"Has the National Interests changed under Globalization?" [Quanqiuhua Beijingxia de Guojia Liyi Gaibian Liaoma?] *Renmin News Network*, http://www.people.com.cn/GB/jinji/222/3802/3832/20010111/376232.html.

8 *People's Daily* editorial, *Xinhua Monthly Newspaper*, No. 10, 2005, p. 43.

9 James Mulvenon, Deputy Director, Center for Intelligence Research and Analysis, Defense Group, Inc. said, "Compared with the widely discussed China's rise in the international arena, I think its return to the international stage is better expression." In fact, there are different interpretations both within and outside China. But its English equivalent is

As a matter of fact, suspicions about China's intent to displace the superpower arise mainly from comparing it with other rising powers in history, particularly the experience of rising powers and world wars in the 20th century. What worries the rest of the world most is a simple analogy between China today and Germany in the 1890s, and Japan in the early 20th century. In this way attention is paid to the result of a rising power, without caring about the process and the period. Though Prussia's neighbors – France, Austria, Russia and Italy – were very suspicious about its intentions, none were willing to sacrifice their own relations with the newly emerging power. As a result most of them tolerated Prussia's unification wars. Due to Bismarck's sophisticated diplomacy, many suspicious neighbors were defeated, one after another. To international relations theorists and politicians today, one conclusion easily drawn is that without a unified Germany the First World War could have hardly broken out in Europe. Similarly, without tolerance of Japan by the U.S. and Soviet Union over its military expansion into Korea and Northeast China, the second World War would have been restricted to a much smaller area in the Asia Pacific. This leads them to regret that actions were not taken to prevent Germany and Japan from rising in power. Recalling these histories, many observers of China's rise would be alarmed, fearing that China would follow the same pattern. Since the rise of such a big power would possibly change existing international rules and regulations, it would inevitably cause worries and arouse vigilance in the rest of the world. An observer even wrote that the development of China is like another sun breaking into the solar system, which influences the velocity and gravitational pull of the system and affects every small planet close to it.[10] The "China Threat" is thus often employed as a call for support mobilization in some Western countries to contain China's rise.

China's development goal for the next 20 years is to reach a $4 trillion GDP with $3000 per capita income.[11] The medium and short-term objectives are to catch up with Europe and the United States so as to improve the people's living standards, rather than to challenge the U.S. hegemony and the existing international order. As some scholars pointed out, China has in fact benefited from American primacy that provides "the peaceful international environment and the international public goods that have enabled the Chinese to focus on an export-led strategy of rapid economic development."[12] Therefore, as Avery Goldstein pointed out, "China's foreign policy behavior continues to conform closely to that typical of a status quo state, especially as Beijing works hard to be welcomed as a responsible member of the existing international community whose acceptance is crucial to China's

---

"rise" and "ascend." In Chinese there are "rise," "recover" and "re-habilitate" into the world community. The author agrees with return to the world arena.

10 Liu Yifei, Yang Zhongxu, "The Chinese Wisdom of Big Power Diplomacy," *Daguo Waijiao de Zhongguo Zhihui*, *China News Weekly*, May 3, 2004. http://www.chinanewsweek.com.cn/2004-05-09/1/3522.html.

11 Hu Jintao, Ceremonial Speech at 2005 Beijing Globe Forum of Fortune, *Xinhua Monthly*, No. 6, 2005, p. 72.

12 Robert G. Sutter, p. 4.

continued modernization."[13] But since China is so big, it is understandable that foreign countries, especially the beneficiaries of the existing international regime, feel worried and are on guard. Whether such a worry could be muted or become an obstacle to China's development would be determined by how China would tackle both domestic and international challenges and how the world would perceive the rise of China. China has to seek to rise peacefully if her development is to occur within a favorable external environment. As President Hu said in his speech at the 60th anniversary of the World anti-Fascist War Victory, history tells us that "using force, or attempting to use force, in order to realize one's own country's interests will only result in failure, and does not conform with the trend of human history, nor is it conducive to each other's interests."[14] In addition, China's outward-orientated economy and its heavy reliance on imported oil and raw materials indicate that its development is dependent on a peaceful international environment and "on the U.S.-military supported security order for the smooth flow of oil to its ports."[15] Future development issues caused by potential shortages of oil and other raw materials have drawn the Chinese government's attention. Under these circumstances the Chinese government has adopted "peaceful development" foreign policy. China will coexist peacefully and work together amiably with other countries in the world, compromise to achieve mutual interests and common goals, promote equality and tolerance, peacefully handle the conflicts caused by different interests, and seek to achieve win-win outcomes, because China has realized that the achievement of the Chinese objectives is reliant upon a peaceful international environment and building on the common interests of nations in the age of interdependence and globalization.[16] On the other hand, being closely connected with the world economy, China's growth has already contributed and will continue to contribute greatly to the world.[17]

Some analysts would argue that China also needs to maintain a powerful military to safeguard its sustainable development and maximize its interests. China's national interests and goals can only be realized by relying on its own efforts. However, times have changed, and history cannot simply repeat itself. Bismarck's diplomacy and expansion through war is no longer applicable in the age of globalization. Chinese leadership has clearly recognized "the negative experiences of earlier rising powers, such as Germany and Japan in the twentieth century, to conclude that China cannot reach its goals of economic modernization and development through confrontation and conflict."[18] Although the United States has attempted to maintain

---

13 Avery Goldstein, *Rising to the Challenge: China's Grand Strategy and International Security* (Stanford, CA: Stanford University Press, 2005), p. 213.

14 President Hu's speech at the 60th anniversary of anti-Fascist war victory, *Xinhua Monthly*, No. 10, 2005, p. 11.

15 Robert G. Sutter, p. 4.

16 Lin Zhibo, "Does China need nationalism," [Zhongguo Shifo Xuyao Minzu Zhuyi], *Renmin News Network*, http://opinion.people.com.cn/GB/1036/3070502.html.

17 Hu Jintao, President of PRC, Ceremonial Speech at 2005 Beijing Globe Forum of Fortune, *Xinhua Monthly Newspaper*, No. 6, 2005, pp. 64–71.

18 Robert G. Sutter, p. 266.

its superpower status and aroused its misgivings about China's rising influence, China-U.S. economic and trade relations have become increasingly interdependent and mutually beneficial, and the two countries have many common interests that would ultimately make them work together rather than fight against each other. Such a strong economic interdependence between China and the United States has become increasingly critical not only to the welfare of the two countries but also to the rest of the world.

Some analysts argue that although the foreign policy environment China faces seems complex, it is actually unilateral as a result of heavy pressure exerted by the United States over its allies and other countries.[19] However, it might be overly simplistic to say that Chinese foreign policy is defined only by its relations with the U.S. As a matter of fact, China's external environment might be summarized as the United States, its allies, and "other" forces. The "other" includes anti-American, fence-sitter and neutralist countries. The current international system is still the one created and dominated by the Western powers, and conflicts among nations are common within it, and China could act accordingly. China's rise and how it will integrate itself into the international community would be the key to international relations in the future,[20] and its relationship with the U.S. would continue to be complicated.[21] But, with a clear picture of international relations in mind, China would be able to navigate through the complex international relations to attain the goal of a rise through peaceful means.

Major International Actors in a Complex Network

With the exception of Japan, not all American allies are obviously its followers. The Iraq war suggests that no matter how powerful the United States is, it can not do whatever it wants in tackling disagreements with its own allies. Furthermore, besides the neutral countries, there are those with anti-American elements, which add complications to the international system. The United States, surrounded by two oceans and two friendly neighbors, has the benefits rarely enjoyed by other great powers throughout history. The potential challengers to its sole superpower status – China, Russia, Japan, Germany and India – are in a very different geopolitical situation. They would pose immediate threats to their neighbors if they sought to

---

19 Liu Lin, Qin Xuan, "Diplomacy forcifully breaks through, China repeatedly says 'no'," *Youth Reference News*, June 27, 2005.

20 Quoted from former U.S. State Secretary Kissinger by Guardian and International Herald Forum, 1990–1993, March. Yang Zheng, *After 1999 – Comments and Forcasts on the International Affairs* (Beijing, China, Zhongguo Guangbo Dianshi Chubanshe, 1991), p. 388.

21 Cheryl L. Hart, "Engagement or Containment: a clear choice," *Assessment of China into the 21st Century*, A.M. Camyon (editor) (New York, Nova Science Publisher, Inc. 1997), pp. 79–80. As President Bush said at a press conference held in the White House Rose Garden in May 2005.

increase their military capabilities to safeguard their own interests or attempt to offset American supremacy. Politics, even international politics, is always parochial. Though American power draws much global attention, the immediate concern for every country is its neighboring states, not the global situation. If a potential challenger takes serious steps to compete with the United States, the regional powers would work together to contain it, thus significantly curtailing its ability to utilize its geopolitical advantages to gain more power in the region while the sole superpower, the U.S. would be able to utilize its unique geopolitical position and a network of military allies to defeat it. Around China, there are several major powerful states that would have no hesitation in helping the U.S. to balance a rising China, thus the external environment for China's rise would be gloomy. However, if China seeks peaceful development, it would not be possible for these states to form an anti-China alliance with the United States, as undermining China would not serve their own interests either. Interdependence exists not only between China and the United States but also between China and other great powers, especially the neighboring states.

The increasingly stronger EU is moving apart from the United States to seek a more independent role after the Cold War, and a strong and unified Europe would make an important contribution to world peace. The widening and deepening China-EU relationship has contributed to the enhancement of both parties' international status and interests.[22] Although China-EU global strategic partnership could discourage American unilateralism, the EU has not acquired sufficient power to compete against the United States, and both sides have too much in common in terms of political ideology and political system. The U.S. and Europe will maintain a good and stable relationship. A stronger and united EU would help to seek a more independent foreign policy from the United States in the future. China-EU relations are currently in their most active and fruitful period, and closer cooperation between China and the EU would increase the EU's political leverage.[23] Though the U.S. has successfully blocked the EU from lifting military sanctions against China, the EU would not indefinitely surrender to American pressure. In choosing between its own economic interests and American interest, it is EU interests instead of American political will that would ultimately shape EU foreign policy making.

Dead set on following the U.S. lead is Japan. Along with its economic growth, expanded political and military ambition, rising right-wing forces, and particularly the American one-sided support, Japan has become more provocative in its foreign policy, and kept making trouble with China.[24] As the number two world economy and China's near neighbor, Japan's active military cooperation with the United States

---

22 Yu Changmiao,*China after the 16 CCP plenary* (Beijing, China, The People's Press, Dec. 2002), p. 360.

23 "To Deepen China-EU relations, Enhance their Comprehensive Cooperation," speech by Premier Wen Jiabao at the summit meeting of China-EU Industry and Business leaders, Dec. 9, 2004.

24 Yu Changmiao, *China after the 16 CCP plenary* (Beijing, China, The People's Press, Dec. 2002), p. 359.

in the West Pacific area would exert tremendous pressure on China, especially in a potential Taiwan cross-strait conflict. The struggle over oil and natural gas resources in East China Sea could turn into a showdown at any time.[25] The friction between China and Japan arises from a combination of Japanese denial of past war crimes and a clash of national interests.[26] Japan has become an eager player in the U.S. policy toward China, particularly in the Taiwan issue. However, it is the U.S. foreign policy that plays a dominant role in the Taiwan issue, and historically the United States has played a balancing role in the East Asian region. Therefore, if China could take a long-range view on the U.S.-supported adversary and the triangle relationships between China, Japan, and the United States, the United States could be seen as a positive role in balancing the potential threat from Japan. If China would concentrate on the immediate objective and ignore the fundamental factor, it could fall into a trap. But, as Japan never feels guilty for its wrongdoing in history and consequently lacks moral support in the region, a U.S. one-sided policy leaning toward Japan as it does to Israel in the Middle East would lose the hearts of many Asian countries that still have a collective memory of the savage Japanese aggression 60 years ago.[27] Therefore, it would be in the strategic interest of the United States to play a balancing role in the region.

Japan, however, is genuinely fearful of China's rise, rather than simply pulling American chestnuts out of the fire. After Meiji Restoration, the Japanese gradually became self important to the Chinese; such national mentality had not changed after WWII. But China's increasingly growing strength makes the Japanese uneasy, for there never has been such a time when both China and Japan are powerful at the same time. "Having both powerful in the same era will be an unprecedented challenge."[28] Though the U.S. and Japan see eye to eye in terms of deterring a rising China, they have conflicting intentions, each expecting the other to be weakened by a conflict with China, which in turn will strengthen its own leverage. It is obvious that for the first time in history both China and Japan are strong simultaneously, which makes them uneasy, something particularly true for the Japanese. China-Japan economic relations are complimentary and thus China's economic development has been of great benefit to Japan economically, as Prime Minister Koizumei has admitted. China should make full use of its economic leverage in dealing with Japan. The economic interdependence between China and Japan in the past three decades has proved that good Sino-Japanese relations will benefit both sides. However, such relations have recently suffered from the Japanese denial of its past war crimes. As President Hu

---

25 Sun Yafei, "East China Sea a Confrontation Sea, the struggle for resources behind China-Japan border demarcation disputes," http://cn.news.yahoo.com/050721/538/2dt19.html.

26 Li Yang, "Behind the puffed up Japan," *China and the World*, May 1, 2005, no. 59.

27 Since Japanese provocation has worsened its relations with South Korea and Russia, an isolated Japan won't be able to recruit sympathy in a potential Japan-China conflict.

28 James F. Hoge, Jr., "A Global Power Shift in the Making," *Foreign Affairs*, July/August 2004. accessed at: http://www.foreignaffairs.org/20040701facomment83401/james-f-hoge-jr/a-global-power-shift-in-the-making.html?mode=print.

said "we emphasize remembering history not out of long lasting hatred, but to learn from history in order to face the future. Only through remembering past lessons can we avoid repeating tragedies."[29] However, the real danger is the tensions and disputes between the two countries over the Diaoyu (Senkaku) islands and the East China Sea that may hold rich gas and oil reserves, as such disputes could strengthen and deepen the sentiments of fear and nationalism in both countries, which could lead two countries into deep trouble. In addition to the "old" disputes, much of the renewed tension between China and Japan stems from the dispute over the definition of "exclusive economic zones" (EEZs). China insists on the UN Law of the Sea definition of EEZs as starting from the edge of the submerged continental shelf while Japan insists on the definition of EEZs as being 200 miles from shore. As a result of both historical and current disputes, there is a widening gap between the economic and political relations between China and Japan. The deterioration of China-Japan political relations calls for a durable solution acceptable by both governments, which would ultimately have to deal with it calmly and cooperatively. Territory disputes could arouse nationalistic fervor that breads distrust and hostility, which could slip out of hand and lead to war. But, it is not necessarily an ultimate outcome, and probably the less possible scenario. Japan has territory disputes with all its neighbors, such as Russia, Korea, China, and Taiwan, while China also has border disputes with some of its neighbors, but all parties involved tend to manage the disputes and crises to avoid the situations slipping out of control even though they cannot find durable solutions as the cost of war is too high for all countries in the age of economic interdependence and globalization. Although the dispute between China and Japan is intensified, the situation is still under control. A durable solution would be ultimately contingent upon the diplomacy, wisdom and strategic vision of the two governments in dealing with the tough issues between the two major power countries, as neither governments nor peoples of the two countries want to repeat the past painful experience. The tightened economic interdependence and mutual benefits would eventually push the two countries closer and bring the two governments back to the negotiation table to find a durable solution acceptable to both sides although the mood so far seems to be running contrary to anything closer to that.

Russia has suffered greatly from its competition with American hegemony during the Cold War, and has a position closer to both China and Europe in terms of advocating a just and reasonable international political order. The July 2005 joint communiqué, signed by President Hu Jintao and President Putin, announced that the development of the China-Russia strategic partnership is the first priority for both administrations, consistent with the fundamental interests of both countries and peoples, and conducive to regional and global peace, stability and development.[30] The large-scale China-Russia joint military exercise in summer 2005 indicated the

---

29 President Hu's speech at the 60 anniversary of anti-Fascist war victory, *Xinhua Monthly*, No. 10, 2005, p. 11.

30 China-Russia Joint Communiqué, *Xinhua Monthly Newspaper*, no. 8, 2005, p. 29.

rising significance of the cooperation between the two countries. Some Chinese analysts even argue that the Shanghai Cooperation Organization could become the only international organization checking NATO in the future.[31] Since Russia could not prevent NATO from expanding eastward, nor could it check the "Color Revolution" from spreading alongside its borders,[32] its indispensable choice is to borrow the increasingly powerful China's strength to deter any aggression from the West, especially the United States. Though many voices warn that the international environment is dangerous, and more attention should be paid to big power cooperation, a certain kind of alliance is useful for China's interests, for friends and allies do help. Though Russia does not have the strength it used to, it still has the capability to completely destroy the whole world, and as a Chinese proverb says, "a camel starved to death is still bigger than a horse."

The above discussion suggests that China could navigate through the complex major power relationship to maintain a balanced, mutually dependent and deterrent, peaceful regional and international environment that is vital for China's continued peaceful development. However, although big power relations and diplomacy would play a determining role in the external environment for China's rise, the peripheral nations are also important and cannot be ignored, and therefore the Chinese government has put forward a good neighbor policy. If the neighbor can tolerate and accept China being strong and rising, then the so-called "China Threat" message or perception would be dampened. A recent case is improved China-India relations. Since China changed its policy of leaning toward Pakistan, China-India relations are experiencing rapid improvement, which counters the Indian attempt to join an anti-China encirclement or coalition. By strengthening economic ties with neighboring states, China is turning the so-called "threat" into an active and benign interaction, and has enormously reduced fears of China, leading neighbors to welcome the idea of common development and prosperity put forward by China. China's deeds during and after the 1997 Southeast Asian financial crisis demonstrate that when Asian countries recognize their common interests with China they can coordinate with a rising China, which helped to maintain the regional stability.[33] China's sincere attitude towards the ASEAN nations has made great progress in the bilateral relationship. The Free Trade Agreement between China and ASEAN nations has greatly improved China's relations with the major countries in Southeast Asia, creating stronger interdependent economic relations between China and the ASEAN.[34]

---

31 He Liangliang, "Shanghai Cooperation Organization makes new rules for Euro-asia Geopolitics," Hong Kong, Wenhui Bao, July 7, 2005.

32 Zhang Jianji, "Shanghai Cooperation Organization and China's Diplomacy," Nanfengchuang, July, 2005.

33 "China quietly marches toward superpower," http://www.5seecn.com/world/2005/9436.html

34 "The interdependent economic relations between China and the U.S. affect the global strategic pattern," http://energy.icxo.com/htmlnews/2005/05/11/593031.htm.

Besides, the position recently adopted by South Korea and Australia, important American allies in East and Southeast Asia, on a potential Taiwan Strait military conflict indicates their disagreement with the United States regarding this vital national interest with China and their unwillingness to fight against China with the United States.[35] This also suggests that the United States will not be able to repeat the Korean War case in which the U.S. was able to lead joint forces from 16 countries. As the focus of national interests in Euro-Atlantic region has shifted from security to economic areas, American allies in that region will be less likely to join the forces with the U.S. in fighting for Taiwan against China if the U.S. decides to intervene in the Taiwan Strait militarily. India would be less eager to join in containing or fighting against China as well.[36] Therefore, the best option for the United States is to maintain the status quo and regional stability, which indeed corresponds to China's "peaceful development" strategy and presents the most important common ground for all regional powers to work with each other or at worse "muddle through." Major power relations should tend to be more cooperative than conflictive.

In the complex international relations system, the United States is obviously the focal point of international relations, interests and contradictions. China's foreign policy strategy "is seen as contingent, and U.S. power and policies play a big role in determining Chinese policy in the region."[37] China-U.S. frictions in many areas could increase, but China has shown its willingness to work with the U.S. rather than to challenge it, unless its core national interests, such as territorial integrity, are threatened while the U.S. has also recognized the important role China has played in economic, political, security, and transnational areas and shown its willingness to maintain a good and stable relationship with China. Unlike U.S.-U.S.S.R. relations during the Cold War, China-U.S. economic relations are interdependent and mutually beneficial, and confrontation would benefit neither side. There are convergence and divergence in China-U.S. relations, but the better choice for both sides is to emphasize convergence and seek a win-win approach to divergence. In the nuclear age, the likelihood of "great power conflict escalating into total war…is lower than at any time in the past century."[38] Interstate relations are based on national interests, and almost every regional power insists on its right to pursue its national interests, which often conflict with American interests.[39] However, as Quincy Wright argues,

---

35 Roh Moo-Hyun declares "American Military based in South Korea should not get involved in Northeast Asia conflict," http://world.people.com.cn/GB/14549/3229226.html. In addition, Austrialia is not willing to fight against China in a cross Strait conflict due to its closer trade relations with China, also see Pang Zhongying, "Australia, between the U.S. and Asia," http://www.people.com.cn/GB/guoji/1030/2030009.html.

36 Analysis: Why is India not willing to fight against China with the U.S.? http://club.backchina.com/main/printthread.php?t=205297.

37 Robert G. Sutter, p. 11.

38 National Intelligence Council Report, Jan. 12, 2005.

39 Samuel P. Huntington, "The Lonely Superpower," *Foreign Affairs*, vol. 78, no. 2, March/April 1999.

with increasing power parity, stability will be maintained,[40] and the United States and China and their major power diplomacy would shape the international landscape in the coming decades.[41]

Major Issues in China-U.S. Relations

Many issues in the world today unavoidably intersect with both American and Chinese interests. Although other countries, especially the big powers, play an important role, the rise of China will involve interaction with the United States more than with any other actors. Since the United States is the sole superpower, and China a potential one, it is not surprising they aim at each other.[42] China-U.S. relations are particularly important for Chinese foreign policy. China's foreign policy toward the U.S. has been based on its mixed perception of the U.S. role in the region and in affecting its core national interests. On one hand, the U.S. supremacy in the region has played a balancing role in maintaining stability which has benefited China greatly and the U.S. has played a major role facilitating China to integrate into the international system and the world economy. On the other hand, China is concerned with the unchecked U.S. superpower that could threaten China's core national interests, particularly territorial integrity, and contain China's rise in the 21st century. However, the U.S. China policy is also two-sided and mixed with engagement and containment at the same time.[43] The international environment for China's rise, to a considerable extent, is defined by American global strategy and its China policy.

The American strategy is to contain any potential power that could challenge its superpower status. According to Martin Jacques, Americans generally believe that China has taken advantage of the U.S. counter-terrorism campaign, especially its persistent involvement in Iraq, to quickly develop its economy and modern weaponry. Therefore, the United States has made an effort to enhance its relations with Japan, India and ASEAN nations to counterbalance China.[44] For the Americans, China is a different matter altogether from Bin Laden, who was never going to pose an even minuscule threat to the position of the U.S.[45] They believe that China clearly could do this, however, and in the long run certainly will. Its growing economic power will, in time, generate greater political and military ambitions.[46] American

---

40 Stanley Hoffman, *Theory of Contemporary International Relations* (Beijing, China, China Social Science Chubanshe, 1990), p. 123.

41 Avery Goldstein, p. 13.

42 Martin Jacques, "Cold War Take Two-U.S. v China will soon be the dominant fault line of global politics," *The Guardian*, Saturday June 18, 2005.

43 Yu Changmiao, *China after the 16 CCP plenary* (Beijing, China, The People's Press, Dec. 2002), p. 354.

44 Martin Jacques, "Cold War Take Two-U.S. v China will soon be the dominant fault line of global politics", *The Guardian*, Saturday June 18, 2005.

45 Ibid.

46 Ibid.

military experts are increasingly aware that there is no comparison between China's future strategic development and past U.S. rivals. Its military strength will be strong enough to challenge the U.S. in military conflicts in about 10 to 20 years. The China threat will be more menacing than the Russian threat was. Therefore, the United States has been promoting its hegemonic goals under the guise of counter-terrorism. The U.S. recent actions in the Asia Pacific area, its penetration into Central Asia, and its returning of military bases to some Southeast Asian nations in the name of counter terrorism campaign, have enormously enlarged its strategic encirclement of China.[47] Therefore, it is obvious that the United States has considered China as its adversary or potential one covertly or overtly. Although U.S. Defense Secretary Rumsfeld does not want to show his hand on this,[48] other hawks are yelling for war aggressively. Kaplan clearly pointed out in *The Atlantic Monthly*, June 2005 that China was the United States' number one enemy, suggesting that the United States must contain it militarily and diplomatically while getting ready to fight and win a war with it.[49] John Mearsheimer, a structural realist, believes that the sooner the better for containing China.[50] Obviously these experts study China only in terms of military and security aspects, paying no attention to other important aspects of development in the world and in China in the age of economic interdependence and globalization.[51]

Another scholar who systematically put forward a theory of opposing any potential challenger to U.S. hegemony is Samuel Huntington. He pointed out in *The Great Chessboard* that the United States should not allow any potential adversary to challenge its status on both ends of the Eurasia landmass. Because of China's rapid development, the United States already looks at China as such a challenger. Now the Bush administration often implies that the American goal is to retain U.S. hegemony and discourage any other party from challenging American dominance or seeking to become a "peer competitor."[52] In the past, a closed and xenophobic China was regarded as evil, so each administration since Nixon's has been working hard to open, evolve, and change China. However, since the Clinton administration, the United States has claimed that a "prosperous, strong and stable China meets the American interests." Opening China's market and integrating it into the international system is exactly the goal the United States has been pursuing, so as to bring it in

---

47 Yue Jianyong, *The Globalization and the U.S. China Strategy*, Hong Kong *Phoenix Weekly*, May 25, 2005.

48 Asked by Cui Tiankai, Chinese assistant minister of Foreign Affairs on June 4, 2005, U.S. secretary of defense Rumsfeld had to admit that China was not a threat.

49 Robert D. Kaplan, "How We Would Fight China," *The Atlantic Monthly*, June 2005.

50 John J. Mearsheimer, *The Tragedy of Great Power Politics* (New York: W.W. Norton & Company, 2001).

51 "China's global influence rises compared to the American in 2004," *Washington Observer Weekly*, Dec. 29, 2004.

52 Harry Harding, "Change and Continuity in the Bush Administration's Asia Policy," in *George W. Bush and East Asia – A First Term Assessment*, ed. By Robert M. Hathaway and Wilson Lee (Woodrow Wilson International Center for Scholars, Dec. 2004), pp. 33–34.

conformity with the international rules. Deng Xiaoping's reform effort catered to the American Strategy, and achieved a series of economic successes. Prosperity is naturally the objective the government and people have long been pursuing. But some Americans begin to believe China has become a challenger, which needs to be contained, and even feel regrettable for agreeing China's WTO status.

Taiwan is another major problem for the China-U.S. relationship. Speaking in Kyoto before coming to visit China on Nov. 19, 2005, President Bush criticized China's lack of democracy and praised what Taiwan has achieved. However, as Wang Jianwei observes, many Americans simplify the confrontation between the mainland and Taiwan into a conflict between authoritarianism and democracy. They believe that, as the leader of the world's democracies, the United States should stand by Taiwan. So democracy becomes the sole standard for judging truth across the Taiwan Strait. This perception only agrees with the justification for Taiwan's pursuit of democracy and freedom, but denies the rationality of the mainland seeking national unification.[53] Though the Chinese people are strong-minded about national reunion, the American government has attempted to prevent their long-delayed dream from coming true.

The huge bilateral trade volume between China and the United States indicates that the United States has truly benefited from Chinese economic prosperity,[54] and this can be one of the main common grounds for achieving the best possible relations between the two.[55] One of the big issues between them is the trade deficit. Due to the differences of development and economic structure, and particularly the American investment in China, it is natural for China to have trade surplus unless the U.S. government allows more high-value added products (high-tech products) to export to China as most of China's exporting goods to the American markets are low-value added products. But, the comparative advantage theory teaches us that such government intervention and regulation in trade and economy are inefficient and counterproductive and could do more harm than benefit to the American economy and consumers. Seeing how the Pentagon has been exerting pressure on the EU, and how the U.S. Congress reacted against the possible lifting of EU military sanctions, Thomas Barnet at the Naval War College, who published "The New Map of the Pentagon: the War and Peace in the 21 Century" in 2005, believes that this is simply a fuss over trivialities. Many American scholars regard the global U.S.-China competition as a zero-sum game, which he believes is "extremely foolish." "That the United States expects China to be successful, but is reluctant to accept any

---

53 Wang Jianwei, "2004 elections and three national isms," http://www.chinaelections.com/readnews.asp?newsid=%7B16D18B32-3ADE-428D-827B-2E69298D7EA5%7D.

54 According to Morgan Stanley, the American companies earned $6 million from the businesses with China, and created 4 billion jobs thus in 2004.

55 The former U.S. secretary of State Powell said that U.S.-China relation was the best in history, and the current secretary of State Rice also expressed the same position during President Bush's visit to Beijing Nov. 19–21.

of the cost is short-sighted."[56] Unfortunately this is not mainstream thinking in the prevailing conservative American political atmosphere.

As President Hu Jintao said during his meeting with President Bush on Sept. 13, 2005 in New York, a healthy, stable and developing Sino-U.S. relationship is beneficial to the common interests of both countries as well as to world peace, stability and development. In order to promote a healthy Sino-U.S. relationship, both sides should maintain high-level exchanges, continue to make full use of and improve consultation and cooperation mechanisms in all fields, and pay more attention to strategic dialogue. He reiterated that economic cooperation between China and the U.S. is growing quickly and is mutually beneficial. With such rapid, large-scale development of bilateral trade, it is unavoidable to encounter frictions and disputes. But China is willing to resolve the trade disputes through dialogue and consultation on the basis of equality, mutual benefit, and common development so as to advance healthy bilateral relations.[57]

China's Possible Countermeasures

Recently, in an evaluation of China's challenges during the next decade by professors from Peking University, none of the top 8 challenges are consisted of foreign threats, suggesting that China's rise is mainly a domestic matter,[58] and that China's foreign policy must be supported by a sound domestic policy. Facing more and more pressure from the joint American and Japanese military operations in the Western Pacific, and the increasing network of encirclement against China, the challenge to Chinese foreign policy is unprecedented, which has led many Chinese to believe that the American containment strategy toward China not only squeezes the space in which China can operate in its neighborhood, but also prevents transfers of military technology to China from much of the world.[59] President Bush describes U.S.-China relations as complex, which is a return to his former position that they are competitive partners. How to tackle the China-U.S. relations will be a key issue in China's foreign policy strategy as such a relationship will influence the overall international environment for China's peaceful rise in a highly interdependent world.

---

56 Dana Priest, "Iraq a new terror breeding ground, war created a haven, CIA advisers report," *Washington Post*, Jan. 13, 2005.

57 President Hu attending the summit meeting of 60th anniversary of UN founding and UN Security Council and delivering an important speech, *Xinhua Monthly Newspaper*, No. 10, 2005, p. 63.

58 Ding Yuanzhu, "2010, the possible three perspectives of China – investigations and consultations to 98 official and non-official experts," the first eight are unemployment, agriculture, finance, gap between rich and poor, eco-environmental issue, Taiwan, social order and public security, *Peking University Yannan Newwork*, http://www.yannan.cn/data/detail.php?id=3055.

59 The U.S. not only pressured EU not to lift arms sales sanction, but also prevented Israel, Ukraine from transferring military technology to China.

The dramatic change in international relations after the Cold War, especially after 9/11, is generally conducive to China's reform and opening to the outside world. The Chinese leaders recognize that, as long as China insists on peace, development and cooperation, carrying out an independent peaceful foreign policy, and insists on the five principles of peaceful coexistence, China will be able to promote a peaceful external environment.[60] China's peaceful development would promote a peaceful international environment and contribute to world peace through its own peaceful development.[61] Thus pursuing a peaceful external context has been and will continue to be a top priority of Chinese foreign policy in the 21st century. Some policy recommendations are proposed as follows.

First, the relations with the United States can be maintained as a contained struggle without breaking out, using struggle to seek cooperation. Joseph Nye said that if the United States takes China as its enemy, then it will be; the contrary is also true, though China-U.S. relations is not decided mainly by the Chinese. The U.S. Defense Secretary Rumsfeld does not want to admit that the U.S. considers China as a threat, so China should also play the same game. Avoiding verbal irritation against each other could provide maneuvering room in the bilateral relationship and diplomacy, avoiding the U.S.-U.S.S.R. style of full confrontation. Rhetoric and deeds need not be identical within a half-genuine and half-false partnership and friendship. As long as both sides could fully appreciate the common interests in regional and world affairs and the profound need for both parties to cooperate in those areas, the two countries would find more benefits than costs in avoiding involving direct confrontation and becoming adversaries, which could help to maintain a stable and cooperative China-U.S. relationship.

Second, China should make full use of "soft power" in economic, cultural, political, and geopolitical areas to minimize the negative effects of China's hard power deficit. Some have described President Hu's diplomatic style as "Tai Qi," using soft power to dissolve American "hard ball" pressure incrementally. Since one of the strategic means the U.S. uses in containing China's rise is to build military and security alliances to encircle China, China would have to make full use of its soft power to weaken or break the chains of encirclement and create agreeable circumstances for peaceful development. In fact, China can neutralize some of America's allies, such as South Korea, within the U.S. alliance system, since it no longer uses ideology to guide its diplomacy. Pragmatic diplomacy has been increasingly popular among nations in the post-Cold War era. In fact, the close trade and economic relations between China and South Korea and their shared concerns about the Korean peninsula nuclear issue have turned the political relations between China and South Korea into a positive situation for China. The key is to take advantage of its rapid economic development and huge market potential to build strong interdependent economic relations with

---

60 *People's Daily* editorial, *Xinhua Monthly Newspaper*, No. 10, 2005, p. 43.

61 President Hu attending the summit meeting of 60th anniversary of UN founding and UN Security Council and delivering an important speech, *Xinhua Monthly Newspaper*, No. 10, 2005, p. 64.

neighboring countries and American allies, and to advocate political and security cooperation with them. However, the application of soft power does not necessitate the absolute abandoning of hard power.

Third, China should consider abandoning its tradition of non-alliance, and establish its own political and military allies in the form of the Shanghai Cooperation Organization, certainly not excluding the possibility of becoming American allies. China was a close ally of the U.S. during the Second World War and a strategic partner during the Cold War after 1972, and has continued to maintain a good, stable relationship with the U.S. since then. China could continue to expand military exchange and cooperation with the U.S. to build mutual trust and cooperative mechanisms in both global and regional security areas and strengthen China-U.S. military relationship and cooperation. U.S. supremacy in the region will continue in the 21st century and China-U.S. bilateral military alliance or security strategic partnership could influence the foreign policy orientation of Japan and the internal politics on Taiwan tremendously.

Fourth, China should maintain frequent high-level communication and exchange with its U.S. counterparts to minimize possible misunderstandings, build an early warning system between China and the U.S. (and Japan as well) to reduce risks of misjudgments and accidents, and to dampen misgivings and enhance mutual trust. China should promote communication and exchanges at all levels and in all areas, such as economic, cultural, legal, political, and social interaction and exchange to shape or influence public opinion, academic community, and thereby have a more far-reaching influence on congressional legislation in the United States. It is also necessary to mitigate the ideological confrontation and try to focus on specific issues in the bilateral relationship. In fact, China has adopted pragmatic foreign policy and diplomacy since reform and opening in 1978. China should continue to water down the role of ideology and emphasize mutual interests and common goals.

Finally, though the United States is the sole superpower today, it faces many kinds of constraints, such as the UN and other major powers. *The New York Times* points out that as an economic power, the United States no longer sets the rules; as a military power it vastly outguns the rest of the world, but it has a hard time translating armed might into influence.[62] Therefore, American influence can be seen world-wide, but the constraints on it are everywhere. In these complicated international relations, if China could make full use of every positive factor, it might be able to navigate through an unfavorable situation and even turn it around.

Great powers rarely rise peacefully, and it would be difficult for China to do so when encountering American antagonism. Although China-U.S. relations have experienced some difficulties in the past, there is no reason to believe that they can not work together to manage the future. Though disputes and conflicts over trade, human rights, etc. will continue, interdependence reflected in closer economic exchanges and trade relations are prevailing, which is totally different

---

62 Fred Kaplan, "China Expands. Europe Rises. And the United States," *New York Times*, Dec. 26, 2004.

from that of U.S.-U.S.S.R. relations. Idealists are often optimists, and we believe interdependence based on mutual interests and common goals would strengthen our relationships with the United States and the rest of the world, and China would be able to preserve a long-term peaceful international environment that is necessary for China's modernization drive.

Chapter 7

Maintaining an Asymmetric but Stable China-U.S. Military Relationship

Xuetang Guo*

About thirty years ago, China and the United States began to establish a cooperative military relationship to deal with a common threat from the Soviet Union. This relationship was asymmetric but stable in terms of nuclear deterrence capability and conventional military power. In 1980s–1990s, China and the United States had maintained a relatively stable military relationship even though there were political stalemates after the Tiananmen Square incident in 1989 and during the Taiwan Strait crises in 1995–1996. However, the fundamental dispute over the Taiwan issue and China's multi-faceted rise in late 1990s deepened mistrust and misperception between the two powers. Since taking office in 2001, Bush government has been not only reassessing the role of China's military power, but also taking corresponding military actions including deploying the Ballistic Missile Defense (BMD) program. Also the adjustment of U.S. military strategy in the Western Pacific in recent years aimed at containing or at least hedging against China's increasing military power will be vital in shaping the future of bilateral relations and regional security as well. Can the asymmetric but stable bilateral military relationship be maintained in the new century? And how? The chapter will explore the evolution of the current security dilemma, and also reassess the international environment for China's rise from the perspective of China-U.S. military relationship.

Given the debate over China's rise and its international significance both in China itself and the United States, this chapter explores firstly China's worries about the U.S. missile defense plans which might destabilize the bilateral military relationship. In the following three sections, the American concerns over China's rise, particularly the rapid military progress backed by the economic modernization, and the U.S. military strategy and policies in dealing with China's challenges are analyzed in order to see how the security dilemma plays and how the bilateral military relationship is becoming unstable. The choice of U.S. military strategy is vital to China's rise, to the overall China-U.S. relations and to the East Asia security environment. An unstable China-U.S. military relationship might essentially damage the peace and

---

* The author wishes to express his gratitude to Dr. Sujian Guo for his kind help and persistent patience for this work, and to Professor Brantly Womack for proofreading this paper and his long-standing and thoughtful academic exchanges.

stability in East Asia. The fifth section assesses the security implications of mutual suspiciousness in the bilateral military relationship for great power relations and the foreign policies of China's neighboring states. The concluding section draws lessons from the assessment of the sensitive and vital China-U.S. military relationship.

U.S. BMD Plans and China's Asymmetric Response

The idea of BMD came from fears of mutual assured destruction during a nuclear war between the United States and the Soviet Union. The Anti-Ballistic Missile (ABM) treaty, signed in 1972 as a guarantee of balance of terror, blocked one dimension of the nuclear arms race and stabilized strategic nuclear relationship in international security in the Cold War. The ABM Treaty continued in force another decade after the collapse of the Soviet Union. However, in the unipolar world, the United States could not escape the allurements of maintaining absolute superiority of military technologies after successes of Patriot missiles in the Gulf War in the U.S., and of protecting absolute national security from potential threats of long-range missile by so-called "rogue" states. "China perceives the advent of U.S. ballistic missile defenses with great alarm...missile defenses are provocative."[1] "[I]n order to prevent new great powers from challenging its hegemonic status in next decades, the United States would prefer to establish ballistic anti-missile defense to deter countries who could challenge (in fact, counterattack) it," Chinese experts argued.[2]

Missile defense includes the lower-tier theater missile defense (TMD) which attempts to intercept shorter-range missiles as they descend toward their targets, and the National Missile Defense (NMD) which focuses on defending North America from intercontinental ballistic missiles (ICBM). On May 1, 2001, U.S. President Bush delivered a speech on missile defense, making clear the United States' determination to develop a multi-faceted and multi-layered missile defense system in order to establish a unilateral absolute strategic superiority. In late December, President Bush announced that the United States would withdraw from the ABM treaty, shaking off the yoke restraining the U.S. from developing a missile defense system. The U.S. stated that the move was aimed at "protecting the U.S. people against missile attacks from terrorists and 'rogue states' in the future." However, according to Xiong Guangkai, Deputy Chief of the General Staff of the Chinese People's Liberation Army, "its real objective was to seize a new commanding height in science and high technology through developing an advanced missile defense system, which would at the same time promote the development of U.S. defense industries and growth of its economy in order to establish an absolute strategic superiority. Therefore, the accelerated development of the U.S. missile defense system is not purely a military

---

1 Brad Roberts, "China-U.S. Nuclear Relations: What Relationship Best Serves US Interests," IDA Document P-3640, pp. 7–8. See www.au/af.mil/au/awcgate/dtra/china_us_nuc.pdf.

2 Xu Yan and Li Li, ed., *Space Shield: American TMD and NMD* (Beijing: PLA Wenyi Publisher, 2001), p. 4.

move, but a major decision made in consideration of its global strategy and all-round national security strategy."[3]

The decision of deploying BMD plan is a heavy blow to international strategic military balance, and meanwhile it is a big challenge to China-U.S. asymmetric-but-stable military relationship. "Without a doubt, the research and deployment of U.S. missile defense programs is a significant challenge to China's security in the twenty-first century. It will bring comprehensive strikes to China's strategic situation, security strategy, political decision, diplomatic capability, development of military power and so on in the new century."[4] From Chinese point of view, Washington's efforts to build national and theater missile defenses inevitably and directly neutralizes China's smaller nuclear deterrent and thus brings overall harmful affects on China's goal of achieving unification with Taiwan. Simply speaking, if the United States had more defense shields, China's sufficient "minimum deterrence" nuclear strategy would be no longer effective, and that would surely deteriorate China's security environment. The bilateral nuclear relationship will be totally asymmetric, but unstable due to necessary Chinese countermeasures.

China's concerns over both NMD and TMD, fall generally into three categories. First, a major Chinese concern is TMD's potential application to Taiwan. "Deployment of TMD in or near Taiwan would reduce China's ability to use missile threats to politically intimidate Taiwan's leaders."[5] Moreover, any U.S. role in such deployment would signal (to both Taipei and Beijing) a greater likelihood of U.S. military support of Taiwan in the event of overt conflict. Thus, China worries that TMD deployment would bolster Taiwanese independence sentiments and the cost of preventing Taiwan from declaring independence would be much higher. A second Chinese concern is the impact of TMD in East Asia. The strengthening of the U.S.-Japan alliance, which conspicuously failed to define the geographic boundaries within which events could lead to joint U.S.-Japan military operations (the Alliance has for the first time urged China to solve the Taiwan issue peacefully in a bilateral joint statement in early 2005), encouraging Japanese remilitarization and opening the door to direct Japanese involvement in a potential Taiwan military conflict. China's third concern focuses on the U.S. itself. NMD has plans which would negate China's nuclear deterrent. Compared to the United States, China's nuclear force remains relatively small, and the U.S. retains a massive retaliation deterrent. Hence, even in the event of direct U.S.-China military conflict, the prospects of China launching nuclear missiles against the U.S. will remain slim. This concern is linked to the first

---

3 Xiong Guangkai, *International Strategy and Revolution in Military Affairs* (Beijing: Tshinghua University Press, 2003), p. 267.

4 Zhu Feng, *Ballistic Missile Defense Plan and International Security* (Shanghai: Shanghai People's Press, 2001), p. 677.

5 Wade L. Huntley and Robert Brown, "Missile Defense & China," *Foreign Policy in Focus*, Volume 6, Number 3 (January 2001). It can be reached through http://www.fpif.org/briefs/vol6/v6n03taiwan.html.

two. "NMD would moderate Pentagon defense planners' concerns over escalation in the event of U.S. intervention in Taiwan or other U.S.-China regional conflicts."[6]

As a predominant political, economical and military superpower, the United States' determination of deploying BMD implied a belittling attitude toward China's response. "The long-term effects of Chinese reactions to pending TMD and NMD decisions are too often overlooked in current U.S. strategic debate. In particular, the debate over NMD is too focused on the pre-existing U.S.-Russia relationship and on emerging concerns over threats posed by small 'rogue' states. Because a direct military conflict over Taiwan would gravely damage U.S. (and Chinese) long-term interests, Washington needs to carefully consider the potential repercussions that deploying TMD or NMD may have for prospects of peacefully resolving the Taiwan question."[7] Whether taken into account or not, Chinese concerns of BMD are understandable and reasonable. "It is very clear to most in China that the proposed U.S. missile defense system will adversely impact their nuclear force, despite American assurance that the system is not aimed at them. A U.S. acknowledgement that missile defense could negate China's deterrent and significantly affect its nuclear decision-making could make it possible for the two countries to have a true strategic dialogue."[8]

Having provided the strategic incentive for China to increase its nuclear arsenal beyond the former standard of minimum deterrence, it is hardly surprising that the Pentagon predicts such developments. The report delivered by the Department of Defense (DoD) early 2002 shows that the U.S. has more interest in deploying tactical nuclear weapons and advanced conventional weaponry to attack and deter its nuclear rivals and non-nuclear enemies in regional wars, including the war with China over the Taiwan issue. "Foreign Missile Developments and the Ballistic Missile Threat Through 2015" report, produced by U.S. National Intelligence Council in December 2001, calculates that although Beijing's future ICBM forces remain considerably smaller and less capable than the strategic missile forces of Russia and the United States, it will increase several-fold by 2015 and be deployed primarily against the United States. For Chinese observers, the countermeasures taken to negate the U.S. defense shield are intended to maintain bilateral asymmetric nuclear relationship, and cannot be interpreted to have strategic military competition with Washington.

---

6   See Wade L. Huntley and Robert Brown, "Missile Defense & China"; and Zhufeng, *Ballistic Missile Defense Plan and International Security*, pp. 678–684. In his book, Professor Zhu Feng lists five direct threats to China's national security from missile defense plans, as introduced generally in the text, and four indirect threats. The indirect threats includes: missile defense plans would change international strategic balance, damage the international arms control process and ignite proliferation of weapons of massive destruction, cause arms races in offensive and defensive TMD and NMD weapons, and deteriorate China-U.S.-Japan relations. See Zhu Feng, *Ballistic Missile Defense Plan and International Security*, pp. 684–688.

7   Wade L. Huntley and Robert Brown, "Missile Defense & China."

8   Joanne Tompkins, "How US Strategic Policy is Changing China's Nuclear Plans," *Arms Control Today*, January/February 2003, p. 15.

As American experts argued, "Beijing will almost certainly regard the plans for the development of NMD as a challenge to its own nuclear deterrent. As a result, Chinese decision makers may even now have begun worst-case planning to offset what they perceive to be an emerging threat."[9]

Under these circumstances, China has to reassess its long-standing nuclear strategy of minimal deterrent for its national security. China should never pursue unilateral nuclear advantages as the Soviet Union did in the Cold War, but should continue adopting a minimum deterrence posture in order to prevent bilateral stable and asymmetrical nuclear balance from being broken by American BMD plans and the shift of nuclear strategy. Chinese countermeasures to the BMD plans can be interpreted as follows:

- To strengthen the survivability of Chinese strategic nuclear weapons which can improve its retaliatory "second-strike" capability.
- To improve Chinese limited nuclear deterrent by deploying a little more long-range and medium-range missile, including ICBMs and submarine-launched ballistic missiles, and
- To reinforce the research and development of countermeasures and capability to break through the missile defenses, including multi-warhead reentry vehicles, parasitic satellite and others.[10]

To develop these asymmetric combat capabilities might raise asymmetric response from the United States, but the key question for both countries should be whether they can maintain a stable China-U.S. military relationship. As American specialists warned, "China may just prefer an open-ended nuclear modernization program to any framework that the United States suggests. But by not putting Chinese intentions to the test, American policy makers risk ending up with the worst of both worlds: missile defenses that are less effective than they might have been, and Chinese and Russian strategic responses that leave the United States less secure than before."[11] Unfortunately, we might see a world in which neither the United States nor China feel more secure than before.

Growth of China's Military Power and U.S. Response

China's military power has been growing rapidly in recent years backed by long-term economic development. The U.S. worries that China's expanding influence would most likely challenge its hegemonic status in Asia Pacific. Realism has been

---

9 Brad Roberts, Robert A. Manning, and Ronald N. Montaperto, "China: The Forgotten Nuclear Power," *Foreign Affairs*, vol. 79, no. 4 (July/August 2000), p. 54.

10 For more details about China's countermeasures, see Zhu Feng, *Ballistic Missile Defense Plan and International Security*, pp. 688–691.

11 Brad Roberts, Robert A. Manning, and Ronald N. Montaperto, "China: The Forgotten Nuclear Power," p. 63.

playing an important role in shaping the American military strategy toward China since the coming of the new century.

China's Rise: An Inevitable Challenge to American Hegemony?

The disintegration of the Soviet Union and the end of the Cold War reawakened close attention to theory of hegemonic stability when our world entered the era of *Pax Americana* in 1990s. This well-known realism approach, developing in the early 1970s, holds that the rise and fall of hegemony is the key for stability of world order. The existence of hegemony is helpful for achieving the international security and the public goods, and otherwise, the disappearance of the hegemonic country brings about chaos and instability of world order. Meanwhile, the theory also insists that the presence of a single hegemonic power is a necessary and sufficient condition for the construction and maintenance of a liberal international economic system.[12] Another theory on hegemonic cycles posits that war results in and from the rise and fall of hegemony. Both approaches assume that challenging powers (or rising powers) are willing to change the status quo of international order and the conflicts between hegemon and challengers are unavoidable.[13] Accordingly, the solution of maintaining hegemonic position is to prevent rising powers from changing the present international order.

During President Bill Clinton's terms, Washington basically realized that China's power, militarily or comprehensively, was far behind the United States. The engagement strategy toward China served American national interests. As an American expert said, "there are no unmanageable U.S.-China conflicts. ...through negotiations with China, the United States can further a wide range of bilateral and regional interests and maintain regional and global stability, while simultaneously promoting change in China that reflects American values... ."[14] Even though there

---

12 See Robert Gilpin, *War and Change in World Politics* (Cambridge, England: Cambridge University Press, 1981); Charles P. Kindleberger, *The World in Depression, 1929–1939* (Berkeley: University of California Press, 1973); Stephen D. Krasner, "State Power and the Structure of International Trade" and David A. Lake, "British and American Hegemony Compared: Lessons for the Century Era of Decline" in Jeffry A. Frieden and David A Lake, ed., *International Politics Economy*, 4th Edition, jointly published by Peking University Press and Thomas Learning, 2000, pp. 19–36 and pp. 127–139.

13 See Immanuel Wallerstein, *The Modern World-System* (New York: Academic Press, 1974); and "Three Instances of Hegemony of the World Economy," *International Journal of Comparative Sociology*, vol. 24 (1983), pp. 100–108; George Modelski, "The Long Cycle of Global Politics and the Nation-State," *Comparative Studies in Society and History*, vol. 20 (April 1978), pp. 214–235. For Chinese introduction on Western studies on hegemony, see Ni Shixiong et al., *The Modern Western Theories of International Relations* (Shanghai, Fudan University Press 2001), pp. 292–305.

14 Robert S. Ross, "China: Why Our Hard-liners Are Wrong," in Eugene R. Wittkopf and Christopher M. Jones, *The Future of American Foreign Policy*, 3rd Edition, jointly published by Peking University Press and Thomas Learning, 1999, p. 214.

were crises, for instance, the bombing of the Chinese embassy in Belgrade by NATO planes in May 1999 made the China-U.S. relations plummet to the lowest level since President Nixon's visit to Beijing, the bilateral military ties had been restored to their former levels by late that year. In April 2000, Defense Secretary William Cohen visited China, and the top American military commander in the Asia-Pacific, Admiral Denis Blair, did later. Because the situation was reversed for the United States after the end of the Cold War, "...military ties between the two countries are now becoming closer than ever, as symbolized by the upcoming five-day stay in Hong Kong of a large U.S. Navy squadron," as an American specialist said, "...the Asia-Pacific region has become the center of the global economy. It is vital to American prosperity. The Euro-Atlantic region, however, has slid to second place in the global roster of American partners. ...the United States has not carried out any hostile action in the Asia-Pacific since the end of the Vietnam War in 1975. This new Asian-Pacific reality accounts for the ever closer cooperation between the American and Chinese military establishments... ."[15]

However, from the very beginning of the twenty-first century, the development of China-U.S. relations has entered a turbulent period. The American new conservative theorists and politicians understood and predicted the future of bilateral ties following the logic of cycles of rise and fall of hegemony. When comparing three powers, China, Russia and India, Washington had cognizance of the challenges from Beijing: China would more likely become the potential rival to the United States since there were more disputes between them.[16] Besides the theoretical foundation from hegemonic studies, the argument of "China Threat" had practical excuses with the growth of China's international influence and successive conflicts over the Taiwan issue in late 1990s. To use an American expert's words: "The return of Chinese students and industrial managers who have studied and worked in the West, like the manager of Hai-Er or the rocket scientist Qian Xuesen, will help China's military-technical development. Prudence and enlightened self (national) interest therefore dictate care in what is sold or transferred to China at this stage of its growth."[17] "A potential China threat" became a real security concern in American strategy and policy toward China.

Due to the wariness of China's rise, Sino-U.S. strategic mutual trust has been very hard to maintain. "As China modernizes its military capabilities, it will seek to play a more active political-military role in the affairs of East Asia. At the same

---

15 Franz Schurmann, "What's The New U.S.-China Military Relationship About?" see http://www.pacificnews.org/jinn/stories/6.02/000128-china.html.

16 Chinese Institute of Contemporary International Relations, *Global Strategy Structure: China's International Environment in the New Century* (Beijing: Shi Shi Publishing House, 2000), pp. 50–55.

17 Larry M. Wortzel, "Comments on 'China's Military-Technical Developments: The Record for Western Assessments, 1979–1999'," in James C. Mulvenon and Andrew N.D. Yang, eds., *Seeking Truth From Facts: A Retrospective on Chinese Military Studies in the Post-Mao Era* (RAND, 2001), pp. 179–180. The book can be accessed at http://www.rand.org/pubs/conf_proceedings/CF160/index.html.

time, U.S. policy calls for the maintenance of strong military forces in the region that "promote security and stability, deter conflict, give substance to [its] security commitments and ensure [its] continued access to the region. The confluence of these two tendencies raised the possibility of potential military conflict between the two countries; at the political level, it poses the question of how 'rules of the game' can be established to reduce the risk of military conflict."[18] The China-U.S. relationship is the most difficult and unstable one during the adjustment of great-power relations in the new century. The differences in ideology and political system and conflict over the Taiwan issue have made the bilateral strategic cooperation not as substantial as that between the U.S. and Russia. China considers itself as "a growing power" or "an emerging power," and would not challenge American leadership in the Asia-Pacific region. But Washington views China differently. For example, in the 2002 U.S.-China Economic and Security Review Report, it says, "China aspires to be a major international power and the dominant power in Asia" and China "believes that the United States is a declining power with important military vulnerabilities that can be exploited." The gap between them on the calculation and understanding of China's power easily stirs up fundamental and structural disputes, multilateral and bilateral. "Because China is not a status-quo country, its size and rapid emergence as a magnet for foreign investment and advanced technologies and the growth of its military capabilities have sounded alarm bells in the U.S., and in other industrialized democracies."[19] As a matter of fact, from the end of September 2001 to the summer of 2002, reports from DoD and intelligence bureaucracies all imply the basic points from theories of hegemonic studies. The rise and fall of hegemony reminds Washington that the military strategy toward China should be readjusted in order to prevent the challenges from China's rise.

China's Military Modernization: A Deepening Security Concern

China set the goal of achieving military modernization about thirty years ago. However, the American concern of China's growing military power has aggravated in recent years. Even after China-U.S. military confrontation in the East China Sea during the Taiwan crises in the middle of 1990s, the United States still calculated that the main threats came from proliferation of Weapons of Massive Destruction (WMD), and China would have no capability to challenge its leadership in East Asia in ten years.[20] This basic judgment of China's military power didn't change until the Bush government took office in early 2001. From then on, the theory of China threat,

---

18 Abram N. Shulsky, "Deterrence Theory and Chinese Behavior," Report of Rand's Project Air Force (MR-1161-AF, 2000), p. 1.

19 "China's Perceptions of the United States and Strategic Thinking," the Chapter in the Report to Congress of the U.S.-China Security Review Commission, "The National Security Implications of the Economic Relationship Between the United States and China," released on July 15, 2002.

20 National Defense University, *Strategic Assessment 1997*, p. xii, The U.S. Government Printing Office, Washington, D.C., 1997.

a debating topic in American academic, business and political circles since early in the post-Cold War era, evolved to be an important and acquiescent security concern in Washington's China policy decision-making process.[21] In almost all China-related official reports on national security since 2001, the increasing vigilance of China's military power is implied.

The Quadrennial Defense Review (QDR) Report 2001 obliquely points out, "The possibility exists that a military competitor with a formidable resource base will emerge in the region [Asia]. The East Asian littoral – from the Bay of Bengal to the Sea of Japan – represents a particularly challenging area." In order to deter the potential threats, the military power would have to be strengthened in Western Pacific according to the DoD's military plan.[22] In early 2002, the U.S. National Foreign Intelligence Board released the unclassified summary of a National Intelligence Estimate on ballistic missile developments and threats, it holds that "China has had the capability to develop and deploy a multiple reentry vehicle system" and presumes that "the overall size of Chinese strategic ballistic missile forces over the next 15 years, ranging from about 75 to 100 warheads deployed primarily against the United States."[23] On March 2002, the Los Angeles Times reported that the Bush administration had directed the military to prepare contingency plans to use nuclear weapons against at least seven countries and to build smaller nuclear weapons for use in certain battlefield situations, including a regional war between Mainland China and Taiwan.[24] On July 12, the DoD submitted the "Annual Report on the Military Power of the People's Republic of China" to the congress, in which said China's military budget was much higher than the figure declared and the accelerating military modernization would counterbalance the U.S. power in Asia Pacific and force Taiwan to unify with China.[25] Just three days later, the U.S.-China Economic and Security Review Report warned that "Beijing is working to counter

---

21 Debates on China's military modernization and its implications to regional security and the United States were popular among American specialists in late 1990s and the debates to a large extent just remained in academics. For elaborations, see Bates Gill and Michael O'Hanlon, "China's Hollow Military," *The National Interest*, no. 56 (Summer 1999), pp. 55–62; James Lilly and Carl Ford, "China's Military: A Second Opinion," *The National Interest*, no. 57 (Fall 1999), pp. 71–77; Thomas J. Christensen, "China, the U.S.-Japan Alliance and the Security Dilemma in East Asia," *International Security*, vol. 23, no. 4 (Spring 1999), pp. 49–80; Most achievements implied China had not posed an immediate military threat against, but a considerable security concern to the national security of the United States.

22 Defense Department of the United States, "Quadrennial Defense Review," Sept. 30, 2001, p. 4.

23 U.S. National Intelligence Council, "Foreign Missile Developments and the Ballistic Missile Threat Through 2015" Report, December 2001.

24 Paul Richter, "U.S. Works Up Plan for Using Nuclear Arms," *Los Angeles Times*, March 9, 2002; "Nuclear Posture Review Report" was submitted to Congress on 31 December 2001 by DoD of the United States.

25 The Defense Department of the United States, "Annual Report on the Military Power of the People's Republic of China," released on July 12, 2002.

U.S. influence and competition by preparing if needed to subdue American forces via military modernization, including asymmetric means of warfare." And the report recommended that the Congress required strict action over export controls.[26] In the report on national security strategy published by the White House in September of the same year, the Bush Government emphasized the United States "welcome[s] the emergence of a strong, peaceful, and prosperous China," but warned that "in pursuing advanced military capabilities that can threaten its neighbors in the Asia-Pacific region, China is following an outdated path…" and it candidly admitted both countries have "profound disagreement" over the Taiwan issue and others.[27] It is well known Washington and Beijing went through a most difficult time in the first half of 2001 due to the collision between a Chinese jet fighter and a U.S. spy plane over the South China Sea. Therefore, it is worthy to note that all these reports, published in 12 months since September 11, 2001, had strategic motivations of assessing and forecasting China's rise and overall China-U.S. relations, not fundamentally influenced by the ongoing worldwide antiterrorism war.

At the very beginning of the Bush Administration's second term, U.S. Defense Secretary Donald Rumsfeld, Central Intelligence Agency director Porter Goss and Defense Intelligence Agency head Admiral Lowell Jacoby delivered a series of warnings on China's military expansion. They focused on the increasing number of missiles that are being deployed across the Taiwan Strait, the acceleration in Chinese defense spending and the rapid increase in the size of Beijing's navy.

In the annual reports on China's military power released in the past three years, the DoD has increasingly publicized the rapidly growing military modernization and power-projection capabilities, indicating that security concerns on China-U.S. military confrontation has been deepening significantly. At a regional security conference in Singapore in early June of 2005, U.S. Defense Secretary Donald H. Rumsfeld argued in his keynote address that China's investment in missiles and up-to-date military technology posed a risk not only to Taiwan and to American interests, but also to nations across Asia. The 2005 annual report on China's military power said "the Cross-Strait military balance appears to be shifting toward Beijing" and "the PLA is generating military capabilities that go beyond a Taiwan scenario." It claimed that PLA military preparations include "an expanding force of ballistic missiles (long-range and short-range), cruise missiles, submarines, advanced aircraft, and other modern systems" and "Such an acceleration of China's military modernization would have direct implications for stability in the Taiwan Strait and the safety of U.S. personnel; it would also accelerate a shift in the regional balance

---

26 Report to Congress of the U.S.-China Security Review Commission, "The National Security Implications of the Economic Relationship Between the United States and China," released on July 15, 2002.

27 The White House, "The National Security Strategy of the United States of America," September 2002, pp. 27–28.

of power, affecting the security of many countries."[28] The 2005 report by the U.S.-China Economic and Security Review Commission had the same tone when it talked about Chinese military.

Furthermore, the booming Chinese economy intensifies the wariness of realist theorists. For example, the proponent of offensive realism, John J. Mearsheimer, argues that economic power could surely back military power. His imagination of China's strength is elaborated in his so many "ifs":

> To illustrate China's potential, consider the following scenarios. If China modernizes to the point where it has about the same per capita GNP as South Korea does today, China would have a GNP of $10.66 trillion, substantially larger that Japan's $4.09 trillion economy. If China's per capita GNP grew to be just half of Japan's present per capita GNP, China would have a GNP of $20.04 trillion, which would make China almost five times as wealthy as Japan. Finally, if China have about the same per capita GNP as Japan, China would be ten times as wealthy as Japan, because China has almost ten times as many people as Japan. Another way of illustrating how powerful China might become if its economy continues growing rapidly is to compare it with the United States. The GNP of the United States is $7.9 trillion. If China's per capita GNP equals Korea's, China's overall GNP would be almost $10.66 trillion, which is about 1.35 times the size of American's GNP. If China's per capita GNP is half of Japan's, China's overall GNP would then be roughly 2.5 times bigger that American's. For purposes of comparison, the Soviet Union was roughly one-half as wealthy as the United States during most of the Cold war. China, in short, has the potential to be considerably more powerful than even the United States.[29]

According to his logic of power transfer, it is not surprising to arrive at his alarming conclusion and prediction:

> If that [China's economy continues modernizing at a rapid pace] happens, it would almost certainly use its wealth to build a mighty military machine. ...for sound strategic reasons, it would surely pursue regional hegemony... . What makes a future Chinese threat so worrisome is that it might be far more powerful and dangerous than any of the potential hegemons that the United States confronted in the twentieth century.[30]

This kind of argument regarding China's challenges shows that "China threat" not only comes from the economic fields in which China and the Unites States have more cooperation, but also from the military competition, even more seriously, backed by economic growth.

---

28 See 2005 Report to Congress of the U.S.-China Economic and Security Review Commission First Session, November 2005, Chapter 3, pp. 115–142. Also see "The Chinese Military Threat," Editorial, *Washington Times*, July 23, 2005.

29 John J. Mearsheimer, *The Tragedy of Great Power Politics* (New York: W.W. Norton & Company, 2001), p. 398; His scenarios of China's potential were simultaneously published by a leading journal of international studies, see John J. Mearsheimer, "The Future of the American Pacifier," *Foreign Affairs* (September/October 2001), p. 55.

30 John J. Mearsheimer, *The Tragedy of Great Power Politics*, p. 401.

Evolution of the Taiwan Issue and East Asia Security Environment

The history of China-U.S. relations shows that the Taiwan issue has been always the most important and sensitive problem in bilateral relationship. A unified China (even by peaceful means) could bring Beijing strategic advantages, especially by accelerating China's naval and air forces.[31] In the last decade, the sharp contradiction between Taiwan forces advocating independence and the determination of Chinese people to achieve reunification emerged not only as a big strategic challenge to China's peaceful rise, but also as a strategic opportunity for the United States to deplete China's capacity to some extent, politically, economically and militarily.

China cannot maintain a stable international environment for economic development when facing rampant separatism in Taiwan. In order to deter creeping independence, the Chinese government formulated the Anti-Secession Law on March 14, 2005. Before the law passed, U.S.-Japan "2+2" Security Consultation Committee meeting (2+2 meeting), between the U.S. Secretary of State Condoleezza Rice, Secretary of Defense Donald Rumsfeld and their Japanese counterparts, issued a joint statement after the one-day consultation that for the first time included "the peaceful resolution of issues concerning the Taiwan Strait through dialogue," which was protested by Beijing for an encroachment on China's sovereignty and meddling in its internal affairs. Eight months later, the United States and Japan announced at the second round "2+2 meeting" a sweeping agreement to reshape their military alliance, including the reduction of marines on Okinawa and the construction of a new generation of radar equipment in Japan as part of a missile defense system. In the middle of November, U.S. President George W. Bush reiterated his support for the U.S.-Japan alliance, vital to the peace and stability of Asia Pacific, when he met Japanese Prime Minister Koizumi Junichiro in Kyoto.

Under these circumstances, the geopolitical configuration has been undergoing fundamental changes: the accelerating speed of China-U.S.-Japan-Russia quadrilateral relations, the long-standing nuclear crisis on the Korean Peninsula involving four great powers, the worrisome stalemate of China-Japan relations, the strengthening U.S.-Japan military alliance and so on. It seems to be inevitable and very difficult to prevent China's rise politically and economically since China has been an important part of world economy and community. Both China and the United States don't want to follow the self-fulfilling prophecy of making an enemy of each other. Over the Taiwan issue, on the one hand, the United States consequently has been promoting Washington-Taipei military cooperation; on the other hand, it is reluctant to see "immediate independence" of Taiwan which most likely brings it into a war with China. Meanwhile, the remilitarization of Japan backed by the United States adds uncertainties and instabilities to the Asia Pacific region.

---

31 Nancy Tucker, "If Taiwan Choose Unification, Should the United States Care?" *The Washington Quarterly* (Summer 2002), pp. 21–22.

Adjustment of U.S. Military Strategy Toward China

As the sole superpower, the United States had considered shifting its strategic center to Asia Pacific in the late 1990s, given the continuing great-power cooperation and the legacy of the end of Cold War. This strategic shift conducted by the Bush Administration has been going well, thanks to China's rise and the essential changes in East Asia. To argue whether or not the American military strategy has changed doesn't make any sense. The question is how it has been changing.

More Antagonistic, Less Friendly

The debate on whether China is a friend or an enemy almost went through two terms of Clinton Administration. The Bush government regards China as a "strategic competitor," not a "strategic partner," based on long-term assessment of China's potential power, not temporary tactical policy consideration. The main characteristic of American strategy toward China might be summarized to be "China is not an enemy, but like an enemy." However, in the military field, the U.S. policy apparently is "more antagonistic and less friendly."

Undoubtedly the strategic mutual suspicions of intentions between China and the Unites States have been increasing inch by inch. And U.S. policy toward China definitely has "no return to Nixon era" as one American scholar puts it, since China is no longer regarded as a strategic leverage to balance a common peer enemy such as the Soviet Union.[32] The nature of China-U.S. military relations has changed fundamentally. With the structural conflict over the Taiwan issue, to see China as a potential military rival or a threat appears to be more convincing. But China is also not regarded rashly as an "existing enemy" in a foreseeable future when the bilateral economic interdependence and non-traditional security cooperation have been expanding and deepening. The military contacts and exchanges are also necessary for the United States to know Chinese military as well as it can and the starting point is to prevent China developing into "*a real enemy*" from its current status as "*a potential threat*." That is to say, in case of bilateral military conflict, the United States is willing to avoid an unfavorable situation by improving military communication and confidence building measures (CBMs). A "more antagonistic and less friendly" strategy toward China will continue in the next decade or more.

Offensive Deterrence at the Core

The readjustment of American military strategy toward China in the new century is certain to be more preventive, taking offensive deterrence strategy at the core and exchange as a supplement. This was a vital reason for blocking China-U.S. military contacts from early 2001 to late 2003. That is why there has been more alertness in

---

32 Jim Mann, "On China, No Return to Nixon Era," *Los Angeles Times*, February 7, 2001.

China-U.S. military relations, but more support and appeasement in U.S.-Taiwan military relations.

With the rapid growth of China's military power and its outreaching capability, the military wariness and strategic precautions will not be diminishing, but will increase sharply. As American Robert Kaplan puts it: "the fight between Beijing and Washington over the Pacific will not dominate all of world politics, but it will be the most important of several regional struggles. Yet it will be the organizing focus for the U.S. defense posture abroad." Therefore, the U.S. Pacific Command has to do militarily, geopolitically, even humanitarianly, to form part of American "deterrence strategy against China."[33] However, it should be noted particularly that the offensive deterrence strategy is mainly for preventive purposes, as Gen. Michael Moseley, appointed to be the next Air Force chief of staff, said with regard to the motivation of U.S. Air Force, "This is not the Air Force saying we want to go to war with China. This is the Air Force saying if we want to avoid war with China, we've got to be able to hold their critical capabilities at risk lest Beijing be tempted to use force to resolve disputes it has with other countries in the region."[34] Military deterrence is not tantamount to confrontation; prevention is not tantamount to cooperation. Deterrence and prevention strategy will not rule out China-U.S. overall cooperation, since cooperation could still be the best choice that might avoid the bilateral military conflicts.

To Establish East Asia Security Net

Given its relevance to China's sovereignty and territorial integrity and geopolitical importance to national interests of both China and the United States, the Taiwan issue is the most likely catalyst of conflict between the two big powers. The Taiwan issue is related to China's sovereignty, unification and China's rise. Thus, in order to deter and prevent a potential enemy, the United States has to establish and has been establishing an East Asia security net by strengthening its military alliances with South Korea, Japan, the Philippines and even Thailand and Singapore. "Although not officially calling its policy in East Asia 'containment,' the United States has ringed China with formal and informal alliances and a forward military presence."[35] It has been carrying out adjustment of military presence in Guam and Japan's Okinawa and military cooperation with Taiwan and the Philippines so that the first ring of defense islands along China's eastern coastal line can be connected. For example, the Guam base is regarded as a deterrent bridgehead that enjoys very high geographic advantage of enhancing long-range strike capability in East Asia.

The United States sees the building of a security net in East Asia has been inherently workable with the reaction of Southeast Asian countries toward China's

---

33 Robert D. Kaplan, "How We Would Fight China," *Atlantic Monthly*, June 2005.

34 "U.S. Struggles on China-war Planning," *Reuters*, June 29, 2005.

35 Ivan Eland, "Is Chinese Military Modernization a Threat to the United States?" *Policy Analysis*, Cato Institute, No. 465 (January 23, 2003), p. 1.

rise. As Abram N. Shulsky explained, "In future crises, China will have to be concerned that its threat or use of force will encourage neighboring states to see her as an emerging strategic threat against which they must band together." He illustrated with an example of China-Philippines dispute on Mischief Reef in 1995 in which The Association of Southeast Asia Nations (ASEAN) drew somewhat closer together in support of the Philippines, one of the members, over the dispute. "This type of regional reaction, encouraged and supported by the United States, may be the best deterrent to Chinese use of force in the region," he concluded.[36] In this way, it will be much easier to strengthen the security net in case China had a military conflict with its neighboring states.

U.S. Military Policy Toward China

The judgment of China's military growth and motivation has made the U.S. military policy toward Beijing in recent years more vigilant and preventive, with four kinds of countermeasures.

Strengthen Pressures through Readjustment of Asia Pacific Military Power

Regional security challenges brought by a rising China are the driving force for the U.S. to shift its military concentration to West Pacific because almost all the possible tensions in East Asia have relations with Beijing, from Korean peninsula, Diaoyu Islands, to Taiwan Island, and to the South China Sea islets. The Pentagon has been redeploying military presence in Korea, Japan, its Guam base and Hawaii.

According to the guidelines of 2001 QDR and other DoD reports, Defense Secretary Rumsfeld has been conducting a fundamental revision in the U.S. defense posture that is intended to counter a potential threat from China basically repositioning the U.S. forces worldwide to increase its capabilities in the West Pacific region. As the report reveals, American defense officials in Washington, at the Pacific Command in Hawaii, and in Asia have spent many months seeking to bring Rumsfeld's policy to reality. They have fashioned a plan intended to strengthen the operational control of the Pacific Command, enhance forces in the U.S. territory of Guam, tighten the alliance with Japan and streamline the U.S. stance in South Korea. The changes include: The U.S. Army headquarters in Hawaii will become a war-fighting command to devise and execute operations rather than one that trains and provides troops to other commands as it does now; The Marines, who have a war-fighting center in Hawaii, will move the headquarters of the 3rd Marine Expeditionary Force (III MEF) to Guam from Okinawa; The 13th Air Force, including three Global Hawk unmanned reconnaissance aircrafts moved to Hawaii from Guam in May to give that service a war-fighting headquarters like those of the other services; a nuclear-powered aircraft carrier is scheduled to replace the conventionally powered

---

36 Abram N. Shulsky, "Deterrence Theory and Chinese Behavior," pp. 54–54.

aircraft carrier Kitty Hawk by 2008. "All in all, these changes will take upwards of three years to complete during which time Beijing can be expected to object in no uncertain terms."[37] As a step of re-enforcing U.S.-Japan alliance and repositioning U.S. forces, the bilateral "2+2 meeting" held in late October 2005 announced that a sweeping agreement to reshape their military alliance, including the reduction of marines on Okinawa and the construction of a new generation of radar equipment in Japan as part of a missile defense system.

At the same time, the U.S. military officials have been researching to win a war with China for the worst case. The appointed Air Force chief of staff Gen. Michael Moseley said at his confirmation hearing before the Senate Armed Services Committee that the Defense Department is struggling to determine the right mix of bombers and other warplanes to fight China if it ever became necessary. A report quoting from a retired military official says that "Moseley likely was referring to the warplanes – manned and unmanned – needed to take out command posts, radar installations, surface-to-air missile sites, air fields and military headquarters. Many such targets are deep in China's interior."[38] At a time of growing showdowns across the Taiwan Strait and on the Korean Peninsula, the plan of readjustment for American military forces in the Asia Pacific region could be highly sensitive and meaningful.

Accelerating Military Relations with Taiwan

The Taiwan problem could be a Pandora's box that will inevitably shape a new military balance in the Asia Pacific region. Although the U.S. sales of sophisticated military equipments to Taiwan have the suspicion of preventing China's unification and China's rise, encouraging radical separatists in Taiwan and anti-American sentiments in the Mainland, the concern of unbalanced Cross-Strait military power has been directly driving close U.S.-Taiwan military ties. The arms sales to Taiwan, a means of both deterring China's military power and gaining economic benefits in the Cross-Strait dispute, will continue as a major leverage in maintaining overall balance in this region.

In April 2001, the Bush administration presented a large package of arms sales including eight diesel-electric submarines, six Patriot antimissile batteries, 12 P-3C antisubmarine aircraft, and other items worth $15 billion to $18 billion. On September 30, 2002, President Bush signed the National Defense Authorization Act for the Fiscal Year 2003, passed by the House of Representatives in which according to section 1206, the United States should regard Taiwan as a "Non-NATO alliance" in terms of arms sales. However, the unbalanced domestic power struggles in Taiwan, mainly among the Democratic Progressive Party, the Nationalist Party and the First Party, unexpectedly have blocked this purchase in the legislature ever since. While requiring Taiwan to do more to prepare for its own defense against a potential attack

---

37 Richard Halloran, "Checking the Threat That Could Be China," *Japan Times*, June 12, 2005.

38 "U.S. Struggles on China-war Planning," *Reuters*, June 29, 2005.

from China rather than rely largely on the United States for its security, the United States has imposed pressures by sending Taiwan a message publicly and privately that, "if it doesn't [buy more weapons to defend itself], the U.S. may be less obligated to come to Taiwan's rescue."[39] The DoD annual report on China's military power released in July 2005 particularly noted that the military balance across the Taiwan Strait "appears to be shifting toward Beijing" and China's military modernization "has increased the need for countermeasures that would enable Taiwan to avoid being quickly overwhelmed."[40]

The U.S.-Taiwan military cooperation and exchange have been improving since the Clinton Administration. The military officers from the Pacific command headquarters were sent regularly to observe Taiwan's "Chinese Glory" military exercise. In May of 2005, the U.S. House of Representatives passed the National Defense Authorization Act for 2006, which contains a section requesting that "the secretary of defense shall undertake a program of senior military officer and senior official exchanges with Taiwan designed to improve Taiwan's defenses against the People's Liberation Army of the People's Republic of China." According to the section, the term "exchanges" means any activities, exercises, events, or observation opportunities between U.S. military personnel or DoD officials and Taiwan armed forces personnel or defense officials, The term "senior military officer" means any active duty general or flag officer of the U.S. armed forces, and the term "senior official" means a civilian official of the DoD at the level of deputy assistant secretary of defense or above. It is expected to see escalating U.S.-Taiwan military exchanges and cooperation in the foreseeable future.

The Unbalanced China-Japan-U.S. Triangle Relations

Geopolitical competition in East Asia is one of the critical reasons for Tokyo and Washington to walk together. Both the U.S. and Japan view China as a strategic competitor and a potential military threat. To some extent, it is not so much a trilateral relationship as a bilateral relationship. The U.S.-Japan's deep cooperation over BMD and anti-terrorism has defeated the utopian idea of a China-Japan or China-U.S. alliance. Furthermore, the U.S.'s unilateral support to Japanese remilitarization also shadows the unbalanced triangle relations.

China-Japan relationship has entered the "Cold War" era because of setbacks in all bilateral fields except trade cooperation, and trade cannot guarantee improvement of political relationships or prevent their deterioration. To make use of Japan as a military leverage of constraining China's rise is a very easy and effective alternative strategically and tactically for the United States. The 2+2 meetings have set up foundation for further military integration between the United States and Japan

---

39 Richard Halloran, "Taiwan Skimping on Defense Readiness," *Japan Times*, August 22, 2005.

40 The Defense Department of the United States, "Annual Report on the Military Power of the People's Republic of China 2005," pp. 6 and 37.

legally and practically and significantly enhanced Japan's growing military power. In its new defense white paper released in August 2005, the Japanese government defined the future role of its Self Defense Forces (SDF) as one that was better able to deal with new threats to national security such as ballistic missile attacks and terrorism, and should be wary of China's increasing defense budget and modernization of its military. As a Japanese military analyst interpreted, "China is now watched as a military power in Asia, and yes, Japan's new policy is to be able to have its SDF ready to respond militarily if there is an attack from that country or any other."[41] In late December 2005, Japanese Junichiro Koizumi's government has formally committed to the joint development of a new sea-based interceptor missile as a main pillar of the U.S.-led missile defense system, marking another significant step toward strengthening Japan's security alliance with the U.S. This decision was seen as being made in breach of the so-called peace clause of the constitution, which specifically renounces the country's capacity to make war. And the joint project, whose products will be sold to the U.S., will also technically break Japan's strict embargo on exporting arms.

Multilateral Export Control to China

Since the U.S.-China Economic and Security Review Commission in 2002 claimed that China had been continuing to supply technology and components for weapons of mass destruction and their delivery systems to terrorist-sponsoring states, the United States has been reinforcing bilateral and multilateral export control efforts, especially hi-tech equipments which might be used or transferred for military purposes. For instance, in July 2005, the U.S. government imposed a fine of $47millions on the Boeing company for violating its American export control regulations, referring to the civilian planes sold as being capable of carrying missile and satellite guiding systems. In late December 2005, six Chinese companies were sanctioned by the U.S. administration for transferring sensitive weapons and technologies to Iran. In 2003, Hughes Electronics Corporation and Boeing Satellite Systems Inc. received a civil penalty in the amount of $32 million for charges by the U.S. Department of State for involvement in reviews of two failed launches of commercial communications satellites on Chinese rockets in 1995 and 1996.

Meanwhile, the United States has also tightened the screws of export control toward China multilaterally. Israel and the United States have been locked in talks over Israel's planned sale to China of spare parts for Harpy drone aircraft and the latter objects on the grounds it would upgrade China's anti-radar aircraft. In June 2005, the Israeli government was forced to cancel the arms deal with China and later the United States demanded a written apology and tighter restrictions on Israeli weapons exports as conditions for lifting military sanctions.[42] Five years ago, the

---

41 Suvendrini Kakuchi, "Japan Bares Its Sword," *Asia Times*, August 5, 2005.
42 Danielle Haas, "U.S. Seeks Written Apology from Israel over China Weapons Deal," *Associated Press*, July 28, 2005.

United States pressured Israel to cancel plans to sell Falcon reconnaissance aircraft to China. "It was the result of a U.S. campaign to block China from obtaining advanced military technology that could be used against Taiwan and U.S. forces supporting the island in any confrontation," as a report says.[43] In July 2005, the European Union was not released as scheduled from the arms sale prohibition against China, under heavy pressures from the United States. The House of Representatives even passed The East Asia Security Act of 2005 on 21 July, requiring new and tougher export licensing requirements for access to sensitive U.S. weapons technology for those selling arms to China, and tightening export controls on their purchase of dual-use items, which have both military and industrial applications.

Implications for China-U.S. Relations and Regional Security

Since Rumsfeld's remarks in early June 2005 in Singapore denouncing the expansion of China's military power, China's military threat seemed to be a fashionable topic and has come to dominate the debate in the American mass media. A blue team member, Bill Gertz, journalist of *The Washington Times*, even wrote two articles on the same day, warning of the coming of China's military threat.[44] Robert Kaplan, an expert in international security, told the public "how we [the United States] would fight China" because "China will be a more formidable adversary than Russia ever was" militarily.[45] Would the American military policy toward China be more assertive and tougher in the next three years of the Bush Administration? As an American journalist commented, "Rumsfeld's remarks seem to be an opening salvo in what could become a public, high-level debate about the threat a modern Chinese military poses to the global balance of power."[46] Generally speaking, the rapid growth of China's missile capabilities, air force and navy might put Asia's military balance at risk, in other words, drive the asymmetric military relationship in an unbalanced direction. People have reasons to worry about "U.S. Sights Are Back on China" when the war on terror seems to be waning.[47] A realist approach has been playing a leading role in U.S. military policy consideration to China. The stability or instability of bilateral military relationship might largely shape the direction of overall China-U.S. relations and Asia security during the twenty-first century. In order to avoid the bad scenarios in which China may confront the United States directly, for students of China-U.S. relations, several factors need to be taken seriously into consideration.

---

43 Edward Cody, "China Scolds U.S. for Blocking Israeli Arms Sale," *Washington Post*, June 28, 2005.

44 Bill Gertz, "Chinese Dragon Awakens," *Washington Times*, June 27, 2005; Bill Gertz, "Thefts of U.S. Technology Boost China's Weaponry," *Washington Times*, June 27, 2005.

45 Robert D. Kaplan, "How We Would Fight China."

46 Mark Mazzetti, "Rumsfeld warns Asia officials of China's military advances," *Los Angeles Times*, June 5, 2005.

47 Michael Vatikiotis, "U.S. Sights Are Back on China," *International Herald Tribune*, June 7, 2005.

First, the role of geopolitics is increasing in Asia and Western Pacific. The United States has been promoting its military influence around China so as to build geopolitical chains in Northeast Asia, Southeast Asia, South Asia and Central Asia since the global war on terror. The Shanghai Cooperation Organization, in which Russia and China are facing geopolitical pressures from the United States in recent years, called for withdrawal of American troops worrying the U.S.-backed "color revolution" could spread in Central Asia countries. Even Mongolia, geographically sandwiched between China and Russia, cannot escape from great-power competition. Alarmed by China's rapid rise, and to a lesser extent by its developing collaboration with Russia, "it [Mongolia] has been steadily drawn into…the 'strategic net' being woven by the U.S. in Asia to 'persuade China to keep its ambitions within reason'."[48] Various pieces of evidence demonstrate the geo-strategic intentions and competitions: in the summer of 2005, China and Russia held the first joint military exercise in Northeast Asia; on October 22 of the year, Defense Secretary Rumsfeld immediately flew to Mongolia after his China visit; only one month later, President Bush again followed the same route for a four-hour visit to Ulaanbaatar. The consequences of geopolitics are apparent everywhere in China-U.S. military relationship.

Second, the evolution of international relations in Asia Pacific is quite complicated and unstable. Most Asian countries are rethinking their positions in China-U.S. relations, bringing political, economic and military concerns into their foreign policies. For instance, The ASEAN countries choose a balancing policy toward China, the United States, Japan, India, and even South Korea, but it hasn't worked well under the "10+3" framework or by building an East Asian community in the recent East Asia summit. How would the Central Asian countries choose their foreign policy directions in the heart of the Eurasian chessboard? The following uncertain problems come from East Asia: will the China-U.S.-Japan triangular relations go in the direction against China's national security? How can the China-Japan relations stop deteriorating and get out of the longstanding stalemate? Where will Japan's remilitarization go in the next decade? What is the future of nuclear crisis on the Korean Peninsula? Nobody can give definite answers to these questions, implying the uncertainties in Asia and Western Pacific.

Third, the politicization and securitization of economic and trade disputes has appeared in Sino-U.S. relations. The strategic intention of constraining or preventing China's growth power can be illustrated from limiting Chinese textile export, pressing Beijing to revalue its currency, to interfering in the business purchasing cases. Compared to the policy of linking China's Most Favored Nation (MFN) status to human rights in the first term of the Clinton Administration, the lawmakers in the Congress took action to link the economic and trade disputes to national security topics. For example, in the summer of 2005, the bidding competition between the Chinese National Offshore Oil Corporation (CNOOC) and U.S.-based oil giant Chevron to purchase California-based oil company Unocal heated up when the U.S. House of Representatives voted 398–15 for a measure calling on President

---

48 Simon Tisdall, "U.S. Pushes at China's Edges," The *Guardian*, August 12, 2005.

George W. Bush to review the CNOOC's $18.5 billion bid, citing security threats, including the possible transfer of military technology to China. As a commentary in *The New York Times* said, "From the dusty plains of East Africa to the shores of the Caspian Sea, China is seeking to loosen the grip of the United States on world energy resources and secure the fuel it needs to keep its economy in overdrive."[49] Actually, in early 2005, China's largest computer manufacturer, the Lenovo Group Ltd experienced similar criticisms for endangering American national security when it wanted to buy the International Business Machines Corp.'s personal computer business. The securitization of economic and trade affairs will be more obvious in the future with the interaction of both economic powers.

Fourth, the military mutual-trust is pressing to be rebuilt between China and the United States. Mistrust and misunderstanding in Sino-U.S. relations exist and have been increasing in recent years. Strategic suspicion begins to affect specific policies over the Taiwan problem, economic and trade disputes, and even more importantly, military contacts and communications. Although the bilateral military contact resumed in 2003 after a two-year break from April 1, 2001, the political implications surpassed its military implications since there were no substantial CBMs established between the two militaries. From early 2004, China-U.S. military communication has been improving. The Joint Chiefs of Staff chairman, Gen. Richard B. Myers said during his Beijing visit in January 2004 that there is a "positive momentum" in the security relationship and "the U.S. seeks a constructive and stable military relationship with China" from which the United States could benefit from expanding bilateral military education exchanges, especially between our academies and war colleges.[50] In late October 2004, chairman of the general staff of the People's Liberation Army, General Liang Guanglie visited the Pentagon and held talks with Rumsfeld. In late January of 2005, Richard Lawless, deputy assistant secretary of defense for the Asia Pacific region led a defense delegation to Beijing and held "the first-ever special policy dialogue" with Chinese counterparts. Both countries also held consultation on maritime military security in July. The first round of bi-annual strategic dialogue was held August 1–3 in Beijing, with topics ranging from bilateral and multilateral concerns. In early December 2005, two delegations led by U.S. Deputy Secretary of State Robert B. Zoellick and Chinese Vice Foreign Minister Dai Bingguo respectively launched the second round of talks in Washington, on trade, energy and international security problems. The senior dialogues were helpful for building strategic military understanding and improving bilateral military exchanges. On October 18, Defense Secretary Rumsfeld made his first official trip

---

49 Joseph Kahn, "Behind China's Bid for Unocal: A Costly Quest for Energy Control," *The New York Times*, June 27, 2005. For more news sources on whether or not the deal would threaten U.S. national security, see the article with collections and analysis by Matthew Clark, "China: A Security Threat to U.S.?" *Christian Science Monitor*, June 28, 2005.

50 Jim Garamone, "China, U.S. Making Progress on Military Relations," American Forces Press Service, see http://www.defenselink.mil/news/Jan2004/n01152004_200401152.html.

to Beijing since he took up his current job in 2001, and held a "straightforward exchange" with Chinese counterpart General Cao Gangchuan, on strategic concerns – including China's military buildup. During his unprecedented visit, he was invited to the headquarters of China's nuclear forces. Contrasting his frequent and sudden secretive visits to Iraq and Afghanistan, the visit to Beijing was largely symbolic. However, this was a very good beginning for high-level China-U.S. military talks and exchanges and opened a new chapter in history since we entered the new century. What both can and should do next is to regularize the meetings between the two defense heads, expand channels and improve substantial exchanges.

Lastly, the militarizing trend of the Taiwan issue will be more apparent. Washington cares more about the rise of China and its overall challenges to American hegemony in a long run than it does about the Cross-Strait problem itself. While posing growing military pressures on China, the Taiwan problem will continue not only politically, but more importantly militarily. The cooperation between the United States and Taiwan has been deepening for decades, from military personnel exchanges to military exercises. Meanwhile, the United States pressures the Taiwanese to purchase defensive and offensive weapons by exaggerating the military threat from Beijing. Under such circumstances, the three "stops" related to the Taiwan issue raised by Chinese government requests to the Uniteds States, would be a very difficult diplomatic task for any Chinese government.[51]

Conclusion

The China-U.S. military relationship is critical for Asia-Pacific security, stability and prosperity in the twenty-first century. Generally speaking, the foundation for an asymmetric-but-stable China-U.S. military relationship has gradually becoming shaky because of growing strategic mistrusts with the rise of China's military power and U.S. military precautions. The key questions are: will the asymmetric and unstable bilateral military relationship evolve to ignite military conflicts? Or is there any possibility of making the conflict manageable and controllable.

On the one hand, the U.S. military strategy toward China is a mixture of "encirclement" and "engagement" which implies deterrent and preventive motivation as a theme. To encircle China is supposed to gain more benefits in the

---

51 During her visit to Beijing in early July 2004, U.S. national security adviser Condoleezza Rice was urged by Chinese Foreign Minister Li Zhaoxing that the United States should "stop selling advanced armaments to Taiwan, stop military and official relations with Taiwan, and stop supporting Taiwan's participation in the activities of those international organizations that only sovereign states can join." On July 24, 2004, Li Zhaoxing told the visiting commander-in-chief of the U.S. Pacific Command Admiral Thomas Fargo that "the United States should clearly understand the seriousness and sensitivity of the Taiwan situation," and he called for Washington to stop arms sales to Taiwan, stop its relevant military exchanges aiming to upgrade the substantial relationship with Taiwan, and stop upgrading the substantial relationship with Taiwan.

military engagement, and to engage China is better to conduct the encirclement purpose. There are critical disagreements between China and the United States, such as Taiwan and non-proliferation issues, but as the White House said: "we will work to narrow differences where they exist, but not allow them to preclude cooperation where we agree."[52] Although not enough, continuing cooperation has been going on between China and the United States in the global war on terrorism, showing strong, early, public support. Now that non-confrontational but preventive motivation exists in American military strategy toward China, the United States is expected to improve the bilateral military exchanges. China has the same conclusion through a different logic of understanding China-U.S. relations because three strategic dilemmas remain as the greatest challenges for the Chinese government in a decade and more.[53] With regard to the Taiwan dispute, human rights and others, it is notable that the bi-annual strategic dialogues since 2005 are very helpful for leaderships in Beijing and Washington to re-establish strategic mutual trust and avoid mutual misunderstanding between them. Neither China nor the United States wants to see the military relationship out of control.

Although it is almost universally accepted in the United States that China is on its way to becoming a military challenge in Asia, on the other hand, most people also agree the military asymmetry will continue for at least two decades. Moreover a large space for cooperation expands in the overall bilateral relations, such as over regional security, trade, environmental protection, anti-terrorism, non-proliferation etc. The unbalanced military power of China is a precondition for a stable military relationship. As a response to U.S. BMD plans, China has to reassess its long-standing nuclear policy of minimal deterrence by seeking survivability and second-strike capability, otherwise, the present stable and asymmetric nuclear balance will be broken by U.S. unilateral shift of nuclear strategy. However, China should never pursue unilateral nuclear advantages as the Soviet Union did in the Cold War, but maintain an asymmetric nuclear capability. In a foreseeable future, the unbalanced military powers will remain, as that will halt bilateral military confrontation and restrain the arms race between China and the U.S.

---

52 "The National Security Strategy of the United States of America," the White House, September 2002, p. 28.

53 Three dilemmas are emerging from the horizon on the way to "great national renaissance": how to balance economic development strategy against the goal of national unification; how to balance a peaceful foreign environment against geopolitical pressures around China; and how to implement "good-neighborly policy" while beating back "Theory of China Threat."

Chapter 8

A Rising China: Catalysts for Chinese Military Modernization

Bang Quan Zheng

The rise of China which coincided with the collapse of the Soviet Union has attracted special attention in the post-Cold War era. Given the huge potential in the Chinese economy and military, many difficult questions arose from the assumption that China might become a "candidate" of great power.[1] Realists believe that a modernized China with a GNP equal to or greater than that of the United States and with roughly comparable military potential would inevitably become a major rival for world power.[2] By contrast, liberals argue that China has come to embrace interdependence and globalization with increasing enthusiasm, and globalization will integrate China into the international community. China can bargain for its national interests within this framework and thus the relative balance of power is not accurately characterized by polarity.[3] To be sure, either positive or negative developments in Chinese behavior in the near future will significantly impact the international system. In the realm of international security, the uncertainty and ambiguity of China's prospective development refer to two critical issues. First, China's increasing defense expenditures derived from its burgeoning economic strength have made it the second largest in the world. China has been continuously acquiring sophisticated armaments from outsiders. Second, the traditional strategy of dependence on manpower and people's war has been replaced with greater reliance on high-tech weapon systems, under the new military doctrine termed "high-tech national defense strategy."[4] Many controversies and speculations have stemmed from the observation of China's emerging professional military. However, whether or not these efforts will translate into practical military power remains to be seen.

Economic globalization has become a great impetus toward incorporating China into the current international system along with its "peaceful development"

---

1 Avery Goldstein, "Great Expectations: Interpreting China's Arrival," September 1996. http://0-www.ciaonet.org.opac.sfsu.edu/wps/goa01/goa01.html.
2 Zalmay M. Khalilzad, et al., *The United States and a Rising China*, Project Air Force, RAND, 1999.
3 Alastair Iain Johnston, "Is China a Status Quo Power?" *International Security*, vol. 27, no. 4, Spring 2003, p. 37.
4 You Ji, "The PLA and regional security," *The Armed Forces of China* (New York: I.B. Tauris Publisher, 1999), p. 1.

strategy. But does this system reassure China about its national security? If China is confident with the current international system, why does it yearn to modernize its armed forces? This chapter attempts to argue that although China has invested tremendous endeavors in modernizing its military power, its military development is still defensive in nature. China's "peaceful development" is based on the stability of current international economic, political and security orders, thus the rise of China would not be a threat to the U.S. and the international system. This chapter is divided into six sections. It will first introduce the Chinese defense strategy, which is crucial to understanding how Chinese leaders perceive its national security and the ways they react to external threats. Second, this will be followed by a discussion of economic engagement and increased dependence on the world economy and peaceful environment, which is important to the understanding of China's attitude toward the current international system. Third, military modernization program reflects China's desire to possess a modern military, which is significant to illustrate China's incentives to upgrade its armed forces. Fourth, related to military modernization, a discussion of Sino-Russian military cooperation will explain the nature of the Sino-Russian military cooperation and why such military cooperation would not be able to alter the military balance between the U.S. and China. Fifth, this section will analyze why the intractable Taiwan issue has a great impact on China's security policy, and extent to which the "peaceful development" strategy had reshaped China's Taiwan policy. Sixth, in the last section, it will explain why U.S. military strategy toward China is the primary security concern for Beijing, and the way the Chinese interpret and react to such strategy is critical to understanding China's calculation of its national security.

Chinese Strategic Culture

Before discussing China's military strategy, I would like to briefly introduce its strategic culture. A national defense strategy is based on a national strategic culture.[5] Andrew Scobell suggests that China's use of force strategic culture should be taken into account as a significant dimension in any analyses, because the subject of national culture has been considered as a crucial dimension in strategy, including the impact of culture on a state's tendency to exercise the armed forces.[6] Thus the contemporary Chinese security policy has been heavily influenced by enduring history and culture.

One of the most critical strategic traditions of China is the maintenance of territorial integrity and sovereignty. Seeking unification is at the soul of Chinese military strategy which has been passed down from traditional Chinese civilization.[7]

---

5   Ibid., p. 236.

6   Andrew Scobell, "China and Strategic Culture," Strategic Studies Institute, May 2002, p. 7. http://www.strategicstudiesinstitute.army.mil/pdffiles/PUB60.pdf.

7   Andrew Scobell, *China's use of military force: beyond the great wall and the long march* (New York: Cambridge University Press, 2003), p. 33.

According to Scobell, national unification is the most important value in terms of national security calculus, on which compromise is impossible.[8] Lieutenant General Li Jijun, former vice president of the Academy of Military Sciences, also states:

> The most important strategic legacy of the Chinese nation is the awareness of identification with the concept of unification, and this is where lies the secret for the immortality of ...Chinese civilization...[s]eeking unification...[is] the soul of...Chinese military strategy endowed by...Chinese civilization.[9]

However, globalization has added a new dimension to the Chinese strategic culture. China has engaged in economic cooperation with the world since its market reform and opening up to the outside world. Economic integration is however a double-edged sword for China – while it enhances its economic leverages, it also brings new challenges to China that deepens its dependence on the outside world. This in turn makes Beijing highly aware of its position in the international system. Since 1996 Beijing has forged a diplomatic strategy with broad purposes to maintain a peaceful international environment that is considered necessary for China's economic development and modernization.[10] Saunders points out that as the Chinese engaged in the world economy has increased, Chinese leaders have sought to maintain a careful balance between the benefits offered by economic integration and the vulnerabilities it creates.[11] This consideration has constituted the basic framework for Chinese international behavior in the era of globalization.

As a new strategic choice, "peaceful rising" has been stressed by China's new leadership, which is different from Jiang Zemin government's advocacy of building a unipolar world structure. The implication of "peaceful rising," as Zheng Bijian reveals,

> the only choice for China under the current international system situation was to rise peacefully, namely, to develop by taking advantage of the peaceful international environment, and at the same time, to maintain world peace through its development.[12]

Hu Jintao also pointed out that in one of his keynote speeches that:

> A country can emerge victorious from tough international competition and enjoy faster development only when it gets along with the tide of the times, seizes the opportunities for development, blazes a trail suited to its national conditions and relics on wisdom and resourcefulness of its own people.[13]

---

8 Andrew Scobell, "China and Strategic Culture," Strategic Studies Institute, May 2002, p. 11.

9 Li Jijun, "International Military Strategy and China's Security at the Turn of the Century," *Zhongguo Pinglun* (Hong Kong), August 5, 1998, in *FBIS*, August 13, 1998.

10 Avery Goldstein, "The Diplomatic Face of China's Grand Strategy: A Rising Power's Emerging Choice," *The China Quarterly*, 2001, p. 836.

11 Phillips C. Saunders, "Supping with a Long Spoon: Dependence and Interdependence in Sino-American Relations," *The China Journal*, No. 40, Jan 2000, pp. 55–81, p. 55.

12 "Peaceful Rise: Strategic Choice for China," www.china.org.com.

13 Ibid.

Beijing has realized that to achieve "peaceful development" domestic and international environments are equally significant. On the one hand, the development of China is based on development within the international system.[14] Although China's economy has achieved impressive growth in the last decades, there are still many serious problems plaguing Chinese society, such as weak economic foundation, underdeveloped productivity, highly uneven development, and a worsening ecological environment.[15] Thus Beijing clearly understands that these domestic social issues would constrain China's national power if it cannot solve them and maintain internal stability. On the other hand, the "peaceful development" also means maintaining the world pace for its development.[16] In international politics, the rise of a country would create an impact on the international balance of power, so China seeks to avoid the competition-inducing policies of Weimar Germany, Imperial Japan, and the Soviet Union in the Cold War.[17] That means it is in China's biggest interest to maintain the existing international system, rather than challenging it, as well as investing in cooperative relationships with other states and remaining unthreatening to any particular country.

A third dimension of Chinese strategic culture is the result of interplay between Confucian and *Realpolitik* strands.[18] On the one hand, China's self-image of strategic culture is basically a Confucian one. Chinese elites believe that their country's strategic tradition is pacifist and defensive in nature. On the other hand, the humiliated history in the last century justifies any use of force including offensive and preemptive strike as for defense purposes.[19] China tries to protect its prestige, existence and integrity by the way of military buildup to counter any external threat. The Chinese have a strong sense of insecurity, and for military leaders in particular, the world is seen from a traditional realist perspective. They believe that the international system is complicated, filled with uncertainty and threats.[20] In fact, Chinese armament policy is heavily influenced by a worst-case scenario based on a comparison of military strength and the order of battle.[21] Although these characteristics are not exclusively applied in China, they indeed tend to set Chinese thinking, particularly that of the powerful conservative leaders' mindset of *realpolitik*.[22] Therefore, Chinese strategists

---

14 "China to be mainstay for peace after peaceful rise," *People's Daily*, June 25, 2004. http://english.people.com.cn/200404/26/eng20040426_141521.shtml.

15 Ibid.

16 "China to be mainstay for peace after peaceful rise," *People's Daily*, June 25, 2004. http://english.people.com.cn/200404/26/eng20040426_141521.shtml.

17 Evan S. Medeiros, "China Debates Its 'Peaceful Rise' Strategy: Is a kinder, gentler Beijing the best route to development?" *YaleGlobal*, 22 June 2004. http://yaleglobal.yale.edu/article.print?id=4118.

18 Scobell, p. 3.

19 Ibid.

20 Ibid., p. 33.

21 Ibid.

22 Hung-mao Tien and Tun-jen Cheng, "The Regional Security Implications of China's Economic Expansion, Military Modernization, and the Rise of Nationalism," *The Security*

want to participate in economic cooperation, yet globalization has not reassured China with its national security.

Chinese Economic Integration and Its Implications

The projection of China's future development can be seen from two perspectives. At the theoretical level, liberals believe that, as China increasingly integrates into the global economy, it would be encouraged to be non-ideological, pragmatic, materialistic and progressively freer in its culture and politics.[23] Following liberal theory, China will be incorporated into the international community, and adopt a role in accordance with international institutions. These international institutions, as John Ikenberry suggests, do not only serve the functional purposes of states, reducing transaction costs and solving collective action problems, but they are also "sticky" – locking states into ongoing and predictable courses of action. In turn, these locked-in relations play a role in restraining the exercise of state power.[24] Since institutions create constraints on state action that serves to reduce their power, China will therefore be less likely to exercise its state power. From this perspective, liberals advocate adopting an engagement policy toward China.

By contrast, realists argue that a rising China will relatively undermine U.S. influence in the region, and that Sino-U.S. rivalry could fit into a wider new international arrangement that will increasingly confront Western, and especially U.S., supremacy.[25] Realists further presume that a stronger China that obtains equal international status with the U.S. will try to change some of these "rules of game" to better reflect its own interests and presence.[26] As Gilpin states, the interests of individual states and the balance of power among them do change as a result of economic, technological, and other developments. As a consequence, those states who benefit most from change in the international system and who gain the power to effect such change will strive to alter the system in ways that favor their interests. The resulting changed system will reflect the new distribution of power and the interests of newly dominant members.[27] That is to say, the U.S. and Chinese relationship is a zero-sum game; a richer and more powerful China on one side will inevitably undermine the interests of the U.S. on the other.

The realist argument is not consistent with the growing volumes of trade between China and the United States. The burgeoning bilateral trade are based on interests

---

Environment in the Asia-Pacific (New York: M.E. Sharpe, 2000), p. 92.

23 Bernstein, Richard and Munro, Ross H. "The Coming Conflict with America," *Foreign Affairs*, March/April 1997, p. 1.

24 John Ikenberry, "Institutions, Strategic Restraint, and the Persistence of American Postwar Order," *International Security* 23: 3, 1998/99, pp. 43–78, p. 2.

25 Bernstein and Munro, p. 21.

26 Khalilzad, et al., p. 19.

27 Robert Gilpin, *War and Change in World Politics* (New York: Cambridge University Press, 1981), p. 9.

Table 8.1 China's Top Export Destinations ($ million)

Rank	Country/region	H1 2005	% change*
1	United States	72,685.9	34.3
2	Hong Kong	52,985.4	22.4
3	Japan	40,298.1	20.5
4	South Korea	16,961.5	39.6
5	Germany	14,562.4	42.5
6	The Netherlands	11,630.7	48.7
7	United Kingdom	8,528.5	35.5
8	Taiwan	7,753.4	28.8
9	Singapore	7,316.2	35.7
10	Italy	5,808.4	34.3

*Percent change over Hi 2004
Source: PRC General Administration of Customs, China's Customs Statistics.

involved, thus it is an error to overlook the economic benefits the United States gains from these practices. Although a stronger and richer China would increase its economic and military leverage vis-à-vis the U.S., one should not overlook that a richer and more dynamic China will have more reasons to cooperate with the United States. In fact, the United State is one of the most important trading partners contributing to China's economic boom. According to the U.S.-China Economic Council, the U.S. has been one of the prominent exporting destinations for China, which accounts for 28 percent of total exports, and the U.S. trade deficit with China had reached $134.8 billions by 2003.[28] Obviously, China is a key benefactor in the U.S.-dominated international economic order, thus Beijing does not have reasons to change the "rules of game."

From Table 8.1 and Figure 8.1, we can see that the U.S. market is the most important export destination for China. Although the United States is currently the powerhouse of the global economy, as China's economic and strategic weight grows the Chinese economy will become an important source of momentum for the global economic growth. Thus, there are no absolute winners and losers between the United States and China. Deng and Moore suggest that whereas recent emphasis has been on China's growing posture in multilateral institutions, more arguments can be made about how informal mechanisms of interdependence, such as Beijing's

---

28 http://www.uschina.org/statistics/tradetable.html.

Figure 8.1   U.S. Exports of Goods

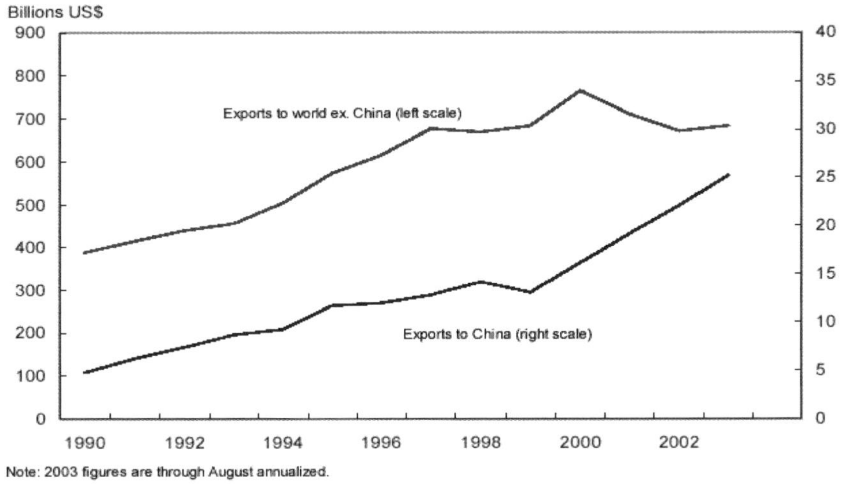

[Chart: Billions US$. Exports to world ex. China (left scale) rising from ~400 in 1990 to peak ~775 around 2000, then ~680 in 2002–2003. Exports to China (right scale) rising from ~5 in 1990 to ~28 in 2003.]

Note: 2003 figures are through August annualized.

Source: "China's Trade and U.S. Manufacturing Jobs" Oct. 30, 2003. http://www.whitehouse.gov/cea/mankiw_testimony_house_ways_and_means_oct_30.html.

burgeoning economic ties, have anchored its relations with other great powers.[29] Moreover, Sino-U.S. commercial relations are deepening into interdependence that China needs the United States as an export market, and the United States needs China's dollar support.[30]

Table 8.1 indicates that the United States is the prominent export destination for Chinese consumer goods. For all of China's oft-cited dependence on the United States as an export market, Washington's desire for foreign borrowing levels the playing field. By virtually any measure, the U.S. government's large spending deficits, Chinese creditors are estimated to possess about 9 percent of U.S. federal government holdings, such as holding of U.S. Treasury bonds, owned by foreign creditors in 2003. It is the second largest foreign holder of U.S. Treasury Bonds after Japan, and a major purchaser of U.S. government-backed mortgage finance bond. Overall Chinese holding of U.S. government (national, state, local) debt instruments amount to $150 billion.[31]

---

[29] Yong Deng and Thomas G. Moore, "China Views Globalization: Toward a New Great-Power Politics?" *The Washington Quarterly*, Summer 2004, p. 132.

[30] Phillip Segal, "Foreign buyers of U.S. bonds are banking on a stable U.S. consumer market," *YaleGlobal*, 2 September, 2003. http://yaleglobal.yale.edu/article.print?id=2365.

[31] Robert Sutter, "Why Does China Matter?" *The Washington Quarterly*, Winter 2003–2004, p. 79.

The emerging Chinese domestic market has become increasingly important to the U.S. economy. The chart above indicates that since 2000 U.S. exports to the world excluding China have fallen, U.S. exports to China, however, have increased rapidly during the same period. In fact, China has become the 7th largest U.S. export market by 2002, which was the 6th largest export destination for the U.S.[32] The result is a historically unusual relationship in which the rising power, developing China, provides both exports (second-leading supplier) and loans (second-leading foreign holder of government debt) to the superpower, the industrialized United States. In this and other ways, China's economic ties with the United States are seen as weakening any impulse the United States may have to view China as a rival that needs to be contained.[33] On such a view, interdependence presents the most viable alternative currently available to China.

Johnston has noted that China is significantly integrated into regional and global political and economic systems. He argues that China has gradually accepted the norms in global trade and anti-proliferation; and even on the most controversial human rights issue, China has no doubt made big progress since the 1970s. Thus he argues that China is no longer a revisionist state. Following the principle of economic globalization China can gain huge economic benefits from the U.S.-dominated international economic system and enjoy the international stability that U.S. hegemony sustains.[34] Moreover, globalization can create constraints on U.S. power that could otherwise be used to promote unmitigated unilateralism in which China thinks it can pluralize and democratize the hegemonic order and strengthen incentives for the U.S. to engage China rather than contain it.[35] To summarize, China's future development still remains uncertain and premature adoption of belligerent policies toward it would create a self-fulfilling prophecy: treat China as an enemy and it will be one.[36] Indeed, China is not the only variable to regional stability and security; instead, the future of the security environment in the Asia-Pacific region will be determined by the power structure which consists of the United States, Japan, Taiwan, China and other regional states. If they accommodate each other's interests and cooperate to strengthen regional and global institutions, as well as comply with the norms and rules set by these institutions to operate their interstate relations, China will be encouraged to cooperate with other powers. If these powers fail to construct a consensual regional order, the result will be at best an armed and fragile peace.[37] Yet, the uncertainty and complexity of these relationships do not reassure China that

---

32 N. Gregory Mankiw, "China's Trade and U.S. Manufacturing Jobs," Testimony before the House Committee on Ways and Means, Washington, D.C. October 30, 2003. http://www.whitehouse.gov/cea/mankiw_testimony_house_ways_and_means_oct_30.html.

33 Deng and Moore, p. 132.

34 Alastair Iain Johnston, "Is China a Status Quo Power?" *International Security*, vol. 27, no. 4, Spring 2003, p. 32.

35 Deng and Moore, p. 127.

36 Ibid.

37 Nathan and Ross, "The great wall and the empty fortress: China's search for security" (New York: W.W. Norton & Company Inc., 1997), p. 236.

its national security or interests can be preserved without the possession of capable armed forces. This, in part, encouraged China to modernize its military.

China's Military Modernization and Its Intentions

Although China's armed forces are roughly 2.8 million,[38] the nation's vast army, supplied with obsolete conventional and crude nuclear weaponry, has relegated China to the ranks of the second-tier powers, and among them perhaps the least capable.[39] At the system level, the PLA's military modernization in the post-Deng era refers to transformation from the motorization age to the mechanization and digitalization age. As the former Chinese president and Chairman of the Central Military Commission Jiang Zemin stressed, the goal of Chinese military forces is to build up information-oriented troops by the middle of this century.[40] Following this principle, the Chinese military will accelerate the enhancement of automatic command systems to integrate information support among combat units.[41]

Realist theory suggests that a strong China will behave more assertively, especially with respect to its desire for deference from neighboring countries.[42] In retrospect, the Chinese have been highly concerned with controlling and neutralizing direct threats to an established geographic heartland originating from a largely fixed but extensive periphery than with acquiring territory or generally expanding Chinese power and influence far beyond China's borders.[43] Structural realists argue that Beijing would intend to retrieve their regional hegemonic status at the expense of U.S. power by asserting sovereign control over territory claimed by China, and take over Taiwan.[44] However, there is no evidence indicating that China is proactively balancing the U.S. on a regional and global scale, at least at nowhere near the degree of the intense competition between the Soviet Union and the United States during the Cold War.[45] While strategic and weapons modernizations are taking place, the rapidly rising PLA does not necessarily mean that China will pose a significant threat to the U.S. in the Asia-Pacific region. Although modernization is underway, it is limited to certain areas, such as cruise and ballistic missiles. Modernizing a handful of key weapon systems could not significantly hamper U.S. operations in the region. From a Chinese perspective, its strategy is based on developing armed forces that do

---

38 Khalilzad, et al., p. 39.
39 Ibid, p. 1.
40 "Chinese Military in Face of Twofold Historical Mission," *Kanwa News*, May 20, 2003. http://www.kanwa.com/free/2003/06/e0619a.htm.
41 Ibid.
42 Johnston.
43 Khalilzad, et al., p. 21.
44 Johnston, p. 27.
45 Ibid., p. 39.

not require a large infrastructure to maintain.[46] That implies the PLA tries to obtain the least defense capability, and its balancing against the U.S. has been hesitant, low-impact. Instead, China will attempt to maintain a peaceful environment and stable relations with the U.S. in the short to middle term.[47]

Although China has altered its "people's war" military strategy, Beijing's increased investment in air and naval forces is exclusively defensive in nature.[48] The new military strategy "people's war under modern conditions," as introduced by Folta, emphasizes the demonstration of China's willingness and growing ability to use different levels of nuclear forces if necessary, including limited strike; preparation of military forces for concentrated defense of particular areas, cities, and industrial assets, instead of being limited to falling back and dispersing for a war of attrition; improvement of military personnel and weapons quality, rather than maintenance of massive ground forces and large quantities of obsolete weapons systems; and enhancement of the capability to conduct combined operations with air, ground, and naval forces.[49] The Chinese government also stresses that:

> China persists in taking the road of peaceful development and unswervingly pursues a national defense policy defensive in nature. China's national defense is the security guarantee for the survival and development of the nation. The main tasks of China's national defense are to step up modernization of its national defense and its armed forces, to safeguard national security and unity, and to ensure the smooth process of building a moderately prosperous society in an all-round way.[50]

In theory, states would mobilize their economic, technological and human resources internally to develop military and strategic power or construct military alliances externally to preserve common interests in balancing a powerful hegemon or dominant state.[51] Observation of Chinese foreign and security policy practices in the recent decade reveals that China does not belong to either of these categories. Chinese military modernization is intended to defend its national security, and to deter the "Taiwan independence" forces from splitting the country.[52]

---

46 Mark A. Stokes, "China's Strategic Modernization: Implications for the United States," *The Strategic Studies Institute*, p. 140. http://carlisle-www.army.mil/usassi/welcome.htm.

47 Ibid.

48 Goldstein, Avery, "Great Expectations: Interpreting China's Arrival," p. 10. www.ciaonet.org.opac.sfsu/wps/goa01/goa01.html.

49 Paul Humes Folta, *From Swords to Plowshares?: Defense Industry Reform in the PRC* (Boulder: Westview Press, Inc., 1992), p. 16.

50 Chapter II National Defense Policy, *China 2004 White Paper on National Defense*. http://www.fas.org/nuke/guide/china/doctrine/natdef2004.html#3.

51 Mark A. Stokes, "China's Strategic Modernization: Implications for the United States," *The Strategic Studies Institute*, p. 140. htpp://carlisle-www.army.mil/usassi/welcome.htm.

52 Chapter II National Defense Policy, *China 2004 White Paper on National Defense*. http://www.fas.org/nuke/guide/china/doctrine/natdef2004.html#3.

Table 8.2 China's Defense Expenditure

	Defense Expenditures (Billion)	Percentage in GDP	Military Expenditure Per capita	Personnel Per 1,000	Nuclear Capabilities
US	420.7	3.9%	953.01	4.7	67,500 ICBMs 10,600 warheads
China	51	4.3%	43.44	2.18	20 ICBMs 250 warheads
North Korea	5.21	33.9%	232.23	52	None

Source: Nationmaster.com, countrywatch.com, the CIA Factbook.

As Table 8.2 shows, China's defense expenditure is $51 billion, which is only 1/8 of the United States. China's 4.3 percent is in contrast to North Korea's 33.9 percent in terms of percentage in GDP. This suggests that Beijing is not attempting to counterbalance the U.S. and does not mobilize its national strength to do so. Moreover, comparing China's military expenditure per capita, as well as its personnel per capita, to its U.S. and North Korea's counterparts reveals that China does not intend to exploit all its national mechanisms to prepare military action to counterbalance the U.S. and its allies in the region. In addition, China's nuclear force posture is primarily geared for strategic deterrence and to achieve a "limited deterrence" capability. In 2000, the U.S. Defense Department claimed that China had only 24 full-range CSS-4 (DF-5) land-based intercontinental ballistic missiles (ICBM) that are capable of attacking the U.S. In the early 1990s, China only deployed four DF-5 ICBMs targeting the United States.[53] Obviously, the nuclear capability serves as a mere symbolic display of national power.[54] Therefore, as Liu Hua-qiu, Director of the Program on Arms Control and Disarmament in China's Defense Science and Technology Information Center, states,

> China's nuclear weapons are not intended for every form of warfare. Instead, they are intended to counter nuclear war...This differs from the nuclear deterrence strategies of the U.S., Russia, English, and France, because the nuclear strategies of those countries include deterring conventional assault.[55]

---

53 Niou, Emerson, "Nuclear Deterrence over Taiwan," July 21, 2003, p. 3. http://www.duke.edu/~niou/teaching/Nuclear%20Deterrence%20Over%20Taiwan.pdf.
54 Ibid.
55 Niou, p. 5.

The PLA's weapon systems are generally backward and their inferiority compared to other major powers has been highlighted in the post-Cold War era. In fact, post Cold War warfare differs significantly in nature. The high-tech warfare demonstrated by the U.S. in the first Gulf War in 1991 indicated that huge human resources with obsolete weapon systems are of limited value in modern warfare in which high-tech weapon systems use their superiority in air and sea control as well as precise cruise missile attacks. If China does not actively upgrade its armed forces, its military leverage will diminish over time.

For China, it is necessary to distinguish between all-out war and limited high-tech war. All-out war refers to mobilizing all available means and resources to fight a war; while the latter refers to modern warfare in which state-of-the-art technologies are demonstrated in sophisticated weapon systems. The PLA is the largest military force in the world, so it is unrealistic to expect upgrades to its armaments in a short period of time. Thus the PLA created a middle course weapons program that attempts to bridge the gap between an all-out war and a limited regional war.[56] Following this principal, the PLA has tried to build up certain military units which are tailored for small-to-medium level conflict. According to the middle course policy, the priorities for funding and modernization are given to fast response units and improving naval and air force hardware.[57] Meanwhile, the PLA also has attempted to maintain its strategic deterrent capabilities which were characterized by the doctrine of strategic return attack, that is, emphasis on strategic attack against the most critical enemy targets. Since the 1960s, the PLA focused on gaining the means, such as ICBMs, to strike strategic targets, thus presenting the prospect of ending a conflict quickly by destroying an enemy's ability to wage war, or by convincing him to desist without first having to fight and defeat his military forces.[58] However, there is no point in using strategic ballistic missiles or nuclear weapons in regional conflicts. To win a war against Taiwan or Southeast Asian states, China must acquire substantial high-tech weapon systems which at least make the PLA stand at the same technological level with their rivals.

Realist theory suggests that a highly efficient weapon's symbolic significance is based on the degree to which it is associated with a state's cultural ideas and images; at the same time, high-tech, unique weapons are more efficient in symbolizing independence and sovereignty than mundane, unremarkable weapons.[59] That is to say, if China wants to regain its great power status, it must obtain lethal military capabilities. China has huge amounts of conventional weapons; however, the quality of those weapons is seriously obsolete. In fact, the Chinese armed forces are still at the motorization stage, and only 15 percent have completed the process of "preliminary mechanization."[60] This implies the majority of China's armed forces

---

56 Ji, p. 57.
57 Ibid.
58 Stokes, p. 7.
59 Katzenstein, ch. 3, p. 7.
60 "Chinese Military in face of Two fold Historical Mission," *Kanwa News*, May 20, 2003. http://kanwa.com/free/2003/06/e0619a.htm.

Table 8.3 Selected Chinese Arms Production Programs

Chinese Name	Original	Type	Date Acquired	Entered Production
T-59	T-54	Tank	1953	1957
J-6	MiG-19	Fighter	1958	1963
J-7	MiG-21	Fighter	1961	1967
Y-7	An-24	Transport	1976	1984
H-6	Tu-16	Bomber	1957	1968
Z-9	Dauphin	Helicopter	1980	1992
Y-8	An-28	Transport	1969	1986

Source: *The United States & a Rising China*, p. 53.

still rely on the old-fashioned weapon systems originating from the 1960s. The PLA's modernization program has to be highly selective with much balancing and sequencing, which causes uneven development (see Table 8.3).

Chinese military modernization is characterized by two perspectives – self reliance and purchase abroad. China is striving to upgrade its own weapon production in line with its belief in the principle of self-sufficiency. The PLA insists that the self-sufficiency principle is the main strategy to achieve modern military capability. Indeed, the Chinese have long possessed self-sufficiency in military production.[61] However, as the table above indicates, Chinese domestic military industries and weapons are basically cloned from Soviet military equipment.[62] By the 1970s, Chinese domestic industry was producing a broad range of weapons and systems, including aircraft, ships, armored vehicles, artillery, and submarines.[63] In turn, the Chinese not only supplied their own armed forces but also became active suppliers of cheap clones of Soviet military equipment for the world market. Chinese armaments are essentially obsolete; the basic problem is not quantity, but quality.[64] Tension with the United States and Taiwan in 1996 explicitly underscored China's limited military capabilities, which were further evidence of its need to modernize its armaments to counter U.S. and Taiwanese capabilities in the region.[65] In order to become a great military power, a nation must rely on its domestic military industry. In particular, to improve the overall quality of military equipments, the PLA has to rely on domestic

---

61 Khalilzad, et al., p. 53
62 Andrew J. Pierre, "People's Republic of China," *The Global Politics of Arms Sales* (N.J.: Princeton University Press, 1992), p. 229.
63 Khalilzad, et al., p. 53.
64 Pierre, p. 226.
65 Tien and Cheng, p. 90.

military industrial complex for the sake of long-term supply as well as reduction of costs.

Of all the branches of military service, the air force was given highest priority.[66] The PLA was convinced that an efficient air force will be a pivotal determinant in future conflicts. After Deng Xiaoping took office, the PLA began to explore and study new strategies which will fit into the development of modern warfare. "Active defense" is a strategy that calls for the air force to shift from a purely defensive to a combined defensive-offensive posture.[67] As Deng Xiaoping stressed: "Active defense itself is not necessarily limited to a defensive concept ... Active defense also contains an offensive element. If we are attacked, we will certainly counterattack ... The bombers of the air force are defensive weapons ... We [must] have what others have, and anyone who wants to destroy us will be subject to retaliation."[68]

In the line with "active defense" strategy, the People's Liberation Army Air Force (PLAAF) adopted new strategic missions, that is, defend strategic points and provide air cover for strategic deployment of mass troops; maintain air domination in the main theaters of operations in support of the army and the navy; launch surprise attacks on high-value targets of the enemy; participate in nuclear counterattack; and conduct strategic aerial reconnaissance. Further, the PLAAF will prepare defense against air raids and support the other services opposing a ground invasion or launching a counteroffensive.[69] Associated with this strategic development, the air force has begun to upgrade their equipment, including medium/long range all-weather interceptors, early-warning systems, electronic countermeasure equipment, and automatic command-and-control systems as the high-priority projects.[70] In the pursuit of these capabilities, Beijing has also tried to exploit foreign air-launched weapons and avionics. Thus Beijing cooperated with a consortium of U.S. companies led by Grumman to install avionics on 55 J-8b fighters. Also, Beijing employed services from other Western countries to upgrade avionics and weapons.[71] However, almost all of these cooperatives efforts with the West were suspended after the Tiananmen event in 1989.

The revolution in air-delivered weapons dramatized by the United States in the first Gulf War shattered Beijing's complacency.[72] Beijing's strategists further assumed that the most likely wars would be limited and held that air domination was a prerequisite for victory. Such war would always begin with air strikes, they declared, and air power would decide "the destiny of the state."[73] So the Central Military Commission (CMC) declared that, by the end of the twentieth century, the

---

66 John Wilson Lewis and Xue Litai, "China's search for a Modern Air Force," *International Security*, vol. 24, no. 1, Summer 1999, pp. 64–94, p. 73.
67 Lew and Xue, p. 78.
68 Ibid.
69 Ibid.
70 Ibid., p. 73.
71 Ibid., p. 74.
72 Ibid., p. 77.
73 Ibid., p. 79.

air force must be able to cope with local wars and contingencies of various types and make preparations for expansion in case of a full-scale war.[74]

Total self-reliance is inconsistent with China's actual industrial capability. In reality, China is still plagued by technological backwardness. First, the technological level of China's domestic defense industrial complex significantly lags behind other industrial developed states.[75] To manufacture modern aircraft requires the creation of a much more sophisticated industrial base, a huge investment, and also would take a long period of time.[76] Further, even though the PLA received technological support from Russia, it still faces difficulties integrating theory and design success into reliable weapon systems.[77] Technological incompetence resulted in delays with development projects and in turn, the obsolescence of systems improvement even soon after their production.[78] The J-7 fighter jet, for instance, is a derivative of the MiG-21 which entered production in 1989, 30 years after the original FISHBED was brought in the Soviet service.[79] Obviously, total self-reliance is not a realistic strategy to make the PLA catch up with the counterparts of the major powers.

In 1992 Beijing and Moscow signed Protocol I to formalize their ties, which included a deal of 26 Su-27 fighters and jet engines as well as the training of Chinese pilots.[80] In the following year, Beijing and Moscow signed Protocol II, which further added to a series of air defense systems, such as the S-300, and TOR-M1 surface-to-air missile systems and itemized areas for further technological cooperation, particularly the areas of communications and electronic countermeasures. In February 1995 China spent $2.2 billion and obtained a license for manufacturing 200 Su-27s over fifteen years.[81] These aircraft are higher-performance Su-27SKS.

China has never been a sea power, having traditionally believed that its major national security threat would come from the land rather than the seas. However, after the 1980s, China realized that threats from the seas in fact far exceed those from land borders.[82] Indeed, China's rapid economic development since the 1980s has significantly increased the importance of protecting its maritime interests, which include the safeguarding of China's territorial waters, coastal economy, seaborne trade and maritime resources, deterring Taiwanese independence and maintaining strategic depth. Since the mid-1980s, China has begun to emphasize a new naval strategy called "offshore active defense" in line with the PLA's new defense

---

74 Ibid.
75 Mark A. Stokes, "China's Strategic Modernization: Implications for the United States," *The Strategic Studies Institute*, p. 135. http://carlisle-www.army.mil/usassi/welcome.htm.
76 Ibid., p. 84.
77 Stokes, p. 135.
78 Ibid., p. 54.
79 Ibid.
80 Ibid.
81 http://www.fas.org/nuke/guide/china/aircraft/j-11.htm.
82 Ji, p. 171.

strategy.[83] "Offshore active defense" means that the People's Liberation Army Navy (PLAN) can exercise an independent battle far away from mainland. That is, the PLAN would wage pre-emptive actions when it regards the situation to be critical, such as when foreign navies intrude into China's territorial waters, seriously violate its maritime interests and threaten its national security.

In their quest for high-tech naval power, the PLAN has worked out detailed short, medium- and long-term plans. The first phase is to develop rapid response task forces capable of operations and deterrence in waters beyond its traditional areas of activity. Its goal is to deter regional threats, from mainly small powers, without fighting, or to win a limited regional maritime conflict with quick, low-cost strikes. In the first phase, the naval attack forces would be composed mainly of land-based medium-range bombers and fleets of attack submarines.[84] Medium-sized surface ships equipped with helicopters will serve as command and escort forces. In the second phase of evolution, which should extend over the first two to three decades of the 21st century, the navy will gradually break away from the West Pacific. For instance, its blue-water fleet may exercise in the Indian Ocean or enter the Atlantic Ocean or pay a port call in the Mediterranean Sea. The third phase will be devoted to developing capabilities to sustain deep ocean warfare. These fleets should possess various kinds of warships to form a three-dimensional system of attack and defense with anti-air, surface and submarine capabilities.[85] At this point China can truly become a regional great power, and may possess more capabilities to challenge the U.S. Seventh Fleet in the Asia-Pacific region.

In line with this strategy, one of the top agendas for the Chinese Navy is to enhance combat capability including upgrading Song class submarines. This ongoing project is currently being undertaken by the No. 701 Research Institute in Wuhan.[86] The major improvements involved changing the original drainage system into a linear drainage system and equipping the vessel with a new command system and a hull-mounted sonar system.[87] Furthermore, a new generation nuclear attack submarine is under construction. The overall design concept is very similar to Russian submarine style namely the hull design is very similar to the Russian KILO 636 in particular.[88] But, as stressed by the Russian Rubin Design Bureau, China's new generation strategic nuclear submarine did not receive any technological assistance from Russia.[89]

Another important area of Chinese military modernization effort is modern information warfare:

---

83 Bates Gill and Taeho Kim, "China's Arms Acquisitions From Abroad – A Quest for 'Superb and Secret Weapons,'" *Stockholm International Peace Research Institute*, 1995, Report 11, p. 60.

84 Ibid.

85 Ji, p. 170.

86 Ibid.

87 Ibid.

88 Ibid.

89 Kanwa Information Center, "Chinese Military In Face of Twofold Historical Mission," http://free/0029/c1010a.htm.

China is actively and extensively engaged in the whole realm of signals intelligence (SIGINT), electronic warfare (EW) and cyber-warfare activities. It ranks as the leader in Asia, at least according to some more quantitative measurements, in some important information warfare (IW) areas. China maintains by far the most extensive SIGINT capabilities of all the countries in Asia and has the most SIGINT ground stations.[90]

"Information offense" and "information defense" are intertwined concepts given high emphasis by the leaders of PLA. Offense refers to combat actions such as weakening and demolishing the enemy's capability to use information effectively, while defense refers to the opposition of the same.[91] To win modern warfare, one must strive to break down the enemy's early warning apparatus and command and control structures. Also missile strikes, combined with an information vacuum caused by heavy jamming and disruption of communications, could seriously complicate the enemy's ability to generate sorties.[92] In this regard, the PLA has embarked on the development of components of a sensor network; once it is complete within the next 15 years it would enable the PLA to detect, identify, and track ships operating around its periphery.[93] Further, the development of electronic reconnaissance and radar satellites would enable the ELINT and radar satellites to work together to detect and identify any vessels in the region. Under this system, if the ship being tracked goes silent, the passive electronic reconnaissance satellite will not be able to pick it up but the SAR satellite will still register its position. If the ship attempts to jam the radar, the ELINT platform can easily pick it up. Using the spacecraft in combination, therefore, makes it extremely difficult for the enemy ships to hide, especially if linked to PLA ground-based SIGINT, surface wave over-the-horizon radar, submarines, and ostensibly civilian sentry vessels operating in the open ocean.[94]

In sum, Chinese military modernization has developed unevenly. Beijing rigorously integrates foreign sophisticated weapon systems, and improves its domestic military industry, in large part, because of the intractable Taiwan issue. The PLA tries to demonstrate its willingness and capabilities in waging war to deter this island from moving to independence. However, the modern weapons system currently represents approximately 5 percent of China's total military arsenal.[95] Thus, these foreign military armaments are not able to change the nature of the backwardness of the Chinese military in general.

---

90 Manuel Cereijo, "China and Cuba and Information Warfare (IW): Signal Intelligence (SIGINT), Electronic Warfare (EW) and Cyber-warfare," http://www.futurodecuba.org/ChinaandInformationWarfare4.htm.

91 www.kanwa.com, Kanwa Information Center, "Chinese Military In Face of Twofold Historical Mission," May 20th 2003. http:// free/0029/c1010a.htm.

92 Stokes, p. 139.

93 Ibid., p. 141.

94 Ibid., p. 142.

95 Kanwa Information Center, "Chinese Military In Face of Twofold Historical Mission," May 20, 2003. http:// free/0029/c1010a.htm.

Taiwan: A Pain in the Neck for China

China's defense culture is firmly constructed on the nation's historical desire to become economically wealthy and militarily powerful. This desire is usually interwoven with popular nationalism and irredentism.[96] Thus to understand China's motives, it is vital to understand the Taiwan issue from a Chinese perspective. Although economic impetus discourages China from exercising its military power, it does not mean that China is not likely to exercise its power in particular scenarios, such as the declared independence of Taiwan. Once Taiwan becomes sovereign, it would constitute the alteration of the status quo in the region. Johnston suggests that status quo powers that face security dilemmas may use military force to secure their territory, and preserve their influence.[97] Supporting Johnston, Art and Waltz point out that status quo powers may acquire offensive weapons to regain territory lost during the opening stage of a war; thus a state would wait to procure these weapons until war seems likely, and only in relatively small numbers, unless the aggressor was able to construct strong defense quickly in the occupied areas.[98] For China, the Taiwan issue represents more than a territorial concern. The first and foremost concerns are nationalism and irredentism. In effect, rapid development of China's comprehensive national power in the recent decade accompanied with increased nationalism highlight the compelling desire for reunification with Taiwan. The importance of territorial integrity is consistently emphasized by Beijing, stating that China suffered a terrible fate under the aggressions committed by the major powers in its recent history; and that the separation of two sides of the strait a half century ago was the result of intervention by the United States,[99] who prevented the Communists from "liberating" this island by dispatching the 7th fleet to the Taiwan Strait in 1949. The rebuilding of a reunified China, including the return of Hong Kong and Macao to China and the unification between the two sides of the strait, has become the basic premise and belief of nationalist revival and self improvement.[100]

Moreover, in the face of intense pressure from economic transformation, an ideological shift from communism to nationalism would help to hold Chinese society together by bolstering a certain intellectual and emotional energy and stability.[101] In turn, advocating Chinese nationalism and national revival became the crucial

---

96 Ji, p. 236.

97 Johnston, p. 56.

98 Robert J. Art and Kenneth Waltz, *The Use of Force: Military Power and International Politics* (Lanham: University Press of America, Inc. 1993), p. 53.

99 Ibid.

100 Lee, p. 75.

101 Johnson, Chalmers, *Blowback: the Cost and Consequences of American Empire* (NY: Henry Holt and Company, 2000), p. 151.

measure of the Chinese Communist Party in uniting its people.[102] As a result, it reinforced the influence of nationalism on Beijing's Taiwan policy.

In terms of political stability, the belief in Chinese nationalism with complete territorial integrity provides an important method for Beijing's leadership to unite its people in the post-communist era.[103] On the other hand, it also limited the room they have in adjusting their Taiwan policy. If a completely reunified China represents something the Chinese leadership has been preaching, it becomes a sacred nationalist mission that must be completed by the entire Chinese people.[104] For this reason, any PRC leader who dares to give up the goal of reclaiming Taiwan is bound to be criticized by his people or attacked by his political adversaries.[105] The leader's legitimacy in leading China will thus be shaken as a result.

In addition to the Chinese leadership's concern with the impact of Taiwan's independence on maintaining the completeness of Chinese territory, the other concern is the importance of Taiwan in terms of geo-politics and geo-economics.[106] First of all, there are problems with nationalist movements by minority groups in the northwest and southwest regions of China.[107] These groups have always posed a threat to China's continuous claim of sovereignty over the territory of these regions.[108] From the perspective of Beijing, if China tolerates Taiwan's independence, it is bound to weaken its own legitimate grounds of claiming sovereignty over the regions of these minority groups. Moreover, Taiwan's independence may even provide a positive example and stimulation to the nationalist movements of these ethnic groups.

Following the principle of "peaceful development," China's new leadership has set a more realistic policy on Taiwan. That is, under Deng and Jiang, unification was the policy, while under Hu, "no independence, no war" is the policy, which is featured by the anti-secession law. In contrast, Jiang Zemin's reign did not take any concrete action to curb Taiwan's rising nationalism except for empty threats.[109] The anti-secession law is a positive development, rather than negative development to the U.S. and Taiwan. The purpose of which is to maintain the status quo instead of seeking unification. Beijing is highly aware that the change in the status quo would bring up the possible conflict between China and the U.S., which in turn would jeopardize the new grand strategy and policy of "peaceful development." On the other hand, the anti-secession law established the legal basis to reunify Taiwan with military force if peaceful means become impossible. It is noteworthy that anti-secession law does not indicate a timetable for unification. It gives both sides of governments more leeway to handle the issue of reunification, while displaying the bottom line of Beijing's tolerance on intention of independence. This means, Beijing

---

102 Lee, p. 77.
103 Ibid.
104 Ibid.
105 Ibid., p. 78.
106 Ibid.
107 Ibid.
108 Ibid., p. 79.
109 "Hu Shows His Color," *China Post* (Taipei), Dec. 26, 2004.

understands the fact that unification is a long term goal, and as long as Taiwan does not pursue independence, Beijing will not intend to reunify with Taiwan by military means and harm the relationship with the U.S. Instead, China is more willing to rely on the U.S. for pressure on Taiwan not to seek independence. Given this consideration, force is only shown as a threat or deterrence to independence. Further, to enhance the deterrent capabilities, acquisition of high-technology weapon systems from outsiders is necessary. Eventually this strategic consideration has led to the Sino-Russian military cooperation.

Sino-Russian Military Cooperation and Its Implications

Structural realists argue that NATO enlargement led to Russia's isolation in the European security environment, and the threat from the U.S. – in the form of upgrading Japan's military power – weakened Russia's strategic importance in Asia. From China's standpoint, the U.S. arms sales to Taiwan, as well as its ambiguous strategy toward the Taiwan problem, and the new U.S.-Japan security guideline were perceived as challenges to its national security. Hence, China and Russia worried that the "unilateralist" Kosovo-style humanitarian actions would apply to Chechnya, Taiwan, and Tibet in the possible future.[110] In addition, Washington's intent to create a National Missile Defense (NMD) system, and thereby abandon the 1972 Anti-Ballistic Missile (ABM) treaty outraged China and Russia. In return, the joint statement of December 1999 stated that both Russia and China publicly criticized the U.S., stating that the establishment of NMD by any signatory state in violation of the 1972 Anti-Ballistic Missile (ABM) treaty would have a destructive impact on a series of international agreements concerning strategic stability, the reduction and non-proliferation of weapons of mass destruction.[111] Based on these common strategic concerns, for some scholars, both Russia and China are seeking to balance the power of the United States.[112] This led to their opposition to "hegomonism" and "unipolarity." Therefore, structural realists believe that China has tried to balance against U.S. power through developing partnership with Russia, building new ties with its neighbors and beyond, and such cooperative relationship between China and Russia might establish an anti-U.S. alliance.[113]

In fact, Sino-Russia relations are still too distant to become an alliance. Many analysts believe that the military cooperation programs with China were largely business deals in nature, similar to its cooperation with other countries. At a time when Russian military-industrial complex has been severely reduced by the move to a market economy, Russia's arms sales to China have become an essential source

---

110 Donaldson, p. 715.

111 Xinhua news agency, "PRC, Russia Leaders Issue Joint Statement," December 10, 1999. http:// russia.shaps.hawaii.edu/ fp/russia/r-c-statcomm991210_eng.html.

112 Ibid., p. 716.

113 Yong Deng, "Hegemon on the Offensive: Chinese Perspectives on U.S. Global Strategy," *Political Science Quarterly*, vol. 116, no. 3, 2001, p. 334 and Johnston, p. 39.

of revenue,[114] which contributes to resolving the problem of Russia's financial difficulty. According to SIPRI, between 1991 and 1997, Russia's military-industrial complex lost 2.5 million workers, bringing the industry's workforce down to 3.6 million employees. In early 1995, the Russia Defense Industry Workers' Union reported that workers were owed more than 160 billion rubles in back pay, while their average wage was only 62.5 percent of the average industrial wage.[115] The decline of world market for arms in developing countries highlighted the importance of China's arms orders. Arms sales to developing countries shrank from $61 billion in 1988 to $28.6 billion in 1991; by 1995 it dropped down to $15.4 billion.[116] Among the arms buyers, China and India together accounted for 70 percent of recent arms sales for Russia.[117] Indeed, Chinese arms purchases in 1995–1996 preserved 835,000 jobs in the industry. By 2000, this figure may increase to 1.2–1.4 million. Therefore, Russia's immediate financial needs will continue to maintain their arms industry and competence coupled with China's desire for sophisticated weaponry, in turn, forms the platform of their deepening relationship.

Sino-Russia military cooperation is a short-term trade off rather than a long-term strategic partnership. Following the structural realist argument, nations are concerned with their geopolitical position relative to other countries.[118] That is to say, all powers have their own reservations in deals with other countries, and they typically will not sell them their most cutting-edge technologies and arms.[119] For Russia, a stronger China will weaken its military leverage. This argument is consistent with the deeply rooted security concerns regarding threats from China. Empirically, the past antagonistic relationship with China combined with the long history of unsettled territorial disputes could cause tension again in the long-term, which reminds Russia that China is still a potential adversary. Theoretically, China is Russia's strongest neighbor in terms of comprehensive power among the neighboring states in the Far East. In addition, the large influx of Chinese into Siberia and the Far East aroused the fear of Sinicization in the areas where the indigenous population is small.[120] As Dmitri Trenin, deputy director of the Carnegie Moscow Center has stressed, "Russians must realize that if they cannot ensure development of the Far East and Siberia, Russia will lose those territories one way or another

---

114 Jennifer Anderson, "The Limits of Sino-Russian Strategic Partnership," *International Institute for Strategic Studies*, December, 1997, Adelphi Paper 315, p. 72.

115 Jennifer Anderson, "The Limits of Sino-Russian Strategic Partnership," *International Institute for Strategic Studies*, December 1997, Adelphi Paper 315, p. 72.

116 Donaldson, p. 713.

117 Ibid., p. 714.

118 Ibid.

119 Kanwa Information Center, "956E II Launching and Military Cooperation between Russia and China," May 2nd 2004. http://www.kanwa.com/free/2004/05/e0504%20956EM.htm.

120 Mitsuo Mii, "Russian-Chinese relations and arms exports" in Russia and Asia-Pacific Security. Stockholm International Peace Research Institute. Stockholm (Sweden), 1999, p. 1. http://projects.sipri.se/Russia/Mii.pdf.

and somebody else will then develop them."[121] In the face of China's growing military strength, Russia therefore needs to maintain a powerful defense. In other words, Russia would not give away its high technology unreservedly and enable China to build up a military industry that will rival them. In this regard, Russia's strategic weapons are still restricted exporting to China in order to maintain its military superiority over the Chinese; Russian military sources have stressed that they will not sell any missile with over 300-km range to China.[122] From China's perspective, the long-term possibility of a resurgent Russia, with sophisticated weapon systems, natural resources, geographic and population size, means it could become a potential enemy.[123]

The comparison of Sino-Russia and Indo-Russian military cooperation may help to explain the nature of the relationship between Beijing and Moscow from another spectrum. Russia's military cooperation with China differs significantly from that with India, who is traditionally a friend of Russia without any hostile history or potential threats. In this context, Russia's reservation in its arms sales to China may not apply to India. The 3M80MBE missile is an example. This is the SSM system for export with the longest range except the BRAHAMS SSM jointly developed by Russia and India. Some similar Russian weapon systems sold to India are more sophisticated than those sold to China in terms of quality. The acquisition of anti-ship missiles is one instance: the range of India's 3M80MBE is 300 km; while Chinese version 3M60ME is only 200 km. India's Su-30MKIs are powered by AL-31FP with thrust vectoring. The engine is steerable in +/- 15 degrees horizontally and +/- 32 degrees vertically which further increased its maneuverability; but Chinese version Su-30MKK will not be equipped with PGO (vector thrust) nor AL-31FP engines.[124]

This suggests that Russia's arms transfers to China are designed to preserve the short-run financial interest of its defense industries. As some analysts believe, the temporary arms sales to China would help to balance the U.S. threat but would not significantly change the military balance with China. In other words, Russia would preserve its long term interests by sacrificing short-term gain. For Russia, arms sales to China may be the only way for Russia to sustain its military industry. For China, there is no alternative armed dealer of advanced weaponry and technology to upgrade their military equipment.[125] In particular, in response to the post-Cold War U.S. military strategy in Asia Pacific, China's demand for modern military armaments has made Russia the most feasible resource.

---

121 Donaldson, p. 722.
122 Kanwa Information Center, "Club Anti-ship Missile and Chinese Navy" http://www.kanwa.com/free/2003/06/e0609a.htm.
123 Nathan & Ross, p. 79.
124 http://www.hudi.republika.pl/Su-30.htm.
125 Ibid.

U.S. Military Strategy and Its Possible Consequences

The United States is increasingly concerned about China's rising comprehensive national power and its behavior in the region; however, if the United States and its allies misinterpret Beijing's motives and overreact to China, it would lead to dangerous and unexpected reactions from Beijing. In fact, China is by no means challenging the international system; rather it wants to acquire minimum capability to deter U.S. intervention in a Taiwan crisis.[126] The new fundamentalists argue that to reassert American primacy globally, military power and willingness to exercise it must return to the center of American foreign policy.[127] Hence, the Bush administration decided not to ratify the CTBT and perhaps resume nuclear testing, to abandon the 1972 Anti-ballistic Missile (ABM) Treaty and actively pursue a national missile defense (NMD) and theater missile defense (TMD) program. The U.S. declared the possible use of nuclear weapons in retaliation against chemical and biological weapon attacks on the U.S. or its allies, and abandoned the qualified no-first-use pledge made by the Carter administration to NPT signatories.[128] Neorealists believe that a challenging power sets a goal for itself which derives from the relation between the military strengths of the two states prior to an arms race. If the relation is one of disparity, the initial challenge usually comes from the weaker state which expects to achieve parity or better. Conceivably a stronger power could initiate an arms race by believing that it required an even higher ratio of superiority over the weaker state.[129]

To sustain a long-term primacy over the region, the U.S. seeks to acquire an overwhelming strategic deterrent capability – the Theater Missile Defense (TMD) system. In fact, the deployment of TMD is a very dangerous move, which would trigger an overall arms race in East Asia. TMD is officially supposed to deal with North Korea, however in reality, analysts have suggested that it is aimed at China.[130] On the technological and strategic level, TMD may only be an intermediary system that would advance on to an offensive system. Once the general public accepts the concept of defense against incoming missiles, military leaders could further convince the public to accept the existence of offensive system that would be able to launch pre-emptive attacks.[131] Indeed, the tactics of American provocateurs in leaking false intelligence reports, prodding Japan into closer military cooperation with the United States, and promoting a theater missile defense (TMD) for the region are not only

---

126 Johnston, p. 32.

127 John Ikenberry, "The end of the Neo-Conservative Moment," *Survival*, vol. 46, no.1, Spring 2004, p. 8.

128 T.V. Paul, "Systemic Conditions and Security Cooperation: Explaining the Persistence of the Nuclear Non-proliferation Regime," *Cambridge Review of International Affairs*, vol. 16, no. 1, 2003, pp. 151–152.

129 Art and Waltz, p. 97.

130 Andrew Hanami, *Military Might of Modern Japan* (Dubuque, IA: Kendall/Hunt Publishing Company, 1995), p. 171.

131 Ibid.

dangerous but potentially illegal.[132] In response to U.S. strategic containment, China might face no choice but to modernize its ICBMs and increase the number of its arsenals to counter this threat, and a new military confrontation between major powers might emerge in East Asia.

Realists suggest that the United States seeks to maintain its superior power position and contain a rising power like China. According to this logic, the revitalization of the U.S.-Japan security alliance is evidently targetted primarily against China.[133] Seen in this light, Beijing has been increasingly worried about the possibility that the U.S.-Japanese alliance could become a tool for defending a permanently separated or even a formally independent Taiwan.[134] In particular, the Chinese policymakers think that a resurgent and militarized Japan would be a threat to China. In effect, the combination of Japanese wealth and technological prowess might create a huge military potential.[135] Japanese production of the F2 fighter jet will dominate the air over the East China Sea for the near future.[136] Moreover, Japan's XSSM-1, capable of use in all weather, is believed to be better than the American Tomahawk cruise missile; Japan's new XAAM-3 air-to-air missile is equipped with an infrared homing system and is expected to outperform American Sidewinders; the new SASM-2 air-to-air missile featuring improved homing infrared image system has an extended range of 62 miles.[137] Combined with sophisticated air power, Japan's large fleet of advanced destroyers and frigates will enable it to be a dominant sea power in East Asia.[138] Furthermore, the PLA interprets the 1996 U.S.-Japanese Common Security and Cooperation Treaty as a pressure from the West. As Japan's former minister Seiroku Kajiyama announced, Japan has expanded its area of security vigilance to cover the Taiwan Strait, and will not lie idle when its allies resort to action in the region.[139] This sentiment plays into Chinese fear and perceptions of past humiliations at the hands of Japanese and Western powers.[140] In response to these external hostile intents, China would accelerate the pace of modernization of their nuclear deterrence capabilities.

Many advocates of the missile defense system believe that a U.S. missile defense would put China in a position of vulnerability without a retaliatory recourse.[141] Indeed, China has begun in recent years to explore new technologies to penetrate this missile defense system. The PLA has made important progress on the development of

---

132 Ibid., p. 160.
133 Deng, p. 353.
134 Johnston, p. 42.
135 Nathan and Ross, p. 79.
136 Robert S. Ross, "China II: Beijing as a Conservative Power," *Foreign Affairs*, March/April 1997, p. 36.
137 Hanami, p. 62.
138 Ross, p. 17.
139 Ji, p. 204.
140 Ji, p. 236.
141 Niou, p. 13.

multiple independently targeted reentry vehicles (MIRV).[142] According to a Japanese newspaper, the PLA in December 2002 test-launched the medium range ballistic missile DF-21 from Shanxi Province equipped with multiple warheads.[143]

Furthermore, since the mid-1990s, the PLA has reactivated its dormant nuclear program, and is gradually modernizing its nuclear forces.[144] China had only one ICBM brigade prior to 1995–1996, since then, it has added two more DF-5 and two DF-31 brigades. Further analysis suggests that China might actually have a third type of nuclear capable ICBM – the DF-4 (CSS-3).[145] China launched a flight test of a DF-4 on 29 August 2002, and the test was monitored by U.S. intelligence as it was fired from Southern China to a remote impact area in the northwestern part of the country. As of mid-2002, China was believed to have about 20 DF-4s with a range of up to 4,340 miles.[146] In 1997, China has acquired new launch vehicle CZ-1D to deliver small satellites into low earth orbit (LEO). The design of CZ-1D consists of a 2-stage vehicle with the first stage burning UDMH and nitric acid whereas the second stage utilizes UDMH and nitrogen tetroxide. The payload capacity of the CZ-1D is 900 kg to LEO and 300 kg to a sun-synchronous orbit.[147] Given that the CZ-1D and DF-4 are identical in length, diameter, and weight, DF-4 can be easily converted into a ICBM: affix the solid rocket motor developed for the CZ-1D on top of the DF-4's 2-stage vehicle and a satellite can be replaced with a nuclear warhead. In this way, the PLA can increase the number of brigades equipped with ICBMs from five to eight, and once each is fully equipped with twelve missiles, the arsenal of China's ICBMs will become ninety-six.[148] That is to say, China's potential nuclear capability might be underestimated by the world. If the U.S. deploys TMD in the near future, the PLA would further increase the number of its ICBMs and modernize them. That would make the region worse off than it is currently.[149]

Another variable affecting China's reactions stems from the ambiguity of U.S. policy toward Taiwan. So far, it is still not clear whether the United States will defend Taiwan if the PLA uses military force to reunify Taiwan. To be sure, if the PLA has capabilities to deter the U.S. or to make the U.S. pay a heavy price on such intervention, Washington would be reluctant to support Taiwan, or only conditionally support it. Thus, the PLA is convinced that supersonic anti-ship missiles are the best weapons that may prevent a U.S. carrier battle group from approaching the Taiwan Strait. For this reason, the PLAN tried to acquire Russian CLUB series anti-ship missiles 3M54E, which is so far one of the most powerful subsonic/supersonic dual-

---

142 Ibid.
143 Hiroyuki Sugiyama, "China Tests Multiple-Warhead Missiles; New ICBMs to be Deployed," *The Daily Yomiuri* (Internet version) in English, Tokyo, 07 Feb 2003 (FBIS Transcripted Text).
144 Niou, p. 12.
145 Ibid., p. 10.
146 http://www.globalsecurity.org/wmd/world/china/df-4.htm.
147 http://www.fas.org/spp/guide/china/launch/cz-1d.htm.
148 Niou, p. 11.
149 Hanami, p. 171.

system anti-ship missiles available. The 3M54E will enable the Chinese Navy to launch effective long range attacks against rival ships. In fact, the first batch of 50 3M54E missiles will soon be delivered to China, and production of these missiles has begun.[150] Combined with 3M54E, KILO 636 and "Soveremenni" destroyers equipped with 3M80E (SS-N-22) will further enhance the PLAN's capabilities to take control of the Taiwan Strait waters and constrain the involvement of the U.S. forces in the Taiwan-China conflict.[151] That does not means the PLAN is capable of defeating U.S. fleets; although it does imply that the price of potential U.S. intervention will considerably increase.

Conclusion

To sum up, the world is increasingly concerned about China's emerging professional military and its impact on regional stability in the Asia Pacific. Structural realists argue that a stronger China will become a rival for the world power, and would strive to challenge the current international system. Following this principle, China will try to upgrade its military power and pose a threat to the region of Asia Pacific. However, the central finding of this study is that a modernized China would not be a threat to the U.S. and the international order; instead, China has sought to be fully incorporated into an interdependent world in the era of globalization.

As we have discussed above, although China's traditional strategic culture has long emphasized on preservation of international prestige, existence, and national integrity, the new strategic choice "peaceful development" has been stressed by Beijing's new leadership, which is intended to maintain a stable domestic and international environment for China's economic development. Moreover, economic engagement in international economic cooperation has gradually incorporated China into the international system, in which China's interests are increasingly interwoven with the world. Given the growth of China's influence in the global economy, globalization has increased China's bargaining power and economic leverages vis-à-vis the U.S. pressures. This does not mean that China would use its burgeoning power to counter U.S. power; rather, a richer and more dynamic China may have more reasons to cooperate with the U.S. There is no question that the U.S. and China are intertwined in one of the world's most important trading partnerships. That is, while China is reliant on the U.S. as an export market, the U.S. also needs China's dollar support. This interdependent relationship constrains the U.S. and China in exercising certain powers. Furthermore, China has one of the largest armed forces in the world, but its weapon systems are serious obsolete. In the face of high technology war, a huge military equipped with obsolete weapons systems does not have much value. Thus Chinese military modernization is designed to enhance its national security

---

150 Kanwa Information Center, "Club Anti-ship missile and Chinese Navy," Nov 20th, 2002. http://www.kanwa.com/free/2003/06/e0609a.htm.
151 Ibid.

by building a sophisticated armed force; otherwise, China's military advantage will diminish over time.

The Taiwan issue is still the most significant strategic concern for Beijing. However, in line with the "peaceful development" strategy, Beijing's Taiwan policy has become more realistic and pragmatic under Hu's new leadership. The passing of anti-secession law indicates that "no independence, no war" is the policy – That is, China does not intend to set a timetable for reunification, but will maintain the status quo. Although China has rigorously modernized its military power to deter Taiwan from independence, and has never renounced the use of military means to reunify Taiwan, China still mainly relies on U.S. pressure for preventing Taiwan from pursuing independence.

The Sino-Russian military cooperation is not aimed at balancing the U.S. presence in the region. From the Russian perspective, Russia's armed sales to China are to preserve its short term financial interests; while from the Chinese perspective, there is no alternative seller to Russia. To date the Sino-Russian military cooperation is still based on economic rather than strategic calculations, and there is no evidence that the Sino-Russian military cooperation can bolster China's military power to great extent, to which it would significantly alter the military balance between China and the U.S. In addition, China has neither the ambition nor the capability to project military power to rival with the United States in the short term. Nonetheless, Chinese military modernization is in part a reaction to the U.S. intention to lock in strategic advantages in response to a rising China in the international system. The ambiguity of U.S. military policy toward the Taiwan issue, and the uncertain future evolution of the security environment in the Asia Pacific, however, do not reassure China with its national security. That in turn has compelled China to upgrade its capability to deter Washington from military intervention in the Taiwan issue and counter any external security threat. Therefore, there are many factors that can affect China's "peaceful development," but if she can manage her external conditions and maintain good relations with the U.S., she will be further incorporated into the international community and play an important role.

Chapter 9

China's Peaceful Rise and Sino-Japanese Territorial and Maritime Tensions

Jean-Marc F. Blanchard*

Introduction[1]

The various contributors to this volume make clear that the prospects for China's "Peaceful Rise" are contingent on a variety of international factors. Needless to say, it also is dependent on China's ability to manage its complex relationship with Japan. Unfortunately, Sino-Japanese political relations are extremely frosty these days. One problem is history. Further aggravating relations is Japan's pursuit of a permanent seat on the U.N. Security Council, which China opposes. In addition, China and Japan seem locked in a competition for friends in South and Southeast Asia. Two other important sources of frictions are the Sino-Japanese dispute over ownership of the Diaoyu (Senkaku) Islands and their quarrel over the delimitation of the East China Sea.[2]

Analysts assessing the prospects for China's peaceful rise must pay attention to these problems because international relations scholars have incontrovertibly shown that boundary disputes are explosive.[3] Indeed, in China's specific case, statistical analyses reveal that it is most prone to use force when territorial issues are at stake.[4] As far as island and maritime disputes themselves are concerned, episodes such as

---

* I would like to thank Joseph Y.S. Cheng, Robert Gamer, Sujian Guo, Greg Moore, and Srini Sitaraman for their feedback on an earlier version of this chapter. I also would like to thank Mikiko Fuse for her research assistance.

1 Chinese and Japanese names are given with the surname first. Publications in English, though, have their names given in the published order. Also, I generally refer to the disputed islands by their Chinese names. This is no way represents any judgment about the respective legitimacy of Chinese or Japanese claims.

2 "China, Japan Relations 'At the Crossroads': Chinese State Councillor," *People's Daily Online*, April 16, 2005, http://english.people.com.cn/200504/16/eng20050416_181364.html.

3 Jean-Marc F. Blanchard, "Linking Border Disputes and War: An Institutional-Statist Theory," *Geopolitics*, vol. 10, no. 4, 2005, p. 689.

4 Alastair Iain Johnston, "China's Militarized Interstate Dispute Behaviour 1949–1992: A First Cut at the Data," *China Quarterly*, no. 153, 1998, pp. 1–30.

Sino-Vietnamese hostilities in 1988 and Sino-Filipino clashes in 1995 evidence the explosiveness of island and maritime disputes.[5]

While the Sino-Japanese territorial and maritime dynamic will shape the prospects for China's peaceful rise, it must be recognized that China's rise (as well as the quest for such) concurrently shapes the territorial and maritime dynamic. On the one hand, it gives China *inter alia* a growing interest in the Diaoyu Islands (the "Islands") and the East China Sea. On the other hand, it provides incentives for Chinese policy makers to temper these controversies in order to facilitate a good working relationship with Japan.

The main objective of this chapter is to evaluate whether or not the aforementioned territorial and maritime problems could end in militarized conflict.[6] To do so, I initially examine the forces driving an escalation of the territorial and maritime controversies. Subsequently, I evaluate the factors that are moderating the disputes. I conclude that the near-to medium-term likelihood of militarized conflict is low despite China's intensifying interest in its boundaries with Japan. One reason is that China still lacks the military wherewithal to challenge Japan. Furthermore, China still has a strong economic and political need for Japan. Over the long-run, however, pessimism is warranted because of China's growing interest in the Islands and East China Sea, strengthening military capabilities, and declining need for Japan.

This chapter has five sections. The second section supplies general background information on the dispute over the Islands and East China Sea, provides a brief history of these problems from 1968 to 1978, traces the Sino-Japanese territorial and maritime dynamic between 1979 and 2000, and details the course of the quarrels from the beginning of the new millennium to the present. The third section develops a three-variable framework for evaluating the conflict potential of the quarrels. The fourth section undertakes a theoretically-guided analysis of these variables. In the concluding section, I summarize my findings, identify some areas in need of further research, and offer some concluding remarks.

An Overview of the Disputes Over the Islands and East China Sea

The Sino-Japanese dispute over the Islands involves rival claims to five uninhabited islands and three rocks situated approximately 200 nautical miles (nm) from the Chinese mainland, 200 nm from Okinawa, and 120 nm from Taiwan. The largest island is called Diaoyu Dao (Uotsuri Shima). Two other noteworthy islands are

---

5   Ji Guoxing, "Maritime Jurisdiction in the Three China Seas: Options for Equitable Settlement," *IGCC Policy Papers* PP19, 1995, pp. 7–8, http://repositories.cdlib.org/igcc/PP/PP19.

6   This paper does not aim in any way to offer a legal analysis. For a list of works that do so, see Jean-Marc F. Blanchard, "An Island of Friction in a Sea of Problems: China and the Diaoyu (Senkaku) Islands and East China Sea Disputes," Paper presented at the 2005 Annual Meeting of the Association of Chinese Political Studies, San Francisco, California, July 30–31, 2005, p. 3 fn(12).

Huangwei Yu (Kuba Shima) and Chiwei Yu (Taisho Shima). These eight islands and rocks roughly aggregate only 3 square miles (7 square kilometers or 7 km^2) of territory.[7] Ownership over the Islands is important because, pursuant to the 1982 U.N. Convention on the Law of the Sea (UNCLOS), it could provide an Exclusive Economic Zone (EEZ) and continental shelf.[8] More specifically, it could provide around 20,000 square nm of EEZ. In geographic terms, the continental shelf associated with the Islands is important for China since a large percentage of China's EEZ entails continental shelf. With respect to Japan, ownership of the Islands would allow Japan to bridge the Okinawa Trough and have baselines from which it could assert rights to what China sees as its continental shelf.[9]

The East China Sea links in the north with the Yellow Sea and connects, in the south, with the South China Sea. It is relatively shallow and thus conducive to resource exploration. Its troughs include the Yangzi, Zhedong, Taipei, and Pengjiayu. Within these troughs lie other troughs that differ in size and depth, but generally possess thick sediment likely to yield oil and gas. The East China Sea also offers

---

7 Raul Lautenschutz, "Japan, China, and the Senkaku Islands," *Swiss Review of World Affairs*, July 1979, p. 32; Phil Deans, "The Diaoyutai/Senkaku Dispute: The Unwanted Controversy," *Kent Papers in Politics and IR*, Series 6, no. 1, February 1996; Han-Yi Shaw, "The Diaoyutai/Senkaku Islands Dispute: Its History and an Analysis of the Ownership Claims of the P.R.C., R.O.C., Japan," *Occasional Papers/Reprints Series in Contemporary Asian Studies*, vol. 152, no. 3, 1999, pp. 10–11; and Daniel J. Dzurek, "Effect of the Diaoyu/Senkaku Islands Dispute on Maritime Delimitation," in M.A. Pratt and J.A. Brown, eds., *Borderlands under Stress* (London: Kluwer Law International, 2000), p. 409.

8 An EEZ generally provides a state with sole rights to exploit all living and non-living resources in the waters, the seabed, and the subsoil out to a distance of 200 nautical miles (nm) from the EEZ's baselines. UNCLOS explicitly states that "rocks which cannot sustain human habitation or economic life of their own" are not entitled to EEZs or continental shelf. Per UNCLOS, the length of a state's continental shelf generally is 200 nm from its baselines. However, in cases where the continental margin represents the natural prolongation of a state's land territory, then it may extend to 350 nm or 100 nm from a depth of 2,500 meters. Even so, natural prolongation no longer serves as an incontestable basis for establishing a country's continental shelf. In any event, in cases where continental shelves overlap, the relevant states are supposed to negotiate a boundary, taking into account circumstances and equity considerations. On UNCLOS's provisions, see Su Dushi, "Some Notes on Problems Concerning the Defense of China's Coastal Areas and Territorial Seas" [Lue Tan Han Wei Wo Guo Hai Jiang Wenti], *Zhongguo Bian Jiang Shi Di Yan Jiu*, vol. 1, 1992, p. 76; Jonathan I. Charney, "Central East Asian Maritime Boundaries and the Law of the Sea," *American Journal of International Law*, vol. 89, no. 4, 1995, pp. 724–749; and Robert W. Smith and Bradford L. Thomas, "Island Disputes and the Law of the Sea: An Examination of Sovereignty and Delimitation Disputes," *Maritime Briefing*, vol. 2, no. 4, 1998, pp. 1–26.

9 Dzurek, "Effect of the Diaoyu/Senkaku Islands Dispute on Maritime Delimitation," 2000, pp. 409, 412; and Victor Prescott and Clive Schofield, "Undelimited Maritime Boundaries of the Asian Rim in the Pacific Ocean," *Maritime Briefing*, vol. 3, no. 1, 2001, pp. 22–23.

rich fishing grounds.[10] The East China Sea controversy relates to the delimitation of China and Japan's respective maritime rights in the sea. Japan claims the median line as the sea boundary while China claims the entire continental shelf on the basis of the natural prolongation principle.[11]

A History of the Sino-Japanese Territorial and Maritime Disputes from 1968 to 1978[12]

In a report based on surveys conducted in 1968, the United Nations Economic Commission for Asia and the Far East (U.N. ECAFE) reported the potential existence of rich petroleum deposits under the East China Sea. Almost immediately, rival claimants began to assert sovereignty over the Islands and assert their position in the East China Sea. In December 1970, China entered the fray, asserting officially for the first time that the Islands were sacred Chinese territory. It also rejected Japanese, South Korean, and Taiwanese plans for joint development of the East China Sea. On June 17, 1971 Japan and the U.S. concluded a treaty, the Okinawa Reversion Treaty, pursuant to which the U.S. agreed to return the Ryukyu and Daito islands to Japanese administration in May 1972. An Agreed Minute attached to the 1971 agreement specified the coordinates of the area to be returned to Japan and these coordinates unquestionably incorporated all the disputed Islands. China decried the treaty, stating that the inclusion of contested islands was invalid and illegal.[13]

---

10 Zou Keyuan, "Sino-Japanese Joint Fishery Management in the East China Sea," *Marine Policy*, vol. 27, no. 2, 2003, p. 125; and Zhao Li Guo, "Seabed Petroleum in the East China Sea: Geological Prospects and the Search for Cooperation," pp. 1–3, Paper prepared for the "Seabed Petroleum in the East China Sea" workshop, Beijing, China, April 12-13, 2004, http://www.wilsoncenter.org/index.cfm?topic_id=1462&fuseaction=topics.documents&group_id=132299.

11 Ji Guoxing, "The Diaoyudao (Senkaku) Disputes and Prospects for Settlement," *Korean Journal of Defense Analysis*, vol. 6, no. 2, 1994, pp. 307–308; Mark J. Valencia, "Asia, the Law of the Sea, and International Relations," *International Affairs*, vol. 73, no. 2, 1997, p. 272; and Prescott and Schofield, "Undelimited Maritime Boundaries of the Asian Rim in the Pacific Ocean," 2001, pp. 19–25. A median line is a line that is equidistant from the nearest baselines of the two countries concerned.

12 The origins of Sino-Japanese territorial and maritime disputes can be traced to 1895. For discussion of the history prior to 1968, see Jean-Marc F. Blanchard, "The U.S. Role in the Sino-Japanese Dispute over the Diaoyu (Senkaku) Islands, 1945–1971, *China Quarterly*, no. 161, 2000, pp. 95–123; and Blanchard, "An Island of Friction in a Sea of Problems," 2005, pp. 7–9.

13 Japan, Ministry of Foreign Affairs, *The Senkaku Islands and the Territorial Issue* (Tokyo: Ministry of Foreign Affairs, Japan, 1972), p. 4; Selig S. Harrison, *China, Oil, and Asia: Conflict Ahead?* (New York: Columbia University Press, 1977), pp. 1–6, 92–100, 174–178, 266–267 fn(7); Su, "Lue Tan Han Wei Wo Guo Hai Jiang Wenti, 1992, p. 81; Ji, "The Diaoyudao (Senkaku) Disputes and Prospects for Settlement," 1994, pp. 286, 293–294, 298; Unryu Suganuma, *Sovereign Rights and Territorial Space in Sino-Japanese Relations: Irredentism and the Diaoyu/Senkaku Islands* (Honolulu: University of Hawaii Press, 2000), pp. 129–133; and Zhao, "Seabed Petroleum in the East China Sea," 2004, p. 4.

In spite of their views about the Islands and East China Sea, Chinese policy makers largely opted in the early 1970s to minimize their territorial and maritime disagreements with Japan. For them, the most pressing objective was to establish diplomatic relations with Tokyo in order to facilitate a front against the Soviet Union and to ease the termination of Japanese relations with Taiwan. Nevertheless, China still took actions to assert its territorial and maritime rights in the wake of the 1972 normalization. For example, in 1973, China attacked a Japanese-South Korean joint development agreement for the East China Sea, stating that the accord was a violation of Chinese sovereignty.[14]

In February 1978, Chinese and Japanese leaders resumed their stalled peace treaty discussions, which had begun in 1975. Beijing's paramount goal of countering the Soviet threat again gave Chinese leaders powerful incentives to shelve Sino-Japanese territorial and maritime tensions so as to smooth the path to an agreement with Japan. In addition, better relations with Japan would support Chinese leader Deng Xiaoping's efforts to reinvigorate the Chinese economy and reintegrate it with the international economy. After all, Japan had the ability to supply China with capital, high end products, managerial expertise, and technology. Furthermore, it could serve as a destination for Chinese exports.[15]

Nevertheless, it proved impossible to completely submerge Sino-Japanese territorial and maritime frictions. In March, anti-treaty forces in Japan began to raise the Islands controversy in an effort to disrupt Sino-Japanese peace treaty negotiations.[16] Among other steps, these forces lobbied the Japanese government to freeze treaty negotiations until after a resolution of the territorial issue. China responded by sending more than 100 fishing vessels, perhaps half armed, into the territorial waters of the Islands. The boats repeatedly traveled around the Islands, displaying signs asserting China's sovereignty. China's dispatch of fishing vessels escalated the controversy to "near-crisis proportions." The dispute, though, did not intensify partly because China opted to mix its display of force with diplomacy.

Shortly after tensions subsided and China and Japan agreed on the anti-Soviet language to be included in a treaty, the two East Asian giants concluded the (August) 1978 Treaty of Peace and Friendship. Two months later, Chinese Vice-Premier Deng Xiaoping acknowledged in Tokyo that China and Japan had different views about the Islands and that a compromise was not yet possible. As far as he was concerned, the dispute should be shelved.[17] Tellingly, China

---

14 Blanchard, "An Island of Friction in a Sea of Problems," 2005, pp. 11–12.

15 Daniel Tretiak, "The Sino-Japanese Treaty of 1978: The Senkaku Incident Prelude," *Asian Survey*, vol. 18, no. 2, 1978, pp. 1235–1249; June Teufel Dreyer, "Sino-Japanese Relations," *Journal of Contemporary China*, vol. 10, no. 28, 2001, p. 373; and Blanchard, "An Island of Friction in a Sea of Problems," 2005, p. 13.

16 This discussion makes extensive use of Tretiak, "The Sino-Japanese Treaty of 1978," 1978.

17 China's Relations with its Neighbors and Its Security Environment [*Zhongguo Zhoubian Guanxi Yu Anquan Huanjing*] (Shaanxi: People's Education Press, n.d.), translated in JPRS-CAR-93-037, June 8, 1993, p. 26.

proved willing to conclude the 1978 Treaty even in the face of continuing Japanese provocations. For example, in August 1978, Nihon Seinensha (the Japanese Youth Federation or Association), a group with ultra-nationalist views affiliations, erected a wooden lighthouse structure ("Number One Lighthouse") on Diaoyu Island.[18]

The Sino-Japanese Territorial and Maritime Controversy from 1979 to 2000

The 1978 Peace Treaty and deepening economic linkages were insufficient to prevent Sino-Japanese initiatives or to eliminate territorial and maritime frictions. To illustrate, early in 1979, Japan started to construct a helicopter landing pad on Diaoyu Island, which China protested by sending 50 fishing boats into the area around the Islands. The same year, Japan sent a team to the Islands whose official task was to gather scientific data and to place markings that would permit satellite surveys of the islands. Even so, China and Japan remained cooperative over conflictual policies for the remainder of the decade.[19]

Late in 1980, China and Japan undertook a joint effort to define an East China Sea border. During their consultations, Beijing claimed a boundary line on the basis of the natural prolongation principle while Japan insisted on using the median line. Given their widely divergent positions, it is not surprising that negotiations failed. Subsequently, China moved to assert its claims by drilling two exploratory wells (Longjing I and Longjing II) in the East China Sea. These actions elevated tensions even though both wells were situated on the Chinese side of Japan's favored median line. China subsequently dampened tensions by withdrawing its rigs and again soliciting Japanese interest in the joint development. For the balance of the 1980s, the Sino-Japanese territorial and maritime controversies were muted. In late 1988, though, differences reappeared when, on the 10th anniversary of its construction of "Number One Lighthouse," Nihon Seinensha spent 3 million yen replacing it with an aluminum structure.[20]

In 1992, the Islands' quarrel dramatically resurfaced because China listed the Islands as Chinese territory in its Law on the Territorial Sea and Contiguous Waters. China also claimed a 12 nm territorial sea around the Islands and a 24 nm contiguous zone. It further required all foreign military vessels to obtain transit permission and all foreign submarines and other submersible craft to sail on the surface. As well, it asserted China's right to authorize scientific research and other activities.[21] In response to complaints, Chinese leaders emphasized that their territorial sea law was

---

18 Shaw, "The Diaoyutai/Senkaku Islands Dispute," 1999, p. 17 fn(15).
19 Blanchard, "An Island of Friction in a Sea of Problems," 2005, p. 16.
20 Ibid., pp. 16–17.
21 "The Law of the People's Republic of China on Its Territorial Waters and Their Contiguous Areas," *Xinhua Domestic Service*, February 25, 1992, translated in FBIS-CHI-92-040, February 29, 1992, p. 2.

nothing more than a formality. Moreover, when then CCP General Secretary Jiang Zemin visited Japan, he called on the two countries to shelve their disputes.[22]

In 1996, China and Japan ratified UNCLOS. The period leading up to these ratifications was fraught with tension. For example, in May 1995, a Chinese government vessel undertook survey work around the Islands and only left after the Japanese MSA and Foreign Ministry demanded that it cease such work. Three months later, Japan dispatched planes to warn off Chinese planes it believed had been sent on a patrol mission over the Islands. In December, Japan reported a Chinese oil drilling ship anchored relatively close to the Islands. And in February 1996, Japan announced that a Japanese MSA vessel had spotted a Chinese oil-drilling vessel off the Islands.[23]

Matters took a turn for the worse after China claimed sovereign rights and jurisdiction over an EEZ of 200-nm and the continental shelf in early June 1996 pursuant to its ratification of UNCLOS. At the time of ratification, China declared that it would settle sea boundaries with states having coasts opposite or adjacent to China on the basis of international law and the equitable principle. Furthermore, it reaffirmed its sovereignty over the Islands. Later in the same month, Japan ratified UNCLOS and passed its implementing legislation. It designated a 12-nm territorial sea, a 24-nm contiguous zone, and an EEZ of 200 nm. It also noted that in cases where another country is opposite Japan the sea boundary shall be the median line, putting it on a collision course with China. As for the continental shelf, Japan limited itself to 200 nm or the median line with opposite states, except as otherwise agreed. Notably, the legislation did not mention Japan's sovereignty over the Islands.[24]

Territorial and maritime relations plummeted when, on July 14, 1996, members of Nihon Seinensha landed on Beixiaodao and built a 5-meter high solar-powered aluminum lighthouse ("Number Two Lighthouse"). Although the Japanese government expressed concern about the lighthouse, it did not dismantle it. In fact, it emphasized that "Japan clearly holds the ownership of the Senkaku Islands" and that the construction of a lighthouse was legitimate. Beijing persisted in demanding that Japan remove the lighthouse, describing it as "a serious encroachment on China's territorial sovereignty." Japan, though, held its ground and denied there was a territorial dispute. The next month, the tenor of the dispute worsened with the *People's Daily* commenting that "No Chinese will surrender the country's territory and sovereignty to anyone. If anybody dares do so, he will be cursed for centuries." Moreover, the Chinese government permitted a Chinese group pushing for war reparations from Japan to present a petition to Chinese President Jiang Zemin that

---

22 Donald W. Klein, "Japan and Europe in Chinese Foreign Relations," in Samuel S. Kim, ed., *China and the World: Chinese Foreign Relations in the Post-Cold War Era* (Boulder: Westview Press, 1994), p. 124; Dreyer, "Sino-Japanese Relations," 2001, pp. 375–376; and Suganuma, *Sovereign Rights and Territorial Space in Sino-Japanese Relations*, 2000, pp. 142–143.

23 Blanchard, "An Island of Friction in a Sea of Problems," 2005, p. 19.

24 Ibid., pp. 19–20.

requested the government to use the Chinese navy to dismantle the lighthouse. Despite this, China sought to dampen Sino-Japanese tensions by again calling upon Japan to consider joint exploration.

In September, frictions escalated after Nihon Seinensha repaired one of its lighthouses which had been damaged. On an unofficial level, there were major protests in Hong Kong and Taiwan. Early the following month, new problems arose when between 30 and 50 boats from Hong Kong and Taiwan traveled to the islands to tear down the lighthouse on Diaoyu Island. To the delight of the activists, six protestors succeeded in landing on the island. During the action, one protest boat sank, which the activists blamed on Japan. Although the Chinese government protested the treatment of the activists as well as the presence of "Number One Lighthouse," the Japanese government responded it could do nothing about the lighthouse because it was built on private land. On the other hand, Japanese Foreign Minister Ikeda Yukihiko reiterated that the Japanese government had no plans to recognize it.[25]

The beginning of 1997 found Chinese and Japanese policy makers working to improve their relationship. In March, for instance, Japanese Foreign Minister Ikeda agreed to defer formal delimitation of an EEZ. He also promised to restrain Japanese nationalists. Even so, Japan stood firm on the Islands. The next month, it was the East China Sea's turn to become a zone of conflict. The Japanese MSA reported not only that a Chinese exploration vessel had entered deeply into Japan's claimed EEZ, but also that it traversed the territorial waters around the Islands and refused to respond to Japanese MSA queries. Contributing to the tense atmosphere of the time, a Japanese group including a Diet member landed on Diaoyu Island on May 6 and hoisted Japanese flags.[26]

In the sphere of fisheries, the news was more positive. In September 1997, China and Japan concluded a Sino-Japanese Fisheries Agreement. It created a Provisional Measures or Joint Fishing Zone (hereinafter PMZ) applicable to both China and Japan's EEZs, which ran between 27°N and 30°40′N and 52 nm from each state's respectively baselines. The accord also established fishing permit requirements, the legal obligations of fishermen, and specified flag-state jurisdiction over vessels operating within the PMZ. Also meriting attention is the fact that the agreement created a joint fisheries committee. Notably, the agreement was silent as to the location of a Sino-Japanese East China Sea boundary as well as the ownership of the Islands.[27]

---

25 Ibid., pp. 20–21.
26 Ibid., p. 22.
27 Mark J. Valencia and Yoshihisa Amae, "Regime Building in the East China Sea," *Ocean Development & International Law*, vol. 34, 2003, pp. 193–196; Zou, "Sino-Japanese Joint Fishery Management in the East China Sea," 2003, pp. 132–137; and Sun Pyo Kim, "The UN Convention on the Law of the Sea and New Fisheries Agreements in North East Asia," *Marine Policy*, vol. 27, no. 2, 2003, pp. 106–107.

In April 1988, a Chinese marine research ship twice entered the territorial waters of the Islands while surveying the ocean floor within Japan's claimed EEZ. This incident was only one of 16 Japanese sightings of Chinese research vessels in Japan's claimed EEZ that year. In June, China began to exploit the Pinghu oil field from a newly established rig in the East China Sea. The same month, five boats, manned by 60 protestors from Hong Kong and Taiwan challenged 50 Japanese MSA ships near the Islands. The incident caused friction because one of the Chinese protest boats sank, with the protestors and the Chinese government blaming the Japanese.[28]

In 1999, the Japanese MSDF listed 30 sightings of Chinese ships in Japan's claimed EEZ. Notably, Japan's MSDF reported four occasions when Chinese ships had entered into the territorial waters off the Islands. The Japanese MSA reported that it requested these vessels to leave and to terminate their research activities, but that these vessels refused. In August, a Nihon Seinensha delegation traveled to the Islands and put three members ashore for a brief time. In response to Chinese protests, the Japanese Ambassador to China expressed regret. At the same time, he called on the Chinese to halt fishing in the area and expressed concern over Chinese oceanographic activities.[29]

The Island and East China Sea Disputes in the New Millennium

In April 2000, members of Nihon Seinensha again landed on one of the Islands and built a small shrine. The Chinese Foreign Ministry expressed indignation and demanded that Japan "honor its commitment, restrict right-wing activists, and prevent similar incidents from recurring."[30] From Japan's perspective, China was the problem as it continued to intrude into Japan's claimed EEZ – Japan reported more than two dozen sightings in 2000. After Japanese Diet members threatened to postpone a $161 million infrastructure loan, Chinese Foreign Minister Tang Jiaxuan agreed to speak with Japanese Foreign Minister Kono Yohei about an advanced notification system for ship activities in disputed East China Sea areas.[31]

After approximately six months of negotiations, China and Japan signed a mutual prior notification agreement on February 13, 2001 (the "2001 Agreement"). Pursuant to it, each side agreed to give two months notice "if either country is to conduct maritime scientific research nearby the coast of the other, except for territorial

---

28 Dzurek, "Effect of the Diaoyu/Senkaku Islands Dispute on Maritime Delimitation," 2000, pp. 409, 411–412; and Valencia and Amae, "Regime Building in the East China Sea," 2003, p. 196.

29 Blanchard, "An Island of Friction in a Sea of Problems," 2005, p. 25.

30 People's Republic of China, Ministry of Foreign Affairs, "Spokesperson on Right-Wing Japanese Landing on the Diaoyu Islands," April 30, 2000, http://www.fmprc.gov.cn/eng/3868.html.

31 Dreyer, "Sino-Japanese Relations," 2001, pp. 383–384; Valencia and Amae, "Regime Building in the East China Sea," 2003, pp. 197–198; and Denny Roy, "Stirring Samurai, Disapproving Dragon: Japan's Growing Security Activity and Sino-Japanese Relations," *Asian Affairs*, vol. 31, no. 2, 2004, p. 96.

waters." Although the 2001 Agreement did not explicitly mention a median line sea boundary, Japan took the position that it implied one. Only two months after China and Japan concluded the agreement, Chinese vessels recommenced research in Japan's claimed EEZ. While, according to Japanese reports, the Chinese violated the 2001 Agreement on several occasions, the most bothersome incident transpired when the Chinese Navy told the Japanese MSDF to stay away from a Chinese hired vessel that was operating on the Japanese side of Japan's favored median line.[32]

In March 2002, there were new tensions as a result of Japan's dispatch of various MSA ships into disputed areas of the East China Sea in order to look for a North Korean ship that had sunk in December 2001 after the Japanese MSDF had chased and fired upon it. China criticized Japan for using force in its EEZ and warned that it would safeguard its rights. Japan retorted that it was its right to fire upon the ship and that it had done so only after the suspect vessel responded forcefully to a Japanese warning shot. Around the same time, Japan started to lease some of the Islands, specifically Diaoyu, Nanxiaodao, and Beixiaodao. According to Japanese newspapers, the government leased the islands for the purpose of enhancing its ability to prevent landings on them. China opined that the lease was invalid and called upon Tokyo to renounce it.[33]

On June 23, 2003, a Chinese boat with 13 protestors entered the territorial waters of the Islands. The protestors were blocked from making a landing by the Japanese MSA. In remarks about the episode, Chief Cabinet Secretary Fukuda Yasuo emphasized that the Islands were an integral part of Japanese territory and that Japan would take whatever legal measures it needed to repel trespassers. Two months later, tensions rose slightly when members of Nihon Seinensha landed on the Islands. Beijing opined that unilateral Japanese actions were illegal and invalid and reaffirmed China's ownership of the Islands. It further called upon Japan to move to eliminate the impacts of the landings and prevent re-occurrences. In October, Chinese activists from the mainland, Taiwan, and Hong Kong set off for the contested islands in a two boat fleet, neither of which successfully landed.[34]

In mid-January 2004 two boats, both from China, traveled to the islands where they planned to set up a monument. Although they got within 10 nm of the islands, they found their progress impeded by Japanese forces. Two months later, seven Chinese activists succeeded in landing on Diaoyu Island. Japanese police arrested them, leading to an angry Chinese diplomatic reaction and three days of relatively low-key anti-Japanese protests in Beijing. In the wake of the incident, which led to a cancellation of bilateral talks concerning continuing Chinese research in Japan's claimed EEZ, Japan moved to ban landings without prior permission. Early in April, Chinese Premier Wen Jiabao repeated Chinese claims to the Islands during a visit

---

32 Selig S. Harrison, "Quiet Struggle in the East China Sea," *Current History*, vol. 101, no. 656, 2002, p. 274; and Valencia and Amae, "Regime Building in the East China Sea," 2003, pp. 198–199.

33 Blanchard, "An Island of Friction in a Sea of Problems," 2005, pp. 26–27.

34 Ibid., pp. 27–28.

by Japanese Foreign Minister Kawaguchi Yoriko to Beijing. In turn, Kawaguchi demanded that China restrain its people from landing on the Islands. The next month witnessed the Japanese Foreign Ministry protesting to China over the intrusion of a Chinese research vessel into Japan's claimed EEZ around the Islands without prior notification as called for by the 2001 Agreement.[35]

In early June, there were new tensions after China built a new drilling facility in Chunxiao (which Japan calls Shirakaba), only 4 km from Japan's favored median line. Subsequently, Japan demanded that China provide it with data on all its exploration activities. The following month, the Japanese Minister for Economics, Trade, and Industry (METI) announced that Japan would launch explorations in East China Sea areas that China claimed, though all of the areas were east of the Japanese-advocated median line. The Chinese Foreign Ministry repeated that China did not recognize and would not recognize the so-called median line. It also informed the Japanese that China could not tolerate Japan's unilateral move and found it dangerous and provocative. Finally, it called upon Japan to immediately stop acts that infringed upon China's interests and sovereignty. For its part, Japan raised complaints about the repeated appearance of Chinese naval survey vessels and government marine research ships in the East China Sea and around the Islands.[36]

In September, Tokyo again asked Beijing to provide it with its exploration data. The Chinese refused, but responded with a proposal that both sides enter into discussions about joint exploration. The next month, Japan sought emergency talks with China after it received reports that Beijing had stepped up its exploration efforts in areas that Japan claimed. Towards the end of the following month, China and Japan held talks, which resulted only in an agreement to continue talking.[37] Not long after the conclusion of the October talks, the *People's Daily* raised alarm about Japanese military plans for the East China Sea, reporting that Japan was contemplating establishing a detection system on it. It further observed that "Since the Chinese-Japan dispute over resources of East China Sea surfaced, Japan has enhanced all kinds of military deployment in this sea area."[38]

In early January 2005, a *People's Daily* opinion piece once again criticized the aforementioned Japanese military plans, which discussed how Japan might repel a foreign invasion against what it considered to be its remote southern islands, including the Islands. The article charged that "what the Japanese military department is trying to do is how it is preparing itself to prevent foreign troops [e.g., Chinese troops] from occupying foreign territories [e.g., Chinese territory]."[39] On February 4, a Chinese Foreign Ministry spokesman called on Japan to settle their territorial and maritime

---

35 Ibid., pp. 28–30.
36 Ibid., pp. 30–31.
37 Ibid., pp. 31–32.
38 "Japan Intends to Set Up Intelligence Station at East China Sea," *People's Daily Online*, November 9, 2004, http://english1.peopledaily.com.cn/200411/09/eng20041109_163229.html.
39 "Japan cannot add Chinese Territory into its Plan," *People's Daily Online*, January 18, 2005, http://english.people.com.cn/200501/18/eng20050118_170987.html.

controversies through negotiation and dialogue.[40] Five days later, Sino-Japanese territorial and maritime problems resurfaced when Japan placed the lighthouse constructed on Diaoyu Island in 1988 under "state control." This move produced a small-scale protest outside the Japanese embassy in Beijing. Moreover, the Chinese Foreign Ministry charged Tokyo with severely violating Chinese sovereignty.[41]

Early in April, Japan began to allocate rights for gas exploration in the East China Sea in Chinese-claimed areas. Japan's action came in the wake of a Chinese refusal to discontinue its exploration activities. China described Japan's move as a big provocation and reminded Japan that China had not agreed on a maritime boundary with Japan. It cautioned Japan not to take action that complicated the situation and again requested Japan to shelve the sea border dispute and pursue joint development.[42] In the following month, the Sino-Japanese territorial dispute flared anew after the Japanese government announced that 18 Japanese nationals had registered permanent addresses on the Islands. A Chinese Foreign Ministry spokesman declared that China would never acquiesce in any of Japan's unilateral moves and reiterated that the Islands belonged to China.[43]

The next month, there were new frictions when the Ishigaki assembly passed a measure that required its mayor and assembly members to inspect the Islands. In an angrily worded commentary, China condemned the assembly's measure and defended its historical rights to the Islands. It added, Japan "not only connives at the right-wing groups' provocative activities, but also goes back on its promise of not taking unilateral actions and tries in vain to capture the Diaoyu Islands as so-called 'Japanese territory'" by *inter alia* starting to rent islands in 2002 and passing resolutions. The commentary warned "If Japan continues to take unilateral actions time and again to challenge China's territorial sovereignty, it can only worsen China-Japan relations."[44] The day after the commentary appeared, China derided Japan's treatment of Chinese fishermen who had been operating in contested areas. It further charged that Japan had rejected China's call for joint exploration and restated that Japan had drawn a sea boundary "without consulting China."[45]

In early July, METI Minister Nakagawa Shoichi announced that Japan had granted, for the first time, test drilling rights in the East China Sea to a Japanese company, Teikoku Oil. Ominously, Japan assigned Teikoku Oil these test drilling

---

40 "China Hopes Sino-Japanese Disputes be Solved through Negotiation," *People's Daily Online*, February 4, 2005, http://english.people.com.cn/200502/04/eng20050204_172917.html.

41 Blanchard, "An Island of Friction in a Sea of Problems," 2005, p. 33.

42 Ibid., p. 34.

43 Ibid., pp. 34–35.

44 "Commentary: A Resolution of Challenging China's Territorial Sovereignty," *People's Daily Online*, June 21, 2005, http://english.people.com.cn/200506/21/eng20050621_191409.html.

45 "Japan 'Violated' China's Sovereignty, FM Spokesman," *People's Daily Online*, June 22, 2005, http://english.people.com.cn/200506/22/eng20050622_191716.html.

rights in an area where Chinese firms were already exploring. A Chinese Foreign Ministry spokesman told reporters, "If Japan persists in granting drilling rights to companies in disputed waters it will cause a serious infringement of China's sovereign right."[46] China further labeled Japan's move a "severe provocation" as well as a violation of UNCLOS. It again rejected Japan's median line, emphasizing that China and Japan should explore a settlement through dialogue. In the interim, it demanded that Japan reverse its decision.[47]

On July 21, the *People's Daily* published a lengthy and vitriolic opinion piece on the Japanese government's decision to grant Teikoku Oil test drilling rights as well as the latter's move to give Japanese names to three oil-gas fields – Chunxiao, Duanqiao (Kusunoki), and Leng Quan – that China regards as its own. It asserted that Japan's move would "make the East China Sea the most dangerous area for possible eruption of conflicts between the two countries" and would damage Sino-Japanese relations. Interestingly, the piece emphasized the Chinese Government's past protests. It also noted that the Chinese Embassy in Japan informed the Japanese Foreign Affairs Ministry that the Chinese Maritime Safety Administration (China's Coast Guard) would continuously patrol China's EEZ.[48]

Not surprisingly, Japan had its own grievances. In early August, Japanese Trade Minister Nakagawa Shoichi told reporters that China was laying pipes in the East China Sea and that China had ignored Japanese protests about the issue.[49] The next month, Nakagawa informed a news conference that China had begun to extract energy at another site, Tianwaitian (Kashi), not far from Japan's EEZ, a fact which Japan protested.[50] This followed the Japanese Maritime SDF's more alarming sighting in early September of a fleet of five Chinese warships, which included a guided-missile destroyer, in the area near the Chunxiao gas field.[51]

---

46 "Japan Stokes China Sea Dispute," *BBC News*, July 14, 2005, http://news.bbc.co.uk/go/pr/fr/-/2/hi/asia-pacific/4681823.stm; and "Japan Grants Drilling Rights in E. China Sea to Oil Firm," *People's Daily Online*, July 14, 2005, http://english.people.com.cn/200507/14/eng20050714_196129.html.

47 "China Lodges Solemn Representations to Japan's Approval of Oil, Gas Drill," *People's Daily Online*, July 15, 2005, http://english.people.com.cn/200507/15/eng20050715_196329.html.

48 "Japan's Provocation in the East China Sea Very Dangerous," *People's Daily Online*, July 21, 2005, http://english.people.com.cn/200507/21/eng20050721_197493.html.

49 "Japan Protests at China Gas Move," *BBC News*, August 10, 2005, http://news.bbc.co.uk/go/pr/fr/-/2/asia-pacific/4137276.stm.

50 "China Accused of Inciting Gas Row," *BBC News*, September 20, 2005, http://news.bbc.co.uk/go/pr/fr/-/2/hi/asia-pacific/4262970.stm; and "Japan Presses China on Gas Fields," *BBC News*, September 30, 2005, http://news.bbc.co.uk/go/pr/fr/-/2/hi/asia-pacific/4296454.stm.

51 Norimitsu Onishi and Howard W. French, "Japan's Rivalry with China is Stirring a Crowded Sea," *New York Times*, September 11, 2005, http://www.nytimes.com/2005/09/11/international/asia/11taiwan.html.

Alarmingly, one Chinese destroyer may actually have aimed its guns at a Japanese MSDF surveillance plane.[52]

Still, the end of September found China and Japan making an effort to deal with their territorial and maritime frictions through diplomacy.[53] On September 30 and October 1, China and Japan held consultations, their third, on the East China Sea. According to Japanese accounts, both sides "shared the common recognition that [the East China Sea dispute] was a matter to be solved urgently." Japan specifically asked China to share information and to discontinue its energy development activities. It also expressed concern about the activities of the Chinese People's Liberation Army Navy (PLAN) in the East China Sea and provided China with a joint development proposal. Japan reported that China refused to accommodate its request to share information, but that China was studying its joint development proposals.[54]

At one-day informal talks that took place in the beginning of 2006, there was little evidence that China and Japan were ready to make progress on their territorial and maritime problems. As in the past, Japan rejected China's joint development proposals while China turned down Japan's. On a positive note, the two protagonists agreed to hold another round of full-fledged talks on the topic and China said it would present a new proposal.[55]

Theorizing the Potential for Territorial and Maritime Conflict

In this section, I develop a model for evaluating the potential for the Sino-Japanese territorial and maritime controversies to erupt in conflict. I initially build this model by analyzing the history of the disputes. Subsequently, I supplement it with insights from the literature on territorial and maritime disputes.

---

52 Hisane Masaki, "Koizumi Plays it His Way," *AsiaTimes Online*, October 18, 2005, http://www.atimes.com/atimes/Japan/GJ18Dh05.html; and J. Sean Curtin, "Stakes rise in Japan, China Gas Dispute," *AsiaTimes Online*, October 19, 2005, http://www.atimes.com/atimes/Japan/GJ19Dh01.html.

53 "China Hopes Sino-Japanese Disputes on East China Sea be Solved through Dialogue," *People's Daily Online*, September 21, 2005, http://english.people.com.cn/200509/21/eng20050921_209778.html.

54 Japan, Ministry of Foreign Affairs, "Japan-China Consultations on the East China Sea and Other Matters (September 30 to October 1, Tokyo)," October 1, 2005, http://www.mofa.go.jp/region/asia-paci/china/consult0509.html; and Curtin, "Stakes rise in Japan, China Gas Dispute," 2005.

55 "Japan-China Tensions Dog Talks," *BBC News*, January 1, 2006, http://news.bbc.co.uk/go/pr/fr/-/2/hi/asia-pacific/4593910.stm; "Japan Accepts China's Proposal to Jointly Develop East China Sea Resources, FM Spokesman," *People's Daily Online*, January 6, 2006, http://english.people.com/cn/200601/eng20060106_233198.html; and "Japan, China Fail to Resolve Gas Row, Set New Talks," *Japan Times*, January 10, 2005, http://www.japantimes.co.jp/cgi-bin/getarticle.pl5?nn20060110a2.htm.

China's Economic Interests and their Effect on PRC Behavior

China's economic interest in the East China Sea is longstanding. It was not until after the late 1960s, though, that China became especially vigorous in defense of its perceived rights to the Islands and in the East China Sea. The reasons for this newfound activism are not surprising. As discussed above, in 1968, the U.N. published a report suggesting that there might be rich hydrocarbon resources in the area. Moreover, legal principles regarding the law of the sea, which were being finalized over the course of the 1970s and eventually codified in the 1982 UNCLOS agreement, increased the economic value of islands and seas. Since 1978, but particularly since the second half of the 1990s, China has become even more assertive in tandem with its expanding interest in natural resources.

Overall, the evidence shows that Chinese decision makers have become more aggressive in pursuing Chinese claims as the economic value of the Islands and East China Sea has increased. Still, China's degree of assertiveness has not moved in lockstep with China's intensifying interests. For instance, despite the publication of the aforementioned U.N. ECAFE report, China made no visible effort in the 1970s to identify or exploit the hydrocarbon resources of the East China Sea. And in the 1980s, even after the conclusion of UNCLOS, the Chinese government never attempted to plant flags on the Islands or to remove Japanese structures on them. This divergence between economic interests and behavior relates in part to China's capabilities.

China's Capabilities and their Ramifications for Chinese Assertiveness

Regardless of China's interest, it can only pursue them if it possesses the requisite capabilities. As far as island and seas are concerned, the requisite capabilities include fishing vessels, Coast Guard naval and air resources, warships, hydrocarbon mapping, test drilling, and drilling equipment, as well as the men, doctrines, and training to use these assets. Generally speaking, Beijing has lacked such capabilities. Thus, it found it difficult to advance its island and maritime interests. It became even more difficult for China to pursue its interests given the existence of opposing forces. For instance, the U.S. administered the Islands between 1945 and 1971.

From the late 1990s into the new millennium, Beijing has become more assertive in tandem with the upgrading of its capabilities. For instance, Chinese vessels are voyaging with increasing frequency into portions of the East China Sea that Japan views as its own. As well, China has become more active in its survey, test drilling, and resource exploitation activities. Another noteworthy trend seems to be the increasing frequency with which China is challenging Japanese actions through Foreign Ministry protests as opposed to *People's Daily* pieces. China, though, has not pursued its interests with reckless abandon even as its rising power has given it a greater ability to do so. In the late 1990s, for instance, after China's naval capabilities had increased, it did not move to repel Japanese activists or parliamentarians who traveled to the Islands. Admittedly, China's overall naval capability was not a match for Japan's. But it would be far fetched to assume that an unfavorable balance of forces alone determined Chinese behavior. In numerous instances, it would not have faced a Japanese military response. In short, China restrained itself. To understand this, one must consider China's operating context.

China's Operating Context and its Effect on Chinese Behavior

In formulating their territorial and maritime policies towards Japan, Chinese policy makers have had to consider *inter alia* the threat environment and economic imperatives. To illustrate, during the Cold War, Chinese leaders faced intense threats from the U.S. and later the Soviet Union. In such a setting, it made little sense to press Japan on boundary issues because, in the former case, Japan could worsen China's threat to the environment while, in the latter, it could help China mitigate it. Thus China did not press Japan. Similarly, Chinese policy makers embraced a temperate policy in the early 1990s because good relations with Japan could help China escape the international isolation into which it had fallen after the 1989 Tiananmen Square massacre. One also should give recognition to the importance of economic imperatives. In the 1970s and 1980s, Chinese policy makers believed a positive relationship with Japan would meaningfully contribute to their country's economic development.[56]

The importance of the broader setting is illustrated by the correspondence between increases in the permissiveness of the politico-economic environment and China's aggressiveness in asserting its claims. To illustrate, from 1995 to 1996, after China's economy had recovered from its post-Tiananmen sluggishness and the international community had re-embraced China, China acted more assertively in defending its perceived rights to the Islands and the East China Sea. Likewise, after the "China-Threat" angst of 1996-1997 and the pressures of the Asian Financial Crisis dissipated, China again became more aggressive in pursuing its interests.

The Lessons of History

In the aggregate, the historical record reveals that China becomes more assertive when its economic interest in the Islands and/or East China Sea increases, when its capabilities improve, and when the broader politico-economic milieu becomes more permissive. Knowing this provides a useful starting point for analyzing the potential for Sino-Japanese territorial and maritime frictions to explode. It is insufficient, though, because an inductively-constructed framework does not allow us to consider non-obvious, but otherwise logically plausible causal factors. To address this defect,

---

56 Andrew J. Nathan and Robert S. Ross, *The Great Wall and the Empty Fortress: China's Search for Security* (New York: W.W. Norton & Company, 1997), pp. 89–90; Klein, "Japan and Europe in Chinese Foreign Relations," 1994, pp. 121–122; and Joseph Y.S. Cheng, "Sino-Japanese Relations in the Twenty-First Century," *Journal of Contemporary Asia*, vol. 33, no. 2, 2003, pp. 262–263, 265.

one must exploit the literature on territorial and maritime conflict, particularly institutional-statist theory, which is designed to explain territorial and maritime conflict.

Institutional-Statist Theory

The fundamental premise of institution-statist theory is that boundaries are legal-politico institutions that perform certain functions. These include military-strategic, economic, constitutive, national identity, ethno-national unity, state building and preservation, and domestic political functions. Boundaries specifically provide value because they serve these functions. Institutional-statist theory argues that this value significantly influences the likelihood of conflict over boundaries; *viz*, as the value of boundaries increases, so does the likelihood of conflict. In individual cases, then, one needs to gauge the functional values associated with the boundaries at stake in a given dispute in order to assess if the dispute will escalate to militarized conflict.[57]

With respect to the Islands and East China Sea, China's preferred territorial and maritime boundaries perform economic, constitutive, national identity, and state building and preservation functions. Consequently, one must consider them in order to evaluate the future course of the Sino-Japanese territorial and maritime dynamic. The aforementioned borders, though, do not serve important military-strategic functions, "facilitate the capture of ethnic kin," or delineate responsibilities among various government ministries. Thus, there is no need to consider how the military-strategic, ethno-national unity, or domestic political functions play into Chinese valuations of their boundaries with Japan.

Combining the foregoing inductive and deductive analyses, three steps need to be followed to forecast the course of the Sino-Japanese territorial and maritime dynamic. First, one needs to consider the functional value, richly understood, of Sino-Japanese boundaries since this affects China's interest in escalating the controversies. Second, one must evaluate China's ability to pursue its interests. Third, one must study the politico-economic environment in which Chinese decision makers construct policy.

China's Rise and the Potential for Militarized Territorial and Maritime Conflict

This section studies China's interests in the Islands and East China Sea. It also assesses China's capabilities. Finally, it analyzes the stimulus that the contemporary politico-economic environment imparts. China's interests, capabilities, and operating context, though, are not static because China is not. Consequently, this section considers, when appropriate, how China's rise is affecting its interests, capabilities, and operating context.

---

57 Blanchard, "Linking Border Disputes and War," 2005, esp. pp. 691–693.

Beijing's Interest in the Islands and East China Sea and China's Rise

China's interests in its Islands and East China Sea boundaries relate to the economic, constitutive, national identity, and state building and preservation functions that these boundaries serve. I examine these functions in sequence, evaluate their worth, and discuss how China's rise will affect them and the values associated with them.

It is widely recognized that China's boundaries with Japan perform an economic function because they enable China to claim rights to the living and non-living resources of the East China Sea. In terms of living resources, the East China Sea is rich in fish.[58] China's large and growing population alone mandates that Chinese policymakers be attentive to this. Beyond this, China's rise is bolstering the country's demand for fish because it is supporting an improvement in Chinese living standards that is nurturing a taste for "luxury" foods like fish (as well as meat). Furthermore, China desires to develop its marine industries as a source of economic growth and employment. However, the need for East China Sea fish, *specifically*, is not great. One reason is that the East China Sea supplies a relatively small and shrinking percentage of China's total fisheries production. Another is that China already has been downsizing the size of its fishing fleets and the numbers of fishermen who exploit the East China Sea. Finally, it seems China can easily meet the bulk of its food needs through domestic production and imports.[59]

In terms of non-living resources, there is great optimism about the hydrocarbon resources under the East China Sea. Various analyses suggest that the continental shelf of the East China Sea may contain between 10–100 billion barrels of oil. As for natural gas, Chinese estimates indicate the continental shelf of the East China Sea may hold between 175 trillion to 210 trillion cubic feet.[60] If these estimates are correct, then the economic function of Sino-Japanese boundaries is *prima facie* precious. China's rise makes this function even more precious. This is because it is producing phenomenal economic growth, rising living standards (which, in turn, are encouraging the purchase of energy-intensive goods), and the expansion of energy-intensive industries such as steel.[61] In turn, these developments are fueling exploding energy consumption. As of 2004, China had become the world's second large oil

---

58 Ji, "The Diaoyudao (Senkaku) Disputes and Prospects for Settlement," 1994, p. 286.

59 This analysis exploits Martin Walker, "China and the New Era of Resource Scarcity," *World Policy Journal*, 1996, pp. 9–10; The World Bank, *At China's Table* (Washington, D.C.: The World Bank, 1997); Li Rongxia, "Marine Economy: New Economic Growth Point," *Beijing Review*, November 30–December 6, 1998, pp. 11–13; and, Zou, "Sino-Japanese Joint Fishery Management in the East China Sea," 2003, pp. 125–126, 137.

60 Harrison, "Quiet Struggle in the East China Sea," 2002, pp. 271–273.

61 Jeffrey Robertson, "China's Power Hunger Trumps Japan Diplomacy," *AsiaTimes Online*, November 2, 2004, http://www.atimes.com/atimes/China/FK02AD01.html; "China's Oil Demand to Remain High in 2005," *People's Daily Online*, January 21, 2005, http://english.people.com.cn/200501/21/eng20050121_171486.html; and Chietigj Bajpaee, "China Fuels Energy Cold War," *AsiaTimes Online*, March 2, 2005, http://atimes01.atimes.com/atimes/China/GC02Ad07.html.

consumer and third largest oil importer, importing over 40 percent of its energy needs. By 2010, analysts believe China will import as much as 50% of its oil needs. Trends with respect to natural gas are similar. Chinese imports are likely to steadily rise, doubling between 2010 and 2020.[62]

Surging energy requirements create a potent stimulus for China to pursue local, offshore energy development. China's actual need to pursue offshore development aggressively, though, depends upon the alternatives. Unfortunately, there are problems with many of them. For instance, China has huge reserves of coal, but coal is costly to extract and relatively inefficient as an energy source. China does possess onshore oil and gas endowments of its own, but these assets are small (or shrinking), costly to extract, and hard to transport. Finally, China has been developing links with energy producing nations such as Iran, Kazakhstan, and Russia. Yet such measures may not yield cheap or secure energy supplies. Furthermore, countries like India and Japan are pursuing energy deals with the same countries.[63] On balance, then, it is likely that China's already strong interest in local, offshore energy supplies will grow.

Examining the economic function of Sino-Japanese boundaries, there is no doubt that they currently perform a valuable service. Furthermore, there is every reason to believe that China's rise will cause policy makers in Beijing to value the economic function ever more. Admittedly, energy from the East China Sea cannot satiate all or even a large percentage of China's energy needs. Nevertheless, it certainly can contribute to them.

It is widely known that Chinese leaders are hypersensitive about sovereignty because of China's 18th and 19th century history when foreign powers annexed Chinese territory, usurped the Chinese government's sovereign rights through measures such as extraterritoriality, and meddled in China's domestic politics. This history has imbued Beijing with an anachronistic Westphalian notion of sovereignty that stresses full independence and no external interference whatsoever in China's internal affairs.[64] Not surprisingly, then, Chinese policy makers have an interest in the constitutive function that their Sino-Japanese boundaries perform. The Sino-Japanese territorial and maritime dynamic chronicled above, in which China repeatedly derides Japanese actions as a violation of China's sovereignty, vividly evidences this.

---

62 Roland Dannreuther, "Asian Security and China's Energy Needs," *International Relations of the Asia-Pacific*, vol. 3, no. 2, 2003, pp. 197–198; Henry J. Kenny, "China and the Competition for Oil and Gas in Asia," *Asia-Pacific Review*, vol. 11, no. 2, 2004, p. 36; and Kosuke Takahashi, "Gas and Oil Rivalry in the East China Sea," *AsiaTimes Online*, July 27, 2004, http://www.atimes.com/atimes/Japan/FG27Dh03.html.

63 Harrison, *China, Oil, and Asia*, 1977, chap. 2; Dannreuther, "Asian Security and China's Energy Needs," 2003, pp. 199–204; and Kenny, "China and the Competition for Oil and Gas in Asia," 2004, pp. 37–41.

64 On this, see, e.g., Yong Deng, "Conception of National Interests," in Yong Deng and Fei-Ling Wang, eds., *In the Eyes of the Dragon: China Views the World* (Lanham: Rowman & Littlefield, 1999), pp. 47–72.

Looking forward, it is not definite how China's rise will shape its valuation of the constitutive function of its boundaries with Japan. On the one hand, it is conceivable that it will modernize Chinese conceptions of sovereignty by enhancing China's security and external leverage. On the other hand, it is intertwining China in a matrix of institutions and interdependence relationships that subject it to threatening new rules and norms. Regardless, it is clear that Chinese policy makers already have a strong interest in the constitutive function of their Sino-Japanese boundaries.

China's boundaries with Japan serve a national identity function in two important ways. First, the Islands were lost during the century of national humiliation and the recovery of the Islands and the surrounding seas would help to cleanse a stain of the past.[65] Second, an important part of the contemporary Chinese national identity is opposition to Japan, which, in the Chinese mindset, was not only an invader and brutal occupier, but is also unrepentant, acting to prevent China from achieving great power status, and hindering China's recovery of Taiwan.[66] In light of this, the Islands perform a valuable national identity function since "there are no other territorial issues that can serve as a focus for the feelings of hostility between China and Japan."[67]

China's rise has no obvious implications for the national identity function that the Sino-Japanese boundary serves. Conceivably, it may offer China alternative sources of identity as a global great power, a regional hegemon, or East Asia's economic leader. Similarly, it might bring China status and pride that makes it less critical to erase the stains of the past. Yet, it could intensify the desire of Chinese policy makers to eliminate all vestiges of the century of national humiliation, the thinking being that great powers do not tolerate past transgressions. In any event, it is the case that China boundaries with Japan currently perform a valuable national identity function.

Boundaries perform a state building and preservation function because they serve as a fount of national unity. It is not surprising, then, that Chinese policy makers have given them greater attention in the wake of the collapse of the Communist bloc in Eastern Europe, the 1989 Tiananmen debacle, and the demise of the Soviet Union. These events revealed that communism no longer sufficed as a wellspring of national unity, that performance legitimacy (i.e., the delivery of economic goods) was an unreliable source, and that new sources were needed. One source to which Chinese leaders turned was nationalism.[68] There is more to nationalism than defense of boundaries. Yet, where states are concerned, nationalism undeniably requires leaders

---

65 "Trouble in Paradise," *Jane's Intelligence Review*, Special Report no. 7, 1995, p. 16; and Daniel J. Dzurek, "Comment on 'Island Disputes in East Asia,'" in Myron H. Nordquist and John Norton Moore, eds., *Security Flashpoints: Oil, Islands, Sea Access and Military Confrontation* (The Hague: Martinus Nijhoff Publishers, 1998), p. 424.

66 Thomas J. Christensen, "China, the U.S.-Japan Alliance, and the Security Dilemma in East Asia," *International Security*, vol. 23, no. 4, 1999, pp. 54–55; and Peter Hays Gries, "China's 'New Thinking' on Japan," *China Quarterly*, no. 184, 2005, pp. 831–850.

67 Harrison, *China, Oil, and Asia*, 1977, p. 182.

68 Recent treatments of Chinese nationalism include Suisheng Zhao, *A Nation-State by Construction: Dynamics of Modern Chinese Nationalism* (Stanford: Stanford University

to vigorously protect their country's territorial interests. As a result, contemporary Chinese leaders place great value on the state building and preservation function of their boundaries.

China's rise is amplifying the value of the state building and preservation function because it is subjecting China to new and powerful stresses. These include high unemployment and underemployment, rising income inequality, and destabilizing economic reforms. These stresses, in turn, are fueling anti-government protests, large-scale riots, and other social problems. To manage these problems, some Chinese elites are calling for even greater use of nationalism. Lin Zhibo, a senior commentator with the *People's Daily*, recently wrote, "today in China an ideological vacuum is emerging" as a result of economic, social, and other pressures. "What can China rely on for cohesion? I believe that apart from nationalism, there is no other recourse." In addition to calling for greater use of nationalism, they are calling specifically for greater anti-Japanese nationalism, seeing Japan not only as a long-term rival, but as an enemy that can unify the people.[69] In short, China's rise suggests that Chinese leaders will see greater value in the state building and preservation function that Sino-Japanese boundaries serve.

In sum, China's boundaries with Japan perform a number of functions including economic, constitutive, national identity, and state building and preservation functions. Contemporary international and domestic circumstances make many of these functions highly valuable. Thus, Chinese leaders already have strong incentives to advance or defend their favored borderlines vis-à-vis Japan. More importantly, China's rise is amplifying the value of the economic and state building and preservation functions of China's boundaries with Japan. Overall, then, China's interests in the Islands and East China Sea will increase the potential for Sino-Japanese territorial and maritime conflict.

Chinese Capabilities and China's Rise

There are two capabilities that matter in regards to the Islands and East China Sea. The first is China's ability to exploit resources. The second is China's naval capabilities relative to Japan's. In regards to the former, China has been continuously upgrading its ability to locate, extract, and transport hydrocarbon and other resources derived from the sea, seabed, and subsoil.[70] In regards to the latter, China has been on an incessant, albeit modest, quest since 1990 to enhance its military capabilities.[71]

Press, 2004); and Peter Hays Gries, *China's New Nationalism: Pride, Politics, and Diplomacy* (Berkeley: University of California Press, 2004).

69 Chris Buckley, "China Commentator Urges Tougher Line against Japan," *Reuters*, January 3, 2006,

70 See, e.g., "Offshore Oil and Gas Exploration Extends to Deep Water," *People's Daily Online*, December 26, 2005, http://english.people.com.cn/200512/26/eng20051226_230901.html.

71 David L. Shambaugh, *Modernizing China's Military: Progress, Problems, and Prospects* (Berkeley: University of California Press, 2002), pp. 1–7.

China's enhancement of its naval capabilities has taken place in both the civilian and military realms.[72] Most visibly, China's upgrading of its military naval capabilities involves the construction or acquisition of new ships such as, respectively, Luhai- and Sovremenny-class destroyers. Beyond this, China is equipping its vessels with modern anti-ship missiles, mines, and radar and weapons control systems. Finally, it has been devoting substantial energies to transforming its submarine force.

In terms of raw numbers, it would seem that China is in highly favorable position vis-à-vis Japan. Yet Japan has far more capable naval armaments. For instance, in the late 1990s, Japan added four super-modern Aegis-equipped destroyers to its fleet. Additionally, it has put or soon will put almost ten modern Oyashio-class submarines into service. To complement its state-of-the-art naval equipment, Japan supports its navy with excellent facilities as well as high quality training. While Japan is constrained by its budgetary problems, the reality is that its modern ships, submarines, and anti-submarine warfare capabilities present the PLAN with a formidable challenge. Indeed, many believe the PLAN's capabilities are decades behind competing Western forces.[73]

In sum, China's existing naval capabilities do not give Beijing complete freedom to pursue its interests. This said, it must be appreciated that China will not have to confront the entire Japanese Navy in every circumstance, if at all. Moreover, China's rise will provide it with the financial, technical, and military tools to shrink the gap between the PLAN and the Japanese Navy. Over time, then, China's growing capabilities will increase the likelihood that the Sino-Japanese territorial and maritime controversy will erupt.

The Politico-Economic Environment and China's Rise

Interests and capabilities do not suffice, on their own, to determine China's behavior towards its territorial and maritime controversies with Japan. History and logic suggest we also need to pay attention to China's operating environment, which includes both political and economic elements. Below, I evaluate the importance of the political context for Chinese policy making towards its boundaries with Japan. Thereafter, I weigh the significance of the economic milieu. In both cases, I consider

---

72 See, e.g., "China Steps Up Maritime Surveillance," *People's Daily Online*, July 15, 2005, http://english.people.com.cn/200507/15/eng20050715_196345.html.

73 This discussion of Chinese and Japanese naval forces draws upon Duk-ki Kim, *Naval Strategy in Northeast Asia: Geo-Strategic Goals, Policies, and Prospects* (London: Frank Cass, 2000), pp. 25–28, 132–192; Bernard D. Cole, "The Naval Component of the Chinese Defense Budget," Remarks prepared for the U.S.-China Security Review Commission, December 7, 2001, http://www.uscc.gov/textonly/transcriptstx/tescol.htm; Shambaugh, *Modernizing China's Military*, 2002, pp. 265–274; Council on Foreign Relations, *Chinese Military Power: A Report of an Independent Task Force Sponsored by the Council on Foreign Relations* (New York; Council on Foreign Relations, 2003), pp. 28, 44–47; and Lyle Goldstein and William Murray, "Undersea Dragons: China's Maturing Submarine Force," *International Security*, vol. 28, no. 4, 2004, pp. 161–196.

how China's rise is shaping the stimuli that these political and economic contexts present.

In terms of the political environment, China presently does not face any dire security threats akin to that presented by the United States in the 1950s and 1960s and the Soviet Union from the 1960s through the early 1980s. Furthermore, unlike in the 1960s, 1970s, and 1980s, China does not need the help of countries like the U.S. and Japan to join or participate in key institutional organizations and institutions. Finally, China, at present, is anything but an international pariah. In the aggregate, then, Beijing no longer has the powerful political need for Japan that it previously did.

Yet China still has various national objectives that Japan can help it achieve. First and foremost, Japan can assist China in its quest to unify Taiwan with the mainland. Clearly, Japan is not going to pressure Taiwan to reunify with the mainland. But Japan could help China by opposing Taiwanese moves to join international organizations. On the other hand, Chinese policy makers may start to view Japan as more of a hindrance than a help as far as the Taiwan issue is concerned. This is so because Japan has been steadily expanding its security relationship with the U.S. to cover a wider geographic range and a broader ambit of security issues, including Taiwan.[74] And Japan may become an even greater obstacle to China's Taiwan goals over time. This is so because Japanese opinion towards China is hardening while becoming increasingly favorable towards Taiwan.[75]

Another area in which Japan can positively contribute to China's national interests is the North Korean nuclear problem. Japan not only can support Chinese calls for dialogue and negotiation, but also can sweeten any economic and political inducements offered to North Korea. On the other hand, Japan can greatly complicate China's efforts to peacefully settle the North Korean problem by, for example, supporting economic sanctions against the hermit kingdom. In Southeast Asia and South Asia, Japan may actually be subverting Chinese interests. For example, Japan has, on occasion, encouraged Southeast Asian countries to take a firmer stance in their dealings with China. Turning to South Asia, we find Tokyo seeking closer political, economic, and military ties with New Delhi in order to counter Chinese gains.[76]

The preceding analysis suggests that China still has a political need for Japan, albeit one that is nowhere near as great as before. Problematically, this need is likely

---

74 Paul Midford, "China Views the Revised U.S.-Japan Defense Guidelines: Popping the Cork?" *International Relations of the Asia-Pacific*, vol. 4, no. 1, 2004, pp. 124–132; Jim Yardley and Keith Bradsher, "China Accuses U.S. and Japan of Interfering on Taiwan," *The New York Times*, February 21, 2005, http://www.nytimes.com/2005/02/21/international/asia/21china.html; and Jing-dong Yuan, "China Seethes at U.S.-Japan 'Meddling,'" *AsiaTimes Online*, February 24, 2005, http://www.atimes.com/atimes/China/GB24Ad01.html.

75 David Pilling, "Issue of Taiwan Raises Stakes between Tokyo and Beijing," *Financial Times*, February 25, 2005, p. 6.

76 Sudha Ramachandran, "Japan-India Ties under China's Shadow," *Asia Times Online*, March 26, 2005, http://www.atimes.com/atimes/South_Asia/GC26Df01.html.

to diminish over time because China's rise is endowing it with the tools needed to achieve its objectives without Japanese help. More alarmingly, China may come to view Japan as an obstacle to its realization of its national interests, rather than simply an unimportant contributor to them.

In terms of the economic context, many are sanguine that Sino-Japanese economic ties can ensure cordial relations between Beijing and Tokyo.[77] To quote one representative statement, "As long as China continues to place a high priority on economic development, China will be unlikely to resort to force to resolve its territorial dispute with Japan."[78] It is unquestionable that economic relations with Japan are important. In the first 11 months of 2005, Japan represented China's third largest trade partner after the European Union and U.S., importing approximately $76 billion from China and exporting $91 billion to it. As of the end of 2004, Japan ranked as the single largest foreign investor in China. Moreover, as of the end of 2004, Japanese companies in China generated around $60 billion in output. Much of this production is exported, which allows China to earn foreign currency. More generally, Japanese investment has upgraded the technology level of China's manufacturing and given it managerial expertise. Beyond this, Japan has been the largest provider of official financial assistance to China.[79] China is well aware of the extensive links that its economy has with Japan's and Chinese leaders routinely describe the Sino-Japanese economic relationship as a complementary rather than a competitive one.[80]

This analysis suggests that China still has a strong economic need for Japan and that it perceives its economic relationship with Japan as a valuable one. Nevertheless,

---

77 See, e.g., Macabe Keliher, "Part 3: Economics Overrides Anti-Japan Sentiment," *Asia Times Online*, February 12, 2004, http://www.atimes.com/atimes/China/FB12Ad07.html; and Howard W. French and Norimitsu Onishi, "Economic Ties Binding Japan to Rival China," *New York Times*, October 31, 2005, http://www.nytimes.com/2005/10/31/international/asia/31asia.html. For a critical view, see Chietigj Bajpaee, "The Price of Asian Conflict," *Asia Times Online*, May 24, 2005, http://www.atimes.conm/atimes/Asian_Economy/GE24Dk01.html.

78 Ashley J. Tellis et al., "Sources of Conflict in Asia," in Zalmay Khalilzad and Ian O. Lesser, eds., *Sources of Conflict in the 21st Century: Regional Futures and U.S. Strategy*, MR897-AF (Santa Monica: RAND, 1998), p. 118.

79 Keliher, "Part 3: Economics Overrides Anti-Japan Sentiment," 2004; J. Sean Curtin, "China-Japan Flames Scald Business," *AsiaTimes Online*, April 19, 2005, http://www.atimes.com/atimes/Japan/GD19Dh03.html; "Japan and China: Joined at the Hip," *TJI (The Japan Investor) Market Letter*, April 20, 2005; "Figures: Top 10 Trade Partners of China's Mainland in January-November 2005," *People's Daily Online*, http://english.people.com.cn/200601/09/eng20060109_233846.html.

80 "Political Chilliness Begins to Affect Economic Ties: Bo Xilai," *People's Daily Online*, April 24, 2005, http://english.people.com.cn/200504/24/eng20050424_182527.html; "Treating Sino-Japanese Economic Cooperation Rationally," *People's Daily Online*, April 27, 2005, http://english.people.com.cn/200504/27/eng20050427_182918.html; and "'Monnet concept' vs Sino-Japanese Friendship," *People's Daily Online*, June 16, 2005, http://english.people.com.cn/200506/16/eng20050616_190625.html.

it is not a given that the economic context will restrain Chinese behavior towards its boundaries with Japan. First, Sino-Japanese trade and investment will not experience anything near the growth rates of the past. Second, the very political frictions that economic relations are supposed to control or eliminate are acting as a drag on the maintenance and further development of economic ties.[81] Illustrating this, frictions are leading Tokyo to reduce its financial assistance to China and to encourage Japanese corporations to diversify away from China.[82] Third, China's rise will put Beijing in a position where the economic relationship with Japan becomes less valuable.

Overall, then, the contemporary politico-economic context moderates the potential for a militarization of the Sino-Japanese territorial and maritime controversies. China still needs Japan politically and economically. This constraint, however, should not be exaggerated. China has a much reduced political need for Japan and may even view Japan as a problem where its national interests are concerned. Nevertheless, China's contemporary economic need for Japan remains great. Still, economic ties are not a panacea. Furthermore, China's rise will diminish its relative economic need for Japan.

Conclusion

The purpose of this piece has been to evaluate the potential for militarized conflict over the Islands and East China Sea. It yields both good and bad news. In the short- to medium-term, the potential for a militarization of Sino-Japanese territorial and maritime controversies is low. Although China's current interests are strong, its capabilities to pursue its interests are limited. Moreover, the politico-economic milieu supplies Chinese policy makers with various incentives for moderation. In the long-run, however, the probability of conflict will grow because various trends, many driven by China's rise, indicate a rising Chinese interest in its Sino-Japanese boundaries, increased Chinese naval capabilities, and a more permissive operating context.

This analysis is incomplete, though. A comprehensive study also must examine how Japan will opt to deal with the disputes and its East Asian neighbor. If Japan assumes a more accommodating stance towards the controversies or aids Beijing in its pursuit of diverse national objectives, then the potential for conflict will decline. Conversely, if Japan decides to adopt a rigid or aggressive stance towards its

---

81 "Political Chilliness Begins to Affect Economic Ties," 2005; and "Economic Price Paid for Sino-Japanese Cold Political Relations," *People's Daily Online*, May 12, 2005, http://english.people.com.cn/200505/12/eng20050512_184750.html.

82 Phar Kim Beng, "Japan Loses Yen to Aid China," *AsiaTimes Online*, November 18, 2004, http://www.atimes.com/atimes/Japan/FK18Dh02.html; "Japan Plans to Cut Yen Loans to China by 10 Percent," *People's Daily Online*, March 14, 2005, http://english.people.com.cn/200503/14/eng20050314_176790.html; and Mariko Sanchanta, "Japanese Companies Warned of China Risks," *Financial Times*, July 2–3, 2005, p. 3.

territorial and maritime issues with China, then the likelihood of a violent eruption will grow. Furthermore, a complete review must analyze the potential U.S. role in the controversy. Lastly, it must evaluate the domestic political situation in China.

China's ability to rise and to do so peacefully will depend upon a host of factors. One of the most important is a successful management of the Sino-Japanese relationship. This will not be easy as China alone will not decide the fate of the Sino-Japanese relationship. However, it seems that China has to stabilize or settle its tense territorial and maritime problems with Japan as she shelved the territorial dispute with Vietnam and Malaysia over the South China Sea. Otherwise, "the worst period of Sino-Japanese relations since World War II," may further decay,[83] which could handicap China's "peaceful rise."

---

83 James Mulvenon quoted in Robert Marquand, "Nationalism Drives China, Japan Apart," *Christian Science Monitor*, December 29, 2005, http://www.csmonitor.com/2005/1229/p01s02-woap.html.

Chapter 10

China's Rise and Contemporary Geopolitics in Central Asia

Oliver M. Lee

Introduction

This chapter will focus on the geopolitical confrontations in Central Asia resulting from U.S. ambitions vis-à-vis Russia, U.S. apprehensions about the rise of China, and the post-Cold War penetration of that region by the United States military. It will examine the interconnected economic and strategic aims of each power; analyze their respective strengths and weaknesses with special attention to the geopolitical conditions in Central Asia, which are a subset of the geopolitical realities of global politics; and will forecast the likely outcome of this confrontation in Central Asia.

The political, economic, and military rise of China actually began more than half a century ago with the success of the Communist Revolution, symbolized by Mao Zedong's dramatic phrase, "China has stood up!" which he uttered at the Gate of Heavenly Peace on October 1, 1949, at the official founding of the People's Republic of China. In the first 27 years of the People's Republic, under Chairman Mao's leadership, China's development experienced periods of dramatic advancement interspersed with periods of terrible hardships and turmoil. On the whole, it is fair to say that in the Maoist decades a strong foundation was laid in China's agricultural and industrial economy, its science and technology, its educational system, its military strength, and its international standing – a foundation for China's astonishing rise since 1978, when the pragmatic Deng Xiaoping took charge.

The U.S. Government's anxiety over the rise of China thus is not of recent origin, but was obvious from the start, when in July 1950 President Truman ordered the U.S. Seventh Fleet into the Taiwan Strait to prevent the Chinese revolution from being extended to the Chinese Nationalists' last holdout – the island of Taiwan. The continuation of that anxiety for the next two decades was manifest in the continued patrolling by the Seventh Fleet in the Taiwan Strait until as late as 1972.

And yet, it is China's incredible sustained economic growth in the past quarter of a century, accompanied by a burgeoning military power and skillful diplomacy, that has given rise to a sense in the U.S. government that China not only has "stood up," but is on its way, in the decades to come, to exceed the U.S. economy in size and thus achieve concomitant economic, technological, military, and diplomatic power. This the American decision makers find alarming. They know there is little the U.S. can do to forestall the rise of China, especially considering that America's economic imperatives cause it to provide capital and technology to China and thus actually contribute to its economic growth.

The U.S. has concluded after bitter experience in the Korean War that never again will it fight a land-war against China, and has confirmed that decision during the Vietnam War by avoiding any provocation that might lead to Chinese entry into that conflict.[1] Nevertheless, the U.S. used its naval and air power, from 1950 to the present, to threaten China militarily in East Asia. And now, in its latest strategic moves threatening the People's Republic of China, the Pentagon established military bases near China's western borders, namely in Uzbekistan (until ordered recently by that country to evacuate) and Kyrgystan. Moreover, American bases in Afghanistan and Iraq and potentially in Azerbaijan lend additional depth to the U.S. power applicable against China's western frontiers. China, in turn, is taking countermeasures against these dangers.

The result of my investigation will be that this conflict of economic and strategic interests in Central Asia between the world's leading seapower (the U.S.) and the leading landpower (China) will not result in warfare between them in the coming decades. For on the one hand the geostrategically expansive U.S. would lack the relevant power in the deeply landlocked Central Asia, while on the other hand the geostrategically defensive China would be able to deploy sufficient strength in a regional war in that area so as to cause the U.S. to reverse its opportunistic penetration of Central Asia, and thus avert warfare between the two giants. China's rise, accordingly, will enable the Middle Kingdom to make effective demands relating to security on its western flank, but, because of this effectiveness, will not lead to warfare in Central Asia.

U.S. Inroads into Central Asia

Ever since the collapse of the Soviet Union in 1991, the United States, under both Democratic and Republican administrations, has pursued a policy of penetrating the former Soviet republics in Central Asia as well as the Caucasus region, something that had been strategically out of the question before the collapse.[2] The U.S. policy

---

[1] See my article, "The Impact of the U.S. War on Terrorism upon U.S.-China Relations," *Journal of Chinese Political Science*, vol. 7, Numbers 1 and 2, 2002, pp. 71–123 for elaboration of these points.

[2] This study will focus mainly on Central Asia rather than the Caucasus because of the former's geographic proximity to China, and the consequent involvement of China in the geopolitics of Central Asia. Located in this region, in addition to Afghanistan, are five of the former Soviet Republics – Kazakhstan, Kyrgystan, Tajikistan, Turkmenistan, and Uzbekistan. It is the last five that are usually defined as constituting Central Asia.

of politically and militarily penetrating Central Asia has had multiple interrelated geostrategic[3] purposes, the main ones being:

(1) to facilitate America's war in Afghanistan and enhance America's future ability to engage in threats and/or warfare in the general region surrounding Central Asia, specifically in Iraq, but potentially also against Iran;
(2) to prevent, by means of gaining political influence and military presence in as many of the former Soviet republics as possible, a re-establishment of Russian domination of its "Near Abroad";
(3) to use its military presence in Central Asia to put pressure on China's western flank, thereby enhance U.S. military encirclement of the Asian Dragon and thus hamper its political, economic, and military capabilities as a potential rival to the United States;
(4) to take steps in Central Asia and environs aimed simultaneously at increasing the diversity and security of oil and gas supplies for America and at minimizing China's political and economic influence in Central Asia, especially its access to oil and natural gas from that region.[4]

In pursuit of these geostrategic objectives the U.S. Congress, as early as October 1992 took the opportunity to pass the Freedom Support Act, which laid the foundation for diverse assistance to the newly independent Central Asian states. Accordingly, in 1993 military officers from Central Asia began receiving training in U.S. facilities in Germany. In mid-1994, four of the Central Asian nations joined NATO's Partnership for Peace Program, which hosted a series of military exercises to provide training in "peacekeeping activities."[5] In August 1995, Kyrgystan and Uzbekistan participated in exercises at Fort Polk, Louisiana. Four months later these two nations, now joined by Kazakhstan, formed a joint peacekeeping battalion. This battalion held exercises at Fort Polk in July 1997, and again in the steppes of Kazakhstan two months later, with the participation of 500 U.S. soldiers from Fort Bragg, North Carolina.[6] It should be noted that Kazakhstan borders directly on China's Xinjiang Uighur Autonomous Region, as do Kyrgystan and Tajikistan also. This modest but unprecedented role of the U.S. military in Central Asia was clearly to lay the groundwork for facilitating

---

3   The difference between "geopolitical" and "geostrategic" is that the former refers to the geographic aspects of political relationships among nations, while the latter refers to a nation's strategic goals and/or pursuit thereof, in the context of geopolitical realities.

4   "Only access to Russian and Central Asian oil can liberate China from dependence on vulnerable sea-borne oil supplies, so the real 'Great Game' is between Beijing and Washington. America's real strategic fear is the rise of China and India. Unlike Russia, they are not beset by demographic decline." Mark Almond, "Ukraine: It's Now or Never for Washington," *The New Statesman* (London), Dec. 6, 2004, p. 31.

5   Elizabeth Wishnick, *Growing U.S. Security Interests in Central Asia* (Strategic Studies Institute, U.S. Army War College, Oct. 2002), p. 16.

6   Walter Schilling, "The Return of Geopolitics in the Caucasus and Central Asia," *Aussenpolitik*, Feb. 1998, p. 53.

future American wars in the region, as was soon to be demonstrated in Afghanistan and Iraq.

In the immediate aftermath of the September 11 terrorist attacks in New York and Washington in 2001, the U.S. decided to overthrow the Taliban government of Afghanistan, which was harboring Osama bin Laden, the leader of the Al Qaeda terrorist network. Within days U.S. officials pressed the Central Asian states for help in the war against the Taliban government. All five states, having engaged in prior cooperation with the U.S., readily agreed to grant American bombers and cargo planes access to their air space.

In October, 2001, Uzbekistan allowed 1,500 American troops to operate out of its Khanabad airbase near the Afghan border, and in December Kyrgystan permitted U.S. forces to build a large air base right next to the Kyrgyz capital, Bishkek. Located a mere 200 miles from China's western border, this base, housing 900 U.S. troops, was said to be strictly for the near-term purpose of supporting the U.S. war in Afghanistan. Ignoring this newly acquired capability to threaten China's western flank, General Tommy Franks, the American commander in Afghanistan, spoke only part of the truth when saying, "The purpose is to be able to use this as a transportation hub, essentially to get closer to Afghanistan so that we can bring large airplanes in and then be able to change their loads into smaller airplanes."[7]

The cooperation of Central Asian nations was prompted by American financial inducements. Immediately after the 9/11 crisis, for example, President Karimov of Uzbekistan

> ...gave Washington the use of a former Soviet air base for operations in Afghanistan, declared all his political opponents to be Islamist terrorists and sat back to reap the rewards. They included more than $500 million for security measures... and an invitation to the White House.[8]

While U.S. military presence in Central Asia did indeed facilitate America's brief bombing war against the Taliban, the stakes were much higher than Afghanistan itself, as was hinted at by Secretary of State Colin Powell when he let slip that U.S. interests in Central Asia are far more important than the conflict in Afghanistan.[9]

Likewise hinting at America's ambitions beyond Afghanistan, Deputy Secretary of Defense, Paul D. Wolfowitz, noted that U.S. bases and exercises would "send a message to everybody, including important countries like Uzbekistan, that we have a capacity to come back in and will come back in... ."[10] And General Franks predicted in Tashkent, twenty months after the ouster of the Taliban regime, "I would expect in the future...that we will see a continuing growth in military relationships between

---

7 *New York Times*, Jan. 9, 2002.
8 Editorial, "Violence in Central Asia," *New York Times*, May 19, 2005.
9 Dai Yan, "U.S. Troops Will Continue to Stay in Central Asia," *Beijing Review*, Oct. 17, 2002, p. 8.
10 *New York Times*, Jan. 9, 2002.

our armed forces and forces here in Central Asia."[11] A Chinese scholar aptly likened the American move to "a chess piece being put at a vital place on the chessboard (which) intensified U.S. influence in Central Asia... ."[12]

Regarding Afghanistan, Gen. Franks took the truly long view when he warned that U.S. soldiers will be in that country for "a long, long time," brazenly reminding reporters that in South Korea, U.S. troops have been based there for more than half a century.[13] By the time the general said this, U.S. Special Forces and U.S. bombers had routed the Taliban and created a pro-U.S. regime controlling the capital city, Kabul, though not much else, as Afghan warlords under nominal Kabul control ran an opium-producing economy in the rest of the country. But the war, at least for the time being, had been won. Nevertheless, after Secretary of Defense Donald Rumsfeld went to Kabul in December 2004 the U.S. decided to set up no fewer than nine new bases in Afghanistan, clearly for purposes other than to find and capture the still elusive Osama bin Laden[14] – in other words, for military purposes in the heart of Central Asia.

Two months later, Senator John McCain, the Number Two Republican on the Senate Armed Services Committee, revealed more than he was supposed to when he told reporters in Kabul that America's strategic partnership with Afghanistan should include "permanent bases" for U.S. military forces. Later his office in Washington awkwardly amended his comments by saying that what the Senator meant was that the U.S. needs to make a long-term commitment, not necessarily involving "permanent bases."[15]

By the summer of 2004, the Pentagon went out of its way to avoid using the term "military base" in such areas as Central Asia, preferring to call these new installations "forward operating sites." Speaking of the new U.S. military presence in Eastern Europe and Central Asia, Secretary Rumsfeld, perhaps to put the provocation of China and Russia in a less alarming light, performed one of his frequent tap dances:

> We're trying to find the right phraseology. We know the word 'base' is not right for what we do.... We have bases in Germany and we will continue to. But we also have had things that we call 'Forward Operating Locations' or sites that are not permanent bases: they're not places where...you have large numbers of U.S. military on a permanent basis... .

---

11 Associated Press, Aug. 23, 2002.

12 Zhou Yihuang, "The U.S. Belt Strategy," *Beijing Review*, Oct. 3, 2002, p. 13.

13 Robert Kaiser, "U.S. Plants Footprint in Shaky Central Asia," *Washington Post*, Aug. 27, 2002.

14 Ramtanu Maitra, "U.S. Scatters Bases to Control Eurasia," *Asia Times* (Hong Kong), March 30, 2005. President Bush initially ordered U.S. forces to capture Osama bin Laden "dead or alive" and placed a $25 million bounty on his head. But when with the passing months, American Special Forces could not produce bin Laden either dead or alive, the President sheepishly downgraded the importance of this mission by saying "he's just one individual."

15 Maitra.

[They are places] where you'd locate people in and out or where you use it for refueling – these types of things.[16]

The Opportunism of U.S. Penetration of Central Asia

Though remarkable for its audacity and unprecedented nature, the Pentagon's anti-Russian and anti-Chinese objective of this military presence in Russia's and China's periphery, including Central Asia, is essentially opportunistic rather than in defense of America's vital, as distinct from non-vital, national interests.

A succinct definition of America's vital national interests was given by the U.S. National Security Council in 1998, as being those interests

> of broad, overriding importance to the survival, safety, and vitality of our nation. Among these are the physical security of our territory and that of our allies, the safety of our citizens, our economic well-being, and the protection of our critical infrastructure.[17]

This definition is couched basically in terms of self-defense rather than aggrandizement, and as such is justifiable – except for its use of elastic concepts such as "vitality of our nation" and "economic well-being," which could be stretched to cover expansionist moves like those the U.S. is making in Central Asia, not to mention even more intrusive and aggressive policies such as the U.S. war in Iraq. Also, the defense of "the physical security of our allies" is not even credible as part of the definition of "vital national interests," since, on the one hand, the U.S. did abandon its erstwhile ally South Vietnam in 1975, and four years later abrogated its 1954 Mutual Defense Treaty with the "Republic of China." On the other hand, this concept leaves room for American expansionist policies in the form of creating new alliances by means of political, economic, or military inducements, alliances which the U.S. would then claim to have a right to protect as part of the "vital national interests" of The Shining City on the Hill. In terms of a strictly defensive definition of America's vital national interests, therefore, America's penetration of Central Asia falls outside of the National Security Council's definition. This penetration was opportunistic in the sense that it took advantage of sudden possibilities to enhance America's power position vis-à-vis two potential challengers to its hegemonic role in the world, namely Russia and China, rather than defending "the physical safety of our territory" and "the safety of our citizens." In this light it is significant that the Defense Department's most recent compendium on U.S. national defense strategy declares that, while "we face a diverse set of security challenges ... we still live in an era of advantage and opportunity" and asserts the need for "an adaptive strategy, predicated on creating and seizing opportunities... ."[18]

---

16 Michael T. Klare, "Imperial Reach," *The Nation* (Washington, D.C.), April 25, 2005.

17 National Security Council, *A National Security Strategy for a New Century* (Washington, D.C., 1998).

18 Department of Defense, *The National Defense Strategy of the United States of America* (Washington, D.C., March, 2005), pp. 2–3.

At a minimum, from Washington's point of view, Moscow could be hampered in its efforts to regain influence in many of the former non-Russian members of the Soviet Union. A maximal though risky objective would be to use political, economic, and cultural techniques to push the Russian Bear along a path of disintegration, similar to the way the U.S.S.R. had disintegrated after four decades of Cold War. All these pursuits could be advanced by a permanent American political and military presence in Central Asia.

As regards China, this potential powerful rival of the United States, it could be "contained" more effectively than before, by means of U.S. augmentation of its military encirclement which includes U.S. naval and air domination of China's eastern front, supplemented by bases in South Korea and Japan, close military ties with Taiwan, Australia and New Zealand, military cooperation by the Philippines, Singapore, and Thailand, and now includes U.S. air and land capabilities anchored on China's western front. As a Chinese scholar put it, "The U.S. deployment around China is increasingly dense, enabling it to possibly make use of the changes to strategically contain China from all directions."[19] Not to be overlooked is the fact that if Washington succeeds in aligning Central Asian nations as client states, it would possess, in addition to its bases in Afghanistan and Iraq, the political and military means to exert disruptive influences in China's Xinjiang and Tibet by means of supporting and backstopping the dissident movements there.[20]

Yet, innovative and ambitious as are America's moves into Central Asia, in geopolitical terms they are no more than opportunistic moves – in the adventurist and gambling sense.[21] This is in contrast with a policy of determined pursuit of vital national interest linked, for example, to strategically crucial territories or maritime choke-points, or indispensable resources such as Saudi Arabian oil. Pointing to the unexpected nature of the new possibilities, Secretary of State Colin Powell confided to the House International Relations Committee that the U.S. "will have a continuing interest and presence in Central Asia of a kind that we could not have dreamed of before."[22] Beijing, however, understood that the American dream had long been cherished, that "The U.S. has had an eye on Central Asia for a long time, but had no way of entering the region," and Beijing realized that "The war on terrorism was

---

19 Zhang Chongfang, "Surroundings Still Steady?" *Beijing Review*, Aug. 8, 2002, p. 8.

20 But Dru Gladney, specialist on China's Muslim population, is not impressed by America's competence in this regard. "America could supply the independence movement with small arms, but similar attempts in the past have shown the United States' ineptitude at supporting independence movements because Washington generally lacks the patience, dedication, and political will required." Dru Gladney, "China's Interest in Central Asia: Energy and Ethnic Security," in Robert Ebel and Rajan Menon, eds., *Energy and Conflict in Central Asia and the Caucasus* (New York: Rowman & Littlefield, 2000), p. 219.

21 The adventurist motive was perceived by a British scholar: "America's drive to dominate the old Soviet Union represents a gamble by today's only superpower to seize the highest-value chips on the table before China and India join the game." Mark Almond, p. 31.

22 Vernon Loeb, "Footprints in Steppes of Central Asia," *Washington Post*, Feb. 9, 2002.

immediately seized as an opportunity for the U.S. to insert its troops into five Central Asian countries."[23]

The moves into Central Asia are adventurist in the same sense that the U.S. invasion of North Korea in October 1950 and its war in Vietnam were adventurist, to wit, pursuing objectives which do not measure up to America's *vital* national interests but were intended to achieve certain territorial and political gains just because U.S. power seemed sufficient to justify a "go for it" gamble. But when the gamble was lost, the objectives were deemed feasible of abandonment, and indeed were abandoned, promptly in the case of Korea (in December, 1950) but most reluctantly in the case of Vietnam.[24]

Washington's current war in Iraq likewise has an opportunistic element in that the Bush administration in the beginning thought American power adequate to the task of not only overthrowing the Saddam Hussein government but thereupon establishing a pro-U.S. government. Yet the prospects are that in the face of a long-term and growing Iraqi resistance movement and heavy costs in American lives and treasury, the domestic pressures for withdrawal from Iraq will increase to the point where the U.S. will ultimately be forced to withdraw.[25] In the meantime, however, Iraq's oil, because of the looming worldwide pressures on oil supplies, will assume increasing importance in the years to come. Hence the Bush administration will no doubt resist these pressures more stubbornly than it would in the absence of the oil question.

In view of the Pentagon's apparently determined pursuit of victory in Iraq,[26] it is in a way surprising that the most recent Defense Department statement of national military strategy contains an explicit public acknowledgment of possible "failure or prohibitive costs in pursuit of strategic, operational, or management objectives," and a recognition "that some objectives, though desirable, may not be attainable, while others, though attainable, may not be worth the cost."[27] In so far as this rare

---

23 Dai Yan, p. 7.
24 Oliver M. Lee, pp. 86–96.
25 Whereas shortly after the fall of Baghdad on April 9, 2003, a celebratory 76 percent of the American people thought that the war was "worth fighting," this percentage steadily declined month after month, year after year, until it sank to 41 percent in early May, 2005, according to a USA Today/CNN/Gallup Poll finding. And according to a Washington Post/ABC poll in mid-March of 2005, 70 percent said the number of American casualties, including more than 1,500 deaths, was an unacceptable price. *Washington Post*, March 16, 2005.
26 Secretary of Defense Rumsfeld said in Baghdad during his ninth trip there, "We don't have an exit strategy. We have a victory strategy." "U.S. Has No Exit Strategy for Iraq, Rumsfeld Says," www.bloomberg.com, April 12, 2005.
27 U.S. Department of Defense, *National Defense Strategy of the United States of America* (March 2005). On the other hand, this oblique acknowledgment that the U.S. war in Iraq may either fail or not be worth the cost may be a reflection of the long-standing opposition of the upper echelons of the U.S. Army to any war that would threaten to bog it down in a quagmire disastrously reminiscent of the hopeless American war in Vietnam. This interpretation is brilliantly put forth by Andrew J. Bacevich in his book, *The New American Militarism* (New

acknowledgement may become specifically relevant to the U.S. war in Iraq, it would be in keeping with my analysis of the adventurist nature of this as well as other regional wars fought in recent decades by the Land of the Free and the Home of the Brave.

Russian and Chinese Response to the U.S. Moves

Initially, both Moscow and Beijing, partly on the assumption that the U.S. bases would have only temporary use for the duration of the Afghan war, reacted with restraint. In fact, Russia's President Vladimir Putin signed on to the U.S. "war on terrorism" partly in order to get Washington to stop badgering Moscow about its policy toward Chechnya, and provided intelligence to the U.S. and allowed the Pentagon to use Russian airspace and Soviet-built airfields in Central Asia.[28] China likewise supported the U.S. 'war on terrorism," partly in return for Washington's agreement to list as a terrorist group the East Turkestan Independence Movement.[29] whose aim is to bring about the detachment of Xinjiang from China.

Within months, however, both Russian and Chinese attitudes toward the U.S. military presence in the region hardened. As one of America's top experts on Central Asia, Martha Brill Olcott, wrote at the time,

> Beijing is determined that China will play a leading a role in the geopolitics of Central Asia, and its size and economic potential seem to ensure that it will. For the Chinese, U.S. military presence may be little more than a temporary annoyance.[30]

And Harvard political scientist Michael Ignatieff predicted:

> In the longer term, the American penetration in Afghanistan, Tajikistan, and Uzbekistan – especially the creation of permanent military bases there – is bound to challenge Chinese and Russian power in the region, and when the opportunity presents itself, they will respond accordingly.[31]

In the light of these insights it is not surprising that in June 2002 China convened a summit meeting of the Shanghai Cooperative Organization (SCO), which grouped China and Russia with four of the Central Asian nations – Kyrgystan, Tajikistan,

---

York: Oxford University Press, 2005), especially in his chapter "The Military Profession at Bay," pp. 34–68. In this light, the statement of the Department of Defense, quoted here, may have represented an end-run by some Army generals around the Secretary of Defense.

28 Katrina Vanden Heuvel and Stephen F. Cohen, "Endangering U.S. Security," *The Nation*, April 15, 2002, p. 5.

29 *Asia Times* (Hong Kong), April 2, 2003.

30 Martha Brill Olcott, "Central Asia," in Richard Ellings and Aaron Friedberg, eds., *Strategic Asia 2002-03: Asian Aftershocks* (Seattle: National Bureau of Asian Research, 2002), p. 251.

31 Michael Ignatieff, "Barbarians at the Gate?" *New York Review of Books*, Feb. 28, 2002.

Uzbekistan, and Kazakhstan. The SCO, when it was founded on Beijing's initiative six years earlier, at first had the modest purpose of confidence-building, border demarcation and trade expansion. But by 2002 it had evolved into a soundstage for asserting opposition to the unilateral policies of the U.S., criticizing its hegemonic status, and urging the establishment of a multipolar world.[32] That year, Kyrgystan became the very first foreign nation to hold joint military land maneuvers with China. The following year saw military exercises involving all SCO members in Kazakhstan and China.[33]

In October 2003, as a countermove to the U.S. air base in Kyrgystan, President Putin surprisingly opened a Russian air base in that same country, intended to provide support for the forces of the Russian-led Collective Security Treaty Organization (CSTO) composed of Russia, Kyrgystan, Tajikistan, Kazakhstan, and Belarus.

At about the same time, former U.S. National Security Adviser Zbigniew Brzezinski expressed concern that "the current geopolitical earthquake in the Persian Gulf" could jeopardize America's political efforts in Central Asia. He added that

> American preoccupation with the mess in Iraq, not to mention the cleavage between America and Europe as well as the increased American-Iranian tension, has already tempted Moscow to resume its earlier pressure on Georgia and Azerbaijan to abandon their aspirations for inclusion in the Euro-Atlantic community and to step up its efforts to undermine any enduring U.S. political and military presence in Central Asia.[34]

On January 15, 2004, the SCO took the step of launching the organization's Secretariat in Beijing, and former Chinese Vice Foreign Minister Zhang Deguang was appointed as its first secretary general.[35] In July 2004, Beijing and Moscow signed a Treaty on Good-Neighborly Relations, Friendship, and Cooperation, including provisions for up to 2,000 Chinese officers to be trained annually in Russian military schools, and for Russian arms sales to China to increase still further.[36] Two months later President Putin was in Beijing to finalize the agreement on the last of the remaining border disputes. This was soon followed up by a major announcement in Beijing that President Hu Jintao had agreed to stage the first-ever joint military exercise with Russia in 2005.[37]

Former CIA analyst Ray McGovern, who after retirement became a severe critic of U.S. foreign policy, sensibly concluded from these developments that "The more…Bush and his neo-conservative helpers throw their weight around in the

---

32 Antoaneta Bezlova, "Beijing Plays down Russia-U.S. Warmth," *Asia Times*, June 5, 2002.

33 www.eurasianet.com, Nov. 26, 2002.

34 Zbigniew Brzezinski, "Hegemonic Quicksand," *The National Interest* (Washington, D.C.), Winter 2003–2004, p. 14.

35 *Beijing Review*, Feb. 5, 2004, p. 43.

36 Central Asia-Caucasus Institute, Johns Hopkins School of Advanced International Studies, *Analyst* (Washington, D.C.) Nov. 21, 2004.

37 *New York Times*, Dec. 14, 2004.

Middle East and elsewhere, the more incentive China and Russia see in moving closer together."³⁸ And, indeed, the foretold joint military exercises were launched on August 18, 2005. Involving 7,000 Chinese and 1,800 Russian troops, the exercise lasted eight days, culminating in an amphibious and paratroop landing on China's Shandong Peninsula.

The Geopolitics of Central Asia

I have shown elsewhere that from the geostrategic point of view, America's "footprints" in Central Asia, even if they were to be permanent, would add very little to America's ability to exert military pressure against China, much less to defeat it in an offensive war against China's homeland, which would be so costly to the U.S. in blood and treasury, and so predictably futile, as to place the very idea of an American war in China in the realm of fantasy, and that a U.S. nuclear attack against China would be out of the question in view of China's ability to retaliate, even if only asymmetrically.[39]

Here, instead, I am focusing on the more realistic question of whether the U.S. would be able to prevail in a limited, regional war in Central Asia *if* it chose to reject determined demands by either China or Russia, or both, to dismantle its military bases there. The following geopolitical analysis will show that the U.S. could not possibly prevail. This analysis does not necessarily point to warfare, but more likely to a situation in which China and/or Russia would be in a position of compelling, without warfare, U.S. withdrawal from Central Asia.[40]

To begin with, Central Asia, being in the "backyards" of both the Middle Kingdom and Muscovy, is militarily much more important to both than it is to the U.S., just as the Caribbean, Central America and South America, for similar reasons of geographic proximity and territorial vulnerability, are militarily much more important to the U.S. than to either Russia or China. This being so, both Beijing and Moscow would be willing to take greater risks and, if it were to come to that, pay a higher price in military confrontation with the U.S. over issues in Central Asia.

Next there is the fact that the American people in recent decades have had an underlying sense that American wars in far-away places really have little to do with America's national interest or with their own lives[41] – which is why in two

---

38 Ray McGovern, "Hu's Not on First," www.truthout.org, Dec. 17, 2004.

39 Lee, pp. 112 and 121–22.

40 As China's most famous military thinker, Sun Tzu, wrote 2,500 years ago, "To fight and conquer in all your battles is not supreme excellence; supreme excellence consists in breaking the enemy's resistance without fighting," and "The skilful leader subdues the enemy's troops without any fighting…. With his forces intact he disputes the mastery of the empire, and thus, without losing a man, his triumph is complete." Sun Tzu, *The Art of War* (New York: Bantam Doubleday Dell Publishing Group, 1983), pp. 15–16.

41 "Until foreign policy issues impinge directly on the personal life of an American citizen, as when his son is drafted or the military base at which he works is closed, the foreign

wars against Iraq the U.S. Government has had to provide frequently shifting and pathetic explanations as to what the wars were "really" about. Given the geographic remoteness and the consequent psychological detachment on the part of the American people, and the isolationist sentiments that lie just beneath the surface in America,[42] it would be quite easy for China and Russia to impose greater casualties on U.S. troops than the American people would be willing to sustain.

Furthermore, America's overall military superiority would be mostly irrelevant to any localized and limited war in Central Asia, because its strategic nuclear weapons by definition would not be used in a limited war, while the use of tactical nuclear weapons would raise the specter of nuclear escalation and therefore would also not be used. Moreover, the U.S. Navy, which is such an important part of America's overall military superiority, would be useless in the middle of the Eurasian continent. As Mao Zedong once quipped, "A battleship is a fearsome thing, but can it climb a mountain?" The closest that U.S. ships can get to Kyrgystan, say, is the seacoast of Pakistan, 1,000 miles away, and the Persian Gulf, 1,200 miles distant. Naval aircraft could cover part of that distance and back, but U.S. planes from air bases in Afghanistan, having nothing to do with the Navy, could do much better. By the same token, American ground troops in the vastness of Central Asia would be deprived of the logistical, intelligence, medical, recuperative, and other services that the U.S. Navy could provide if its ships had access to the combat zone.

Apart from the fact of being fundamentally a seapower, the U.S. would be hamstrung by the enormous distance of its homeland from the heart of Eurasia.[43] That the distance factor is independent of the maritime factor can be appreciated by noting that England, the dominant sea power in its day, was geographically quite close to most of the theaters of war in Europe and yet was handicapped in warfare on the Continent *because* it was a seapower rather than a landpower. On the matter of distance, in America's 1990–1991 build-up to the first war against Iraq, it was the great geographic distance that accounted for the fact that it took the U.S. five months to transport and deploy 500,000 troops and their weapons, equipment and supplies to the Persian Gulf, even though much material had already been "pre-positioned" in

---

involvements of his government touch him somewhat less than a television drama or a football game. He may follow a war or a negotiation in the newspaper or on television to see who is winning. He is unlikely to know much about the issues at stake or to care deeply unless he feels his country to be spectacularly triumphant or humiliated." Richard J. Barnett, *Roots of War* (Baltimore: Penguin Books, 1972), p. 243.

42 "Shaken by the Iraq war and the rise of anti-American sentiment around the world, Americans are turning inward, according to a Pew survey of United States opinion leaders and the general public. The survey, conducted this fall and released today, found a revival of isolationist feelings among the public similar to the sentiment that followed the Vietnam War in the 1970's and the end of the Cold War in the 1990s." Meg Bortin, "Survey Shows a Revival of Isolationism in U.S." *New York Times*, 11/17/05.

43 Zbigniew Brzezinski pointed out that "America is too distant to be dominant in this [Central Asian] part of Eurasia but too powerful not to be engaged." Brzezinski, *The Grand Chessboard* (New York: Basic Books, 1997), p. 148.

the small Gulf states of Oman and the United Arab Emirates, but more massively on the giant U.S. naval base in British-controlled Diego Garcia, an island in the Indian Ocean.[44]

In contrast, both China and Russia have large troop concentrations and supply bases practically next door to Central Asia. In the case of China, they are based in the Lanzhou Military Region and the Chengdu Military Region. Nationwide, besides a People's Liberation Army of 2,250,000 men, of whom 1.7 million men are ground troops, China has 10 million militia members in the primary category alone, which comprises rapid reaction detachments, infantry detachments, and specialized technical detachments, among others.[45]

Regarding methods of troop mobility, former U.S. Ambassador to China (1989–91), James Lilley, reports that

> Chinese forces depend on an elaborate network of existing supply and support facilities all over China, connected primarily by road and rail. The network can sustain the PLA in combat for extended periods of time over vast geographic areas. While the PLA's logistics infrastructure is best suited for protracted defense of its homeland, it can be adapted to support modest forays outside China.[46]

The distance factor affects the comparative costs of troop mobility, Political Scientist Roger Burbach, referring to the fact that the U.S., situated between the Atlantic and the Pacific Oceans, is in the global context an "island" country at least 3,000 miles away from the Eurasian continent, points out that the costs of applying U.S. firepower in Asia or the Gulf are enormous, whereas China "can move its military forces anywhere in the Asian theatre at a fraction of what it costs the U.S."[47]

As to the vulnerability of Chinese troops to U.S. air power, this would be a serious factor if the U.S. could have total control of the air as is the case in Afghanistan and Iraq, and was the case in Kosovo, Panama, Grenada, Cambodia, and Vietnam. The conservative columnist George Will exults that U.S. air dominance vastly simplifies the tasks of American ground forces "because they cannot be threatened from the air, and enemy ground forces cannot concentrate."[48] Against China, however, to achieve air dominance is easier said than done, as the Chinese Air Force possesses at least 180 very powerful fighter jets (Sukhoy-27) and

---

44 In 1974, the U.S. converted its communications station in Diego Garcia into a full-blown naval base," extended the airport runway to 12,000 feet, deepened the lagoon to accommodate a carrier task force, and store a thirty-days' supply of fuel there for ships and aircraft." Chalmers Johnson, *The Sorrows of Empire* (New York: Henry Holt & Co., 2004), p. 221.

45 *China's National Defense in 2004*, cited in *People's Daily* (Beijing), Jan. 2, 2005.

46 James Lilley and Carl Ford, "China's Military: A Second Opinion," *The National Interest*, Fall 1999, p. 74.

47 Roger Burbach and Jim Tarbell, *Imperial Overstretch* (New York: Zed Books, 2004), p. 209.

48 George Will, "The Hour of Air Power," *Newsweek*, March 31, 2003, p. 66.

fighter bombers (Su-30), and is engaged in co-production with Russia of 200 more Su-27s.[49] In addition, China owns a variety of indigenously developed modern and versatile combat aircraft such as the J-10, the FC-1, and the FB-7.[50] American bombers would also be targeted by China's modern surface-to-air missile defense by means of the SA-10 and SA-11.[51]

Not only would U.S. forces be greatly handicapped by America's distance from Central Asia, but the very stakes conceivably giving rise to such a war, namely whether the U.S. military bases will or will not be dismantled, hinge on the survivability of those bases in the face of determined China and/or Russian attacks. These bases are vulnerable to attacks by several hundred Chinese highly accurate supersonic ballistic missiles, the DF-15, which can be launched from deep inside Xinjiang and reach their targets within minutes, and even more numerous cruise missiles which can skim low over the terrain and thus evade radar detection. As Paul Bracken of Yale University has pointed out,

> Ballistic missiles are made to destroy bases. They can disarm an opponent before he can move to an offensive position. ...The U.S. is far ahead of China and other countries in tanks, jet planes, and guided missiles... . But these are the wrong comparisons to make. Staying in Asia is not a game about who has better weapons; it is a contest of missiles against bases.[52]

As already stated, America's penetration of Central Asia was a response to windfall opportunities, but by the same token, if and when conditions turn out to be less than opportune, it is predictable that the U.S. will pull back its horns, as it had done over the years in North Korea, Vietnam, Cambodia, Beirut, and Somalia. The benefits of its bases and troops in Central Asia, once the Afghan war has ended one way or another, would continue to be significant to the U.S., but as Kenneth Weisbrode wrote in 2002,

> American difficulties in the Middle East, and growing rivalry with China, are likely to make geopolitical competition with Russia in Central Eurasia less significant to the U.S. than its declaratory policy for much of the 1990s would seem to suggest.[53]

By mid-2005, Beijing and Moscow were ready to make the first of their formal demands regarding the American bases in Kyrgystan and Uzbekistan. On July 5 the members of the Shanghai Cooperation Organization, at a meeting in Kazakhstan, announced that,

---

49 *Washington Post*, July 19, 2001.
50 Michael D. Swaine and Ashley J. Tellis, *Interpreting China's Grand Strategy, Past, Present, and Future* (Santa Monica: RAND Corporation, 2000), p. 163.
51 Ibid., p. 163.
52 Paul Bracken, "America's Maginot Line," *Atlantic Monthly*, Dec. 1998, pp. 85–93.
53 Kenneth Weisbrode, "Central Eurasia: Prize or Quicksand," *Adelphi Papers* (London: The International Institute for Strategic Studies, 2001) no. 38, p. 82.

Member states of the Shanghai Cooperation Organization believe that participants in the anti-terrorist coalition should define a deadline for the temporary use of infrastructure and their military presence on SCO member state territory.[54]

Accordingly, on July 11, Kyrgystan's newly elected President Bakiyev stated, albeit prematurely, that the situation in Afghanistan had stabilized and that therefore it was "time to discuss the necessity of U.S. military presence in Kyrgystan."[55] Within two weeks Defense Secretary Rumsfeld rushed to Bishkek to change Bakiyev's mind. He managed to do so by making a promise of "considerable increase" of Washington's annual $50 million contribution to Kyrgystan's budget.[56]

Rumsfeld saw no point in visiting President Karimov of Uzbekistan, as the latter already in June had limited flights by America's C-17 and other heavy cargo aircraft taking off from the Khahanabad air base, and had thus compelled the U.S., in its efforts to send supplies to Afghanistan, to divert its cargo planes to its Manas airbase in Kyrgystan.[57] This is hundreds of miles farther from Afghanistan, which means much longer and costlier trips for trucks that pick up the supplies to haul to Kabul. Constrained by the fact that the U.S. military was stretched to the limit in Iraq, the most that Rumsfeld could do in response to Karimov's move was to say that it would not set back U.S. military operations in Afghanistan.[58]

Four days after Rumsfeld's bypassing of Uzbekistan, Karimov tightened the screws by formally ordering the U.S. to leave Khanabad air base altogether by January 2006. In November, Karimov took things still further. Speaking to reporters before departing for Moscow he said:

> ...the resentful forces that have been told to leave the Khanabad airfield will not rest. They never tire of subversive activities. I would say their main goal is to discredit Uzbekistan's independent policy, disrupt peace and stability in the country, and make Uzbekistan obey.[59]

After arriving in Moscow, Karimov met with President Putin and signed a new treaty which further hampered any possible U.S. military action against Uzbekistan, as the treaty established an alliance between Russia and Uzbekistan, stating in Article 2 that:

---

54 "Central Asian States Ask When U.S. Troops Will Leave," Reuters, July 5, 2005-12-13.

55 *People's Daily*, July 21, 2005.

56 Erica Marat, "Rumsfeld in Kyrgystan: Halting America's Faltering Position in Central Asia," *Analyst* (Central Asia-Caucasus Institute, Johns Hopkins School of Advanced International Studies), July 27, 2005.

57 Bradley Graham and Robin Wright, "U.S. Shifts Flights out of Uzbekistan," *Washington Post*, June 15, 2005.

58 *U.S.A. Today*, July 25, 2005.

59 Daniel Kimmage, "Uzbekistan: Between East and West," www.Eurasianet.org, Nov. 17, 2005.

If an act of aggression is committed against one of the sides by any state or group of states, this will be viewed as an act of aggression against both sides. In the case of an act of aggression against one of the sides, the other side… provides necessary assistance, including military assistance, as well as giving aid through other means at its disposal.[60]

It is likely that to add credibility to the Russian pledge to defend Uzbekistan, Russia will be granted the right to establish a military base in this former Soviet Republic.

The Geopolitics of Eurasia

For the United States, one great geopolitical advantage is America's unchallenged naval power. The U.S. Navy has been dominant throughout most of the 20th century, continues to be dominant today, and will remain dominant for decades to come. However, as the dominant seapower the United States does not have the advantage as the landpower, China, can leverage in Eurasia, particularly Central Asia, although the U.S. could be able to establish and/or maintain and/or expand its beachheads on the periphery of the Eurasian continent.

The maritime power's focus on the periphery of Eurasia derives from its acceptance of the fact that it cannot control the continent itself (despite the modern seapower's ability to strike deep inland with strategic bombers, ballistic missiles and cruise missiles) but also the sea power's consequent determination to at least constrict the military and economic environment of the continental power or powers and thereby prevent their maximal use of the resources, manpower, capital, markets, etc., of the entire Eurasian continent. Such maximal use would have adverse power consequences for the seapower, for, as the geostrategist Brzezinski has pointed out,

> About 75 percent of the world's people live in Eurasia, and most of the world's physical wealth is there as well, both in its enterprises and underneath its soil. Eurasia accounts for about 60 percent of the world's GNP and about three-fourths of the world's known energy resources. Eurasia is also the location of most of the world's politically assertive and dynamic states… . All of the potential political and/or economic challengers to American primacy are Eurasian. Cumulatively, Eurasia's power vastly overshadows America's.[61]

Brzezinski adds that "Fortunately for America, Eurasia is too big to be politically one," but points out that "the struggle for global primacy continues to be played" on this "chessboard" which is Eurasia.

The seapower's control of the outer edges of the Eurasian continent of course has the added benefit of augmenting the resources, markets, etc. available to the seapower – most crucially the oil and natural gas of the Persian Gulf region, and the industrial productivity and markets of Western Europe. The multiple uses of controlling the fringes of Eurasia were described by strategic analyst Colin Gray

---

60 Ibid.
61 Zbigniew Brzezinski, *The Grand Chessboard* (New York: Basic Books, 1997), p. 31.

when the Soviet Union still existed, but in terms which are still valid today vis-à-vis China and Russia:

> The Soviet security position in Eurasia is imperiled by a resistance around the periphery that is organized, underwritten, and even substantially provided by an effectively insular superpower [the U.S.] of continental proportions.[62]

The geopolitical realities are such that the maritime power is willing to limit its ambition to containment or constriction if circumstances are compelling. Thus it was that Britain, the dominant seapower in the 18th and 19th centuries, was willing to reach an agreement in 1907 with Tsarist Russia, the behemoth landpower, whereby the influence of each was delimited within Persia, then in the north of Afghanistan, and to the borders of Tibet, which was agreed to be "no-man's land." Similarly, during 45 years of the Cold War, America, the dominant seapower then, was willing to accept the existence of the Soviet Union and its control of Eastern Europe as facts of life and contented itself, with the exception of a misadventure in North Korea in October 1950, with controlling the earlier-mentioned bridgeheads on Eurasia's periphery.

The converse of this willingness to limit its ambitions, however, is that as soon as circumstances permit, the sea power will pursue a course more ambitious than containment. Thus, following the liberation of Eastern Europe in 1989–1990 and the collapse of the Soviet Union in 1991, the U.S. became the sole superpower in the world and, as described earlier, began for the first time to make inroads upon the heartland of Eurasia. Now there arose opportunities for enhancing the "multiple uses" of controlling the periphery of Eurasia by enlarging the periphery. Consequently in 1991 the U.S. invaded Iraq, although President Bush, the elder, did not feel up to conquering the country. In Kosovo in 1995 the U.S. Air Force contributed to the further disintegration of Yugoslavia. In Europe, Washington successfully pushed for the admission of several former Soviet satellite nations into the U.S.-dominated North Atlantic Treaty Organization (NATO). In Afghanistan the U.S. has endeavored since 2001 to make it a viable client state, and in Iraq, President Bush the younger has been trying since 2003 to accomplish what his father did not attempt.

In its power relations to any major Eurasian power or powers, the U.S. not only strives to maintain its bridgeheads on the periphery of the Eurasian continent, but constantly to expand these bridgeheads. It is therefore, vis-à-vis the major Eurasian powers, fundamentally an expansionist and offensive power.

However, a Eurasian power like China, on the other hand, not yet in the short run but clearly in the long run, has the capability of satisfying almost all its needs for raw materials, advanced technology, capital, labor power, markets, and international cooperation entirely within the Eurasian continent, preferably by peaceful means. It has less reason to scramble for natural resources or markets or cooperative nations

---

62 Colin Gray, *The Geopolitics of Super Power* (Lexington: The University Press of Kentucky, 1988), p. 95.

outside Eurasia. It thus has less reason to possess a dominant navy[63] or to challenge the dominant naval power on the high seas, not to mention trying to project its power against the coastlines of the dominant seapower. It does, however, need to prevent the dominant sea power from expanding its beachheads on the eastern part of the continent, which is why in November 1950 China blocked the adventurist General MacArthur from conquering North Korea, and why during the Vietnam War China stood ready to enter the war if U.S. troops were to invade North Vietnam.[64]

Moreover, China has an interest in creating conditions for the maritime power's withdrawal from its East Asian beachheads altogether so as to be less vulnerable to the latter's "power projection." Such withdrawal took place in 1975 upon the U.S. expulsion from South Vietnam and Cambodia, and, after more than fifty years of U.S. military presence in South Korea, has begun to take place on that peninsula. To prevent the dominant seapower from re-establishing beachheads on the continent, the landpower needs to develop the capability of denial of coastal access to the U.S. Navy and ground forces and hampering its "power projection" capability.[65] In its power relations with the dominant seapower, therefore, the continental power is fundamentally a defensive power.[66] This defensive character is not negated by the fact China is developing a "brown-water" navy which will have the mission of

---

63 It is a fascinating historical fact that between 1405 and 1433 China did have an impressive navy which carried out seven large naval expeditions to Southeast Asia, India, the Persian Gulf, and East Africa, nearly a century before Portuguese ships managed to round the Cape of Good Hope to also reach East Africa. At the time the Chinese ships were superior in construction and in navigation techniques, were much larger than the Portuguese ships. And yet by 1433 the Ming Emperor put a sudden end to the expeditions. Harvard historian John K. Fairbank persuasively wrote: "The similar capabilities of the Chinese and Portuguese voyagers make the contrast between their motivations all the greater. The Chinese simply lacked the expansive urge which the Europeans had, and this fact made all the difference…. [T]he main point demonstrated by the Ming voyagers and their cessation fifty years before Vasco da Gama was China's self-sufficiency." John K. Fairbank, *The United States and China* (Cambridge: Harvard University Press, 4th edition, 1979), p. 151.

64 China's Premier Zhou Enlai in a 1964 interview with a Pakistani newspaper committed China to giving support and help to Vietnam. He warned that "Should such just action bring on U.S. aggression against China, we will unhesitatingly rise in resistance and fight to the end." He ominously added, "Once the war breaks out, it will have no boundaries." *Peking Review*, May 13, 1964, cited in *China & the U.S., 1964–72* (New York: Facts On File, Inc., 1975), p. 114.

65 The U.S. Navy in 1992 defined its new, post-Gulf War doctrine as focusing on operations off the coastlines of the world more than on the high seas, and also "power projection" against land powers by use of Marine expeditionary forces, carrier-based aircraft, Tomahawk missiles from attack submarines, and naval gunfire support "to apply offensive military force against the enemy." Colonel Harry Summers, Jr., *The New World Strategy* (New York: Simon and Schuster, 1995), p. 114.

66 This does not at all mean that a continental power is ipso facto non-expansionist, but only that a continental power's expansionism, if it exists, tends to be targeted within the continent, as countless intra-Eurasian expansions historically have demonstrated, including

contesting U.S. naval dominance in the East China Sea and South China Sea so as to make U.S. "power projection" against the Chinese mainland still more difficult.

Along with China's rapid economic growth and the sudden collapse of the Soviet Union, China's influence in Central Asia has significantly increased. Through the Shanghai Cooperative Organization initiated by Beijing and other methods, Beijing has engaged in a rash of diplomatic activities in the region. As described by Bates Gill of Washington's Center for Strategic and International Studies,

> The Chinese are sending people all the time to meet prime ministers and presidents and generals and all the way down the diplomatic ladder.... This is all about soft power, and strategic and diplomatic relationships... . Central Asia is a fantastic lens, or model for what China is trying to do all over its periphery: reaching out and settling old scores, and trying to establish a benign kind of hegemony.[67]

As a result, despite the existence of some anti-Chinese feelings in Central Asia rooted in centuries of complex relations between the Chinese empire and the nomadic "barbarians" of the west and the north, plus the lingering effects of Soviet propaganda against the Chinese Communist Party during much of the Maoist period, the Central Asian states since the beginning of their independence were eager to be on good terms with Beijing as well as with Washington. The presidents of Kazakhstan, Kyrgystan, and Uzbekistan have all stressed their special relationships with China's leaders.[68] On this matter, geographic proximity is the most salient geopolitical factor.

At the level of implementation, there has been a remarkable influx of Chinese merchants throughout Central Asia in recent years, selling goods manufactured in Xinjiang. For example in Kazakhstan's capital, Almaty, the Chinese market Ya Lian

> ...has become one of the city's largest marketplaces, attracting thousands of shoppers to its stalls, which offer everything from household appliances and clothes to consumer electronics. It is a scene repeated at hundreds of Chinese markets across Central Asia.[69]

These Chinese goods are a result of two decades of impressive industrialization and economic growth in Xinjiang, following the overall trend in China since the early 1980s. By 1988, when Doak Barnett of Johns Hopkins University traveled in China's western provinces, he already saw some factories in Xinjiang producing consumer durables, including TVs, washing machines, and refrigerators on a small scale.[70] By 2002, the pace of economic development had been such that:

---

those of Alexander the Great, Attila the Hun, Tamerlane, Ghengis Khan, Ivan the Terrible, Napoleon, Hitler, and Stalin.

67 *New York Times*, March 28, 2004.

68 Jeremy Bransten, "Central Asia: China's Mounting Influence," www.Eurasianet.org, Nov. 23, 2004.

69 Branston.

70 A. Doak Barnett, *China's Far West* (Boulder: Westview Press, 1993), p. 395.

Towns everywhere are being modernized, with clean and up-to-date shops replacing old-fashioned ones.... The capital Urumqi now has modern freeways, highways, supermarkets, and high-rise apartments. A town like Aksu, which not so long ago was a backwater, has assumed a modern appearance with clean and modern shopping malls.[71]

Xinjiang's economy is developing much more rapidly than the economies of the neighboring Central Asian states.[72] This is largely because after the demise of the Soviet Union they had followed the policies demanded by the International Monetary Fund, which turned out to be economically disastrous. By 2003, Xinjiang "has enjoyed a decade of 8 percent GDP growth, on average, compared with negative growth in Kyrgystan, Tajikistan, and Turkmenistan, while Uzbekistan and Azerbaijan recorded minor GDP rises... . Now, Xinjiang is their new role model."[73]

The attraction of this role model for the Muslim populations of Central Asia is based on more than Xinjiang's economic performance in general. It has an extra glitter due to the fact that the benefits of economic development are not limited to the Han nationality but are shared to a significant degree by the Muslim populations there. Thus in 2003 Colin Mackerras observed "an emerging Uighur middle class whose members have better jobs, are more prosperous than their parents, and are accessing better education for their children than they themselves received."[74]

Some might argue that Beijing is making special efforts in Xinjiang to create opportunities for the Uighur minority so as to weaken the appeal of the Uighur separatist movement. Such indeed has been the effect of the policies. And yet it is clear that China has pursued poverty alleviation programs in all minority areas for two decades, and promoted economic development in those areas to the extent that adverse natural conditions allowed. Xinjiang has developed faster than other poor provinces partly because it had been the beneficiary, back in the early 1950s, of Beijing's decision to allocate, for strategic reasons, big investment funds to Xinjiang and to send a great many skilled technicians and workers there to develop the oil industry and to build a major railway reaching as far as Urumqi, plus a string of modern factories along the railway.[75] Beijing thus had authentic developmental motives in Xinjiang. Using geopolitical advantages, economic interdependence, and strategic partnership, China will likely continue to gain political and economic influence in Central Asia in the future.

In what follows, we will shift our focus to the broadly diverse geostrategic interests of China, Russia, the European Union, and the U.S. within the entire Eurasian

---

71 Colin Mackerras, "Ethnicity in China: The Case of Xinjiang," *Harvard Asia Quarterly*, Winter 2004, p. 6.

72 Graham E. Fuller and S. Frederick Starr, *The Xinjiang Problem* (Washington, D.C.: Central Asia-Caucasus Institute, Johns Hopkins School of Advanced International Studies, 2003).

73 Laurence Brahm, "Banking on the Xinjiang Model for Central Asia," *South China Morning Post* (Hong Kong), Nov. 24, 2003.

74 Colin Mackerras, p. 7.

75 Barnett, pp. 385–87.

continent. These interests are not only more diverse than geostrategic interests of the U.S. and China but also more extensive than the geopolitics of Central Asia.

America's geostrategic interest on the Eurasian continent has, since the founding of NATO in 1949, been the mainstay of this military alliance between most of Western Europe and the United States and Canada, ostensibly for defense against potential Soviet invasion of Western Europe. But, in view of the fact that American leaders in reality did not believe that Moscow had any intention of invading,[76] it is evident that America's geostrategic interest in having a foothold in Western Europe by means of NATO was other than defense, namely to maintain its grip on the European bridgehead on the continent and patiently await, and benefit from, the day when the Soviet Empire would collapse of its own internal contradictions.[77]

By 1982, NATO's initial membership had been enlarged to 16 nations. With the disintegration of the Soviet Union in 1991, NATO's original stated purpose became obsolete. Yet, instead of being dismantled, NATO not only was kept alive but, under American leadership, expanded eastward to include ten former East European satellites of the former Soviet Union, reaching as far east as the Baltic states: Estonia, Latvia, and Lithuania. Under the new circumstances, America's geostrategic purpose in Europe had become more expansive. As Brzezinski succinctly described it in 1997,

> America's central goal in Europe... is to consolidate through a more genuine transatlantic partnership the U.S. bridgehead on the Eurasian continent so that an enlarging Europe can become a more viable springboard for projecting into Eurasia the international democratic and cooperative order....[78]

By now the states in the Caucasus and Central Asia clearly are targets for NATO expansion which, if successful, would extend the encirclement of Russia all the way to Mongolia. The same expansion would bring NATO to the western borders of China, thus amplifying the U.S. encirclement of China, and would hamper China's

---

76 At the time of the major U.S. initiatives after World War II, namely the Truman Doctrine and the Marshall Plan, "U.S. officials certainly did not believe that the Kremlin was contemplating unprovoked and premeditated military aggression." Melvin P. Leffler, *The Specter of Communism* (New York: Hill & Wang, 1994), p. 56. George F. Kennan, Director of the State Department's Policy Planning Staff, wrote in a secret memorandum in November 1947, "The Kremlin does not wish to have another major war and does not expect to have one." Quoted in Thomas H. Etzold and John L. Gaddis, eds., *Containment: Documents on American Policy and Strategy, 1945–1950* (New York: Columbia University Press, 1978), p. 96.

77 George Kennan wrote in July 1947 under the pseudonym "X" in an historic article which became one of the main pillars of Washington's Cold War strategy: "But the possibility remains (and in the opinion of this writer it is a strong one) that Soviet power... bears within it the seeds of its own decay, and that the sprouting of these seeds is well advanced." George Kennan, "The Sources of Soviet Conduct," *Foreign Affairs* (New York), July 1947, p. 580.

78 Brzezinski, p. 86.

access to Central Asian oil and natural gas, thereby weakening this rising competitor on the world scene.

The other major European organization, the European Union (EU), is torn between the "Old Europe" centered on France, Germany, Holland and Belgium, which envisions a gradual disengagement from the American Eagle's embrace, and the recently admitted East European nations which hope to benefit from American investments and trade and military alliance through NATO. EU membership has recently increased from 15 nations to 25. Most of the ten new members are, as was the case in NATO's expansion, East European, reaching as far eastward as Poland and the Baltic states. Aiming still further east, the EU plans to admit Bulgaria and Romania in 2007.

In so far as the European Union, despite recent setbacks caused by French and Dutch voters, remains under the influence of the powerful "Old Europe," there will continue to be a tension between it and NATO.[79] This tension will most likely increase not only because of America's unilateralist, hegemonic foreign policy but because the "Old Europe" more and more realizes that its previous self-identification as part of the "democratic West" in opposition to the Soviet bloc East had caused it to lose sight of a deeper, more historically rooted cultural identity which had little to do with America. How democratic, after all, was Europe historically, when, before World War II, there was Fascist rule in Italy, Germany, Spain, Portugal, Austria, Poland, Hungary, Bulgaria, and Romania, and fascism had significant presence in England, France, and most other West European countries?

A penetrating analysis of this divergence of cultural identities and of foreign policies was published recently by Lanxin Xiang (相蓝欣), a Chinese professor at the Graduate Institute of International Studies in Geneva and also at the East China Normal University in Shanghai. Xiang writes that,

> The deeper undercurrent of a possible transatlantic divorce is that the U.S. and Europe are projecting two different models of the West. The U.S. model is that of an individual-rights based democracy whose foreign policy is determined by national self-interest alone. The EU member states, by contrast, pursue a model of communitarian social democracy, and a worldview that is 'rites-based' – that is to say, based on the rites of international institutions, norms and rules. The recent split within the EU over Iraq does not alter this general trend.[80]

Xiang acknowledges that after the end of the Cold War the transatlantic partners did agree to NATO's enlargement, but points out that from the very beginning the two sides had different purposes in mind. Washington preferred to treat Russia as

---

79 "The political integration of the EU presents the greatest challenge to continuing U.S. influence in Europe since World War II...." Jeffrey L. Cimbalo, "Saving NATO from Europe," *Foreign Affairs* (New York), Nov./Dec. 2004, p. 112.

80 Lanxin Xiang, "China's Eurasian Experiment," *Survival* (London), Summer 2004, p. 109.

a defeated power, defined it as a potential threat, and used NATO's enlargement as a mechanism for holding the political West together, including a European role for the U.S.

On the Eurasian continent, on the other hand, the end of the Cold War meant that the more enduring concept of the cultural West was back. At the same time, the communitarian element in European civilization found common ground between all of Europe and the Asian part of Russia as well. Moreover, the turn of events required a new approach to Moscow. Thus:

> The Europeans, who must live with Russia on the same continent, had to find ways of integrating Russia to avoid another disastrous division of Europe. A united Europe is the only sure way of opening up a path to Russia for its integration into the common European house.[81]

Accordingly the EU Treaty of Amsterdam in 1996 created a special instrument called "Common Strategy" which was offered to Moscow in 1999. President Putin responded enthusiastically, in contrast with his negative attitude toward NATO.

Almost simultaneously, notes Xiang, "a second organic Euro-Asian link has been nurtured." Russia and China decided shortly after the Cold War to significantly improve their bilateral relations, including their joint membership in the Shanghai Cooperation Organization. Thus on the Eurasian continent there were created strategic links between the EU and Russia, and between Russia and China.

But until the first half of 2003, there was still lacking a direct strategic link between the EU and China, but by 2004 things had stunningly changed, such that "the EU is at the top of the Chinese leadership's agenda." One factor was that China passed Japan in 2002 to become the EU's second largest economic partner. Furthermore, China was playing an increasingly important role on the world stage. Thus when, in the wake of the 2003 U.S. invasion of Iraq, the EU issued its fifth joint statement on China, "the tone was drastically different. China was considered a strategic partner in the 'global governance'." This led Beijing to respond within three days "with the same enthusiasm as Putin had shown in 1999," and the forming of enduring Eurasian links was underway. Not the least of Beijing's motivations in this new approach to Europe, Xiang maintains, is geopolitical:

> The geopolitical instincts of the Beijing leadership tells it that a Eurasian orientation is safer for its foreign policy than a Pacific one. In the Pacific, potentially explosive issues are abundant: the real or imaginary Sino-American strategic rivalry; the crisis on the Korean Peninsula; a rearming and more assertive Japan; and last, but not least, the intractable Taiwan problem. In policy terms, China would prefer a quiet eastern front and an intense interaction with the [continental] West.[82]

While Xiang may be right about Beijing's preference regarding the eastern front, I have shown earlier that China has been and will continue to be assertive on that very

---

81 Ibid., p. 111.
82 Ibid., p. 118.

front, But of course I would agree that China, for obvious geopolitical reasons, feels less vulnerable on its western front to potential "power projection" by the world's dominant seapower. And by forming strategic partnerships with Russia, Central Asia, and the European Union, China has enhanced its geopolitical security on its western flank, which in turn counterbalances its vulnerability in the east. Referring to the pioneer of 20th century geopolitical analysis, Xiang points out that "China needs Mackinder's 'heartland' to reduce the enormous strategic pressure coming from the Pacific East."[83]

Conclusion

In this chapter we began by showing that in the wake of the collapse of the Soviet Union, the U.S. Government seized the opportunity to forge cooperative relations with the newly independent nations in Central Asia, thus establishing an unprecedented American foothold in that region, including the building of a large air base in Kyrgystan and permission to use a former Soviet air base in Uzbekistan. This foothold served the economic purpose of obtaining American access to new oil fields in the region, plus the military purpose of threatening the interests of both Russia and China in their respective "backyards."

The study showed that Beijing and Moscow, jointly as well as independently, took steps to counteract the American moves. We predicted that in the face of Chinese and Russian determination in future years to demand U.S. withdrawal, the Pentagon, knowing that its penetration of Central Asia had been an opportunistic gamble, and realizing that for geopolitical reasons the foothold could not be maintained, will decide that retreat is the better part of valor.

The study showed that in the absence of non-nuclear regional war with the U.S., and nuclear war being ruled out by the facts of nuclear deterrence, China will be in an especially favorable situation in Central Asia. Her geographic proximity combined with industrial and commercial prowess and developmental experience make her a natural partner and even a model for the Central Asian republics, with the likelihood of economic benefits and cooperation and peaceful coexistence all around. China will thus have shown that its rise in economic, political, and military power will not, at least not in Central Asia, result in any unwarranted use of power.

Yet China's geostrategic vision transcends that. The vision is that China's political and economic achievements in Central Asia, when combined with the foreseeable steady enlargements of the networks of Eurasian rail, highway, pipeline, and air transportation, will lay the groundwork for a strategic partnership linking together China, Central Asia, Russia, and Europe, and potentially the Middle East and India as well. Beijing anticipates that the European Union will flourish, that NATO will consequently wither away, thus depriving the United States of its long-standing military bridgehead on the western end of the continent. America's maritime

---

83 Ibid., p. 118.

superiority will thus become more and more irrelevant to the political, economic, cultural, and technological partnerships on this massive Eurasian continent, which Beijing believes will be guided by the Five Principles of Peaceful Coexistence declared by Premier Zhou Enlai half a century ago.

Index

Headnote: *f* or *ff* indicates figure(s); *n* or *nn* indicates note(s); *t* or *tt* indicates table(s).

Afghanistan 42*t*, 180, 238–51 *passim*
Al Qaeda terrorist network 240
Amnesty International 97*n*, 105
Amsterdam Treaty (1996) 259
An, Chen 64
Anti-Ballistic Missile (ABM) Treaty (1972) 160, 202
anticorruption campaign
  See corruption
antidiscrimination
  See discrimination
  as result of corruption 64
ASEAN (Association of Southeast Asian Nations) 150, 173, 178
Asia Pacific region 6, 27, 144, 190–1, 202–4
Asian economic zone 142
Asian financial crisis 23–4, 69, 77
  China's response to 86, 150, 226
  and Kang's thesis 70*n*
authoritarianism 118–19, 135, 154
Azerbaijan 238, 246, 256

Bakiyev, Kurmanbek (President) 251
balance of power 68–70, 81–2, 87, 177, 183, 186–7
Baltic states, NATO expansion into 257–8
Bang, Quan Zheng 183–209
Barnett, Doak 255
Beixiaodao
  See territorial and maritime disputes
bin Laden, Osama 240
Blair, Denis 165
Blanchard, Jean-Marc F. 211–36
blind eye 92*f*, 93, 93*n*, 94, 106, 114
BMW (Baoma An) case study 131
Bo'ao Forum for Asia 1–2, 27
boundary disputes
  See territorial and maritime disputes
Bracken, Paul 250
Brzezinski, Zbigniew 11, 35, 246, 252, 257

Buddhists 103
Burbach, Roger 249
Bush, George H.W. (President), meeting with Hu Jintao 155
Bush administration
  See also United States
  China Threat theory of 166–7
  on CNOOC-Chevron-Unocal deal 178–9
  military containment strategy of (*See under* United States)
  missile defense strategies of 160–3, 167–8
  as strategic competitor 171

Cao, Gangchuan (General) 180
Cao, Siyuan 13
capital flight, and corruption 85, 87
capitalists, as socialist builders 50
Cardinal Kung Foundation 103, 112*t*
case studies
  BMW 131
  of corruption 78–9
  HBV carrier discrimination 124–5
  Nujiang River dam 131
  of repression 123–6
  Sun Dawu 125, 125*n*
  Sun Zhigang 56, 123–5, 124*n*
  Xiamen Yuanhua 78
  Yu Huafeng 125, 125*n*
Catholics
  See Christians
cell phone and SMS as agents of change 131–2
Central Asia, and contemporary geopolitics 237–61
China
  See also economic growth/development; peaceful development *(heping fazhan)*; peaceful rise *(heping jueqi)*; territorial and maritime disputes
  air mobility of 249–50

and Asian economic zone 142
and Asian financial crisis 86, 150, 226
Ballistic Missile Defense (BMD) program 159
constitution of 49
contrasted with Soviet Union 36
defense expenditure 193, 193*t*
as a developing country 37
electoral system of 121–2
food supply 228
governance indicators 62*t*
as holder of U.S. debt 189–90
as a hybrid regime 122 (*see also* hybrid regime)
international integration and participation of 26, 142–3, 146–52
maritime history of 254*n*
military modernization (*see* military modernization)
political liberalization of 122–34
PSI ranking of 42*t*
reemergence of 27, 39
as responsible stakeholder 39
security strategy of 37
strategic culture of 184–7
China Reform Forum 2, 27
China Threat theory 1, 39, 41, 144, 150, 165–70
Chinese Communist Party (CCP)
blueprint for good governance 126–7
characterizations of 39, 52–4, 79
and corruption 63–4, 79
and democratization 5, 13, 40–1, 53–4, 119–20, 119*nn*–120*nn*, 137–8
economic development measures of 22–3
on nationalism and Taiwan 201
reform measures of 24–5, 36–7, 48–50
Chiwei Yu (Taisho Shima)
See territorial and maritime disputes
Christians
detention of 105*t*–106*t*
growth and repression of 101–14, 102*ff*
spatial distribution of arrests 111*t*–112*t*
Chunxiao/Shirakaba Island
See territorial and maritime disputes
civil liberties 122, 134
civil service reform 75–6, 87*n*, 130*n*
civil society and citizen politics 123–6, 130–4
clientelism (patronage) 65, 67–8, 73, 80–1

Clinton, Bill (President), and Sino-American relations 164–5
Committee for the Investigation of Persecution of Religion in China (CIPRC) 103, 105*t*, 111*t*
communications, and military strategies 199
Confucian system 52, 128, 143, 186–7
constitutionalism 123–30
corruption
anticorruption policies 82, 84–5
assessment of control of: neutral 82–5; optimistic 79–82, 85–7, 128–9; pessimistic 74–9
case studies of 78–9
checked by democratization 35
comparative studies of 67–74
Corruption Perception Index (CPI) 51, 51*t*
intensification of 82–4
of macroeconomic management 72–9
networks of 78–9
as protest-precipitating factor 63*n*, 64
and regime stability/instability 74–85
rise of, in market economy 23, 50–2, 64–5
shift from nontransaction forms of 80
spectrum of 88*f*
and state-society structures 83*t*
as threat to peaceful development 5, 25, 50–2
varieties of 83*t*
CSTO (Collective Security Treaty Organization) 246
cults
See religious dissent/repression
Cultural Revolution (1966–76) 47

Daito islands
See territorial and maritime disputes
Dali, Yang 79
deep reform 4, 23–6, 34–7
democratization
and elections 121–2
hybrid regimes as pathway to 134–8
and peaceful reform 5, 13–14, 34–5, 39–60, 132
and state-society relationships 133–4
as supply/demand process 135–7
varieties of 118, 118*nn*–120*nn*
Deng, Xiaoping
on deep reform 22

domestic policies of 18
foreign policies of 19, 154
on island/maritime dispute 215
philosophy and strategy of 20, 24–5, 47–8, 63
as a pragmatist 237
taoguang yanghui concept of 2
Deng, Yong 188
development
  See peaceful development *(heping fazhan)*
Diamond, Larry 120–2
Diaoyu/Senkaku Islands dispute
  See also territorial and maritime disputes
  Lighthouse incidents 216–17, 219–20, 222
Ding, X. L. 77
Ding, Xueliang 64
diplomacy, and international stability 149–152
discrimination, case studies 124–5
Doner, Richard 72–3
Dui Hua Foundation 97, 97*n*, 98*t*, 103–4, 104*f*

East Asia, economic comparisons with China 67–74
East China Sea
  See also territorial and maritime disputes
  and China's capabilities 231–2
  China's economic interests in 219, 225, 228–31
  and disputes in the new millennium 6, 9, 148–9, 166, 206, 212–31, 234
economic growth/development
  See also peaceful development; peaceful rise
  CCP development measures of 22–3
  containment of (*see under* United States)
  and corruption 61–88
  deep reform of 23–6
  East and Southeast Asia examples of 67–74
  and East China Sea 219, 225, 228–31
  and embedded state autonomy 67–8
  and energy needs 228–9
  and environmental challenges 28–9
  and foreign policy 18–21, 141–2
  and globalization 5–6, 141–58, 190–1, 208–9
  and national identity 230–1
  and natural resources 28–9
  optimistic outlook for 143
  peaceful rise as basis for 25–7, 143, 185
  and regime stability 61, 63
  and social instability 29–30, 34–7

and "soft power" 3–4, 156
and state-business relationship 69
economic integration implications 187–91
elections, as democratization criteria 121–2, 134
energy consumption, oil, coal, electricity 28–9, 145, 228–9
ethics, and regime stability 50–4
eudemonic reasoning 44, 47, 54–9, 55*t*
Eurasia, geopolitics of 252–60
European Union (EU) 142, 147, 258–9
Evans, Peter 68
Exclusive Economic Zone (EEZ), 20 149, 213, 213*n*, 217–19
exports
  by China 24; destinations 188*t*; to EU 234; to Japan 215, 234; to U.S. 234
  by U.S.: to China 189*f*, 190; value of 21*t*

Falun Gong 103–4, 104*n*, 109–10, 114
Fascism, in Old Europe 258
Folta, Paul Humes 192
foreign direct investment (FDI) 9, 20–1, 24
foreign policy 1–2, 11–12
  and economic development 18–21, 141–2
  under Mao 18
  as a status quo state 3–4, 8–9, 144–5, 200–1
  and U.S. hegemony 150–4
foreign trade 20, 21*t*
four modernizations 18
Franks, Tommy (General) 240–1
Friedberg, Aaron L. 10

Gang of Four 47
GDP (gross domestic product) 18–19, 19*ff*, 143–4
geopolitics
  in Central Asia 237–61
  distinguished from geostrategy 239*n*, 247
  of Eurasia 252–60
Gertz, Bill 177
Gill, Bates 255
Gilpin, Robert 187
Gini coefficient increase 57
globalization
  and challenges to China 24
  and Chinese strategic culture 185–6
  and economic interdependence 5–6, 141–58, 190–1, 208–9

Goldstein, Avery 9, 20, 144
Gong, Li 33
good government 126–9
Goss, Porter 168
grand strategy for peaceful rise 20, 25
Gray, Colin 252–3
Great Western Development Program 58
Guo, Baogang 39–60
Guo, Xuetang 159–81

happiness
  See eudemonic reasoning
harmonious society, defined 55
health care system, in rural areas 58
hegemonic stability
hegemony and heterodoxy
  defined 91n
  interplay between 91, 93–4, 106–14
  unipolarity of U.S. 2, 36, 143–4, 149, 153–4, 160, 164
hepatitis B virus (HBV) carriers, discrimination against 124
heping fazhan
  See peaceful development
heping jueqi
  See peaceful rise
High-Speed Train case 131
homelessness
  See human rights
household consumption gaps 29, 30t, 31
Hu, Jintao (President) 2n
  on a harmonious society 55, 185–6
  meeting with President Bush 155
  on peaceful development 2, 145
  pragmatism of 156
  restoration of Three Represents 53, 56
  on socioeconomic development 31
  Tai Qi soft-power diplomacy of 156–7
  on Taiwan 3, 201
  on value of history 149
Huangwei Yu (Kuba Shima)
  See territorial and maritime disputes
human rights 56, 96t, 178
Human Rights Watch 100
Huntington, Samuel 64, 118n, 153
Hutchcroft, Paul 72
hybrid regime 5, 118–22, 134–8
hydrocarbons
  See natural resources

ICFTU (International Confederation of Free Trade Unions) 99
idealistic altruism, and regime stability 50, 56, 141–2, 158
Ignatieff, Michael 245
Ikeda, Yukihiko 218
Ikenberry, John 187
illiberal democracy
imports 21t, 24, 228–9
income disparity 57–8, 57t
  See also socioeconomic disparity
India 32, 204, 233
Indonesia 69, 70n, 79, 83t, 86, 88f
information technology, as agent for change 130–2
interest-based civil organizations 132–3
international interdependence 146–52, 208–9
International Monetary Fund (IMF)
international relationships 145–52
Internet, as agent for change 131–2
Iraq war 240, 244–5, 253

Jacoby, Lowell 168
Jacques, Martin 152
Japan 206
  See also Sino-Japanese relations
  2+2 meeting, with U.S. 170, 175
  demonstrations against 131, 131n
  economic comparisons with China 67–74
  Lighthouse incidents (see Nihon Seinensha)
  METI (Ministry for Economics, Trade and Industry) activities 221–2
  MSA (Maritime Safety Agency) activities 217–20
  MSDF (Maritime Self-Defense Force) activities 219–20, 224
  naval capabilities of 232
  remilitarization of 170
  security alliance with U.S. 206
  territorial and maritime disputes 211–36
Japanese Youth Federation/Association
  See Nihon Seinensha
Jiang, Zemin
  on deep reform 22
  market oriented reforms of 48
  on military goals 191
  multipolar world concept of 2
  on rule of ethics 52–3

on territorial/maritime dispute 217
Three Represents theory of 24–5, 46, 48–9, 56
Jiao, Yulu, as model icon 50
Jie, Chen 54
Johnson, Chalmers A., *MITI and the Japanese Miracle* 67
Johnston, Alastair Iain 190

Kang, David 69, 70*n*
Kaplan, Robert D. 153, 177
Kawaguchi, Yoriko 221
Kazakhstan 238–9, 255
Kennedy, Scott 80
Koizumi, Junichiro (PM) 170
Kono, Yohei 219
Kyrgystan 238–40, 355

labor unrest 99–101, 106*t*, 114
Lam, Willy Wo-Lap 13
land reform, under Maoism 47
Lanzhou Military Region
Lardy, Nicholas 76
Law on the Territorial Sea and Contiguous Waters 216
Lawless, Richard 179
Lee, Oliver M. 237–61
legal system
  See also rule of law
  checks and balances proposals for 126–8
  limits to government power 128
legality and ritual *(fa li)* principle 44
legislation, law on *(lifa fa)* 128
legitimacy
  See political legitimacy
Lei, Feng, as ideal man 50
Li, Deshui 29
Li, Jijun (Lt. General) 185
Li, Peng, on deep reform 22
Li, Qingsi 141–58
Li, Zhaoxing 180*n*
Liang, Guanglile (General) 179
Liaoyang and Daqing protests
Lilley, James 249
Lin, Zhibo 231
Liu, Guoli 17–37
Liu, Jie 26
looting 71, 73
Lu, Xiaobo 75

Luxembourg, Rosa 53

MacIntyre, Andrew 75
Mackerras, Colin 256
Mackinder's "heartland" 260
Mandate of Heaven *(tian ming)* 44, 46
Manion, Melanie 74, 84
Mann, Michael 79
Mao, Zedong
  foreign policy 18
  on founding of PRC 237
  ideology of 47
  self-reliance policy of 18, 23
Maoist communism, and political instability 46–8
maritime interests
  See territorial and maritime disputes
market economy
  as deep reform measure 23
  importance of rule of law 123
  and rise of corruption 50–4
  and socialism 23
Marxism 46, 48
McCain, John 241
McGovern, Ray 246
Mearsheimer, John J. 34, 153, 169
Medeiros, Evan S. 14
migrant laborers 58–9
military modernization 6, 166–71
  See also PLA; PLAAF; PLAN
  arms production programs 195*t*
  communications/information systems 199
  goals of 191–200
  naval defense strategy 197, 232–3
  and self-sufficiency 195–6
military strategies, of U.S. and China 6, 146, 152–4, 159–81
minzhu kengtan 133
missile defense strategies
  of China (*see* military modernization; weapons systems)
  of U.S. (*See under* United States)
Mongolia 105*n*, 178
Moody, Peter 46
Moore, Thomas G. 188
Moseley, Michael (General) 172
Most Favored Nation status 178
multilateral organizations 2, 26
Muslims, opportunities for 256

Myers, Richard B. (General) 179

Nakagawa Shoichi 223
National People's Congress, adopts the
    Three Represents 49
national security strategy 37, 184
nationalism/national identity 230–1
NATO (North Atlantic Treaty Organization)
    202–3
  expansion into Eurasia 253, 257–8
  natural prolongation principle 213–14, 216
  Partnership for Peace Program 239
  SCO as foil to 150
  split from EU 258
natural resources.
  See also East China Sea
  and China's capabilities 231–2
  China's reserves 229
  competition for, in Central Asia 257–8
  energy/hydrocarbon consumption 28–9,
    145, 228–9
  exploration for, and Sino-Japanese
    disputes 219, 222–3, 225–6
  of the Islands 149, 213–14
  living and nonliving 228–9
  and sustainable growth rate 28–9
Nihon Seinensha, Lighthouse/island
    incidents 216–17, 219–20, 222
nonperforming loans 77
North Korea, China's attitude to 32–3, 233
Nujiang River dam case 131
Nye, Joseph S. 27, 156

oil
  See natural resources
Okinawa Reversion Treaty 214
Olcott, Martha Brill 245
Old Europe 258
openness/open door policy 20–1, 23–4,
    128–30
organized crime/mafia 60, 83*t*

Pan, Yue 49
Parsons, Talcott 42
Pax Americana 164
Peace and Friendship Treaty (1978) 215–16
peace breaker (Taiwan) 9, 32, 147–54,
    161–3, 168, 170–4, 180
peaceful development *(heping fazhan)*
    and the American factor 10, 146–7, 157–8
    challenges to 5, 8–14, 25, 50–2, 94–101
    and deep reform 4, 22–6, 34–7
    domestic preconditions for 20, 186–7
    and ecological concerns 17–22, 29, 186
    and hybrid regime 117–38
    and political reform 24–5
    and regime stability/political legitimacy
        39–60, 91–4
    and Taiwan policy 3
    use of term 1, 1*n*, 2
peaceful rise *(heping jueqi)*
    as basis for economic development 25–7,
        143, 185
    challenges to 26–34, 141–58; and
        countermeasures, 155-158 26–34, 152–4
    and China's capabilities 231–2
    and grand strategy 20, 25
    and hybrid governance 137–8
    and military strategy 163–70, 183–209
    and national rejuvenation *(minzu fuxing)*
        27, 27*nn*
    and nationalism 230–1
    and Sino-Japanese relations 211–36
    use of term 1, 1*n*, 2, 27, 27*nn*
Pearson, Margaret 75
Pei, Minxin 86
people first *(men ben)* principle 44, 56
People's Republic of China (PRC)
    See China
per capita income 37
Pinghu oil field 219
PLA (People's Liberation Army) 191–200,
    248–50
PLAAF (People's Liberation Army Air
    Force) 196–7
PLAN (People's Liberation Army Navy),
    East China Sea activities 224
political legitimacy
    Chinese understanding of 42, 43*t*, 44
    and hybrid regimes 126, 128
    Jiang's reforms 49
    and peaceful development 39–60
    relational hypotheses for 45–6
    and Sino-Japanese relations 233
    three-dimensional view of 60
    two-dimensional view of 44
political reform measures 22–6, 134–8
    and idealism 10, 56, 141–2, 158

Political Stability Indicator (PSI) 41–2, 42*t*
Powell, Colin 240
PPP (per purchase power), China's ranking 143
privatization, and corruption 64–5
profit-seeking/sharing 71
   See also rent-seeking behavior
   and capital flight 85
   as moral hazard 50
property rights, under 2002 constitutional amendments 56
Protestants
   See Christians
protests
   See social unrest
Provisional Measures (PMZ) joint fishing zone 218
public opinion, as agency for change 131–2
Putin, Vladimir (President) 245–6, 259

Quadrennial Defense Review (QDR) 167
Quah, Jon S. T. 73, 84

Ramsay, Ansil 72–3
realist theory 8, 34, 153, 169, 177, 183, 186–8
   on military goals 191, 194, 206, 208–9
   on NATO enlargement 202
regime categorization 120–2
regime stability
   See also repression
   analytical framework for 41–6
   and the CCP 5
   Chinese understanding of 43*t*, 44–6
   and corruption 61–88
   defined 62–3
   and eudemonic appeals 54–9
   and hybridization 5, 117–37
   and legitimizing ideology 46–50, 59–60, 452
   and official ethics 50–4
   and peaceful development 39–60
regional income disparity 57*t*
religious dissent/repression 95, 101–13
   heretical cults 107, 107–8*nn*
rent-seeking behavior 50, 66–7, 71, 80
repression
   See also regime stability
   case studies of 123–6
   forms of 5, 89–115, 93*n*, 106*t*

   and regime stability 89–115
   religious (*see* religious dissent/repression)
   of separatism 107*t*, 108–9
   strategic 92*f*
   and toleration 113–14
Rice, Condoleezza 170, 180*n*
Rose-Ackerman, Susan 82, 84
rule by virtue *(ren zhi)*, and political legitimacy 44
rule of ethics, to counter corruption 52–3
rule of law 24, 52, 123–30
Rumsfeld, Donald
   on Afghanistan pull-out 251
   bypasses Uzbekistan 251
   on China's military expansion 168, 177
   sees China threat 153, 156, 168, 173
   on Taiwan Strait 170
   talks with Liang Guanglie 179
   visits Beijing 179
   visits Bishkek 251
   visits Kabul 241
   visits Mongolia 178
rural subsidies 58–9
Russia
   See also Sino-Russian relations
   air mobility of 249–50
   arms sales to China 202–4
   domination of its near abroad 239
   response to U.S. moves 245–7
Russia-Uzbekistan treaty 251–2
Ryukyu islands
   See territorial and maritime disputes

Saunders, Phillips C. 185
Schleifer, Andrei 70, 73
SCO (Shanghai Cooperation Organization) 150, 157, 246
   influence of, in Central Asia 255
   July 2005 meeting on US military presence 250–1
   June 2002 summit meeting 245–6
Scobell, Andrew 184–5
sectarianism
   See religious dissent/repression; specific groups
security
   See national security strategy
separatism
   See under repression

Shambaugh, David 33–4
Shanghai Cooperation Organization
Shieh, Shawn 61–88
Shulsky, Abram N. 173
Sino-American relations 33, 37, 141–3, 145–6, 149–52
  asymmetric military relationship 159–81, 247
  China as strategic competitor 171
  and China Threat theory 165–70
  China's response to U.S. moves 160–3, 245–61
  and economic integration 187–91
  major issues 152–4, 156–7, 178–9, 205
  and regional security 177–81
  triangular relationship with Japan 147–9, 157, 161–2, 174–8, 190
  triangular relationship with Taiwan 202
  U.S. as debtor 189–90
  U.S. containment strategies 205–8, 257–8
  and weapons of mass destruction (WMDs) 33
  as zero-sum game 187
Sino-ASEAN relationship 150
Sino-EU relations 259
Sino-India relations 150
Sino-Japanese relations 6–7, 9, 32–3, 148–9
  2001 Agreement (for prior notification) 219–20
  and economic growth 232–5
  Fisheries Agreement (1997) 218
  militarized conflict potential 227–35
  and military modernization 231–2
  and national identity 230–4
  Peace and Friendship Treaty (1978) 215–16
  and territorial/maritime tensions 211–36
  triangular relationships 147–9, 157, 161–2, 174–8, 190
Sino-Russian relations 32–3, 149–50, 170, 178
  Good-Neighborly Relations, Friendship, and Cooperation Treaty 246
  military cooperation 202–4, 209; joint military operations 246–7
  and Protocols I and II 197
  structural realist view of 202–4
Sino-Soviet relations 214–15, 226
SIPRI (Stockholm International Peace Research Institute) 203
social reform 34–7, 133

social unrest 89–94, 89n, 94–101
  See also regime stability; repression
socioeconomic disparity 23, 29, 30t, 31, 56
Songhua River contamination 129, 129n
South China Morning Church 113
South Korea, collusion and corruption in 70
Southeast Asia, economic comparisons with China 67–74
Soviet Union
  See Sino-Soviet relations
state-owned enterprises (SOEs), and corruption 77
state-society relationships/structures 66–7, 74, 83t, 116, 131, 133
status quo power 3–4, 8–9, 144–5, 200–1
strategic culture
  See under China
strategic repression
  See repression
Suharto 69, 70n, 79, 83t, 86, 88f
Sun, Tzu 247n
Sun, Yan 65, 72–3, 80
Sun Dawu case 125, 125n
Sun Zhigang case 56, 123–5, 124n
Sun Zhigang Incident 56, 123–5
Sutter, Robert G. 8, 12

Taiwan
  anti-secession law 170, 201
  arms purchases from U.S. 174–5, 180n
  Japanese opinion about 233
  and nationalism/irredentism 200
  no independence, no war (budu buwu) policy toward 3, 201
  one country, two systems policy 32
  opposition parties of 32
  as a pain in the neck 200–2
  as peace breaker 9, 32, 147–54, 161–3, 168, 170–4, 180
  triangular relationships: with U.S. and China 202; with U.S. and Japan 207
Tajikistan 239
Taliban government, of Afghanistan 240
Tang, Jiaxuan 219
Tanner, Murry Scot 90
taoguang yanghui (low profile) concept 2
taxes 23, 58
technology 131–2, 183, 194

Index

Teikoku Oil Co., drilling in East China Sea 222–3
Teng, Wensheng 48
territorial and maritime disputes 6–7, 149, 211–36
  See also East China Sea
  and China's capabilities 231–2
  and China's operating context/behavior 226
  conflict potential 6–7, 224–7–236
  institutional-statist theory on 227
  Law on the Territorial Sea and Contiguous Waters 216
  in the new millennium 219–24
  Provisional Measures (PMZ) joint fishing zone 218
Thailand, autonomous corruption in 72–3, 86–7
theater missile defense
Three Represents 24–5, 46, 48–9, 56
Three Self patriotic movement 101
Tiananmen Incident, effect of 22, 24, 48, 196, 226
Tianwaitian/Kashi exploration 223
Tibet, as challenge to peaceful development 9
transparency
  See openness/open door policy
Transparency International, Corruption Perception Index 51
treaties
  See also CSTO; NATO
  Amsterdam (1996) 259
  Anti-Ballistic Missile (ABM) 160, 202
  Good-Neighborly Relations, Friendship, and Cooperation 246
  Okinawa Reversion 214
  Peace and Friendship (1978) 215–16
  Russian-Uzbekistan 251–2
Trenin, Dmitri 203
Truman, Harry (President), and Taiwan 237

Uighur Autonomous Region
  See Xinjiang Uighur Autonomous Region
underground church
  See Christians
United Nations
  as constraint on U.S. 157
  Convention on Law of the Sea (UNCLOS) 149, 213–14, 213*n*; and China's economic interests 225; ratified by China and Japan 217; violations of 223
  Development Program (UNDP), on China's income disparity 57
  Economic Commission for Asia and the Far East (UN ECAFE) 214, 225
United States
  See also Sino-American relations
  2+2 meeting with Japan 170, 175
  as adventurist 243, 243*n*, 244
  air mobility of 249–50
  arms sales to Taiwan 174–5, 180*n*
  balancing role of 10–11
  and Central Asian geopolitics 178, 237–61; geostrategies 238–42
  Central Asian penetration 242–5
  and China's foreign policy 151–2
  citizens' distaste for warfare 247–8
  containment strategy of 10, 155–6, 159–81, 190, 239, 243–4, 257–8
  creditors of 189
  East Asia Security Act (2005) 172–3, 177
  Eurasian geostrategy 252–3, 257–61
  expulsion from Central Asia 254–5
  Freedom Support Act 239
  military policy toward China 6, 146, 152–4, 173–7; adjustment of 171–3; possible consequences of 205–8
  missile defense strategies of 160–3, 202, 205–6
  and Pacific Command 173–4
  and Russia 149, 242–3
  and Sino-Japanese territorial/maritime disputes 214
  split with EU 258–9
  trade deficit with China 188
  triangular relationships: with China and Japan 147–9, 157, 161–2, 174–8, 190; with China and Taiwan 202; with Japan and Taiwan 207
  unipolar hegemony of 2, 36, 143–4, 149, 153–4, 160, 164
  vital national interests, defined 242
United States Navy 248, 252–3
United States Navy Seventh Fleet 237
urbanization 58
utilitarianism, and political legitimacy 44, 54–5
Uzbekistan 238–40, 251–2, 355

Vishney, Robert 70, 73

Wang, Beili
Wang, Jisi 36
Wang, Zhengxu 117–38
Wank, David 81
war on terrorism, as U.S. entry into Central Asia 243–7
warfare
  as economically disruptive 3, 21, 26, 149
  geopolitical analysis for Central Asia 247–60
  PLA strategies for 194–5
weapons systems
  high-tech 183, 194
  of mass destruction (WMDs) 33
  modernization goals for 191–200
  nuclear 32, 193–4, 207
Weber, Max 60
Wedeman, Andrew 69, 71, 84, 89–115
Weisbrode, Kenneth 250
Wen, Jiabao 28, 31, 59, 220
Wenling City 133
Will, George 249

Wolfowitz, Paul D. 240
Womack, Brantly 35
World Bank 41, 62t
World Happiness Rank 55t
World Trade Organization (WTO), China's entry into 24, 26
Wright, Quincy 151–2

Xiamen Yuanhua case 78
Xiang, Lanxin 258–9
Xinjiang Uighur Autonomous Region 9, 105, 239, 256
Xiong, Guangkai 160

Yan, Xuetong 1n
Yang, Dali 75
Yu Huafeng case 125, 125n

Zhang, Deguang 246
Zhao, Ziyang 24
Zheng, Bijian 1–2, 25–7, 31–2, 39n, 185
Zhou, Enlai, Five Principles of Peaceful Coexistence 261
Zoellick, Robert 39